BOUND FOR GROWTH

BOUND FOR GROWTH

How to Pick Winning Stocks Using Industry Analysis

DAVID WANETICK

Editor of the Market Maneuvers Publications

IRWIN
Professional Publishing

Chicago • London • Singapore

This publication is designed to provide accurate and
authoritative information in regard to the subject matter
covered. It is sold with the understanding that neither the
author or the publisher is engaged in rendering legal, accounting,
or other professional service. If legal advice or other expert
assistance is required, the services of a competent professional
person should be sought.

*From a Declaration of Principles jointly adopted by a Committee
of the American Bar Association and a Committee of Publishers.*

◤▼ Times Mirror
◣ Higher Education Group

Library of Congress Cataloging-in-Publication Data

Wanetick, David.
    Bound for growth : how to pick winning stocks using industry
analysis / David Wanetick.
       p.   cm.
    Includes index.
    ISBN 0-7863-0979-2
    1. Stocks. 2. Speculation. 3. Investment analysis.   I. Title.
HG6041.W34   1997
332.63'22—dc20   96–28997

Printed in the United States of America
1 2 3 4 5 6 7 8 9 0 3 2 1 0 9 8 7 6

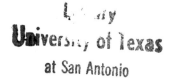

*To my grandmother, Kressie Rothbarth,
whose wisdom and devotion have been
with me every day of my life.*

C O N T E N T S

Chapter 8

Financial Services   205

Chapter 9

Health Care   250

Chapter 13

Other Industries   369

PART ONE

KNOW WHAT YOU'RE BUYING

1

CHAPTER

Introduction

Buying a stock is like buying anything else. You must know what you are purchasing; if you don't, you probably won't be happy with what you get.

But what do you get when you purchase a stock? Quite simply, you become a part-owner of the business whose shares you hold. Thus, stockholders share in the bounty of successful businesses. The stock market eventually rewards shareholders of prosperous companies with rising stock prices. Also, shareholders of growing companies often benefit from increasingly generous dividend payout policies.

There are, however, no assurances that you will reap such rewards. After all, investing in stocks is risky business. Stocks of poorly managed companies are sure to lose value over the long term. Also, dividend payouts can be reduced or even eliminated.

So then the question becomes, How can you maximize your purchase of winning stocks while minimizing your exposure to losers? I already gave you the answer! *You must know what you are buying.*

But wait! Buying a stock is not like buying apples and oranges. For heaven's sake, average people do not know how to compare one stock against another.

One of the goals of this book is to demystify the process of profitably investing in stocks. Too many would-be investors avoid the stock market because they believe that they lack the intelligence to successfully invest. These people think that choosing good stocks requires the application of some kind of arcane alchemy.

It doesn't. Prudent stock selection requires much more research and common sense than mastery of mathematics or never-ending number crunching.

The first step in demystifying the stock market is to take a step back and forget about which stocks to buy. First, look for outstanding companies. Remember, stockholders own parts of companies. As a business owner you will want to invest your money where it will work the hardest. Serious investors search relentlessly for the companies with the best prospects.

In Part I, Know What You're Buying, I will convince you of the importance of understanding the *business* of the companies in which you are contemplating investment. Part I is broken down into the qualitative factors and the quantitative factors that you should consider in your search for outstanding companies. A review of the qualitative factors is an appeal to your common sense, but it is also important to understand the quantitative criteria that financially sound companies must demonstrate.

Okay, let's suppose that you have found an outstanding company that meets our qualitative and quantitative requirements. What are you supposed to do now? The second step of successful investing is to make sure that stocks are purchased at reasonable prices. After all, no prudent shopper would buy something unless the price was reasonable. This is more complicated than buying a stock for the fewest dollars possible. Thus, Part I discusses the traits that make the stock of an outstanding company worthy of your investment dollars. I accomplish this by explaining the valuation gauges that fundamental analysts employ to determine whether or not a particular stock merits investment.

Let's rehash. Successful investing requires adherence to two simple rules:

1. Only buy shares of outstanding companies.
2. Only accumulate such stocks when they are trading at exceedingly attractive levels.

If you read Part I and think about the issues that are discussed, you will avoid many costly mistakes. And if you follow the advice that is provided here you will be able to boost your investment performance. Of course, finding stocks that meet these stringent criteria is not easy. However, as Peter Lynch wrote, "If you uncover enough rocks you will find some good stocks."

Part I is a necessary narrative on successful stock market investing, but it's simply a small piece of the puzzle. No one can really gain a true understanding of a business unless they understand the industry in which the business operates. The fortunes of businesses are, in part, influenced by the health of the relevant industries. Thus, companies cannot be prudently analyzed in isolation of the industries in which they operate. This would be like trying to gain a genuine understanding of the Civil War without understanding the context in which this war was waged.

Each industry faces its own unique set of advantages and disadvantages. Competition, access to inputs, distribution channels, and capital requirements vary from one industry to another. Also, changes resulting from demographic shifts, legislation, and technological advances will impact different industries in different ways. Furthermore, changes in one industry impact other industries. These very changes play a large role in determining the investment worthiness of a stock. Finally, the tools for measuring the financial performance and financial position of companies differ depending upon the industry in which a company operates.

In addition to providing much needed insight into how dozens of industries operate, industry analysis reconciles two sound investment practices that are at odds with each other: specialization and diversification.

As discussed above, investors must know what they are buying. With this dictum in mind, many investors wisely focus on the industries with which they have the greatest knowledge and expertise. These are usually the same industries in which the individual builds his career. For instance, it is prudent for bankers to seek investment opportunities in the banking industry. Similarly, pilots judiciously look to the airline industry as a source of investment ideas.

This tactic makes sense because investors are well versed in the particular industry's terminology, conditions and challenges. Additionally, sticking to one's area of expertise has other advantages. For instance, the banker or pilot may belong to trade associations that keep its members informed of changes impacting the particular industry. Thus, by sticking to your area of knowledge, you can be privy to actionable information before the herd of other investors. This is, of course, an inherent advantage.

The other sound strategy that investors often employ in modeling their portfolios is diversification. Diversification is like an insurance policy. Even though prudent investors attempt to purchase inexpensive shares of outstanding companies, sometimes even the savviest investors miscalculate. Thus, diversifying one's portfolio limits the losses that an investor will sustain if one of his stocks falls in value. Similarly, investors may want to spread their exposure over different industries. This step is taken as a precautionary measure in the event that an entire industry is, unexpectedly, adversely impacted.

Focusing on one's area of expertise and diversification are both sound investment strategies. However, these methodologies are at odds with each other. To wit, how can an investor create a truly diversified portfolio and still limit his positions to the one or two industries with which he is intimately familiar?

The answer to this question lies in Part II (Look before You Leap). By gaining a keen understanding of many industries, you can broaden your range of competence. Thus, you can more sensibly diversify your portfolio since you will have a better sense of how businesses in various industries operate.

I believe that an understanding of numerous industries will sharpen your analysis and will allow you to be more critical of each industry that you follow. This is because you will have a broader spectrum from which to choose your investments. Having a choice in investments is critical because it forces you to compare and contrast the risk/reward ratio of one investment against others.

On the other hand, devoting all of your energies to one industry may cause you to become biased. If you confer solely with analysts, company spokesmen and trade association officials affiliated with one industry, you may become partial to that industry. With a limited investment scope you will always be able to rationalize the purchase of shares of one company in that industry, regardless of better opportunities in other industries.

In addition to widening your field of knowledge, I discuss a multitude of industries in order to give you a more thorough understanding of how industries impact one another. A simple example of this is determining the effect that a strike by steel workers will have on car manufacturers. A more indirect example of how intertwined industries are is how advances in biotechnology may be a negative development for grocery stores (to be explained later).

Also, I thought it would be wise to discuss a variety of industries since companies do not always fit into neatly defined industries. For example, in what industry does PepsiCo Inc. lie? There is no simple answer to this question. Pepsi is not solely in the beverage industry because it operates restaurant chains (e.g., KFC and Taco Bell) and owns the Frito-Lay™ line of snack foods. And due to its Pepsi® products and snack foods, it is not solely a restaurant company. Finally, Pepsi is not simply a snack food company, because soft drinks and restaurants account for much of its business. Thus, in order to analyze companies in multiple business lines, the investor must be familiar with several industries.

Another advantage of analyzing numerous industries is that today industries are converging at an unprecedented rate. For instance, pharmaceutical companies are buying drug distributors; thus, without learning about both the pharmaceutical industry and the drug distribution industry, you will not be adequately equipped to evaluate the prescription benefit managers. Likely, it is impossible to analyze the coal mining industry without also analyzing the electric utility industry.

While it is important to ascertain the industry-specific issues and to apply industry-specific financial tools, reading about so many industries will make your mind more flexible. This flexibility is valuable since, to some extent, some of the concepts are portable. For instance, in the chapter on restaurants some of the comments regarding franchising are applicable to franchising in the lodging industry as well. Also, the discussion on strike funds in the automobile chapter is also applicable to the integrated steel industry. Additionally, the discussion on geographic variances in the homebuilding industry is applicable to other region-sensitive industries such as banks, grocery stores, and electric utilities. Thus, your familiarity with the industries described in Part II will have more benefit to you since you will be able to apply the principles contained in Part II to industries and situations that are not specifically addressed in this book.

Of course, the portability feature requires thought. The development of a more intense investment methodology is perhaps the underlying objective of *Bound for Growth* The content of this book will undoubtedly improve your investment performance. However, the timeliness and appropriateness of any particular sentence may vary. Nevertheless, the rigorous application of the industry analysis methodology that you will acquire by reading this book will serve you well.

I believe that industry analysis is more important now than ever before. One reason is that more money is currently under professional money management than in any time in history. Since these money managers do not get paid to hold cash, they are forced to find value wherever it exits; thus, there will be more sector rotation. In order to invest in the soon-to-be-hot sectors, investors will have to understand what drives industry performance.

Industry analysis is indeed an unexplored investment methodology. Reading this book will thus give you an advantage over the millions of investors that do not factor industry analysis into their investment-related decisions.

Bound for Growth was written not as an academic treatise but rather as a vehicle for imparting thought-provoking ideas that will add another layer of diligence to your stock-selection process. Thus, I want you to consider the contents of this book when you make your regular investment decisions.

2

WHY INVEST IN THE STOCK MARKET?

The primary reason for investing in stocks is *to enjoy superior returns on your investments.* Historically, no other investment medium has yielded returns as large (over extended periods of time) as common stocks. The following point, made by Peter Lynch, the legendary money manager of Fidelity's Magellan Fund, illuminates the enormous potential of common stocks. According to Lynch, if you had invested $1,000 in each of the following four instruments in 1927 and the money had compounded tax-free, your investment would have appreciated to the following amounts 60 years later:

Treasury bills	$ 7,400
Government bonds	13,200
Corporate bonds	17,600
Common stocks	272,000

Remember, these initial investments were made two years *before* the Crash of 1929. If this $1,000 was invested after the Crash, common stocks would have appreciated significantly more. In addition to stocks' yielding the highest returns, common stocks are the best protection against inflation's diminishing the real value of investments over time.

Another advantage of investing in common stocks is that the *potential returns are unlimited.* Since, in general, there is no limit as to how large a corporation can grow or how profitable it can become, there is no limit as to how high your shares can soar. On the other hand, there are definite limits to the returns that you will receive on other investments. For example, bondholders only receive pre-determined interest payments regardless of how well the issuer is performing. Thus, if you buy shares of IBM, there is no limit as to how far these shares can rise. However, if you purchase IBM bonds and IBM does extremely well finan-cially, Big Blue will not increase interest payments to bondholders.

While stocks offer unlimited profit potential, *exposure to losses is limited to the amount of money that you invest.* If you buy shares of Whirlpool® at $60 a piece and Whirlpool goes bankrupt, the most you can lose is $60 a share. However, if you are a general partner in a partnership, your liability is unlimited. For exam-ple, somebody could injure themselves on the partnership's premises and sue you. Or the EPA could determine that the partnership was improperly disposing of its waste, resulting in penalties that exceed your ownership stake in the partnership.

Not only do common stocks offer the most lucrative investment potential, but compared with other investment activities, the procedure of *investing in com-mon stocks is simple.* Generally speaking, you can arrange to purchase or sell any stock in a few minutes by placing an order with your stockbroker. You simply tell your stockbroker which stocks you wish to buy or sell and the order is usually exe-cuted while you wait on the phone. This is a significant contrast to the time and effort it takes to invest in other media. For example, in order to consummate a transaction in real estate, you may have to have the property inspected by apprais-ers, consult with accountants, and negotiate with lawyers.

The fifth advantage of investing in stocks as opposed to other medium is that *common stocks are liquid assets.* In virtually every situation, you will be able to acquire or dispose of your securities without any trouble. On the contrary, in real estate and in other types of investments, it may not be possible to find the corre-sponding buyer or seller needed to carry out the proposed transaction within your desired time frame.

In addition to stocks being liquid assets, you can easily determine the cost or proceeds of executing a stock transaction. This is because daily stock quotations are readily listed in financial newspapers as well as major general interest newspa-pers. Thus, you simply multiply the number of stocks you are trading times the price of such stocks (plus or minus commissions) to determine your costs or pro-ceeds. On the contrary, consider all of the factors that must be taken into consider-ation to determine your proceeds on selling a vacation home; you would have to consider federal, state, local, and school tax issues, repairs, rents collected, use of the home as an office, and how the home was purchased.

The sixth advantage of investing in stocks is that *reliable information is available* for all companies that trade on established domestic stock exchanges. The audited income statements, balance sheets, and statements of cash flows that all publicly traded companies are required to file provide you with more informa-tion than you would likely receive about partnerships or small business ventures in which you are considering taking an interest. No other country in the world exercises as much oversight over its public companies as does the United States. The Securities and Exchange Commission (as well as other regulatory agencies) has a commendable record of monitoring the accuracy and thoroughness of the financial reports that public companies are required to file with it.

The seventh advantage of investing in stocks is that *you can create a diversified portfolio with relatively little money.* For instance, a $25,000 portfolio can represent five positions of $5,000 each in companies whose operations are exposed to different sectors of the economy. In contrast, it would be difficult to find a promising investment in areas such as real estate or collectibles (e.g., paintings or antiques) for $25,000. And even if a suitable investment could be found in such a medium for $25,000, you would forfeit diversification since such investments are not divisible.

Yet another reason to consider investing in stocks is that *stocks can be proxies for other investments* that you would not ordinarily make on your own. For example, you can try to profit from growth in foreign countries by buying shares of closed-end country funds (e.g., the France Fund or the Brazil Fund). (Closed-end country funds invest their assets abroad but their shares trade on established domestic exchanges just like all other stocks.) You can also buy shares of closed-end regional or closed-end emerging market funds (e.g., the Asia Pacific Fund or the Morgan Stanley Emerging Market Fund) in hopes of benefiting from growth in different parts of the world.

The domestic stock markets can also serve as proxies for entire foreign equities markets. Thus, aggressive investors can wager on the direction of foreign stock or currency markets by trading call or put warrants, which trade like common stock but are pegged to the indexes of foreign stock markets or currency markets (e.g., Paine Webber Nikkei Put Warrants or Merrill Lynch Deutsche Mark Put Warrants).

There are other examples of how stocks can be proxies for other investments. You can pursue opportunities in real estate by buying shares of real estate investment trusts (e.g., Washington R.E.I.T.) or play bonds by buying closed-end bond funds (e.g., Kemper High Income Trust). You can also purchase a basket of securities by buying general purpose closed-end mutual funds (e.g., Royce Value Trust).

The stock market can also be a proxy for commodities. For example, you can buy shares in gold mining companies when you believe gold is undervalued or you can buy shares of oil or gas companies when you believe that these industries will prosper. You can also buy into shares of companies whose earnings are contingent on the prices of commodities (e.g., Thorn Apple Valley's fortunes may be inversely tied to hog prices). You can also play collectibles either by buying shares of auctioneers (e.g., Sotheby's), manufacturers of novelty items (e.g., Topps or Score Board) or by buying shares of companies that have large collections of art or antiques (e.g., *Reader's Digest*). Furthermore, when you think that turmoil is ahead and a strong cash position is judicious, you can either leave your cash in you brokerage account and receive a money market rate of interest or you can accumulate the shares of companies that hold large amounts of cash (e.g., Chemed or Hanson).

SOURCES OF INVESTMENT ADVICE

There are a few basic sources of investment literature that all investors will come across. Foremost among these sources are the general media, corporate documents, informed industry sources, and friends and colleagues. Since these sources supply most of the readily available information regarding public companies, a short discussion about each is warranted.

General Media

One of the more useful sources of information is the popular media. Magazines such as *Business Week, Barrons* and *Forbes* and newspapers such as *The Wall Street Journal* and *Investor's Business Daily* uncover a wealth of information about companies and industries. Trade journals and local newspapers offer unique insight into industries and regional developments that could impact different companies. However, such articles usually do not thoroughly analyze the financial position and prospects of the companies and industries under review from an investor's point of view. Therefore, an upbeat article about a company in a general interest publication should not be misconstrued as a well-reasoned buy recommendation. Also, it is imperative to understand that articles that come from the general media should supplement, but not replace, diligent research.

Corporate Documents

Due to stringent disclosure requirements, annual reports, 10-Ks, 10-Qs, 8-Ks, and prospectuses can be sources of valuable insight into the company under review. However, the investor must have a sound understanding of accounting principles to be able to interpret the financial data provided in those reports. Further, this financial information should not always be accepted at face value but rather should be compared with historical figures and against the company's competitors. Also, the press clippings and press releases that are collected by public companies (or their public relations firms) provide the investor with useful information. However, you must be able to wade through the meaning and importance of these announcements and guard against overly solicitous companies.

Discussions with Informed Sources

After you have gathered, digested and synthesized information pertaining to the company or industry under review, you can try to speak with the securities analysts, corporate executives, regulators, consultants, trade association representatives, and reporters for the trade publications that relate to the topic you are reviewing. However, you must respect these people's time; thus, do not seek to interview them until you are prepared to ask insightful questions.

Friends and Colleagues

Investors should never impulsively react to *tips* or *rumors* from friends or colleagues. As Peter Lynch said, you should spend as much time studying a stock as you would buying a refrigerator. However, as part of your research, you can seek *information* from friends and colleagues. In fact, friends and colleagues that work in the industry you are researching can be good sources. These people may be more candid than the experts cited above. For example, your pilot friend may give you a more genuine account of the airline industry's relations with its workers than the head of the Federal Aviation Administration.

PRELUDE TO INVESTING IN THE STOCK MARKET

You should *invest your time before you invest your money.* Peter Lynch said you should only buy a stock if you can give a convincing five-minute explanation for doing so. Thus, you should be able to answer general questions about the companies in which you invest. For instance, you should have an idea about the companies' strategies, competitive environment, labor relations, marketing strategies, and so forth.

You should also save time by avoiding the sectors of the market that are beyond your zone of comfort. At a minimum, this means to *stay away from companies and financial products that you honestly do not understand.* Do not buy a company that produces semiconductors, if you do not know what a semiconductor is and do not buy a put warrant on a foreign index if you do not understand the risks associated with that put warrant.

Investors should heed the old adage *"When in doubt stay out."* Never feel compelled to constantly make decisions about the direction of future stock prices. You should only make an investment when you think you will be able to eat well and sleep well. However, when you find a stock that you feel strongly about you should have the courage to aggressively accumulate it. After all, to profit handsomely you must be willing to act boldly.

Mark Twain summed up our aversion to reckless speculation by saying, "There are only two times when you should not speculate in the stock market; one is when you can't afford to speculate and the other is when you can." Investors must understand that the stock market is not an instant accession to wealth and that *even the most aggressive trading strategies take time to ripen.* If your investment horizon is less than at least a few months, you should rethink your outlook before you commit any funds to the market. Myopia and a distorted view of reality will lead not only to disappointment but to the destruction of an otherwise sound investment program.

To be a successful investor you must *act as if you do not need to invest* in the stock market. Wealthy people don't need the market to meet their financial objectives. Therefore, they can better restrain greed and overcome the fear of investing because their actions are grounded on objective reasoning, not on the hope of supplementing their income by dabbling in stocks. Extremely wealthy investors would not risk squandering their resources on a stock that was not truly appealing. Neither should you.

Since investing in stocks is riskier than socking money away in certificates of deposit (CDs) or money market accounts, shareholders demand a higher return on their stock investments. It is critical, however, to be realistic about the kinds of returns that investors can expect to receive. *Stocks are, after all, alternatives to other investments, not lottery tickets.* In an environment in which CDs and money market accounts yield 4 or 5 percent, a 12 percent annual return would be extremely worthwhile. This 12 percent may not sound as glamorous as 35 or 45 percent, but huge risks would have to be taken to obtain these (usually) illusory returns. Losses would almost certainly be incurred while undertaking such risks. Therefore, the prudent investor will only invest in those stocks that have higher risk-adjusted returns than other investments.

This 12 percent annual return will look more attractive when considering *the power of compounding.* A $10,000 investment that appreciates 12 percent each year will be worth $528,000 at the end of 35 years. Keep in mind that most investors will invest more money each year. If you invested an extra $5,000 for each of the next 34 years and gained a 12 percent annual return, your total portfolio would be worth $2,451,000 at the end of 35 years. True, 35 years is a long time. However, the alternative to setting realistic expectations will usually lead to huge losses. After all, Warren Buffett, the first man to become a multibillionaire just by making good stock picks, generates about a 25 percent annual return on his investments. This doesn't sound as glamorous as the 35 or 45 percent that one money manager or another will get each year, but consistency is the key. In the final analysis, $10,000 invested with Buffet in 1956 would have been worth over $30,000,000 in 1992.

Another important thing to keep in mind is *to not overextend yourself in the market.* Stocks should only be purchased with funds that will not be needed in the foreseeable future. If you overcommit yourself in the market, your personal obligations may force you to liquidate your holdings when the market is temporarily weak. Committing too large a percentage of your wealth in stocks may cause you to become a stock jockey. This will lead to more risk taking and to investing more on hope than on intense analysis.

John Neff, the manager of Vanguard's Windsor Mutual Fund, said that *as many people lose money in the stock market because they are too smart as people who lose money in the market because they are too dumb.* This means that it is unwise to take a position in a stock for reasons that are too complicated for most of the investing community to understand, because the lack of interest or buying power will fail to push the price of the stock higher. Furthermore, it is better to avoid aggressive trading strategies, speculative situations, and sensational story stocks.

Also, *it is important not to lose perspective* when analyzing the merits of a stock. Make sure that the fundamentals of the companies under review are in order before analyzing the ancillary attributes of the stocks under review. Thus, if a company in which you are considering making an investment has two divisions—one accounting for 95 percent of the company's revenue, the other accounting for just 5 percent—95 percent of your research should be devoted to the division that accounts for 95 percent of the company's revenue, while only 5 percent of your time should be spent researching the smaller unit.

There should be some diversification in a stock portfolio so that any single holding going sour will not decimate your portfolio. However, and equally important, *there should not be too much diversification.* If you try to hold too many securities, you will not have the time or energy to adequately monitor the underlying companies' performances. Furthermore, it must be understood that diversification is not a substitute for research. Casually purchasing stocks just to increase the number of issues in your portfolio will undoubtedly diminish your returns.

3
CHAPTER

KEEPING TRACK: FUNDAMENTAL ANALYSIS

Investors who adhere to the fundamentalist school of thought (i.e., investors who look at companies' fundamentals such as product, management, and finances) select their stock purchases as if they were businessmen who were considering acquiring the entire company under review. Fundamentalists quite simply invest in shares of the best companies that they can find and that are trading at the cheapest possible prices. In determining which are the best companies, the fundamentalist considers a wide range of qualitative and quantitative factors regarding the company under review. In discovering the cheapest stocks, the investor will rely upon valuation ratios. Since fundamentalists have a very long-term investment horizon and a grave aversion to losses, they forgo most of the opportunities that come to their attention. Fundamentalists wait until an opportunity comes along that meets their rigid criteria and then they invest a large part of their resources in such a company. (Some of the favorable traits that fundamentalists seek when reviewing companies are set in the next section.)

While fundamentalists conduct exhaustive examinations of companies' fundamentals, they disregard the strength or weakness of the stock market. Since they believe that the stock market is merely the place where one can buy and sell pieces of companies, they do not allow any market indicators to sway their judgment about investing in stocks. Therefore, high market indexes, topping formations, or bearish breadth indicators would not preclude the fundamentalist from making commitments in the market.

Since the fundamentalist sees no correlation between a company's earnings power and the random walk of the stock market, he would not try to time his purchases and sales to the valleys and peaks in the stock market. After his initial investment, the fundamentalist monitors the performance of the company but not the daily fluctuations in the market price of the shares. If the company's operations were still sound, he might continue to purchase a fixed dollar amount of the company's shares on a regular basis. Even a sharp decrease in the market value of his holdings would not dissuade him from adhering to his program of accumulating shares of undervalued companies. To paraphrase Warren Buffett, you shouldn't own a stock if a temporary 50 percent decline in price would cause you to lose sleep. Subsequent to acquiring the shares, the fundamentalist would continue to hold his shares until the market priced them near their intrinsic value.

QUALITIATIVE FACTORS

Some of the *qualitative factors* that fundamentalists seek in their investments include:

- *Noncompetitive businesses.* Fundamental investors shy away from businesses that are too competitive. Excessive competition often results in price wars, which lower revenues, squeeze margins, and reduce earnings. Also, too much competition can result in competitors poaching each other's key executives, leaving a hollow management structure.

- *Barriers to entry.* Fundamentalists like to invest in companies that benefit from barriers to entry because an existing business will benefit if potential competitors have difficulty entering the same industry. Such barriers to entry include extremely high start-up costs, lack of access to essential raw materials, proprietary databases, or difficulty in developing a sufficient distribution system.

  One example of a barrier to entry is capital intensity. Since it takes so much money to build an aerospace company, few new competitors will be able to raise enough capital to enter the aerospace industry.

- *Unfair advantage* Unfair advantages can result from owning intangibles such as patents, trademarks, and superior production processes. No other company can use these intangibles to compete against the company that owns the intangibles. Other examples of unfair advantages include management expertise, years of intensive marketing, and exceptional customer service.

  Franchises benefit from tremendous customer loyalty and have an important unfair advantage. Extreme customer loyalty precludes customers from substituting their products. Harley Davidson® is a great example of customer loyalty. Since Harley Davidson customers are loyal enough to have the Harley Davidson trademark tattooed all over their bodies, they are unlikely to switch to another company's motorcycles.

- *Simple, stable businesses.* Fundamentalists also try to avoid companies that are subject to continuous technological change. This is because rapidly changing businesses produce goods that have short life cycles. Such acceleration in obsolescence often requires these companies to discount their older products. As a result of discounting, revenues plunge and margins erode. Also, companies in rapidly changing industries must devote enormous resources to research and development, marketing and promotion of their new products in order to compete.

Conversely, businesses that produce simple products are easier to manage, face less obsolescence, and require less development and promotional expenditures. The essence of a good business is one that takes readily available commodities and, with minimal effort, creates a premium-priced product.

- *Distance from government regulation.* Since the government often limits the returns on investment that regulated companies (e.g., utilities) are allowed to earn, it is preferable to find companies that are not subject to such restrictions. The cost of implementing regulations that are stipulated by the various governmental authorities are high, while the benefits therefrom are dubious.

   Similarly, fundamentalists search for companies that have the ability to raise their prices without attracting political opposition. Examples of this ability include cigarette and alcohol manufacturers because politicians do not want to encourage the consumption of such products in the first place. On the contrary, neither utilities companies nor insurers have the ability to raise prices without attracting political opposition because most lawmakers consider utilities and health insurance to be vital to their constituents' well-being.

- *Prestige appeal.* In some high-end niche areas consumers equate higher-priced goods with being more valuable than cheaper alternatives, and thus, actually prefer to pay for the higher-priced goods. This desire to pay up for products reduces the usual difficulty in convincing customers to buy top-of-the-line products. Another benefit of prestige products is that customers often become the manufacturers' best sales force by bragging about and showing off their purchases. Thus, using prestige appeal as a sole criterium, it is better to invest in a prestigious confectionery maker than a discount confectioner; better to have an interest in an up-scale perfume maker than in a generic perfume manufacturer.

- *Difficult to comparison shop.* It is preferable to invest in companies that sell merchandise for which it is difficult for the customer to comparison shop. Futher, customers have the most difficulty comparison shopping when they shop for that line of merchandise infrequently. Thus, it is preferable to invest in a chain of furniture stores as opposed to a chain of grocery stores.

- *Adequate size.* The most ardent fundamentalists typically search for larger companies since they generally set the quality standards, dictate pricing, and have a dominate market share in any industry. The larger companies usually have larger advertising, marketing, and research budgets, as well as easier access to credit than their smaller competitors.

- *Proven track record.* A proven track record is important because it discounts the hype surrounding a company's future potential and provides concrete indications of how efficiently the company has used its assets, adapted to changes in its operating environment, and overcome unforeseen obstacles.

- *Repeat revenues.* Repeat revenues occur when customers make a habit of purchasing a product or service from a company. Since it is easier and cheaper to retain customers than it is to continually find new customers, it is advantageous to provide goods or services that are conducive to long-term relationships with customers. The newspaper, pharmaceutical, and insurance industries have enjoyed the advantages of repeat revenues. Also, manufacturers of products that are arguably addictive, such as cigarettes, benefit from repeat revenues. Other sources of recurring revenues include licensing agreements, royalties, and maintenance contracts.

- *Large customer lists.* It is preferable to find a business that has many customers instead of only a handful of large customers. Businesses that only have a few customers (e.g., defense contractors) are beholden to those customers; the loss of any one large account could be catastrophic. However, for businesses that have large customer lists (e.g., newspapers and magazines), the loss of a few customers is not terribly problematic.

- *Motivated workforce.* A company's workforce is an asset often overlooked by securities analysts because there is no place to put it on the balance sheet. However, a dedicated workforce can make a major difference in productivity, sales generation, customer satisfaction, and customer retention. A company that has low employee turnover and an incentive program is preferable to a company that has high employee turnover and no incentive program.

- *Insider ownership.* Fundamentalists also search for companies that have a large degree of insider ownership. When insiders own large interests in their company, their interests are aligned with the shareholders' interests. Furthermore, fundamentalists like to see insiders buying more of the company's stock since this indicates that insiders are confident about their company's future. Moreover, insider ownership should be widely dispersed.

- *Stock buybacks.* Another indication of management's optimism for its company's future prospects is evidenced by the company's buying back a significant percentage of its own shares. Additionally, the reduction of shares outstanding bolsters earnings-per-share growth.

     However, since there is no liability for not buying back the shares that a company is authorized to repurchase, you should not assume that every company will complete its repurchase program. Instead, you should compare companies' previous announcements of repurchases with their actual repurchases. Then give credence to the companies that have demonstrated the least divergence from their authorizations to actual repurchases.

QUANTITATIVE FACTORS

Included among the financial considerations with which the fundamental investor is concerned are the earnings growth, drivers and quality of earnings, the value of the company's assets, the efficiency in which such assets have been employed, the company's capital structure, the price that must be paid for the shares, and the company's dividend policies. An overview of each of these considerations is set forth below.

Earnings Trends (Components of Earnings)

In searching for superb companies you should scrutinize at least 5, preferably 10, years of financial data. A company can legitimately calculate its earnings in a number of ways that are in accordance with the Generally Acceptable Accounting Principles (GAAP) and report radically different results. Reviewing and averaging several years of data will smooth out reported earnings and render comparisons between competing companies more useful. A span of years is also studied to determine how the company performed throughout economic cycles.

Not surprisingly, fundamental investors like to see a steady, predictable ascendancy in the company's earnings; they like to see the company earn more money each year, even during recessions; and they want to make sure that the growth in earnings exceeds the inflation rate and population growth.

Next you should determine how a company's earnings compare with those of its competitors as well as ascertain which factors contributed to the earnings. In order to review the company's earnings you must consult the income statement. Unlike the balance sheet, which depicts a company's financial position for a point in time, the income statement summarizes a company's activities over a period of time. The advantage is that you can glean a clear insight as to how the company operates as a going concern.

Revenues

The first item that appears on the income statement is sales or revenues. This extremely revealing data should indicate that sales (revenues) are growing impressively and consistently. Growth in the total dollar amount of sales should be accompanied by a corresponding growth in the number of units sold. Ideally, the fundamentalist likes to invest in companies that are both raising their prices and selling more units. When prices are rising for a given product, profit margins widen. Also, when more units are being sold, the company is likely selling products with wide appeal. The combination of both higher prices and more units sold indicates that consumer demand for the company's products is price inelastic.

Also, the number of units sold gives us insight into the company's product mix. The product mix is basically the number of each of the company's various products being sold. Since different products vary in the degree of profitability that they contribute to the company, reviewing the product mix is one of the first steps in projecting the company's future earnings. Fundamentalists like to see the greatest sales growth coming from the products that are the most profitable to the company and perhaps a discontinuation of the products that are only marginally profitable.

Increasing sales growth is not always an indication of future profitability. First, we know that if sales are increasing and the gross margins are decreasing then the company is slashing its prices just to generate volume at the expense of its profits. Excessive discounting may signal that the company's products are obsolete or are otherwise not competitive. It is also dangerous for a company to constantly discount its products because consumers become conditioned to such discounts and refuse to pay full prices.

Second, you should be cautious about investing in a company that is too aggressive in reporting its revenues. For example, a company whose products are sold by a commissioned sales force may book its revenues shortly after a salesman makes a presentation. It would be far better if the company were to wait until firm orders were received, products shipped, and payment made before booking its revenues.

Third, it is problematic when a company's accounts receivables are growing faster than its revenues. Such a situation could indicate that many customers are not paying their bills on time.

Gross Margins

Gross margins are sales minus the cost of goods sold divided by sales. For example, if a company sold a lamp for $100 and the materials used to produce the lamp cost $60, then the gross margin would be 40 percent ($100 − $60 = $40/$100 = 40%). The higher a company's gross margins are, the more revenues the company can allocate to advertising, marketing, and research and development—all of which are ingredients that lead to even more growth. The tremendous impact that gross margins have on net income is made apparent by comparing the ABC Company to the XYZ Company below:

	ABC	XYZ
Sales	$100,000	$100,000
Cost of goods sold	40,000	70,000
Gross margins on sales	$60,000	$30,000
Operating expenses:		
Marketing and selling expenses	$7,000	$7,000
Administrative expenses	3,000	3,000
Research and development expenses	10,000	10,000
Income before income tax	$40,000	$10,000
Income tax expense (rate 30 percent)	12,000	3,000
Net income	$28,000	$7,000

As is made apparent, the ABC Company is a much more profitable company solely due to the fact that its gross margins are so much larger than those of the XYZ Company. In the coming years, chances are that the ABC Company will even be stronger than the XYZ Company because it has more money to spend on research and marketing, among other things. Additionally, the ABC Company would be able to survive a price war whereas the XYZ Company might not. Let's see what happens when these companies are forced to discount their prices by 15 percent.

	ABC	XYZ
Sales	$85,000	$85,000
Cost of goods sold	40,000	70,000
Gross margins on sales	$45,000	$15,000
Operating expenses:		
Marketing and selling expenses	$7,000	$7,000
Administrative expenses	3,000	3,000
Research and development expenses	10,000	10,000
Income before income taxes	$25,000	$(5,000)
Income tax expense (rate 30 percent)	7,500	0
Net income (net loss)	$17,500	$(5,000)

As you can see, when faced with a difficult operating environment the companies with large gross margins will survive while the companies with low gross margins may perish. The above example illustrates why fundamental investors like to see gross margins of 50 percent or more. Also, higher sales can significantly bolster gross margins. As sales increase, the company's buying power grows. Thus, the company can use its buying power to force concessions from suppliers. As a result, revenues rise faster than the costs of goods sold, resulting in much wider gross margins.

Operating Margins and Net Profit Margins

You should search for companies that have wide and expanding operating margins. Operating profit margins are operating income (which correlates to income before income taxes in the example above) divided by sales. Thus, the operating margins for the ABC Company are 29 percent ($25,000/$85,000).

Fundamentalists try to determine how much of every dollar of sales falls to the bottom line by analyzing the net profit margins. Net profit margins are net income divided by sales. For example, the ABC Company has an after-tax profit margin of 20.6 percent ($17,500/$85,000), whereas the XYZ Company has no net profit margins because it incurred a loss. Fundamentalists like to see the net profit margins at 5 percent or higher. While they favor companies that consistently increase their net profit margins, it should be understood that this is not easily accomplished if the company's tax rates are being increased.

Earnings Quality

In order to better analyze a company's performance you must first weigh the sources of a company's earnings. The company's operating earnings (earnings from the company's primary operations) are given much more weight than irregular gains and losses caused by accounting conventions such as extraordinary events, the impact of discontinued operations, or the cumulative effect of accounting changes. In other words, operating earnings have higher earnings quality than gains from unusual occurrences because operating earnings are recurring in that they are derived from the company's principal business segments.

Let's assume that both the ABC Company and the XYZ Company, as presented below, are in the retail furniture business. Additionally, suppose that the $8,000 gain that the XYZ Company realized was from an extraordinary event such as selling a lot of land that it happened to own as opposed to selling furniture. Even though both companies earned $1.40 per share, the ABC Company would be deemed to have higher earnings quality than the XYZ Company because all of its income was generated from its main business.

	ABC	XYZ
Sales	$100,000	$100,000
Operating income	21,000	13,000
Extraordinary gain	....	8,000
Income taxes (33.34 percent)	$7,000	$7,000
Net income	14,000	14,000
Average shares outstanding	10,000	10,000
EPS	1.40	1.40

You should search for companies that have not reported a loss in the last 10 years. This is because if no losses were reported, the company could not overstate its losses in one year (by recording an extraordinary loss) in order to clear the decks for positive earnings comparisons in future years.

There is one caveat to discounting the impact of extraordinary events. If the company reports extraordinary losses either too often or the extraordinary losses appear excessive in terms of the company's historical earnings or equity, such losses should not be disregarded. Frequently reporting extraordinary losses is a sign of bad management and an indication that the company is trying to cover up its operational problems by classifying the operating losses as extraordinary events.

T I P

There is one consolation for a company that has reported losses in the recent past: Companies can carry over their net operating losses to future years, thus shielding the company's earnings from federal income taxes in the future.

Also, all extraordinary losses should be reported net of the associated tax savings. For example, if a company reports an extraordinary loss of $1,000,000, there is a concomitant tax savings of $340,000 ($1,000,000 × 34%) due to the fact that extraordinary losses can offset income. Therefore, the company should report an extraordinary loss of $660,000 ($1,000,000 – $340,000). Failure to factor in the tax benefits when reporting extraordinary losses will result in overstating the subsequent years' gains.

Quality of earnings is enhanced when the company is conservative in its accounting procedures. Some indications of conservative accounting are using the last-in-first-out (LIFO) method rather than the first-in-first-out (FIFO) method for inventory valuation, expensing costs as opposed to capitalizing costs and choosing an accelerated rather than a slower method of depreciation, amortization, and depletion. For instance, let's see how two companies can legitimately report radically different results merely by employing different accounting criteria:

	ABC	XYZ
Sales	$1,000,000	$1,000,000
Costs and expenses:		
Cost of goods sold [1]	400,000	350,000
Depreciation [2]	100,000	80,000
Amortization expense [3]	50,000	30,000
Exploration costs [4]	75,000	50,000
Pension costs [5]	60,000	40,000
Asset impairments [6]	30,000	
Compensation:		
Base salaries	75,000	75,000
Bonuses [7]	50,000	
Total costs/expenses	840,000	625,000
Pretax income	160,000	375,000
Tax Expense (34 percent) [8]	54,400	54,400
Net income	105,600	320,600
EPS (on 100,000 shares outstanding)	1.06	3.21

[1] The ABC Company uses the LIFO inventory valuation method and the XYZ Company uses the FIFO method. In an inflationary environment, LIFO firms report higher costs of goods sold because the most recent additions to their inventory are counted as being sold at higher prices than the earlier-acquired inventory. On the contrary, FIFO firms report lower costs of goods sold because the costs of their earlier purchases are counted at lower prices for purposes of computing cost of goods sold.

[2] The ABC Company uses an accelerated depreciation method with shorter lives than the XYZ Company uses.

[3] The ABC Company amortizes intangible assets over shorter time periods than the XYZ Company.

[4] The ABC Company expenses all exploration costs while the XYZ Company capitalizes all such costs.

[5] The ABC Company has a more conservative assumption of the rates of return on its pension assets than the XYZ Company.

[6] The ABC Company decided to report a loss on the market value of its long-term marketable securities while the XYZ Company has not yet made such a determination.

[7] The ABC Company pays its employees bonuses in cash while the XYZ Company pays their employees bonuses in stock options.

[8] The ABC Company simply has a tax liability equal to 34 percent of its pretax income ($160,000 x 34 percent = $54,400). However, the XYZ Company makes use of a $73,100 net operating loss incurred in previous years to reduce its current tax liability from $127,500 ($375,000 x 34 percent) to $54,400.

A few of the other pitfalls to avoid when analyzing the quality of companies' earnings include the following:

Deferred taxes will most likely act as a drag on future earnings and should be included in the company's debt structure.

Other deferred charges, such as organizational costs, should be treated with skepticism. Such deferred charges are often not assets representing future benefits, but rather deferred losses that are being carried forward so as not to cloud the current earnings reports.

You must consider the potential adverse impact of contingent liabilities such as litigation, claims arising from product warranties, or self-insurance risks.

The inclusion of bank debt in the current liability section of the balance sheet may mean that the company cannot obtain a refinancing arrangement with a lender. If there is not a valid reason for the current liability classification of the bank debt, then the company may have problems that are not readily apparent from its disclosed financial statements. (One valid reason for including bank debt in the current liability section is that short-term bank debt is needed to finance the slower periods of a highly seasonal business.)

Although the fundamental analyst will carefully read the footnotes to the financial statements in order to get a more in-depth understanding of the company's accounting practices, there are a few overwhelming indications that a company has quality earnings:

1. An increasing cash position without a concomitant increase in debt.

2. Book value and shareholders equity consistently increasing over the years.

3. Consistently increasing cash dividend payments over many years.

The Power of Positive Cash Flow

The calculation of cash flow and the interpretation of cash flows statements are difficult concepts to understand and will only be briefly dealt with here. The definition of cash flow is net income plus depreciation, amortization of intangible assets and other charges (such as increases in deferred cash liability, amortization of bond discounts and warranty expenses). Cash flow is an attempt to measure the differences in the cash inflows and the cash outflows that a company has over a period of time.

As mentioned before, earnings reports are liable to manipulation. Also, the concept of earnings is dubious in that earnings are not tangible. However, cash flow is extremely important because it is cash rather than earnings that must be expended to finance capital expansion, repay loans, initiate stock repurchases, and pay dividends. Fundamentalists like to see a continuous growth in cash flow.

Also, the company should always have a positive free cash flow, meaning cash flow is greater than the sum of the dividend payments and capital expenditures. If a company does not have positive free cash flow, it may have difficulty making its dividend payments or investing in capital-intensive projects.

Analysts use cash flow to determine the company's ability to repay debt and interest. For instance, the cash flow-to-debt ratio tracks the firm's ability to meet scheduled long-term debt and interest payment requirements. Also, the cash flow-to-interest ratio determines how many times free cash flow will cover fixed interest payments on long-term debt. The higher these ratios are, the easier it is for the company to repay its obligations to creditors.

Adequate Returns on Equity/Acceptable Returns on Assets

As an investor, you will want to measure the returns that the management teams of your holdings are generating on your investments. Thus, you should determine the return on shareholders' equity (ROE) that your various companies are generating. ROE is a measure of how efficiently management has used the shareholders' equity to generate income. ROE is net income divided by the average common shareholders' equity throughout the period under review. Many fundamental investors insist that the companies in which they invest have achieved an uninterrupted ROE of at least 15 percent over the last 5 to 10 years. A 15 percent or greater ROE is an indication of solid managerial performance. A less conservative

T R A P

> ⊘ You should not be impressed with a company that posts a very strong ROE ratio if the ROE was generated because equity had been reduced as a result of special charges.

investor might accept a slightly lower ROE if he thought that a management shake-up was imminent, an unprofitable business might be sold or discontinued, or the company was plotting a foray into a rapidly growing business segment.

Value investors are also interested in tracking companies' use of all of their assets. The return-on-assets (ROA) ratio is computed by dividing net income by the average total assets that the company had on hand for the year. This ratio gives an indication of how efficiently management utilizes *all* of the assets under its control (regardless if such assets were funded by debt or equity).

Sound Capital Structures

Fundamental investors only give serious consideration to companies that have sound capital structures. This is because it is capital structure, along with cash flow, that determines if and how a company will be able to fund future expansion.

T I P

☞ Intangible assets should be considered as valuable assets. Thus in calculating the return on assets (ROA) ratio, the value of intangible assets (such as goodwill, patents, and trademarks) should be included in the denominator. This may seem logical, but analysts sometimes calculate ROA by subtracting intangible assets from total assets, distorting the ROA by making the ROA ratio higher than it normally would have been.

Ideally, a large part of future expansion will be funded from cash flow even though there may be legitimate circumstances, such as aggressive competition, that require capital expansion to be accelerated through the assumption of debt. Companies should not have too much debt in relation to their equity or else their access to the debt markets will be limited in the future and onerous repayment obligations may cripple normal corporate operations.

However, companies can safely assume some debt. In fact, it can even be advantageous for a company to have some debt on its balance sheet since interest expenses are a tax-deductible expense. As a rough rule of thumb, long-term debt should not exceed roughly 30 percent of equity. However, companies that operate in noncompetitive or heavily regulated industries (e.g., utility companies) or companies that produce goods for which their customers have an inelastic demand (e.g., food and tobacco companies) may safely employ higher levels of debt.

Also, the value investor would scrutinize the financial reports to determine if the company is resorting to tactics to understate the amount of debt that is effectively utilized. A company can take such tactics by underfunding its pension obligations or by failing to capitalize its lease expenses. (Leases are similar to debt in that lessees are required to make a series of payments, which often have interest components, into the distant future in order to enjoy the use of assets. Therefore, GAAP requires the capitalization of leases—recording the lease as an asset and an obligation on the balance sheet—when such leases resemble debt.) Finally, you should read the footnotes to the financial statements to determine whether or not the company is subject to overly restrictive covenants.

You should calculate a few ratios designed to determine how easily the company can cover its fixed charges. One of these ratios, the fixed-charges ratio, is simply earnings available to meet fixed charges divided by fixed charges. (Fixed charges include interest payments, interest implicit in lease obligations, preferred-stock dividend requirements of the majority-owned subsidiaries, principal repayment, and long-term purchase contracts in excess of normal requirements that are not subject to cancelation.) The higher the fixed-charges ratio, the more easily the company can pay its fixed charges from earnings.

Another ratio that indicates how easy it will be for the corporation to meet its fixed charges is the cash flow coverage ratio:

$$\frac{\text{Pretax cash provided by operations}}{\text{Fixed charges}}$$

This ratio may be more revealing than the fixed-charge ratio because pretax cash flow provided by operations is a more accurate measure of available cash on hand than earnings. Of course, it is cash, not illusive earnings figures, that is used to pay fixed charges. The higher the cash flow coverage ratio is, the less of a detriment the company's debt becomes.

T I P

An overfunded pension plan strengthens the company's capital structure. "For one thing, an overfunded plan means a company does not have to make cash contributions to the plan, leaving more cash for expansion or other corporate expenditures. Overfunded plans can tap into the surplus to cover hefty retiree medical costs. Surplus assets also give a big boost to earnings. And a pension surplus can be a strategic weapon, affording a company the flexibility to sweeten early retirement packages in downsizings."

Source: Suzanne Woolley, "Corporate America's Clean Little Secret," *Business Week* March 18, 1996, pp. 104–5.

One of the formulas that analysts use to determine the ease with which the corporation will meet its interest payments is the total interest coverage ratio. This ratio, which determines the number of times total interest charges were earned, is computed by dividing the sum of the pretax income plus total interest expense by total interest expense. This quotient should be at least 5 or 6, but always the higher the better.

One of the ratios used to determine whether or not the company is liquid enough to meet its short-term obligations is the current ratio. This ratio is determined by dividing current assets by current liabilities. The current ratio should usually be 2:1 or higher, meaning the company has at least $2 of current assets for every $1 of current liabilities.

The Importance of Dividends

Since the fundamental investor is a long-term investor he likes to be paid while he waits for his stock to appreciate. Therefore, he prefers to make commitments to companies that have long, uninterrupted histories of increasing their dividend payouts; rising dividends indicate that the management feels that the future earnings will be sufficient to cover the increased dividend expense. (The fundamental investor knows that the Board of Directors would rarely increase the dividends only to make a retraction shortly thereafter because this would be a highly noticeable indication of incompetent stewardship.)

For many reasons, the conservative investor prefers that some of the company's earnings be paid out in dividends as opposed to its plowing back all of its earnings into future operations. Because fundamentalists tend to invest in the more dominant companies, they feel that the company should already be in a strong enough financial position to afford to pay dividends and maintain a capital expansion program. The fundamentalist would argue that a company that has been in business for several decades cannot use the excuse that all of the earnings should be retained in order to fuel rapid growth. This may be legitimate reasoning for a company that has only been in business for a few years and is rapidly growing but not for an older, slower-growing concern.

Conservative investors also like dividends because dividends do not lie. Investment relations specialists, securities analysts, and others often make rosy predictions regarding a stock's capital-appreciation potential. Unfortunately, many of these predictions never come to pass and the projected capital gains turn into realized capital losses. On the contrary, dividends are real money that investors can deposit in their bank accounts.

Also, conservative investors like dividends, thinking it unwise to let management retain all of the earnings when management's agenda often differs from that of the shareholders. Fundamental investors become stockholders solely to make money; management is not always exclusively interested in making money for them. Management is often more concerned with increasing market share at the expense of profits, bestowing largesse on their officers, or sponsoring community activities.

Finally, dividend payments can act as insurance policies in that they usually prevent the stock from falling too far. This is because the lower the stock goes, the

T I P

> The higher the dividend yield, the better—as long as the dividend is secure. You can get a feel as to whether the dividend is secure by evaluating the dividend in terms of the company's earnings and cash flow: The dividend payout should not be greater than about 65 percent of earnings or in excess of roughly 50 percent of cash flow.

higher the dividend yield becomes. For example, if a company pays $1.00 per share a year in dividends and the conservative investor pays $15 for each share, his yield would be 6.67 percent ($1/$15). Then if the market experienced some turbulence and these shares fell to $9.00 the dividend yield would rise to 11.11 percent ($1/$9). Such a high dividend yield would usually entice more people to purchase these shares, which in turn would push the price of these shares up.

Acceptable Valuations

After finding a solid company with a promising future, you want to make sure that its shares can be purchased at reasonable prices. Do this by comparing the market price of the shares with the company's book value, earnings, earnings yield, cash flow, dividends, and sales.

The fundamental investor seeks companies selling beneath their book values. Book value is the difference between assets (recorded at historical costs minus accumulated depreciation) minus liabilities. This difference is also referred to as owners' equity, which is the measure of the shareholders' investment in the company. Therefore, a company that has $150,000,000 in assets and $60,000,000 in liabilities would have a book value, or owners' equity, of $90,000,000. If there were 5,000,000 shares outstanding, the book value per share would be $18.00 ($90,000,000/5,000,000). Thus, if this company's shares were quoted at less than $18, the investor could reasonably expect to get more than he paid for. *Buying stock whose price-to-book value ratio (P/BV) is less than one is generally considered to be a good buy.*

The fundamental investor will try to purchase shares that have a reasonable price-to-earnings ratio (P/E). This very common ratio is found in most newspapers for most stocks and is simply the market price of a share divided by the previous

TIP

Because book value reflects historical costs and not current asset values, it provides only a rough and ready benchmark for determining the fair market value of a company. Quite often a company's book value may be severely misstated in terms of its fair market value. For instance, book value will be understated when a company records land purchased in 1960 for $500,000 as an asset even though the same land is now appraised at $5,000,000. Such an understatement of book value in terms of fair market value provides a margin of safety in the fundamental investor's calculations.

years' earnings per share (EPS). The P/E also represents the number of years that it will take the company to earn the purchase price that the investor paid for the stock. For example, if the ABC Company earns $2.00 per share each year and the market values the shares at $28, the P/E would be 14. Thus, it would take about 14 years for the company to earn the purchase price of the stock. As a sweeping generality, a stock with a P/E between 6 and 9 is undervalued while a stock with a P/E above 16 is usually overvalued.

The P/E ratio is more meaningful when it is compared with the growth rate in earnings per share. The P/E to growth rate (PEG) is P/E divided by the growth rate in EPS. If the PEG is less than one, the stock is generally considered to be cheap. Thus,

TRAP

⊘ One problem with the price-to-book value ratio is that a company's human assets are not factored into book value. This omission distorts the validity of book value because human capital is often more valuable than tangible assets, especially in a knowledge-based economy.

For instance, there could be two software companies endowed with the same tangible assets. Assuming that the market capitalizations for these two companies are the same, they would have identical P/BV ratios. However, one company could be staffed with people of (Microsoft® CEO) Bill Gates' ilk while the other could be staffed with laymen. Obviously, the company with computer programming capabilities similar to those of Bill Gates would be more valuable. However, the P/BV ratio would indicate that the company with top-notch programmers is no more valuable than the company with laymen doing the programming.

if the ABC Company had a P/E of 14 and was growing at 20 percent a year, the PEG would be .70 (14/20) and thus would not be considered overvalued.

When examining the P/E ratio, keep the following important tips in mind:

1. Look for shares selling below their average P/E ratios.

2. Take the average of several years' worth of earnings when computing the P/E ratio.

3. Compare the P/E of the company under review with the P/E of its competitors as well as with various market indexes (such as the Dow Jones Industrial Average, Standard and Poor's 500, etc.).

4. Remember that the market rewards companies with higher P/E multiples if they generate consistent earnings growth rather than unpredictable earnings.

Another way to evaluate the P/E ratio is to calculate the earnings yield by simply dividing the P/E into 1. Thus, the earnings yield for the ABC Company would be 7.14 percent (1/14). This is, at least theoretically, the earnings that the company would yield the investor on an annual basis. This earnings yield should be compared with the current rate on AAA Corporate bonds; since stockholders face more risk than bondholders, they should be rewarded with a higher yield. Thus, if the current rate on AAA corporate bonds was 8 percent and the ABC Company had an earnings yield of 7.14 percent, the stock would not be attractive.

Realizing that the earnings figures are far from being a perfect measure of a corporation's performance, the fundamental investor will try to relate the price of the shares to the cash flow per share. The price-to-cash flow ratio (P/CF) is merely

T I P

☞ You should add-back "nonrecurring" charges recorded by the company in re-evaluating its P/E multiple. For instance, assume that a company that you are reviewing recorded a total net income of $150 million over the past five years; announced $50 million in "one-time nonrecurring charges" over the same period of time and has shares that are trading at a P/E multiple of 18. In re-evaluating the multiple, you should subtract the charges from net income ($150 million – $50 million = $100 million). Since this reduced net income by 33 percent, you should increase the P/E multiple by 33 percent, to reach 24 ((18*1/3) + 18)).

the market price of the stock divided by the cash flow per share. The stock will generally appear cheap if the P/CF is 4 or 5 and expensive if the P/CF is 9 or above. Also, a low P/CF provides companies with a compelling reason for buying back their stock.

A simple way to relate the price of a share of stock to the dividend payout is to calculate the dividend yield—the amount of the dividend that is paid out divided by the price of the stock. Thus, if a company paid a $1.50 dividend each year and the stock cost $17.00, the dividend yield would be 8.8 percent ($1.50/$17.00). Generally, less than a 3 percent dividend yield indicates that the shares are overvalued, while a dividend yield that is more than 6 percent indicates that the stock is undervalued.

You should also evaluate the price of the shares in terms of sales or revenues. The price-to-sales ratio (P/S) is merely the market capitalization of the company (number of shares outstanding times price per share) divided by the company's previous year's sales. As a sweeping generality, a company is considered to be undervalued if the P/S is .75 or less for small capitalization companies and 0.4 or less for large capitalization companies. The P/S is an especially useful tool for detecting small companies that are basically sound but have experienced temporary setbacks.

The P/S has several advantages over the more common P/E ratio:

1. Sales are a more consistent measure of a company's activities than earnings; the level of sales indicates the demand for the company's products and is not subject to nearly as much manipulation as are the earnings figures.

2. The P/E ratio can, at times, be rendered inoperative when the company reports losses and not earnings.

3. The sales and revenue figures are usually released several weeks before the earnings figures.

Buying Stock for Less Than the Company's Assets

Because fundamental investors are highly selective about the commitments they make to the market, they are primarily concerned with finding a bargain—they want to make sure they get more than they pay for. As discussed above, investors can be reasonably assured of this if they buy the company's stock for less than the net assets or book value that each share represents (or buy a stock with a price-to-book value ratio of less than 1).

An excellent indication that a value investor is getting a bargain is when he finds a stock that is selling below its "cash per share." The cash-per-share calculation starts with unrestricted cash in the company's coffers and subtracts all of the claims on the company prior to the claims of its common shareholders. This difference is divided by the shares outstanding. For example, if the ABC Company has a cash balance of $82,000,000 and total liabilities (which includes all debts, payables, pension payments, uncapitalized leases, deferred taxes, etc.) amounting to $32,000,000, the company would have $50,000,000 in unrestricted cash. If there were 5,000,000 shares outstanding, then there would be $10 of cash per share ($50,000,000/5,000,000 = $10). If the market price was less than $10 per share, the investor would get the remainder of the company's current assets and all of its fixed assets for free. Thus, the cash-per-share figure can lead to the discovery of a tremendously undervalued company.

A similar strategy would be to find a company selling below its "net-net current assets." Net-net current assets are working capital (current assets minus current liabilities) minus all other claims prior to the claims of the common shareholders. Thus, if the XYZ Company had $132,000,000 in working capital and $27,000,000 in other claims prior to those of its common shareholders, the net-net current assets would be $105,000,000. Therefore, if there were 7,000,000 shares outstanding the net-net current assets per share would be $15 ($105,000,000/7,000,000). If the market price was less than $15, it would be indicative of an undervalued company.

A simple modification can be made to the net-net current assets approach. Since most companies would be able to realize some cash proceeds by liquidating their fixed assets, we could add 25 percent of the value of the fixed assets back to the net-net current assets. In the above example, if the XYZ Company had $210,000,000 booked as fixed assets, we should add $52,500,000 ($210,000,000 ×

T I P

A company that is growing its earnings through increased sales will be rewarded with a higher valuation than a company that is growing its earnings just as rapidly through cost reductions.

25%) to the net-net current assets ($105,000,000) to get $157,500,000. Thus, $157,500,000 divided by 7,000,000 shares equals $22.50 per share in adjusted net-net current assets. Again, if the market values these shares at less than $22.50, a profitable opportunity is probably at hand.

Tying It Together

Finally, there are a few formulas that tie together several of the concepts just described. First, there is the *investment value ratio:* The return on assets divided by the P/E ratio. For example, if the ROA was 24 percent and the P/E was 10, the investment value ratio would be 2.4. A company with an investment value ratio of above 1.5 is good, but the higher the better.

Second, the fundamental investor would apply the *return value ratio:* Add the ROA to the after-tax dividend yield and then divide that sum by the P/E ratio. For example, let's assume that the company under review has an ROA of 24 percent and a 5 percent dividend yield. The after-tax dividend yield to the shareholder would be 3.3 percent [5% × (1 − .34)]. Adding the 24-percent ROA and the 3.3-percent after-tax dividend yield equals 27.3 percent. Then the final step is to divide the 27.3 percent by the P/E, which we will assume is 12. Therefore the return value ratio is 2.28. A Return Value Ratio above 1.75 is good, but, again, the higher the better.

One formula that ties book value (BV), ROE, and an investor's required return (RR) together is called the expectancy value (EV), which indicates the highest price that should be paid for a share of stock. The expectancy formula is EV = BV(ROE/RR). Let's say that we can get a 7-percent return on investment by purchasing risk-free Treasury bonds. Since investing in stocks is riskier than holding T-bonds, we will require a higher return than the 7-percent opportunity cost that can be obtained by buying the T-bonds. Under these circumstances, let's suppose that the required return is 10 percent and the company under review typically generates 14-percent ROE. By application of the expectancy formula, the fundamental investor would be unwilling to pay more than 70 percent of book value for the shares of said company (.14/.10 = 1.40). Therefore, if the book value per share was $30.00, the fundamentalist would not want to buy any shares for more than $42.00 per share ($30.00 × 1.40).

Additionally, the fundamental investor may apply what John Neff calls *the terminal relationship figure*—the total return (the sum of the growth rate in the earnings per share and the dividend yield) divided by the P/E. Therefore, if the EPS (earnings per share) were growing at 15 percent each year and the dividend yield was 5 percent, the total return would be 20 percent. Then we would divide the total return by the P/E, which we will say is 8 in this example. The terminal relationship figure would then be 2.5 ((15 + 5)/8). The higher the terminal relationship figure the better. This figure should be compared with the other investment alternatives to determine how expensive the earnings growth and dividend yield are in comparison with other opportunities.

Another simple ratio that I like compares the net profit margins with the price-to-sales ratio. The higher this ratio, the better. Let's say that company A has net profit margins of 6 percent and a price-to-sales ratio of 1.2, while company B has net profit margins of 4 percent and a price-to-sales ratio of 1.0. So assuming that everything else about the companies is the same, which stock is the better buy? The answer is company A, since 6/1.2 = 5 while 4/1 is only 4.

Finally, the fundamental investor may wish to calculate the capital value (CV) figure, the maximum price to pay for a share of stock:

CV   =   BV((AIBV+DYBV)/OC) $10.67 = $8.00((10%+6%)/12%)

where

CV   =   capital value

BV   =   book value per share ($8.00)

AIBV   =   average annual increase in book value (10%)

DYBV   =   dividend yield on current book value (6%)

OC   =   opportunity cost (12%)

By application of the formula, the capital value in this example is $10.67. Therefore, shares of this company should only be purchased for less than $10.67.

PART TWO

LOOK BEFORE
YOU LEAP

4

Retail

The retail sector is huge. Depending upon how you wish to define retail, this chapter could include everything from after-market automotive retailers to grocery stores to drug stores to sporting goods stores. While the scope of the retail industry can be bewildering, it may help to segment the retail industry by lines of merchandise offered, service levels, formats, and locations. The main advantage of doing so is to facilitate comparison with the performance of companies serving similar markets. You can only obtain a clear picture of a company's relative performance by making apples-to-apples comparisons. Thus, department stores should be compared with other department stores while discounters should be compared with other discounters.

Despite the wide variety of retailers, a few generalities apply to the retail industry. For instance, retailers do not change the form of items that they sell. Thus, they cannot embellish the attributes of the individual goods that they stock. However, retailers change the *perception* of the goods that they stock. For example, if some items are only available at exclusive high-end retailers, greater value will be associated with such product. Also, retailers can favor one manufacturer over another by giving the preferred manufacturer prime shelf space.

Power Shift

In general, retailers have increased their power vis-a-vis manufacturers over the last 10 years or so. It used to be that a retailer had to satisfy the manufacturer in order to retain the privilege of selling the manufacturer's goods. For instance, retailers had to commit prime shelf space to ensure that they would receive shipments from manufacturers.

Now, retailers decide which manufacturers they wish to deal with. There are a couple of reasons for this transition:

- Retailers have only recently made the transformation from family management to professional management. (Manufacturers made this transformation long before retailers.) Accordingly, manufacturers can no longer use their internal economic forecasts or customer satisfaction surveys to demand concessions from retailers. Now retailers can use their own statistics generated from the widespread use of scanning data to demand preferable terms from manufacturers.

- *There has been a proliferation of products while retail space has risen only marginally.* For example, in the consumer-packaged-goods industry, the number of stockkeeping units (SKU) grew 16 percent each year from 1985 to 1992, while shelf space only advanced 1.5 percent during each of those years; the result is that retail space has become more valuable. Thus, the new paradigm is *he who controls shelf space determines the products customers have to chose from.*

While there has been a power shift from manufacturers to retailers, there is still friction between these two players. For instance, manufacturers object to large retail chains' selling their products at excessively low prices. While the largest retailers can always threaten to stop selling an uncooperative manufacturer's products, manufacturers of well-known products also have leverage over retailers. For instance, major sporting goods chains such as The Sports Authority must carry Nike™ products. Similarly, national book store chains such as Barnes & Noble must carry books published by Irwin Professional Publishing.

While manufacturers by law cannot dictate prices that retailers charge, they still have recourse:

- They can use minimum-advertised-price policies (essentially floor prices below which they will not contribute their percentage of an advertising campaign's cost) if the retailer sells the products below such prices.

- They can stop shipping to customers that sell below their cost. (In fact, Whirlpool® suspended shipment of its washing machines and dryers when Best Buy wanted to sell such appliances at very low retail prices.)

- They can diminish their retailer support (including the training of the retailer's sales force).

- They can delay the shipment of the manufacturer's new products.

With this brief background in mind, it is now time to begin our analysis of the retail industry. The retail industry becomes manageable to analyze by doing two things: first, you must consider macroeconomic indicators; second, you must consider sector-specific criteria.

Macroeconomic Factors

To a large extent, the health of the retail sector is dependent upon current general economic conditions and expectations of future prosperity. In other words, people must have the means to spend as well as the confidence to make purchases.

To ascertain the general condition of the economy, you can simply look around yourself. If you, your colleagues, and your friends are generally becoming more prosperous, then the local economy is probably growing. On the other hand, if you and your neighbors are facing difficulty finding employment, paying your bills, and saving, then the economy could very well be deteriorating.

However, for a more formal method of ascertaining the strength of the economy, you can simply keep abreast of the direction of the major economic indicators. A good starting point is gross domestic product (GDP), which measures the value of all goods and services produced by the domestic economy in a year. Retail sales should rise when real GDP (which factors out inflation) is growing since this indicates that the economy is genuinely expanding.

There are a few things you should keep in mind when considering how growth in real GDP may impact the retail industry. First, you should put the growth in context. Since the United States economy is so large, it cannot grow at very high rates. Thus, even a 3-percent growth rate in real GDP is encouraging.

TRAP

⊘ You should be careful not to extrapolate excessive GDP growth onto the long-term profitability of retail stores. Thus, if GDP is growing by 5 percent annually, it does not necessarily follow that the revenues of retail stores will consistently rise by a similar rate into the distant future. This is because the Federal Reserve may boost interest rates in order to dampen accelerating economic growth. Rising interest rates act as a brake on economic growth, which will be felt by retailers. Additionally, higher interest rates make it more expensive to charge purchases on credit cards.

When real GDP rises above 3 percent, economists believe that the economy is growing very quickly.

Another tool that you can use in projecting macroeconomic growth is the Index of Leading Economic Indicators, which projects the future vitality of the economy (over the coming nine months) by averaging 11 forward-looking economic barometers. In addition to simply considering the growth rates (or contraction) of this index, investors can get a feel for the breadth of the economy's strength by considering the number of this index's components that are advancing versus the number of the components that are declining. Obviously, the greater the number of components that are rising, the broader the economy's strength is.

Employment Measures

While macroeconomic gauges such as GDP and the Index of Leading Economic Indicators give investors a rudimentary feel for the direction of the overall economy, investors wishing to take positions in retail stocks should focus on economic indicators that better measure consumers' capacity to spend.

One such set of factors hinges on employment levels; as employment levels rise, more people will have income to spend. One way to gauge employment levels is to consider how many people are being added to payrolls. This can most easily be done by referring to the Labor Department's nonfarm payroll reports. The more workers that the Labor Department indicates have been added to the nation's payrolls, the better the outlook becomes for retail spending.

Another method of gauging the employment picture is to monitor the unemployment rates. Reductions in the number of people applying for unemployment insurance indicate that more people are finding jobs (or fewer people are losing jobs), the falling levels of these applications are thus a harbinger of strong retail spending. On the contrary, the higher the unemployment rate climbs, the gloomier the outlook for retailers becomes.

However, unemployment rates can vary significantly from one region to another. Thus, variations of unemployment rates in different parts of the country point to areas of strength and weakness for retailers. For instance, rising unemployment rates in New England may indicate difficulty for northeastern retailers such as Caldor, while declining unemployment rates in Wisconsin may be a precursor of greater retail sales for Wisconsin-based stores such as Kohls.

It is important to realize that all unemployment numbers are highly volatile. Therefore, you should not place too much emphasis on one week's numbers. Rather, it is best to compare the current four-week moving average to the four-week moving average of the applications for unemployment insurance from a year earlier.

The above employment gauges are useful for measuring the current employment situation. But to stay one step ahead of other investors you must formulate an outlook for employment in the more distant future by considering a number of factors. For instance, the Conference Board's Help-Wanted Index can be relied upon to determine how much hiring employers intend to do in the future. The higher this index rises, the brighter job prospects become.

You should also consider the results of surveys that attempt to predict future staffing requirements of American firms. Organizations such as the American Management Association and the Gallup Organization, for example, periodically poll large firms to ascertain what such firms' plans are regarding the hiring or firing of employees. Similarly, the National Federation of Independent Businesses conducts inquiries of smaller businesses' staffing plans.

Personal Income

While employment levels are helpful in determining future consumption, investors should also consider the trends in personal income, which correlate directly with consumer spending. When incomes rise, people feel freer to spend. Conversely, lower incomes are a precursor to lower retail spending. Additionally, *expectations* of future income levels are important for future spending: When people believe that they will be awarded with bonuses and raises, they will spend more freely; conversely, when workers anticipate wage freezes or concessions they will draw their purse strings tighter. Changes in personal income levels are published monthly by the Commerce Department. As a diligent investor you should try to get a sense of *future* income growth to stay ahead of the pack.

Your ability to project future employment levels is a good foundation for determining trends in personal income. This is because wages and salaries are the largest component of personal income, accounting for roughly 57 percent. Thus, when wages and salaries rise, so too will personal income.

Wages and salaries are likely to rise when the labor market is tight. For instance, when employers have difficulty recruiting and retaining workers they may try to attract and appease workers with higher wages. Thus, the retail sector could benefit from a double whammy when employment levels rise. (Higher employment levels and higher wages boost consumers' ability to spend.)

One precursor to higher wage levels occurs when employees work increasingly long hours. (The length of the average workweek is published by the Bureau of Labor Statistics.) Longer workweeks are an early indicator of an economic upturn because employers would rather work existing workers longer hours than hire additional workers.

There are two major benefits associated with longer workweeks:

1. *Wages rise due to workers receiving greater overtime payments.* Since most workers are paid at least time-and-a-half for working overtime, longer workweeks result in a disproportionate amount of money falling into workers' paychecks.

2. *Excessively long working hours are a harbinger of higher employment growth.* There is a limit as to how much overtime people can work. Working too many hours for an extended period of time often results in work-related injuries, mistakes, and worker disgruntlement. Thus, in

order to avoid these problems, employers eventually must begin to increase their headcount.

While wages and salaries constitute the largest component of personal income, these elements are by no means the only components of personal income. The next largest category of personal income is transfer payments, which includes welfare payments, disaster relief disbursements, and farm subsidies. Other compo-

T I P

You should monitor changes in consumers' wealth since wealth is a determinant of consumers' willingness to spend. If your net worth is decreasing you will be less likely to increase your discretionary spending than if your net worth is rising. (Therefore, falling real estate and stock values should depress consumption.) Thus, you should consider the changes in the value of residences and equities because these are sources of a large degree of consumers' wealth. Similarly, the less equity people have in their homes (due to reverse mortgages), the less likely they are to spend. On the other hand, refinancing mortgages at lower interest rates puts more money into homeowners' pockets.

nents of personal income include interest payments, dividend payments, and rent payments. The trends in each of these components should also be monitored in order to gauge consumers' ability to spend.

Savings Rate

Consumers do not solely finance their purchases with income; purchases are also made from savings or borrowings. Thus, it is important to factor developments in consumers' saving rates into your projections of future retail sales levels. (The national savings rate is published by the Commerce Department.)

More important than the savings rate at a given point in time are the trends in the savings rate. When analyzing changes in the nation's savings rate it is important to maintain a keen perspective of time. When the savings rate falls due to more money being spent on retail purchases, the better off retailers are *in the near term*. This is simply because retail sales are being funded from savings accounts.

On the contrary, if consumers become increasingly frugal, their savings rates will rise but they will, by definition, spend less on consumer goods *in the near term*. Lower spending on consumer goods translates into less revenue for the retail sector.

However, when considering the future of retail sales, we change our opinion regarding the direction of the savings rate. Decreasing savings rates *over the long term* are problematic for the retail sector. The lower the savings rate falls, the less of a reservoir of buying power consumers will have to finance future purchases. On the other hand, the higher the savings rate rises, the better the prospects for retail sales become in the distant future because consumers have more ability to spend.

Debt Levels

One problem associated with low savings rates is that consumers are more quickly forced to resort to financing their purchases with debt. Similar to savings rates, there is a profound difference between the impact of debt levels over the short term and over the long term. For instance, rising credit card debt levels are positive for retail sales in the near term. This is obvious because credit card–financed purchases translate into retail revenue.

However, there are limits as to how high consumers' debt levels can rise before the long-term viability of retail sales becomes imperiled. (One good source to use in determining the overall growth in total consumer credit card indebtedness are reports issued by the Bankcard Holders of America. Other telling sources of changes in credit card usage include reports by Visa U.S.A. and Master Charge International.) Nevertheless, reports of significantly greater charges by one of these issuers is not always a sign of trouble ahead. For instance, such growth could be attributable to more merchants' accepting a given card or to there being more of a particular card in circulation.

Consumers will find that if they use their charge cards too aggressively, they will hit their credit limits sooner. When this happens, retail sales are likely to plunge. (In determining how close consumers are to hitting their credit limits you can review statistics regarding credit limits from the *Nilson Report,* a credit card industry trade publication.) However, when it appears that consumers are rapidly approaching their credit limits, you should consider a number of factors. Some credit card companies liberally raise credit limits as long as their customers are

T R A P

⊘ While liberalized credit policies by retailers will usually result in higher sales, they could present receivable problems later. For instance, I was extremely concerned when, in December 1995, Best Buy announced that its customers could buy merchandise before Christmas but would not have to pay for it until the beginning of 1997.

making their minimum payments on time. (The thinking behind such policy is that consumers will use a competitor's card when they exhaust all of the credit from their card. Thus, failing to raise credit limits results in lost business.)

Credit card companies can take other action to make consumer expenditures easier to finance. For instance, billing can be deferred for a number of months and interest rates can be lowered. Additionally, minimum payments (as a percentage of the balance outstanding) can be reduced.

TRAP

⊘ You should be cautious about investing in a retailer that is factoring (selling its accounts receivable at a discount) more than 60 percent of its accounts receivable.

On the other hand, when billing is not deferred or when interest rates and minimum payments are increased, retail sales may be dampened. However, the retailers will face fewer collection problems and will receive higher financing fees when they undertake such policies.

The investor should consider the percentage of sales made on cash and credit terms. The greater the percentage of sales made on credit terms, the more receivable problems will likely arise in the future.

One of the traditional tools that investors use to determine how well consumers can handle their debt levels is to consider the ratio of installment debt (which includes credit card debt and auto loans) that consumers have outstanding in relation to their disposable income. The higher this ratio becomes, the more likely it is that consumers will have no choice but to scale back their purchases.

Confidence Levels

So far, this chapter has discussed consumers' *ability* to fuel retail sales. Aside from having the ability, consumers must also have the *confidence* to spend. Such confidence hinges, to a large extent, upon future expectations—more specifically, upon projections of future changes in personal income and levels of wealth.

There are, however, other considerations that impact consumer confidence:

- The expectations of higher taxes will adversely affect consumer confidence, while anticipated tax reductions boost consumers' spirits.
- Political turmoil, such as anxiety over elections, is another factor that has been attributed to dampened consumer confidence.
- Discussions regarding higher payroll deductions for employees' medical coverage can reduce consumer confidence.
- A growing number of consumers shopping at discount stores (versus regular retailers) could indicate that consumers are losing confidence.

The Conference Board and the University of Michigan issue separate reports regarding changes in consumer confidence on a monthly basis. However, some analysts believe that it is better to monitor actual consumer spending because consumer spending indicates what consumers are actually doing, not what they are saying in surveys. Thus, you should refer to changes in spending as reported monthly by the Commerce Department. Also, Salomon Brothers' index of 22 retailers provides a general reading on the retail industry. Finally, reports issued by Johnson Redbook Service illuminate same store-sales trends in the retail sector.

Geographic Variances

When analyzing the economy, it is important to realize that different regions of the country will be in different stages of the economic cycle. For any given period of time, some regions will be experiencing rapid growth while others will face economic deterioration. These considerations are important for analyzing regional retailers. Generally, you should seek to invest in those regional retailers that will benefit from being positioned in the regions of the country experiencing economic resurgence.

As a diligent investor, you should consider the health of the industries that drive regional economies. Then you should search for retailers that are concentrated in the most promising regions while avoiding investing in the shares of retailers most exposed to deteriorating industries. For instance, if you believe that the forestry industry is about to earn record profits, you should invest in a

T I P

There *is* a prudent way to invest in a retailer whose stores are largely exposed to a region of the country that is deteriorating economically. The logic of investing in a chain of close-out stores in an area of the country that is deteriorating economically would be that an increasing number of people would have to shop in these stores since they could no longer afford to shop at regular retailers.

retailer that is concentrated in the Northwest. Or if you believe that the computer industry is the most promising industry of the future, you should invest in the retailers that will benefit from such growth by virtue of their being concentrated in the Silicon Valley area. On the other hand, if you believe that oil and natural gas prices are about to plummet you should avoid investing in retailers that serve Texas.

Cyclicality

Earlier discussion in this chapter advised investors to monitor the strength of the economy in order to gauge the health of the retail industry. This is an important first step in analyzing retail stocks because there is a loose correlation between the health of the economy and the profitability of retailers. However, as a savvy investor, you should determine which segments of the retail industry are most closely tied to the general health of the economy. Some segments are early cyclicals and begin to experience increased profitability sooner than late cyclicals, which experience a lag in benefiting from economic upturns.

One advantage of separating the early cyclicals from the late cyclicals is that you will be able to determine when various sectors of the retail industry will perform the best: When the economy begins to rebound from a recession, the shares of the early cyclicals will rise in value first; when the economy begins to experience a downturn, the shares of the late cyclicals should be the last retail stocks to fall in value.

Another advantage of segmenting retail stocks by cyclicality is that investors will know which sectors of the retail industry are undervalued and which are overvalued. For instance, when the economy begins to experience a downturn, investors may sell shares of retail stores indiscriminately. The result is that most retail stocks will fall in value. Thus, the late cyclical sectors of the retail industry may become undervalued since their share prices will have fallen faster than their profitability (representing a buying opportunity). On the contrary, when the economy begins to rebound from a recession, many investors might purchase retail stocks indiscriminately. As a result, most retail stocks will rise in value. Thus, stocks of the retail sectors that experience lags in performance will be overvalued (representing a selling opportunity) since the late cyclical retailers' earnings will not have significantly improved so quickly.

So, which sectors of the retail industry are early cyclicals and which sectors are late cyclicals? The answers to these questions largely hinge on the related companies' sensitivity to interest rates. This is because interest rates are a major driver of the economy. (Generally, the strength of the economy is inversely related to the direction of interest rates. When interest rates fall, economic activity usually accelerates; conversely, rising interest rates dampen economic growth.) Thus, the retailers that are most affected by changes in interest rates are early cyclicals while those retailers that are least impacted by changes in interest rates are late cyclicals.

Which sectors of the retail industry are most dependent on interest rates? Think about it. I know you can answer this question correctly. Want a hint? Ask yourself which purchases you are most likely to finance with debt. There lies your answer because you pay interest for the privilege of borrowing money. The higher interest rates rise, the less willing you are to finance your purchases with debt. On the contrary, the further interest rates fall, the less resistant you become to assuming debt.

Well, I bet you are more likely to finance purchases of big-ticket items rather than lower-priced merchandise with debt. The more expensive a product is, the fewer people can afford to buy it with out-of-pocket funds. Therefore, durable goods (which are designed to last at least three years) are early cyclicals since they are most sensitive to interest rates. Examples of durable goods sold by retailers include household appliances (such as washing machines) and entertainment apparati (such as stereos). Companies like Whirlpool® and Sony®, then are considered early cyclicals.

Also, many goods that go into the home are considered early cyclicals. This is because when interest rates fall, mortgage rates soon follow suit. Therefore, many homeowners refinance their mortgages. Since such homeowners benefit from lower monthly mortgage payments, they have more disposable income with which to make larger purchases. Thus, furniture and household fixtures are also considered early cyclicals.

Other goods are less dependent on a strong economy to maintain steady sales levels. For instance, food and apparel sales are less cyclical (or are later cyclicals) than more discretionary items. People have to buy food regardless of the state of the economy. Also, since the average piece of clothing is much less expensive than a durable good, fewer people need to resort to financing their wardrobes with debt.

Moreover, some segments of the retail industry are highly dependent on an extremely strong economy to realize above-average sales gains. Most of these segments consist of goods that are highly discretionary such as jewelry or recreational vehicles. The consumer who buys a recreation vehicle with debt must be highly

T I P

The liquidity of wealth is one factor that boosts sales of luxury items. Thus, initial public offerings (IPOs) and corporate insider sales of stock are helpful in selling more luxury goods. So too is the lack (or repeal) of any luxury taxes.

confident about the future soundness of his finances. This is because it takes a large degree of confidence to purchase items that are both discretionary and expensive. This is especially true of merchandise that is financed with debt.

Seasonality

The seasonality of retail sales varies from one segment of the retail industry to another. For example, children's apparel sales are strongest in the fall (for the back-to-school season). Also, Christmas presents the best selling opportunities for toy retailers. Therefore, retail stocks usually rise a few months before the strongest selling season. Accordingly, stocks of toy stores such as Toys "Я" Us® usually rise in the fall in anticipation of strong earnings related to Christmas sales.

However, you should not project a company's financial results for an entire year based upon the results it achieved during its best season. Let's say you are considering investing in a retailer of winter clothing. Let's further assume that this retailer earned $1.00 a share the previous year. Then you see that this retailer posted earnings of $.40 for the quarter ended March 30. It would be a mistake to extrapolate these earnings gains onto your projections for the entire year's results. Thus, you should not assume that this company will post earnings that approximate $1.60 for the year. Nor should you assume that earnings are rising 60 percent ($1.60 – $1 = $.60/$1.00). This would be faulty logic since retailing winter clothing is a seasonal business with one of the best quarters ending in March. Sales during the summer months will most definitely be slower for this retailer, and therefore earnings during these quarters will fall far short of $.40.

RETAIL STORES

Of course, there are a variety of retail formats, ranging from department stores to outlet malls to close-out stores. Similarly, the product lines carried by these formats vary. Some stores have narrow product lines but deep inventory levels. Other stores (known as "category killers") stock broad product lines with limited selections in each category. Some stores appeal to the masses, while other stores carry only merchandise that appeals to a limited audience. Different strategies work for different product lines and different customers.

When you analyze a retailer you must be very careful to make apples-to-apples comparisons. Failure to use comparable frames of reference will cause you to unfairly rate companies. Some categories of retail stores will inevitably have

T I P

There are isolated instances when declining same-store sales are not problematic. For instance, declining same-store sales growth due to a store's placing its units in close proximity to one another may be acceptable if such cannibalization prevents competitors from entering the market. Retailers that implement this strategy believe that the lack of competition will eventually allow their store to raise its prices.

Also, declining same-store sales growth in the second year of a store's existence is not always indicative of future problems. It is often difficult for a store to improve upon the first year's results. This is due to new stores' generating abnormally high revenue because there are usually promotions such as grand store openings associated with these new stores.

higher average ticket sales, while other types of retailers will inevitably have higher inventory turnovers. Thus, you cannot fault high-end retailers like Tiffany's for having lower inventory turns than a close-out retailer. Similarly, you cannot fault close-out retailers such as Consolidated Stores for having lower average purchases than high-end retailers.

Revenues

As previously discussed, you should look for companies that are consistently increasing their revenues. However, it is not sufficient for a retailer merely to increase its top line. A retailer that is increasing its store count by 15 percent annually but only achieves 10-percent total revenue growth is not preforming satisfactorily. Such results would indicate that same-store sales growth is faltering. Instead, you should search for companies that are posting impressive same-store sales growth, which indicates that each store is increasing its productivity.

Managements of some retailers boast about their store's *volume* of transactions while executives of other retailers boast of their *average* store transaction. For example, the CEO of Company A might try to impress investors with the fact that his company averages more customer transactions per day than its competitors. Also, the President of Company B might try to entice you to invest in his company's stock by telling you that his store's average transactions exceed those of its competitors. In reconciling average store transactions with the average number of transactions for a given store, you should compare the product of these two averages with companies that have similar strategies and product lines. This procedure should help determine which of the following fictitious retailers may be the more promising investment.

Let's assume that Company A has an average store transaction of $33 and averages 250 transactions per store per day. Let's further assume that Company B

TOOL

You should consider how efficiently the retailer under review generates revenues. One tool for making such determination is the sales-per-square feet ratio. This ratio is derived simply by dividing the company's sales by number of square feet of selling space the company controls. For example, if a given company has $1 million in monthly sales and 10,000 square feet of selling space, the sales-per-square-foot ratio is $100, meaning that the retailer generates $100 for every square foot of selling space that it controls. The higher this ratio is the better. You should thus search for companies that are consistently increasing their sales-per-square-feet ratio, indicating they are making better use of their real estate.

has an average store transaction of $43 and averages 200 transactions per store per day. Company B may be the better investment because its product of average store transactions and average number of transactions is $8,600 while the product of Company A's two averages is $8,250.

It would also be helpful to determine what percentage of people that enter the store end up actually making a purchase. Some stores are always crowded but realize lower sales than you might think. This is because many people are just

TIP

☞ The retailers that will be the most damaged by the overbuilding of selling space will be the ones with the greatest future lease obligations on their company's balance sheets.

browsing through the store. This is often the case with retailers that sell exotic or new-age products. Pier 1, a retailer of imported furniture, and Sharper Image, a merchant that is heavily stocked with high-tech gadgetry, have been said to have had this problem.

Investors should monitor changes in selling space in the retail industry. When the selling space (square feet)-per capita ratio becomes too high, retailers are expanding their selling space faster than the population is growing. Thus, a rapidly rising sales space-per capita ratio may indicate that retailers are overexpanding. Such overexpansion is intensified when more shopping is being done through catalogs and electronically as well as when the local economy is deteriorating.

On the other hand, when the sales space-per capita ratio is falling, retailers may be able to achieve greater revenues per square foot since the population is growing faster than retail selling space.

Employee Relations

You should also seek to invest in those retailers that utilize their employees most efficiently. Ideally, the retailer should try to generate as much revenue as possible with the fewest number of employees. One way to measure retailers' success in doing this is to compute the revenue-per-employee ratio. This ratio is calculated merely by dividing the retailer's revenues by the number of employees that the retailer has on its books. For instance, if a retailer generates $1 million in revenue and has 25 employees, the revenue-per-employee ratio is $40,000. This ratio should be compared with that of retailers with similar formats, retail lines, and levels of service.

Retailers can improve their revenue-per-employee ratios by operating with leaner inventories and exerting leverage over their suppliers. When a retailer

T I P

> Declining revenue-per-employee ratios are less problematic for retailers that largely compensate their employees on the commission basis. Commissions are largely a variable cost for retailers. When business is slow, payroll expenses will remain low for these retailers since salaries account for a small part of workers' pay. Thus, the retailers' profitability will not be as adversely affected as if the store had paid its employees on straight salaries.

requires its vendors to retain the store's inventory until such inventory can be placed directly on the store's shelves, the retailer can eliminate the labor-intensive step of moving inventory from the delivery truck to the stock room and from the stock room to the selling floor. Some retailers are even successful in requiring their suppliers to set up their displays in the store's selling space. For example, apparel manufacturers such as Ralph Lauren and Nautica set up store-within-a-store sections in department stores. Since such store-within-a-store concepts relieve the retailer of the need to stock such shelves, the retailer's revenue-per-employee ratio rises.

You should also try to gauge the extent of a retailer's inventory shrinkage due to pilferage and theft. Such expenses are typically the second largest variable operating expenses for a retailer, right after payroll costs. Also, shrinkage due to employee theft is a measure of employee disgruntlement. However, it is difficult to measure shrinkage because retailers do not like to publish this data. Not only is it embarrassing, but the publication of such information may result in higher insurance premiums.

Inventory Turnover

Investors should also consider how fast the retailer moves its inventory. The more times that a retailer turns its inventory. the more units of merchandise the retailer can sell in a given year. Often times, the retailer will publish its inventory turns in its annual reports of quarterly reports. Also, publications such as *Value Line* often publish the inventory turns for retailers. If you cannot find the inventory turns for the retailer that you are considering investing in, you can calculate the inventory turnover ratio by dividing the cost of goods sold by the average inventory that the retailer had on hand throughout the year. (The costs of goods sold figure can be located on the second line of the income statement. Average inventory is calculated by dividing the sum of the inventory at the beginning of the year and the inventory at the end of the year by 2.)

It is important to realize that retailers can have different strategies regarding inventory turnovers. One strategy is to turn inventories as fast as possible, the

T I P

☞ Rising average wages are not always problematic for retailers. One reason is that higher wages often result in longer employee retention. Retailers that have low rates of employee turnover save tremendous expenses associated with the hiring and training processes. Also, better compensation of loyal employees results in greater job satisfaction which often translates into better customer service.

advantage being that inventory is converted into cash faster; the fewer days that inventory is sitting on a retailer's shelf, the sooner that inventory will be turned into cash.

The formula for determining the number of days to sell inventory is 360 days/average inventory turns. If retailer ABC averages 12 inventory turns a year, it will take an average of 30 days to sell its inventory. On the other hand, if retailer XYZ averages six inventory turns a year, it will take an average of 60 days to sell its inventory. Thus, the higher the turnover ratio, the more liquid the company's financial position is.

The downside for retailers that have rapid inventory turnovers is that markdowns are often aggressively tacked onto merchandise in order to generate higher sales. The result of such markdowns is that profit margins are compromised.

However, there are situations when slower inventory turnovers should not be a cause for concern. For example, a retailer that begins to stock a different line of merchandise will probably experience slower inventory turns on the new lines of merchandise. This is because the regular customers may not be accustomed to buying such merchandise from that retailer. Also, a company that is expanding the rate of new store openings may experience slower average inventory turns because the newer stores have not yet hit full stride.

A second inventory strategy is to maintain wide profit margins at all costs. The result is that inventory can turn over much more slowly than under the first strategy. However, since these retailers are not consumed with accelerating their inventory turnovers, fewer markdowns (and less margin erosion) are realized under this strategy. Retailers that implement this strategy are often merchandisers of high-prestige items.

Therefore, you cannot analyze retailers' inventory turns or profit margins on goods sold by themselves. Since you want to invest in a company that has the best combination of inventory turns and profit margins on units sold, you can multiply inventory turns by profit margins. This formula will help you decide which of the following companies presents the better investment opportunity. Suppose Company A has 5.7 inventory turns a year and profit margins of 3.2 percent.

T I P

☞ The number of days to collect receivables should be considered in conjunction with the number of days to sell inventory in order to determine the conversion period of turning inventories into cash. For example, if the number of days to sell inventory is 30 and the days to collect receivables is 60 the total conversion period of inventories is 90. The shorter this total conversion period, the better.

Further assume that Company B has 4.4 inventory turns a year and profit margins of 4.7 percent. Which company represents the better investment? The product of Company B's inventory turns and profit margins is 20.68 while the product of Company A's inventory turns and profit margins is 18.24. Thus, Company B is the better investment.

Determining the Relative Attractiveness of Competing Retailers

Many times investors contemplate which one of two competing retailers will come to dominate its niche. For example, several years ago, you may have wondered if Kmart® or Wal-Mart® would become the dominant mass-merchant retailer. Or if you are considering investing in a chain of low-priced men's clothing stores, you might be trying to determine whether Men's Warehouse or Today's Man has more loyal customers.

What follow are two ways of determining which of two competing retailers in a given niche has the winning formula:

1. *If both of the retailers compete in the same markets, the retailer whose customers largely bypass its competitors in commuting to that given retailer will usually be the more successful retailer.* For example, it was revealed at the end of 1995, that 49 percent of Wal-Mart's customers pass a Kmart store when driving to shop at Wal-Mart. This is a perfect illustration of consumers' preference for Wal-Mart over Kmart.

2. *When the retailers operate in different geographic markets, the one with the larger total annual chain revenue relative to the population served will have the greater staying power.* Let's assume that you are considering investing in a chain of sporting goods stores. After conducting preliminary research, you have narrowed your choice down to two sporting goods retailers. Both of these retailers have similar strategies and carry similar lines of merchandise, and the regions in which these stores operate are very similar in terms of demographics, weather, and economic trends.

More specifically, let's assume that sporting goods retailer ABC operates in Dallas while sporting goods retailer XYZ operates in Atlanta. (Dallas and Atlanta are said to be very similar cities.) Further, assume that ABC has 80 stores with each store generating $300,000 in annual revenue, while XYZ has 60 stores with each store generating $500,000 in annual sales. Finally assume that Dallas has 1 million people while Atlanta has 1.5 million people. So which store does a better job of selling to its population?

The answer to this question is determined by the following formula:

$$\frac{\text{Total annual chain revenues}}{\text{Population served}}$$

Thus, the ratio for ABC is $24 per potential customer (($80 \times \$300,000)/1$ million) or $2.4 million per every 100,000 people. On the other hand, the same ratio for XYZ is $20 per potential customer (($\$500,000 \times 60)/1.5$ million) or $2.0 million for every 100,000 people. Since ABC derives $2.4 million per every 100,000 of its potential customers while XYZ only derives $2.0 million from each of its 100,000 potential customers, ABC has the more popular format. Thus, ABC could pose a serious threat to XYZ if ABC were to move into the Atlanta market. However, if XYZ were to move into Dallas, ABC would not be threatened since ABC is so much more capable of penetrating the local population.

DEPARTMENT STORES

While department stores are not growing in terms of overall units or revenues, neither are they likely to go the way of the dinosaur. They appeal to many shoppers because they offer one-stop shopping. This convenience is especially popular with people between the ages of 35 and 50, which is a very attractive segment of the population in terms of wealth and buying power.

Also, in the early and mid-1990s, a number of inefficient retailers went out of business. As a result of mergers among the survivors, the remaining department stores are stronger than they were before the shakeouts experienced in the latter part of the 1980s and early 1990s. (Indeed, Sears' shares rose 70.7 percent, while shares of Federated Department stores rose 41.6 percent in 1995.)

The remaining department stores can wring a lot of concessions out of their suppliers, which reduces department stores' costs. However, they can also damage themselves by forcing too many concessions out of their suppliers. For instance, the consolidation among the department stores has resulted in their becoming very demanding towards their suppliers with regard to shipping instructions; they demand that items be shipped at certain times, on certain days, to very specific locations, on specific kinds of hangars, in certain kinds of boxes, with very specific invoices placed on certain parts of the boxes. Failure to comply with any of these requirements can result in deductions from the department stores' payments to the suppliers. One problem arises, then when small suppliers are not able to comply with all of these requirements. The lack of supply of clothing, for example, from small designers will make it more difficult for department stores to differentiate themselves.

T I P

Shopping malls lose their appeal during a weak economy because it takes longer to enter and leave a mall than, say, a strip center. During times of economic hardship shopping becomes less of a pastime and more of a chore. Thus, people do not like to spend any more time shopping than they have to when the economy is weak.

Challenges for Department Stores

The perception of department stores has been transformed from a place to conduct one-stop shopping to a category of stores that are neither cheap nor carry deep lines of merchandise. Thus, department stores are caught in a crossfire. On the one side are the general mass merchants (e.g.. Wal-Mart), which offer representative samples of every product category at very low prices. Thus, department stores cannot attract customers with rock-bottom prices. On the other side are the category killers (e.g., Bed, Bath and Beyond) that offer every variation of merchandise in one category of products (e.g., linens). Thus, increased competition from niche retailers is forcing department stores out of many lines of merchandise.

Analytical Considerations

Since department stores are usually located in shopping malls it is important to analyze the status of malls in determining the outlook for department stores. The popularity of shopping malls turns upon the strength of the overall economy—the stronger the economy, the more popular malls become, and vice versa (because people do not like to window shop when they cannot afford to buy the merchandise).

Since 70 percent of the shoppers that frequent malls enter or exit through a department store, it is important to consider the traffic entering the malls in which the company that you are interested in has stores. The more traffic that frequents such malls, the more optimistic the outlook is for department stores. You should also consider the average amount of time that shoppers spend in shopping malls. The more time shoppers spend in malls, the greater the chance is that they will buy something from a department store. Finally, you should consider the average number of stores that shoppers visit during their trips to the malls. The fewer stores that are visited, the better the business for department stores. When shoppers visit fewer stores, they are probably more purposeful in their shopping and will want to find what they need quickly. Since department stores offer one-stop shopping, it is likely that efficient shoppers will spend most of their time in department stores rather than in numerous boutiques.

OUTLET FACTORIES

Discount factory outlets have become very popular, especially with clothing designers. Clothing designers benefit from establishing their own factory outlets in several ways.

- They allow designers to dispose of flawed, out-of-season, floor models and overrun merchandise in an economical way.
- They can be used to test new merchandise, to test in-store displays, and to experiment with new product categories.
- They have low advertising costs since their brands are so well known and since so many outlets are located next to one another.

Despite these advantages, clothing manufacturers face a number of risks in establishing their own outlets:

1. Upscale retailers may refuse to carry a designer's line of clothing if the manufacturer sells too much of its clothing through outlet factories; retailers do not want the image of their merchandise depreciated by the discounts found at outlet stores, and they fear that customers will buy the designers' products at the factory outlet rather than at the upscale merchant. Designers try to avoid such competition with their retailers by placing their outlets a good distance from their retail customers. However, some of these outlets have become so popular that they have actually become tourist destinations. For instance, the outlet stores in my hometown of Vacaville, California, have become a magnet for busloads of shoppers from as far away as Sacramento.

2. The growth of outlets has resulted in a more liberal return policy by the retailers since returned merchandise can be resold at the outlet store.

3. Building too many factory outlets may cause customers to believe that the quality of a designer's line is deteriorating.

TIP

It is difficult for close-out stores to generate repeat revenues in a strong economy.

4. Overbuilding may further lead to the commoditization of designers' labels.

5. Too many outlets could cause the designer to suffer losses at its retail stores.

CLOSE-OUT STORES

Close-out stores such as MacFrugals obtain most of their merchandise from other distressed retailers and from factory overruns. These stores do well when other retailers are hurting since their merchandise can be between 50 and 80 percent cheaper than at discount stores. Thus, when the economy is very weak, customers shop at close-out stores first.

Close-out stores lose their novelty when the economy improves for the following reasons: people become tired of the treasure-hunt atmosphere; it is depressing to see heaps of junk; and the consumer does not like to go to the store when the merchandise is unpredictable.

Furthermore, you should be aware of some of the secular developments that could adversely impact the close-out retailers. For instance, better inventory management by manufacturers and large retailers is detrimental to close-out stores since there will be less old inventory for the close-out retailer to purchase and thus they may have difficulty finding enough close-out merchandise to fill all of their stores. Also, lower prices at discounters heighten the competition for close-out stores.

CONSUMER ELECTRONICS RETAILERS

Two of the nation's dominant consumer electronics retailers (Best Buy and Circuit City) have very different strategies. Best Buy's stores are designed much like most other retailers. Customers push shopping carts through the stores and place the items that they wish to buy in the carts. Best Buy employees are available to answer customers' questions. These employees are paid on a salary basis so they have no incentive to oversell. When the customer is finished shopping he pays for his merchandise at the cashier and then takes the goods out to his car.

Circuit City is completely different. For instance, there is usually only one floor model of each product for the customers to look at. Whenever a customer wants to buy something, he has to approach a commissioned salesperson who will write out an order form for the customer. Then the customer takes the order form to the cashier. The cashier accepts payment for the items and relays the customer's order to the supply room. After the customer pays for his merchandise, he goes to the supply room to take receipt of his items.

What is the logic behind Circuit City's merchandising method? First, only one model of each item is available so as to force the shopper to interact with the commissioned salesperson. Circuit City hopes that this interaction will allow the salesperson to sell more merchandise (or more-expensive merchandise) to the customer. Second, Circuit City's selection and purchasing process is segmented so as to maximize the time that its salespeople spend selling. At Circuit City, salespeo-

T R A P

⊘ Manufacturers of consumer electronics dislike electronics retailers' liberal return policies. Many customers take advantage of these return policies by essentially borrowing electronic equipment. For instance, some consumers "purchase" a camcorder only to return it a few days later. Retailers that foster such liberal return policies may find that the best manufacturers refrain from shipping to the retailer.

ple just sell; the segmented shopping process ensures that they will never have to spend their time stocking shelves or helping the customer bring merchandise to the cashier or to their car.

Commissioned salesforces at stores such as Circuit City can sell highly profitable products to customers who otherwise would never buy such products. For example, Circuit City can sell many more extended warranties (than a store like Best Buy), which are extremely profitable for retailers since malfunctions in consumer electronics usually occur in the first year of purchase (when the manufacturer's warranty is still in place) or after the fifth year of purchase (when the extended warranty has expired).

However, there are a number of disadvantages associated with the Circuit City model of retailing. First, many customers do not like to go through so many steps to make a purchase. Second, many industry observers claim that paying salespeople commissions results in inferior customer service since the salespeople are in such a hurry to close sales and thus do not really sell customers the most suitable items. As a consequence, stores with a commissioned sales force often have lower levels of repeat business. Furthermore, dissatisfaction with merchandise often results in higher return rates.

APPAREL

Within the retail sector, women's clothes are earlier cyclicals than men's clothes since women are more fashion conscious than men. Thus, shares of women's apparel retailers should be purchased before shares of men's apparel retailers once a weak economy begins to rebound.

The profitability of top clothing designers is often severely eroded by knock-offs or cheap copies of a top designers' clothing. Clothing designs are virtually impossible to patent. A copycat designer can simply add another button to a dress or shorten the hemline another inch without precisely duplicating the top designer's version of the same garment. Copycat designers have been known to rummage through thrift shops for "inspiration" or even to copy designers' clothing directly from fashion shows. In fact, knockoffs can be produced so quickly (with the help of facsimiles of clothing and overnight mail services) that they can beat the original product to market.

Women's Apparel

Twice as much money is spent on women's clothing as on men's and children's clothing combined. Women also do a great deal of shopping for men and most of the shopping for children. However, the stocks of women's clothing retailers do not always represent sound investments for the following reasons:

1. An aging population can mute the attractiveness of women's retail stores. Middle-aged women generally spend less on their wardrobes than younger women because they are less fashion conscious. Thus, middle-aged women prefer to wear what fits rather than what is in style. Also, while middle-aged women may earn more money than younger women, middle-aged women may have less disposable income since they spend more money on their homes, their children, caring for their parents, and saving for their retirement.

2. When many different kinds of fashion are acceptable, women can recycle their clothing by retaining their clothing for longer periods of time. Similarly, when the fashion industry teaches individual women which kinds of apparel best suit their figures and complexions, these women will be less sensitive to fashion changes in general. Thus, these women will not embellish their wardrobes when new clothing is introduced each season.

T I P

☞ When considering investing in a retailer that serves working women, you should consider trends in women entering or leaving the workforce. When more women enter the workforce, stores like Ann Taylor that specialize in dressing the professional women should benefit.

3. Industry observers have stated that America's obsession with gorgeous models can have a backlash on women's clothing. Most women realize that they will never look as good as the top models. Eventually, many women simply stop trying to look as attractive and thus stop buying

expensive clothing (and cosmetics). Similarly, frivolous fashion shows that parade unwearable costumes have been said to contribute to women's flagging interest in new styles. Conversely, women's fashionable apparel becomes more profitable when conspicuous consumption is in vogue.

Cosmetics and Perfumes

Discount perfume stores such as Perfumania have made a big splash with investors over the past three years or so. Many investors believe that the popularity that these stores enjoy with women will lead to substantial and sustainable earnings growth. (These stores are popular because they allow women to buy expensive perfumes at reduced prices. Also, these stores have wide selections.)

While low prices and a vast selection are enough to attract customers, the investor should delve deeper into the operations of these discount perfume stores. In doing so, you will realize that they face a number of challenges:

1. *Their sources of supply are not reliable.* The stores are able to sell perfumes for discount prices because they either obtain their merchandise from distressed retailers, from manufacturers' overruns, or from the gray market (unauthorized copies of high-end perfumes). The unreliability of these sources is a problem, as perfume buyers tend to be loyal to their favorite fragrances.

2. *The shallow depth of assortment* is problematic for discount perfume stores because entire ensembles of merchandise may not be available. For instance, a customer may not be able to find the lotions, perfume, and powder of the same scent.

3. *Some branded perfume manufacturers insist that discount perfume stores not advertise their wares.*

4. *Sometimes cosmetic and perfume manufacturers force their retailers to reduce their discounts.* Thus, the risk in investing in such stocks is that many customers may come to realize that a 5- to 10-percent discount is not worth the effort of visiting a discount perfume retailer and learning that the perfumes that they really want are not in stock.

5. Since the female population in the United States and Canada only represent 5.4 percent of the world's women, *cosmetics companies are looking abroad for expansion opportunities.* However, cosmetics manufacturers must be sensitive to local considerations (e.g., aromas, mix of products and shades, degree of lather that skin care products create, pork proteins in skin care products in Muslim countries), and many countries treat cosmetics as drugs, strictly regulating their import. Nevertheless, some companies try to circumvent these obstacles by establishing factories in target countries.

Men's Apparel

The men's tailored clothing market has been shrinking as a result of more businesses instituting casual-dress policies. The trend toward more casual dress will be strengthened by the following:

- More businesses being incubated in the home.
- More white-collar workers telecommuting.
- More people moving to the suburbs.
- More people moving to warmer regions (where the dress code is more casual).
- Fewer people frequenting their place of worship, which is one place suits are usually worn.

Thus, men's apparel retailers should emphasize casual clothing. Since men need help coordinating casual clothing, customer service is becoming especially important. Some men's apparel companies and retailers have been visiting offices to teach men how to dress casually while still looking like they mean business.

Failure to realize the growth in casual clothing can be seriously problematic. At the end of 1995, it was revealed that Today's Man was on the brink of bankruptcy, one reason being that the company had not devoted enough selling space to casual clothing.

Since most men do not enjoy shopping (compared with women), men's retail stores should be designed to facilitate expeditious shopping. For instance, clothing of the same size should be laid out together (rather than by designer), and exit signs should be clearly marked. Accordingly, Men's Warehouse's strategy is to blanket an area with men's stores since stores closer to the customer save the customer time. Convenience is especially important since men usually have to visit the store twice when their clothing is altered.

Children's Apparel

In analyzing the stocks of children's clothing designers or retailers, it is important to analyze demographics:

- The higher the birth rate, the more bullish the outlook for such companies becomes.
- Average age of parents is another consideration since the longer they wait to have children, the more money they are likely to spend on them.
- Smaller families generally spend more money on the clothing of each of their children.
- When children are being born to working mothers, their parents may try to substitute expensive clothing for time spent with their children.

- The longevity of grandparents is an important consideration since they are not very price sensitive when buying their grandchildren clothing.

MAIL ORDER

Shopping by catalog has been growing increasingly popular due to the convenience that it offers, ordering merchandise from catalogs allows the customer to shop whenever he wants from the convenience of his home. Other benefits of shopping at home include saving time and sometimes avoiding state sales taxes. Also, catalogs are completely portable and do not require sophisticated equipment to use.

Retailers also benefit from offering catalogs for the following reasons:

- Customers are willing to pay for the convenience, thus profits are high because prices are usually not discounted.

- Catalog retailers that have low response rates can prudently continue to send catalogs to people who do not buy merchandise from the catalogs if they do buy merchandise from their stores. For instance, Talbots (a women's clothing retailer) uses its catalogs to determine where it should establish new stores.

- Catalogs eliminate the expense of maintaining retail outlets. Also, catalogs make inventories and logistics easy to manage.

However, one risk associated with retailers' (such as Land's End®) selling their merchandise through catalogs is that catalogs represent a fixed cost. Once catalogs are mailed, it is impossible to remedy any flaws contained in the catalog—for instance, Gander Mountain (a sporting goods catalog retailer) found its earnings severely affected after it mailed a flawed calender at the end of 1992. Conversely, flaws with displays at retail stores can quickly be corrected.

You should realize that large mail order houses have huge advantages over smaller mail order houses in terms of warehousing costs, supplies, and phone rates. Larger houses can afford to presort catalogs by zip codes, bundle them in packages, and ship them to bulk mail centers or other dropoff locations around the country. Small carriers aren't staffed for that kind of sorting and thus pay higher mailing costs.

In analyzing a retailer that derives a large part of its revenue and earnings from catalog sales, you should consider paper and postage costs. Of course, the higher these costs rise, the less profitable the retailer's catalog operations will become. Other investment considerations include the sales-per-catalog ratio and the average number of items that are purchased from each catalog sent to each customer. Obviously, you should seek to invest in the catalog retailers that generate higher-than-industry-average sales-per-catalog ratios and that have a rising average number of items purchased from each catalog mailed.

Many catalog retailers are venturing into television shopping. This is generally an easy transition for such retailers since there are no stores (and no distribution problems) with either retailing method. One advantage of TV shopping is that responses to advertised products can be instantaneously advertised. Thus, when all of the inventory of a particular product is sold, the retailer can begin to promote another item.

Some catalog retailers such as Spiegel are beginning to try to sell their merchandise over on-line computer systems. However, you should be aware of some of the potential pitfalls in such selling strategies:

1. Transmission times are now too slow and graphic displays are not yet sufficiently attractive.

2. People are reluctant to pay to learn about merchandise when they can simply visit retailers to have their questions answered for free.

3. Consumers enjoy the socializing (such as spending time with friends, window shopping, talking with salespeople, and people watching) that comes with shopping.

4. Some retailers do not know how to display their products.

5. Retailers dislike electronic butlers that are programmed just to find the lowest prices. (Some retailers are configuring their software so that these electronic butlers cannot be used.)

FURNITURE

The American Furniture Manufacturer's Association reports industry shipments and makes projections relating to furniture sales. However, you can gain a sense of the outlook of the furniture industry by taking a few developments into account. First, the fortunes of the furniture industry usually follow new and existing home sales because people need to furnish their homes after they move in. Therefore, you should monitor housing completions as well as sales of new and existing homes as reported by the Commerce Department.

The prospects for the furniture industry also brighten as the *size* of new homes increases. There is a disproportionate amount of spending on furniture for larger homes. For instance, consumers spend 3.5 times as much money on furniture for a 2,000-square-foot house as for a 1,000-square-foot house, and they spend *nine* times as much money on furniture for a 3,000-square-foot house as for a

T I P

You should seek furniture stores that provide their customers with prompt delivery and have low real estate expenses.

T I P

☞ Another interesting niche of opportunity within the furniture industry is the manufacturers of ready-to-assemble furniture (RTA) such as Ameriwood Industries. The characteristics of RTA furniture are appealing to consumers for a number of reasons:

- The aesthetics and durability have markedly improved over the past few years.
- RTA has low price points.
- RTA can be carried out of the store (meaning that customers do not have to wait for delivery).
- People can easily move RTA furniture around in their homes.
- RTA furniture is especially appropriate for home entertainment, home offices, and computer work areas.

Retailers are also very receptive to RTA furniture because

- It does not take up too much floor space.
- It can be readily stacked on shelves.
- It can be shipped with density.
- There is less of a damaged-goods problem since RTA comes in packages.

1,000-square-foot house. This is because people need to purchase more furniture for bigger homes and people that purchase larger homes can afford more-expensive furniture.

The furniture industry should benefit from people's spending more time at home because furniture will wear out faster resulting in a faster replacement cycle. Reasons for people spending more time at home include fear of crime, business start-ups being incubated at home, telecommuting, and the greater sophistication of home entertainment systems.

Furniture retailers such as Haverty Furniture and The Bombay Company face several obstacles: Transportation costs are high, the incidence of damaged goods is high, furniture is sold at expensive price points, and inventory turnover is usually slow.

However, furniture stores benefit from the infrequency of customer's visits there because this makes it difficult for consumers to comparison shop.

TOY MANUFACTURERS

Toy manufacturers (e.g., Hasbro and Mattel) and toy retailers (e.g., Toys "Я" Us) share a number of benefits by being in the toy industry.

1. While toys are discretionary purchases, sales of toys are not highly cyclical. It is difficult to deprive children of their toys.

2. Sales of toys are less weather-dependent than sales of many other leisure products, such as sporting goods.

3. Popular toys can be relaunched every few years.

4. Toy manufacturers do not face competition from generics or private-label manufacturers since children demand specific toys and are not price sensitive.

5. U.S. toy manufacturers have more leverage in winning license agreements from major American movie studios than any other nation's toy makers since the studios believe that the American manufacturers can best serve the U.S. toy market, which is the world's largest. American licensing agreements are extremely valuable since U.S. movies and TV shows are internationally popular. These licensing agreements can be highly profitable due to the heavy advertising outlays expended by the movie studios to popularize their (animated) characters. However, the major movie studios realize the value of their licensing agreements to the toy manufacturers and are therefore raising their royalty rates. Thus, you should consider the royalties that toy companies pay to movie studios.

6. American toy manufacturers benefit from the large U.S. retailers aggressively expanding abroad. For instance, the U.S. toy makers can relatively easily sell their goods through the more than 300 units that Toys "Я" Us operates outside of the United States.

T I P

In estimating the size of the toy market, you should consider the birth rate over a few years, starting about five years ago.

However, toy manufacturers face several significant secular obstacles. The first is age compression, which means that children are maturing faster and therefore have less time to enjoy playing with toys. Over the past few years there has been a growing amount of literature suggesting that children today are forced to mature faster since they are exposed to life's difficulties at an earlier age than children were a few generations ago. For instance, there are more out-of-wedlock births, parents are getting divorced when children are younger, and children are more likely to see their parents lose their jobs. Thus, children are assuming more of the domestic chores such as grocery shopping, preparing meals, and housekeeping, which accelerates their maturity.

Second, toy retailers are consolidating and thus asserting their influence. In the United States, four toy retailers (Toys "Я" Us, K mart, Wal-Mart, and Kay-Bee Toys) account for the overwhelming majority of toy sales. Accordingly, toy manufacturers are forced to grant their retailers very lenient payment terms. In fact, it is not uncommon for toy retailers to take as long as 180 days to pay toy manufacturers.

Also, retailers place their orders on a just-in-time inventory basis. If the manufacturer cannot fill such orders fast enough, the result may be stock-outs (lost sales) and possibly the loss of shelf space. However, it is very difficult to fill such orders because the manufacturers do not know what to produce until a short time before the orders are needed. This is because the toy business is a "hits" business. (This year's popular toys will not be popular next year.) This is compounded by a large degree of manufacturing being conducted in Asia.

Another problem that toy manufacturers face is that toy retailers are quick to cancel orders when sell through is uncertain. Since children are not price sensitive, marking down a toy will not move the item any faster. Thus, some major toy retailers such as K mart are only accepting deliveries of toys on consignment. If these retailers cannot sell the toys, the manufacturers will have to take them back.

5

The Food Industry

GROCERY STORES

The grocery store industry is mature. While everyone must eat, many Americans are trying to *reduce* their food intake. Thus, population growth is one of the primary determinants of the volume of food sold.

Also, since grocery chains are largely regional businesses, it is important for the investor to monitor the population growth and economic vitality of the region in which the particular grocery chain operates. The population can be affected by movements of people to or from other regions of the country or by the arrival of immigrants. When a healthy Seattle economy attracts more people to the area, Quality Food Centers should become increasingly profitable. On the other hand, emigration from California due to economic deterioration will make a California-based chain of grocery stores such as Albertson's a less-attractive investment.

The economy is an important factor in determining how much consumers will pay for grocery store merchandise. The weaker the economy, the more likely consumers are to price compare. Consumers can become very sensitive to food prices since they shop frequently. For instance, many people know exactly how much various local groceries charge for common items like milk and bread. Moreover, a weak economy leads to more people trading down (e.g., buying hamburger meat instead of steak). On the other hand, when the economy is expanding people are not only less concerned with comparing food prices but they may actually trade up (e.g., choose steak over hamburger meat).

Before investing in grocery stores, you should consider the state of inflation or deflation. If there is both general economic inflation and food deflation (i.e., falling food prices), then union contracts can be especially damaging. This was a problem that originated at the end of the 1980s. At that time, union contracts were pegged to the Consumer Price Index, which was rising; food prices were falling. Thus, the grocery stores' labor costs were rising while their revenues were falling. Consequently, the grocery stores' profit margins contracted.

Grocery stores benefit when people buy food closer to the time that they

TIP

 Food deflation results in restaurants' becoming more competitive with grocery stores because the restaurants' service costs can be more easily absorbed in their customers' checks.

consume it. When people shop on an empty stomach they are generally not discriminating shoppers. Single people are more likely to shop on an empty stomach than families because the wife/mother is more likely (than the single person) to plan her family's meals in advance. Also, low-income people are more likely to shop on an empty stomach since they live "hand-to-mouth."

Analytical Considerations

Traditional grocery stores can be analyzed using many of the same tools that are used to analyze other retailers, such as same-store sales growth, sales per square foot, and sales per employee.

Also, the greater the percentage of a store's square footage devoted to selling space the better because the store can derive greater revenues if more of its square footage is devoted to selling. Also, having a small percentage of square footage dedicated to warehousing indicates that the store has significant leverage over its distributors—that is, the distributors are forced to supply the warehousing.

On a regional level, the investor should consider selling space per capita. When this ratio rises dramatically, it will be difficult for any of the grocery stores in the given region to maintain their pricing levels. However, should the selling space-per-capita ratio decline, it may be possible for the grocery stores to raise their prices.

Areas that have a lengthy construction-approval process can slow down expansion, which enhances the selling space-per-capita ratio. Other factors that can present difficulties to expanding selling space include a lack of available real estate, high real estate costs, little unemployment, high unionization, and high transportation costs.

T I P

It is often preferable for stores to remodel (rather than expand) since remodeling does not increase the square footage in the local market. Another benefit of remodeling is that remodeling is cheaper than building new stores.

Another tool for analyzing this industry is average customer transactions (average ticket prices in the restaurant industry), representing the average amount of money that each customer spends in the store. Obviously, the higher the average customer transaction is, the better for the store. Finally, store cleanliness is important to customers and therefore should be considered by the investor.

Preferred Customers

It is preferable for grocery stores to attract wealthier customers. While everyone must eat, wealthier customers are preferable to low-income customers since the shopping patterns of the former are more predictable. Wealthy customers do not have to wait until an item goes on sale before they purchase it. Thus, a wealthy customer may consistently shop on one particular day of the week. On the other hand, stores in low-income areas may be very busy when special sales are offered but largely idle at other times. Thus, grocery stores that operate in wealthier areas benefit from greater predictability in executing routine functions such as employee scheduling and shelf stocking.

Some stores have established value-added kiosks that feature such foods as Chinese and Italian fares to attract the wealthy customer. While these units may not always be wildly profitable in and of themselves (due to their high labor intensity), they bring wealthy customers into the store. Moreover, the supermarkets that are adding gourmet food and prepared dishes can recapture some of the business that is lost when shoppers dine out.

Nevertheless, many people believe that stores operating in low-income areas are hugely profitable since they can charge high prices to people that have few alternative places to shop. True, the prices that these stores charge are sometimes higher than what wealthy people pay because poor people are condemned to shop locally (since they are sometimes immobile) while wealthy people can travel more freely (and seek the better buys). However, stores that operate in low-income areas face higher expenses in terms of employee training (due to high turnover), processing of food stamps, higher pilferage, greater vandalism, and higher risk of robbery. Consequently, stores located in inner cities typically have extremely high security costs.

TIP

> Some stores located in low-income areas choose to absorb the higher costs of running such stores since passing high prices on to customers may result in charges of price gouging or unfair trade.

Men and Women Shoppers

Both grocery stores and branded food manufacturers benefit when more men (than women) shop for food. Thus, the greater the percentage of men that are their family's primary shopper, the better off grocery stores and branded food manufacturers are.

Men are hunters while women are gatherers. Since men are prone to shop in a hurry, they generally do not compare prices and sizes (of packaged food) as diligently as women. Thus, men are more likely to buy branded food. Men also feel that they are doing the right thing when they buy branded food. Furthermore, men do not plan their shopping routines as diligently as women and thus shop more often, which generates more traffic for the store. Finally, men often shop on empty stomachs, which leads to overbuying.

On the other hand, women are better shoppers than men. It has even been said that part of a woman's self-esteem is being a good shopper. Thus, private labels fare better when more women do the shopping since women are more likely to comparison shop than men. On the contrary, the more women that enter the workforce, the better it is for branded labels since more men will be relegated to the shopping duties.

Another development that is beneficial to both grocery stores and branded food companies is grocery stores' accepting payment with debit and credit cards. Consumers are less discriminating when they pay for their groceries with debit or credit cards because they are less price sensitive than when they pay with cash.

Merchandising Methods

There are two fundamental methods that grocery stores can employ to sell their merchandise. Under the promotional (or "high/low") method, selected merchandise is sold on a special "sale" or other deal basis such as the "buy-three-get-one-free" basis. Under the every day low price ("EDLP") method, all of the store's merchandise is always sold at consistently low retail prices. Grocery stores prefer the promotional method of merchandising while the food manufacturers favor EDLP, and therein lies a major source of contention between the two.

Grocery stores prefer high/low pricing to EDLP for the following reasons:

- The items that are on sale lure many shoppers into the store.

- The manufacturers sponsor such promotions by granting the grocery stores promotional allowances.

- Since only a small percentage of the store's merchandise is promoted at any given time, higher prices are usually realized on most items sold.

- Grocery stores can make wide profit margins when they overbuy merchandise from food producers during promotions and then sell the excess inventory at the full retail price when the promotion expires. For example, a grocery store can boost its margins 50 percent under the following scenario. Assume that a grocery store normally buys a can of soup from the soup company for $1.00 and sells it at retail for $1.50. (Thus, the regular profit margin is 50 percent, $1.50 − $1.00 = $.50/$1.00 = 50%.) During the promotion, the store buys each can of soup for $.75. Once the promotion is terminated, the grocery store can sell each can of soup for the regular price. Thus, the grocery store can achieve a 100 percent profit margin ($1.50 − $.75 = $.75/$.75 = 100%, which is double the regular profit margin of 50 percent) by overbuying during the promotion and then selling the merchandise for the regular price when the promotion is over.

The Importance of Scanning Systems

The advantages associated with stores' installing scanning devices include the following:

- Scanning systems provide grocery stores with information that the store can use to demand promotional allowances from the manufacturers. For example, a grocer can use data derived from scanning systems to alert a supplier that they are losing sales to a competitor. The store can then cajole the supplier to either sponsor a promotion (to sell at least as many products as its competitors) or risk having the store reduce the supplier's allotted shelf space.

- Scanning helps managers reduce inventory levels, which consequently lowers warehousing costs, security costs, insurance costs, and the risk of shrinkage and lack of demand (i.e., loss of inventory due to theft or perishability).

- Scanning relieves the retailer of the burden of waiting for periodic (and time-consuming) stock takes to find out what needs to be reordered. With scanning, the store manager immediately knows what has been purchased and therefore what needs to be reordered. In fact, some scanning systems are so sophisticated that they are tied into the manufacturers' factories; thus, when an item is purchased, the manufacturer automatically arranges to deliver another item to the particular store.

- Scanning bar-coded prices allows for faster check-out times, reducing the store's demand for labor and increasing customer satisfaction.

- Point-of-sale data help determine the optimum number of cashiers that will be needed for each part of the day.

- Grocery stores can use the data generated by scanning to learn more about their customers' shopping habits or even sell such data to food manufacturers. For instance, Food Emporium uses a savings club card to get data about its customers' buying patterns. Under this program, Food Emporium automatically deducts manufacturer's rebates for items that a customer purchases (even if no coupon is presented) in return for swiping its savings club card through its scanners to register the customer's purchases.

Private Labels

One of the primary reasons for grocery stores' introducing private-label foods and other merchandise is to pressure the branded-label manufacturers to maintain their promotions. These pressure tactics often work since private labels are so much cheaper than their branded competitors; many customers will choose the private-label product unless the branded good is sold on some sort of a deal basis. Thus, grocery stores use private labels as a wedge against branded food companies' insistence on resorting to the EDLP method.

Another benefit of private labels is that they allow the grocery store to differentiate itself from other stores. For example, a grocery store that sells to a Hispanic community can label its foods with Hispanic-sounding names. This is important because stores look basically the same since they carry identical products. Thus, private labels allow grocery stores to enhance their image with customers.

However, not all grocery stores are successful in launching private-label lines. In order for private labels to work, the grocery store should generate sufficient volume in order to offset the initial costs of launching a line of private labels.

Also, private labels are usually most successful in the categories that consistently raise their prices. This is because sustained price increases in branded categories provide an umbrella under which private labels appear very inexpensive. For instance, the price increases that cereal companies have been imposing make that category vulnerable to private labels, while the relative price consistency in the soft drink industry has proven to minimize competition from private labels. On the other hand, private labels are not suitable for the product categories that have many price points since the price points in the lower range will lower the ceiling under which private labels appear inexpensive.

Moreover, the locality where the grocery chain operates should have relatively weak patent and trademark protections so that the private labels can produce products that closely resemble the branded versions without risking patent

TIP

There are drawbacks for grocery stores launching private labels even when such launches are successful. For instance, grocery stores cannot generate slotting fees (i.e., fees that grocery stores charge branded-food manufacturers for placing their products on the stores' shelves) on private label foods. Additionally, grocery stores must have their own employees stock their shelves with private labels. On the other hand, grocery stores can sometimes avoid this allocation of labor by requiring branded vendors to stock their stores' shelves with the vendor's brands.

Finally, the grocery stores that contract with food manufacturers for the production of their private labels face a business-interruption risk. If the manufacturers face rising orders for their branded foods, their production capacity may become strained. As a consequence, they may choose not to renew their contracts with the grocery stores for the production of their private labels. Thus, the grocery stores may not be able to obtain their private-label goods.

infringement litigation. Weaker patent and trademark protections in the United Kingdom is one of the factors attributable to British grocery stores' (such as Sainsbury) selling more private labels than the American grocery stores.

Grocery Stores' Defenses against Mass Merchants

Contrary to the opinions of many analysts, the grocery stores have a number of strengths that will ensure that they are not overwhelmed by the mass merchants. First, even though mass merchants allow shoppers to buy large volumes of food at reduced prices, consumers cannot buy too many perishable goods at one time. (Obviously, shoppers cannot buy huge volumes of milk since much of it would spoil before it could be consumed.) Thus, mass merchants are largely ineffective in selling perishable items. As a result, grocery stores such as Food Lion are distinguishing themselves from mass merchants by refocusing on the merchandising of perishable products.

One benefit of being a better merchandiser of perishables is that perishables are staple products—such as dairy, meats, and fruits and vegetables—that consumers cannot do without. Also, stores known for their produce, meat, and dairy aisles will benefit from more frequent-shopper visits. For instance, shoppers who cannot buy too much milk in one visit must return to the store a short time later. Additionally, perimeter departments (which is where perishable foods are found in grocery stores) afford interactions with the customer. For instance, butchers often come to learn how their customers prefer their meat cut.

T R A P

⦸ There are challenges to grocery stores' superior management of perishable goods. Of primary concern is that biotechnology may reduce the advantage that grocers have traditionally had over mass merchants. For instance, biotechnically enhanced fruits and vegetables would exhibit reduced spoilage. As a result of enhanced shelf life, inventory would be easier to control, which would add to the benefit of mass merchants. A separate challenge is that some mass merchants such as Wal-Mart have subcontracted with firms that specialize in managing the perishable food sections of supermarkets.)

The grocery stores have other competitive advantages vis-a-vis the mass merchants. First, grocery stores have much deeper selections than the mass merchants. (Thus, supermarket pricing does not have to be as low as mass-merchant pricing.) Also, supermarkets have begun to mimic the mass merchants by stocking large amounts of products at reduced prices on crates. For instance, many stores have achieved "qualified club status," which allows the store the same discounts that the mass merchants receive. Therefore, grocery stores can offer both wide selections and rock-bottom prices (on selected merchandise).

Finally, grocery stores have discovered a way to mute the advantage of mass merchants' having many services under one roof. By locating grocery stores in strip centers next to banks, bakeries, florists, video rental stores, and the like, grocery stores can essentially offer one-stop shopping. By locating in these strip centers, grocery stores offer the customer the convenience of one-stop shopping without the grocery store's having to provide the services that are beyond its core competence.

MASS MERCHANTS

Competitive Advantages

Mass merchants are fierce competitors with grocery stores. Mass merchants are appealing to customers because they offer one-stop shopping and very competitive prices. These companies are able to offer the customer extremely low prices because they can use their huge volume to demand price concessions from suppliers. Additionally, mass merchants only buy from the biggest and most-sophisticated manufacturers thus streamlining their merchandising and further reducing their costs by eliminating wholesalers.

Another reason mass merchants can afford to offer comparatively lower prices on food is that they can subsidize food prices from the attractive profit margins they derive from selling general merchandise.

Mass merchants generally have advantages over grocery stores in terms of labor expenses because mass merchants usually do not use unionized labor. However, mass merchants often motivate their employees by awarding stock. For instance, Wal-Mart proudly features employees who hold over $100,000 of Wal-Mart stock in its employee newsletter.

TRAP

Ø One problem with incentivizing employees with stock is that morale might sink when the price of the stock falls. In fact, many customers complained about Wal-Mart's deteriorating customer service in 1993 and 1994, which just so happened to coincide with a retreat in the price of Wal-Mart's stock.

Separately, dealing with large units of merchandise is less labor intensive than selling smaller units. For instance, it takes less time to stock and ring up a four-pack of soap than to stock and ring up one bar at a time.

Mass merchants are more competitive with the supermarkets when people are more conscious of their time (when more women enter the workforce, for example). This is because people tend to shop at grocery stores twice a week but shop at general merchandise stores roughly twice a month.

Limits to Mass Merchants' Growth

"At Wal-Mart's (the leading mass merchant in the United States) current growth rate of around 18 percent, its sales would reach $200 billion by the year 2000—possibly making it the world's largest company." [1]

Nevertheless, there are constraints on mass merchants' growth potential:

- Mass merchants have such large stores that they cannot open new stores too close to existing ones without cannibalizing the original store's sales.
- Some communities are opposed to the entry of a mass merchant and are thus blocking it from obtaining the necessary zoning permits.

---

[1] "Change at the Check-out." *The Economist,* Mar 4, 1995, p.3.

Mass merchants are also reluctant to locate in areas predominately populated by older people

- Because the parking lots are so large that most customers have to park too far from the stores' entrances.
- As indicated by customer satisfaction surveys, mass merchants' outlets are so large that older people often get confused and become tired from shopping. In fact, Eckerd's drug stores run commercials in South Florida that poke fun at the inconvenience of shopping at mass merchants by asking"Why go shopping when you can pick it up at Eckerd's?"

Mass merchants are not well suited for low-income areas either since the population there cannot afford to buy large quantities of food at once. Even if low-income people could afford to purchase large quantities of food in one shopping spree, they would have difficulty transporting the food home since they often

TRAP

> 🚫 It is extremely problematic for membership clubs such as Price/Costco to eliminate their membership fees since such fees are pure profit. (There are no associated costs of goods sold.)

travel on public transportation. Conversely, mass merchants are so large that they can become unappealing to time-conscious wealthy people since it can take too long to shop in these stores.

Additionally, mass merchants would be hurt if courts find them guilty of predatory pricing. (Grocers have alleged that mass merchants sell some of their merchandise below their costs in order to drive out the competition.) Losing predatory-pricing cases would likely result in the mass merchants' being forced to raise their prices, which would render these superstores less appealing to the shopper.

It is important for the investor to realize that when mass merchants lose their appeal, their earnings can erode very quickly, one reason being the tremendous expense involved in operating these huge stores. When revenues can no longer cover expenses, earnings turn to losses.

FOOD DISTRIBUTORS

Food distribution is largely a fixed-cost business. Thus, food distributors such as Sysco Corporation try to increase their volumes in order to better leverage their fixed costs. In other words, higher volumes of food distributed yield wider profit margins.

Given that bigger is better, food distributors try to serve the growing mass merchants. However, supplying mass merchant chains is problematic since these chains eventually get so big that it becomes economical for them to do their own distribution. In response, some distributors such as Fleming Companies have tried to offset potential losses from their mass merchant customers by establishing their own stores. However, the food distributors' existing customers despise this strategy since the distributors become competitors of their stores.

Food distributors are usually more prosperous during times of inflation. Inflation helps food wholesalers since their markups are based on the cost of goods sold. Since the cost of goods sold rises during inflationary cycles, so too do the markups that wholesalers charge.

Inflation also helps food distributors' margins since the goods that they sell to grocers are sold out of inventory. For instance, suppose that a distributor buys a box of canned vegetables in January then sells it to a grocer in July. If there is rampant inflation, there will be a wide disparity between the price that the distributor receives for the canned vegetables and the price that the distributor paid for it.

One positive trend in the food distribution industry is that these distributors are not as sensitive to economic downturns as they previously had been. This is because grocery stores now carry more discretionary items, such as flowers, which can be eliminated during a recession. Since the grocery stores reduce their costs by eliminating the discretionary merchandise, they may put less price pressure on their distributors for the delivery of staple food products.

PACKAGED FOOD PRODUCERS

Merchandising Methods

Packaged-food companies favor the every-day-low-price method of merchandising for a number of reasons:

1. Most of the packaged food companies' largest customers (the mass merchants) already operate on the EDLP basis; thus, the packaged food companies do not believe that they should have to reconfigure their merchandising strategy for grocery stores that only account for a small percentage of their business.

2. Promotions are extremely difficult for manufacturers to administer. For instance, two different products can be promoted different ways—one product's price can be reduced by 30 percent, for example, while the other product can be promoted on a buy-three-get-one-free basis. These products can be sold through different stores located in different geographic regions, and the effective dates of the promotions can vary. Of course, a large packaged-food manufacturer would multiply these vari-

ables by all of the products that they produce, all of the regions that they serve, all of the stores that they sell to, all of the different types of promotions that they sponsor, and all of the different durations of time during which their promotions are effective. Thus, it is easy to see that promotions can quickly become very complex for packaged food manufacturers to execute. As a result, the promotional method lends itself to many errors, which can lead to customer dissatisfaction.

Couponing, in particular, is difficult for branded-food manufacturers to administer:

- Couponing hurts the perception of branded goods being of high quality.

- It is not unusual for a $.50 coupon to cost the manufacturer $.75 because the coupons must travel from the manufacturer to a marketing firm to a newspaper to the retailer and back to the manufacturer.

- When a customer forgets to bring a coupon to the store, he is discouraged from buying the product because he feels like he is overpaying.

3. EDLP is more conducive to efficient manufacturing because orders are more predictable and consistent. Under the promotional method of merchandising, orders are more volatile; thus, manufacturers pay extensive overtime during periods of peak production and underutilize people and facilities when the promotions expire.

4. Food producers dislike EDLP because it leads to diversion. Diversion occurs when grocery stores take advantage of promotions by buying far too much merchandise from branded-food companies at discount prices then sell their excess inventory to diverters at a markup. (Diverters are independent companies that specialize in arbitraging merchandise sold on the promotional basis.)

For instance, a grocery store might traditionally buy 1,000 boxes of cereal for a week's worth of sales. Assume that the wholesale price is normally $1.25 and the retail price is $2.00. However, during times of a special sale the store might buy 2,000 boxes of cereal at $.75 a box and sell each box of cereal for $1.50.

Under diversion, a grocery store might buy far more boxes of cereal than it would be able to sell even during the week of the special sale. For instance, the store might buy 5,000 boxes of cereal at $.75 a box. However, the store can only sell 2,000 boxes during the week of the promotion. The other 3,000 boxes might be sold to a diverter. The diverter might buy these 3,000 boxes from the grocery store at $.95, yielding the store a $.20 profit on each of the 3,000 excess boxes. (These profits are one reason why grocery stores favor the promotional method of merchandising over EDLP.) Then the diverter would sell the 3,000 boxes to another grocery store for $1.10. Since the $1.10 is lower than the regular $1.25 wholesale price, the other grocery store could reduce its retail price without reducing its normal profit levels. Thus, under the promotional method of merchandising, the branded-food companies lose control of their pricing.

5. EDLP is more conducive to building brand equity (the value that a consumer perceives that a branded product has in excess of a generic substitute) than the promotional basis. When a company's products are too

T I P

Effective advertising campaigns by packaged-food companies (rather than promotions) can turn retailers into mere way stations between the warehouse and consumers' shelves.

often marketed on some kind of a deal basis, the customer will become conditioned to basing his buying decision merely on the price of a product. However, when promotions are eliminated, the food company can direct its marketing dollars towards sustainable advertising campaigns, which builds brand equity. The creation of brand equity builds genuine demand for a product even though the product sells for a higher price than a substitute. When genuine demand for a product exists, the retailer's power is diminished (relative to the food manufacturers' power) since the store will have to carry the product.

Private-Label Competition

Generally, branded-food producers are averse to private labels since private-label foods take market share away from branded foods. Additionally, the success of private-label foods reduces the pricing flexibility of branded foods. For instance, branded-food companies are more likely to resort to discounting when their products compete with private labels.

However, branded foods have the following advantages over private labels:

- Grocery stores do not have much expertise in the production of food.
- All of the marketing behind branded food does result in the generation of genuine demand for such products.
- Grocery stores cannot stock too much private-label food since the grocery stores rely upon the slotting fees that branded-food companies pay to secure shelf space in the stores.

- Branded goods are less dependent on low commodity prices than store labels. This is because both branded and private-label foods pay the same prices for commodities but branded foods sell for higher retail prices. Thus, sharp surges in commodity prices (e.g., caused by droughts or floods) do not adversely impact the profitability of branded foods to the same extent as store labels.

- Foods that require complicated manufacturing processes are not suitable candidates for being sold under private labels. The reason is that expensive manufacturing processes prevent such foods from being produced at low prices.

- Branded-food manufacturers are more responsive to consumers than store-brand manufacturers. For example, many branded goods offer toll-free phone numbers and Internet addresses that consumers can call or log on to if they have questions or comments. These toll-free numbers and Internet sites are good public relations ploys and also prove to be sound research tools.

Contract Manufacturing

In some instances, grocery stores contract with branded-food companies to manufacture private-label goods. Such arrangements allow the branded-food companies to boost their factory utilization rates. Also, producing private-label goods can be profitable for the manufacturer since there are no marketing costs associated with private labels. Additionally, there are no inventory risks associated with private labels since they are made to order.

However, branded-food companies should not jeopardize the image of their goods by producing private labels to an excessive extent. If the public becomes aware that both branded foods and private-label foods are produced at the same facilities by the same companies, they will come to believe that there is no difference between the two foods. Thus, branded-food makers often manufacture private labels of goods for which they offer no branded competition. For instance, a leading catsup company makes private-label soups but not private-label catsup.

Relations with Mass Merchants

Mass merchants offer some benefits to leading food manufacturers:

- Since mass merchants only offer two or three of the leading brands in each category, the dominant food makers face little competition in the mass-merchant format.

- Since branded-food companies do not need to put any advertising or promotional money behind their products that are placed in mass-merchant outlets, the leading food companies enjoy profit margins that are almost as wide as their products sold in grocery stores.

■ Foods that are traditionally loss leaders at grocery stores are not threatened by the growth of mass merchants since mass merchants cannot profitably sell loss leaders. (Loss leaders are foods that are sold at a loss with the mindset that the retailer will recoup its losses by charging a higher price on a complementary item. For instance, ice cream topping may be sold at a loss in order to encourage the purchase of ice cream that is sold at a healthy markup.) This is because loss leaders already sell at low prices in grocery stores and would have to be discounted to a point that eliminates profitability for the mass merchant.

Niches of Opportunity and Adversity

Despite the maturity of the food industry, I believe that there are opportunities for a food company to boost its sales. For instance, branded-food companies should focus on selling more of their food to institutions (e.g., restaurants, cafeterias, airports, schools, prisons) since more meals are being consumed outside of the home.

T I P

One area of potential adversity for the food manufacturers is the frozen-dinner segment. The concern is that the greater emphasis on prepared take-out foods at restaurants and grocery stores will become increasingly competitive with frozen dinners.

Also, sales of natural foods should continue to rise steadily due to heightened concerns about the safety of pesticides, food additives, preservatives, and chemicals.

Food companies should be successful in selling food to foreign markets. Many of these markets are growing economically, have young populations, and are enamored with Western culture. Moreover, the American (and to a lesser extent European) food companies are much more powerful marketers, efficient producers, and aggressive distributors of their products than their foreign rivals.

International sales should grow the quickest for those foods that enjoy wide visibility since people want to be seen consuming chic American foods. (Thus, sodas should sell better than cereals.) Also, foods that are laden with preservatives should do well in developing countries since much of the food currently sold in these regions spoils before reaching its market. On the cost side of the equation, international free-trade agreements such as GATT make it easier for food companies to source their ingredients.

However, one of the problems with manufacturing food in countries with weak patent protection is that counterfeit products can cause injury. For instance, it was reported that Pabst Blue Ribbon beer had been tampered with in China, causing dozens of consumers to fall ill and even killing one.[2] Such incidents hurt the brand equity of the bootlegged product worldwide.

Vertical Integration

Some analysts have argued that food producers should not be too vertically integrated. (Vertical integration occurs when one company controls all of the steps in its manufacturing process; it is the opposite of outsourcing.) Their reasoning is that the company's stock would trade at a lower multiple (of earnings) since the related commodities business would typically be valued at a low multiple. Commodities businesses are generally valued at a low multiple since their dependence on the weather makes their earnings unpredictable. However, the analyst must weigh this argument against the benefits of vertical integration as discussed in the section on slaughterhouses.

SUPPLIERS—FERTILIZER PROVIDERS

The outlook for fertilizer stocks is largely contingent upon the supply and demand for fertilizer itself. There are a number of factors that influence the demand for fertilizer:

T O O L

One ratio used to determine how much future crop planting there will be is the stocks-to-use ratio. The lower the ending stock of a given crop is in relation to the usage and exports of such crops during a given year, the more planting (and more usage of fertilizer) there will be. For instance, if the Agriculture Department reported that the stock of wheat at the end of 1994 was 500 million bushels while the usage of such wheat during 1994 was 2 billion bushels, the stocks-to-use ratio would be 40 percent (500 million/2 billion). If the Agriculture Department reported that the stock of wheat fell to 200 million bushels in 1995 while the usage of such wheat was 2 billion bushels in 1995, the stocks-to-use ratio would fall to 10 percent (200 million/2000 million). The decline in this ratio is bullish for fertilizer stocks since it indicates that there will be greater planting of wheat.

---

[2] *Wall Street Journal,* November 3, 1995, p. B1.

1. Of course, the more crops that are planted, the more fertilizer will be used. However, there are earlier indicators of demand for crop planting. For instance, low crop inventories (on a worldwide basis) forces farmers to plant more crop and use more fertilizer.

2. The existence of bumper crops in previous years means the soil has been drained of its nutrients and requires more fertilizer per acre.

3. Fewer acres of government set-aside programs are beneficial to fertilizer producers since more acres are put back into production.

4. Population growth in foreign countries can cause foreign countries to import U.S.-produced fertilizer. U.S. fertilizer producers especially benefit from foreign countries' establishing or restoring subsidies for imported fertilizer.

5. As diets in developing countries change from grains to meat, more fertilizer is required to produce bigger crops to feed livestock.

Since all of these demand factors were in place in the beginning of 1995, several fertilizer stocks such as The Vigoro Corporation doubled in value from January of 1995 to December of 1995.

However, there are a few factors that could reduce the potential demand for fertilizer. For instance, environmental laws that put stiff requirements on fertilizer use force farmers to economize on their use of fertilizer. Also, biotechnology is problematic since new breeds of plants absorb more nutrients more readily and are more resistant to disease and drought. Therefore, farmers planting such genetically enhanced crops will have less demand for fertilizers.

On the supply side of the equation, supply should be reduced as a result of free-trade agreements that require the elimination of subsidized fertilizer production. For instance, GATT will reduce competition from heavily subsidized European fertilizer exports.

Investors should also consider capacity utilization at fertilizer production facilities. The higher such capacity utilization is, the higher fertilizer prices should rise which should propel the shares of fertilizer producers higher. The fertilizer companies further benefit from tight capacity since it is very expensive and can take a very long time to expand production capacity in this industry. For example, it can take five years and cost over $600 million to build a world-class potash mine. Thus, once supplies of fertilizer inputs are tight, they should remain that way for quite a while.

SEEDS

The stocks of seed producers such as DeKalb Genetics usually behave in a fashion similar to the stocks of fertilizer companies in that the stocks of seed producers move in accordance with the supply of and demand for those seeds. One factor that could boost the demand for seeds is the elimination of farm subsidies that would bring more acres into production. On the other hand, government set-aside programs that are meant to boost crop prices result in less planting; less planting results in less demand for seeds.

T I P

One of the best measures of a seed's value is the average additional bushels per acre of yield the given seed produces. Of course, the more crops yielded because of the seed, the higher the demand for the seed will rise.

Demand for seeds should grow as genetic engineering in seeds is used to enhance the functionality of crops. For example

- Some seed suppliers are manipulating plant genes to invent new crops with traits such as unusually high oil or protein levels or lower fat content. Seeds that ensure nutritionally enhanced crops will benefit from growing demand by farmers. Farmers that feed a large percentage of nutritionally enhanced crops to their livestock will be able to reduce the expensive nutritional supplements that they currently must insert into their animals' feed to ensure their livestock's well-being.

- Some genetic seeds are resistant to herbicides, which is important since some herbicides not only kill weeds but also crops.

- Genetic seeds that are laden with natural insecticides render crops resistant to insects and thus improve yields. These biotechnologically engineered seeds reduce the need for farmers to use chemical insecticides.

- Seeds are being developed that will have high tolerances to drought. Drought-tolerant crops will allow farmers more leeway in terms of the planning of irrigation channels. However, if the government has a generous crop-insurance program that bails out farmers during times of droughts, farmers are more likely to buy seeds that boost crop yields rather than ones that offer protection against drought.

Genetically enhanced seeds should do well in developing countries because these countries are particularly adversely impacted by problems such as drought, herbicides, and insecticides. Also, foreign expansion by American restaurants should help this industry since these restaurants demand consistency in their produce.

SLAUGHTERHOUSES

Just like any other industry, slaughterhouses benefit when the costs of their raw materials (in this case, livestock) are low. Some slaughterhouses such as Thorn

Apple Valley attempt to keep their livestock costs low by buying animals from breeders. By doing this, the slaughterhouse does not have to invest in the infrastructure (e.g., automated feeding machines, scientifically formulated feed mixing, climate-controlled pens, and in-house veterinary care) that is required to raise livestock.

Further factors that can lead to low prices of acquiring livestock are overbreeding by animal breeders and low costs of animal feeds, such as grain in the case of hogs. On the other hand, extreme heat or drought can kill livestock, which is likely to raise the costs of acquiring the surviving livestock. Similarly, poor harvests and heavy exports of crops result in higher feed bills, which translates into more-expensive livestock.

Some slaughterhouses take a different tactic in sourcing their raw materials. These vertically integrated slaughterhouses, such as Smithfield Foods, believe that they can maintain better product quality and consistency if they raise their livestock in-house. While these companies must invest in infrastructure, they believe that this investment is worthwhile since the consistency of livestock makes production more efficient.

Vertically integrated slaughterhouses believe that they can boost the number of pounds of product that are yielded from their animals. Also, these slaughterhouses are confident that, through proprietary genetic engineering, the percentage of lean meat obtained from their animals will exceed the industry average. (Of course, the leaner the animal, the better.) Moreover, vertically integrated slaughterhouses feel that they can increase the percentage of protein, iron, and zinc that their company's products contain.

Vertically integrated slaughterhouses argue that they can offer their customers more predictable product quality through the use of proprietary genetic engineering. One example associated with the failure to achieve genetic consistency is provided by the beef industry. The fierce independence of cattle ranchers virtually ensures the continuance of high variability in cattle, making it impossible for the beef packers to process beef efficiently. Moreover, the lack of uniformity in beef processing makes it extremely difficult to sell beef products to the food service industry, which demands uniform supplies so as to minimize internal handling costs. This obstacle to catering to the food-service industry will prove to be a growing opportunity cost as Americans continue to eat more meals outside of the home.

Other investment considerations relating to the slaughterhouses include the following:

- The length of time that slaughterhouses need to wait before the animals are processed. (The shorter, the better.)
- The average number of pounds of feed that the animals consume before they are processed. (The fewer, the better.)
- Labor costs. (The lower, the better.) Attempts by slaughterhouse workers to unionize in 1995 was a factor that kept stocks of slaughterhouses such

as Tyson Foods flat during that year. In addition to wages, health care exposure could rise for slaughterhouses as "nearly half of the people working in swine buildings complain of bronchitis, asthma-like conditions, inflamed sinuses, or flu-like illnesses from breathing dust and gases from pig feces and urine." [3]

T I P

You should consider the reception to processed food that constituent distribution channels will display. For example, unionized butchers at grocery stores oppose the packaging of beef the way that chicken is purchased because packaged beef could make the butchers obsolete. Such opposition could make it virtually impossible for a slaughterhouse to successfully launch a new processed-beef product.

- Since the rapid processing of livestock can be dangerous, it is important to consider the incidents of accidents and work stoppage.
- Less-stringent inspections and labeling regulations are generally beneficial to slaughterhouses. However, more-stringent inspections can benefit slaughterhouses if they result in fewer accidents and less downtime. Slaughterhouses that have the lowest standards in terms of sanitation and safety have the most to lose from increasingly stringent inspections since they will have to make the greatest efforts to comply with new regulations. On the other hand, slaughterhouses, such as those operated by Tyson Foods, whose standards exceed new industry regulations may not be adversely impacted since they will have no operating changes to make.
- Proximity to markets is important to ensure freshness of the processed food with minimal transportation expenses. However, the stench from slaughterhouses is so bad that many communities are averse to the establishment of slaughterhouses nearby.

NONALCOHOLIC-BEVERAGE PRODUCERS

The nonalcoholic-beverage industry in the United States is mature. For instance, Americans already drink more soft drinks per capita per annum than any other nationals in the world. Additionally, there is little domestic population growth to support further soft-drink sales.

---

[3] *Wall Street Journal,* July 11, 1995, p. B7.

This industry maturity was largely achieved as a result of the pervasiveness of beverage products (especially colas); that is, soft drinks are available in all regions of the United States. Moreover, the soft-drink companies have saturated their distribution outlets. Thus, the large soft-drink companies (e.g., Coca-Cola® and Pepsi®) have largely been successful in achieving their goal of ensuring that there is a can of cola within everyone's reach. As one beverage-industry executive said, "Whenever someone extends his arm, there had damn well better be a cola sitting there for them."

However, the producers of nonalcoholic beverages benefit from a few redeeming features. First, the fierce competition that is resulting from maturity in the soft-drink industry is helping to ensure that private labels do not capture too much market share. Second, there are niches for potential growth in the "alternative beverage" segment of the nonalcoholic beverage industry. Third, exceptional growth opportunities for American nonalcoholic beverage companies lie abroad.

Competition

Competition from private labels is not particularly fierce in the soft-drink industry because the major soft-drink companies have not aggressively raised their prices over the years. Thus, the pricing umbrellas under which private-label beverages could exist has been extremely shallow. Additionally, when it appears that private

T I P

> The cost of the elaborate distribution systems that the major beverage companies command is exorbitant and therefore produces a barrier to entry.

labels may begin to encroach on the major cola companies' market share, the large beverage companies have successfully been able to reduce their costs. Lower costs allow the major nonalcoholic-beverage companies to aggressively use promotions and advertising to protect their market shares without sacrificing profitability.

Determinants of Demand

Soft-drink sales are somewhat cyclical. Thus, more gallons of soft drinks are sold when the economy is strong than when the economy is weak. (When the economy is weak, many consumers will substitute cheaper drinks for soft drinks.) However, since the large beverage companies are now global players, domestic economic sluggishness is usually offset with economic growth in another part of the world, therefore, the investor should not become automatically disenchanted with beverage stocks when the domestic economy is weak. Nevertheless, it is equally important to realize that rapid growth in consumption of soft drinks in a region that is selling a small amount of soft drinks will not compensate for weakness in major markets. For instance, torrential growth in consumption in Latin America will not make up for decreases in consumption in the United States and Europe.

It is important to consider how restaurants' policies influence soft-drink sales. For instance, so-called value meals sponsored by fast-food restaurants boost the sales of soft drinks since value meals usually offer medium or large drinks, rather than small ones. Also, liberal refill policies at restaurants will boost the gallonage of soft drinks sold. However, when patrons take out and receive deliveries from restaurants, lower levels of soft drinks will be sold than if people ate in restaurants. This is because people may need to offset the expense of eating prepared food by drinking inexpensive beverages such as water, Kool-Aid® or milk.

The beverage companies will be able to sell more gallonage when the weather is hot. Therefore, beverage analysts often factor in projections of temperatures in the summers into their earnings models. Moreover, subtle shifts in exposure to weather could impact sales of beverages. For instance, migration to the Sunbelt could be a long-term advantage for beverage companies. On the contrary,

T I P

☞ Some large beverage companies have resolved the dilemma of owning bottlers versus contracting with them by taking equity stakes in bottlers that are large enough to have significant influence with their bottlers. Under these terms, the beverage company conserves capital by entirely avoiding the costs of building and maintaining its own bottling operations.

the transition from physical work (performed on farms or in factories) to more intellectual work (performed in air-conditioned offices) could be a long-term disadvantage for beverage companies. Similarly, children's preference to play video games instead of sports could result in reduced demand for beverages.

Production

You should consider whether or not the company under review owns its own bottlers. The major advantage of a beverage company's owning its own bottlers is that such a company will gain control over its own production. When bottlers are not owned outright, a number of problems can arise. For example, new product launches can be a source of contention since such launches often require new bottling equipment, new packaging, new label designs, different cap sizes, and different warehousing procedures. Often times, the bottler will be unwilling to make all of these changes for a product that may be short-lived.

On the contrary, one advantage of contracting with independent bottlers is that such contracting is much less capital intensive than is building and maintaining bottling operations internally. With reduced capital commitments it is easier to increase the rate of expansion of a brand.

T I P

It is favorable when the beverage industry avoids legislation requiring beverage companies to establish programs to collect and recycle returnable bottles.

Also, not owning bottling operations can allow a company to increase its prices. For example, some large beverage companies only sell their concentrate to bottlers. Since the price of such concentrate is only a small cost to the bottler, the beverage company can raise its concentrate prices substantially without hurting the bottler too much.

Expenses

On the expense side of the equation, you should pay especially close consideration to packaging prices and prices of other ingredients. As far as packaging goes, you should try to gain a sense of the relative utility and direction of aluminum, glass, polyethylene terephthalate, (PET a.k.a. plastic soft-drink containers) and paper prices.

One advantage of aluminum is that it is stackable and largely unbreakable. On the other hand, while glass is breakable it has an upscale feel, which is popular with producers of juices, iced teas, and beers. Additionally, certain juices can only be processed at very high temperatures, which glass can accommodate but plastic cannot. However, packaging made from PET is not labor intensive, features low breakage on assembly lines, low breakage in transportation, light shipping weights, and resealability. Finally, while both glass and PET are relatively easily recyclable, glass is harder to shape than plastic.

One telling signal of the direction of packaging costs (regardless of the material used) is factory capacity-utilization levels. When capacity utilization levels are high, packaging prices will likely rise; when capacity-utilization levels are low, packaging prices will usually fall. Obviously, low packaging costs will add to the benefit of beverage companies.

With regard to ingredients, you should consider the direction of sugar and sugar-substitute prices. International trade agreements (such as GATT) may reduce sugar price supports, which would result in sugar prices falling. Also, a greater selection of sugar substitutes would generate competition in this sector and therefore reduce costs of sugar substitutes. (Beverage companies are interested in substitutes to aspartame since this sugar substitute has a limited shelf life.) Of course, the lower the prices of sugar and sugar substitutes fall, the better for beverage companies.

The investor should consider the impact of changes in labeling requirements. Some labeling requirements can both increase costs and lower revenues for beverage companies. For instance, under some proposed labeling laws, beverage companies would need to disclose all of the ingredients, which would require the use of larger, thus more costly, labels

Also, the Nutrition Labeling and Education Act requires producers of juices to list the juices in descending order of predominance by volume. Thus, juices may have to be called by names that are not as appealing, which could lower sales. For example, an "Apple-Cranberry" juice that contains more cranberry juice than apple juice would have to be renamed "Cranberry-Apple" juice.

Niche Beverages

Beverage companies introduce niche beverages to generate excitement in the entire nonalcoholic-beverage industry. Also, new beverages can usually be sold at a premium since they benefit from being a novelty—in fact, some people believe that drinking a particular brand of bottled water is a status symbol. In other instances, niche beverages can be targeted to a narrowly defined segment of the population. For instance, sports drinks were introduced to meet the needs of athletes.

The large beverage companies are well suited to generate niche beverages. The reason is that they have many permutations of beverages that are designed to appeal to people in different parts of the world. Thus, when a niche becomes popular in one part of the world, the large beverage company can simply take one of its formulations off of its shelf and plug it into its local distribution system.

T R A P

⊘ Since there are no (FDA) compliance standards for bottled water, consumers may lose their confidence in consuming bottled water and thus purchase more water-purifying devices instead of bottled water. However, bottled-water producers could circumvent that situation if they were to adopt their own standards.

However, since New Age beverages cannot grow indefinitely, the prudent investor should ponder where some limitations to niche beverage growth lie:

- Some bottled drinks (such as iced tea) are much more expensive than their homemade versions, which are very easy for consumers to make.

- Many niche beverages are only sold in single servings, making it difficult for such drinks to gain significant volume.

- Some new beverages may not fit into a defined category in grocery stores. For instance, grocers were uncertain as to whether they should place iced coffee with the ground coffee, dairy products, or New Age beverages. Since grocery stores did not consistently place iced coffee in one part of the store, customers did not know where to find it resulting in lost sales.

- Some New Age drinks are not as healthy as they hold themselves out to be. For example, despite all of the advertising claims that it is made from the best stuff on earth, Snapple labels suggest most Snapple drinks are sugar water containing less than 10 percent fruit juice; thus, many customers may stop buying Snapple when they realize that they really are not buying a healthy drink.

- Some New Age beverages just do not taste as good as traditional colas. One problem with citrus-based juices, for example, is that consumers' mouths get tired of citrus.

Many analysts believe that consumption of bottled water, on the other hand, will be a long-lasting trend. These proponents hold that bottled water will grow because it is healthy and light. Also, heightened concerns about the safety of municipal water systems are said to help increase the consumption of bottled water. This is especially true if sanitary standards for drinking water are loosened or related funding becomes more scarce.

Specialty Coffee

Many analysts believe that specialty coffee bars (such as Starbucks) will, to a large extent, replace traditional bars. These analysts argue that aging baby boomers will not be able to consume as much alcohol but will still enjoy going out for something to drink. Also, heightened sensitivity toward drinking and driving and declining social acceptability toward drinking alcoholic beverages in general will be a boon to gourmet coffee bars.

However, the prudent investor should question the likelihood of coffee bars' replacing regular bars:

1. Coffee bars do not offer the same social experience that regular bars offer. Many people go to bars just to meet other people which is

facilitated by the presence of alcohol, music, and dancing. Since coffee bars lack the excitement that regular bars offer, they are thus not destinations for socializing.

2. In a regular bar, crowds draw additional traffic. That is, people want to go where the excitement is. However, crowds in gourmet coffee shops actually discourage additional patrons because people feel that they might not be able to sit at a table. Similarly, people will not feel comfortable sitting in a gourmet coffee shop for too long when other people may be waiting for a table. Furthermore, coffee bars have much less capacity (to accommodate patrons) than regular bars because people sit down when they are drinking coffee while they often stand up when drinking at regular bars.

3. Even when people do spend a lot of time in a gourmet coffee shop, they cannot consume nearly as many cups of coffee as they can consume bottles of beer. The same young man that can easily chug 15 beers at a bar will seldom drink more than three cups of coffee at one sitting. Thus, there is not a direct correlation between the amount of time that a customer spends in a gourmet coffee shop and the revenues per customer received by the coffee shop.

4. Compared with regular bars, coffee bars do not benefit from the advertising and marketing by their vendors since the individual coffees sold by gourmet coffee bars are usually not advertised.

Aside from the disadvantages that gourmet coffee shops have versus the regular bars, there are other limits as to how pervasive coffee bars can become.

- Since coffee bars serve hot beverages, they are not suitable for many warm climates.

- Since the coffee served in these bars is expensive (a cup can easily cost $3), these bars are only suitable for wealthy areas.

- A lot of coffee is consumed just for the jolt of caffeine, thus consumers may be largely indifferent to the taste. For instance, people who buy coffee in the morning "just to get going" would most likely prefer to buy coffee at a doughnut shop rather than at a gourmet coffee shop. (Doughnut shops also offer faster service than gourmet coffee shops.)

- Many of the coffees that gourmet shops serve cannot be marketed as being healthy. Some small cups of specialty coffee are laden, for example, with several hundred calories each. Also, latte is not really a cup of coffee at all, simply one ounce of espresso and seven ounces of steamed milk. Latte drinkers do not even get the benefit of the calcium because it passes through the body without being fully absorbed.

International Opportunities

In a presentation that I attended, Roberto Goizueta, the chairman and CEO of Coca-Cola, once described the opportunity that his company is presented with abroad with the following story:

> On a voyage across the Atlantic Ocean, one passenger remarked to the other that the ocean is very expansive. The other passenger's rejoinder was that what they could see was just the surface. The ocean is also very deep.

In this story, Mr. Goizueta related that the foreign opportunities that soft-drink makers are presented with lie not only along geographic lines but also in terms of repeat business. American soft drinks are just beginning to be introduced to large populations all over the world, and demographics are positive in most developing countries as these emerging markets have large percentages of young people with whom soft drinks are especially popular.

T R A P

⊘ Increased sensitivity toward drunk driving hurts bars and helps the volume of beer consumed at home but not enough to offset the loss at the bars. Bars charge higher prices and people tend to drink more on a night out on the town than at home.

Moreover, these drinks are easy to sell on a repeat basis since it is chic to drink American products and there is not much of a cultural change from drinking water to drinking soft drinks. (On the contrary, there is a significant cultural change from eating sushi to eating hamburgers because there are major changes as far as preparing and eating these foods.)

Additionally, soft drinks are relatively affordable for large segments of developing countries' populations. In fact, the liberal provision of soft drinks has been substituted for air conditioning in some factories in developing countries.

In estimating the demand for soft drinks in emerging markets, consider the number of hours it takes the average consumer to earn enough money to purchase a serving of the soft drink. The fewer the hours, the more affordable the soft drinks are and thus the brighter the prospects become for the beverage company.

However, there are some obstacles that American beverage companies are confronted with in selling their products abroad:

- The same symbolism of Americana that American colas represent that is popular with consumers is sometimes a target of the ire of foreign politicians. In the most extreme cases, soft-drink companies are forced out of promising markets as Coca-Cola was once driven out of India.

- U.S. cola companies have to deal with a lack of infrastructure in developing countries. Consequently, U.S. companies may have to make large investments in bottlers, delivery trucks, and sales training.

ALCOHOLIC-BEVERAGE PRODUCERS

The alcoholic-beverage producers also face a mature domestic market. Moreover, foreign beers have a great deal of appeal to American consumers. (However, U.S. brewers often benefit from the popularity of foreign beers since they produce such beers for the domestic market under licensing agreements.) In response to sluggish domestic demand, many beer producers are introducing microbrews and are expanding internationally. Much of the U.S. brewers' international expansion is targeted toward those countries that have a lower (but rising) per-capita consumption of alcohol.

Determinants of Demand

Reasons for a secular decline in demand for alcoholic beverages include an aging population, growing sensitivity toward drunken driving, less tolerance toward underage drinking by college students on the part of college administrators (due to liability concerns), and declining social acceptance of drinking.

T I P

> You should consider the percentage of a brewer's barrelage sold at full price versus a discounted price. (Of course, the fewer barrels of beer sold on a promotional basis, the better.) Similarly, when discounts are offered, the smaller the discounts are, the less dramatically brewers' profit margins will be eroded.

A strengthening economy and warm weather are cyclical factors that are helpful to beer sales. The economy is an important determinant of demand for beer for two reasons:

1. The volume of beer consumed is proportional to the strength or weakness of the economy, as the purchase of beer is largely discretionary.

2. When the economy turns weak, beer drinkers have a greater propensity to "trade down" to cheaper beers. Similarly, trying economic times result in brewers' launching more discounts and other promotions. However, sales of alcoholic beverages other than beer, especially wines, are less

economically sensitive. This is because the people that are wealthy enough to drink (and collect) the best wines can still afford to purchase such wines even when the economy is weak.

Moderately hot weather is beneficial for brewers because people like to drink beer when the weather is hot. However, extreme heat is bad for alcoholic-beverage companies because alcohol is a diuretic and people need to have sufficient liquids in their systems to prevent dehydration when heat is extreme.

Similar to the cigarette manufacturers, the alcoholic-beverage companies have difficulty segmenting their markets for advertising purposes. As in the tobacco business, the targeted constituent groups will take umbrage at being the focus of an alcoholic-beverage campaign. However, the difficulty that brewers have in segmenting their market is less problematic than the difficulty that cigarette manufacturers face since most beer advertising is aimed at men. (Men consume 80 percent of the beer in the United States.)

Alcoholic Content

Some alcoholic beverage producers are reducing the alcohol content in their drinks to appeal to women. Another advantage of offering drinks with lower alcohol content is that more distribution outlets will stock such drinks, which is important since many women have an aversion to frequenting liquor stores. Similarly, some of these distillers are adding fruit flavorings to drinks such as wine coolers to appeal to women.

Nonetheless, brewers have not always been well rewarded for introducing nonalcoholic or low-alcohol beers to the market. (A beer is generally considered nonalcoholic if it has less than 0.5 percent alcohol by volume. The alcohol content in a low-alcohol beer is generally less than 1.2 percent.)

- Demand for these "nonbeer beers" has been lackluster since many people are no longer embarrassed to be seen not drinking a beer. Now, many people feel comfortable drinking specialty coffees or sodas in social settings.

- Beer does not taste very good without alcohol.

- Alcohol acts as a preservative, and thus, the nonalcoholic beers have a shorter shelf life than regular beers. This reduced freshness is especially problematic for bars since bar owners need to sell the contents of an open keg quickly to avoid waste.

Nevertheless, low- or nonalcoholic beverages have two advantages over high-alcohol-content beers:

1. Since there is usually a direct relationship between a beer's alcohol content and its calorie content, lower-alcohol beers are usually lighter (in terms of calories) than high-alcohol beers.

2. Nonalcoholic brewers should enjoy bright growth prospects in Islamic countries since their authorities forbid alcoholic beverages.

New Introductions

It is important for brewers and distillers to introduce new products to the market in order to reinvigorate the alcoholic beverage industry. Also, new launches allow the new beverages to sell at higher prices because they are different from the existing products. (However, the free market is not the final arbiter of prices in the alcoholic-beverage industry. This is because, in some states, control agencies regulate the retail prices of alcoholic beverages.)

Additionally, the large brewers have been implementing "momentum marketing" techniques to reduce the marketing and testing expenses associated with new product releases. Momentum marketing occurs when a new beer is introduced in just a few cities initially. This not only creates a mystique, but results are determined faster and it is easier to discontinue these new beers if they do not perform well.

Microbreweries

Consumers have been gravitating toward beers with more of an individualized or local taste. Since the fewer than 15,000 barrels of beer a year that microbreweries produce are targeted at narrow geographic markets, microbreweries have become increasingly successful in meeting the demand for beers with a provincial feel.

While the microbrewers may produce less beer than the major brewers spill, the large brewers cannot use all of their muscle in competing with the microbrewers. For instance, large companies that make microbrews realize that using all of their resources in advertising their microbrews will cause the microbrew to lose its novelty appeal. Thus, some large breweries are trying to tap into the popularity of microbrews by "phantom branding" their beers. In phantom branding, the label on a beer indicates that the microbrew came from a fictitious brewery, rather than the true major brewery.

Additionally, microbrewers benefit from lower federal excise tax rates than are levied on the major producers. Major producers are currently levied a federal excise tax of $18 a barrel, whereas brewers that produce fewer than 2 million barrels a year only have to pay a federal excise tax of $7 a barrel on the first 60,000 barrels that they brew.

Despite the excise tax advantage, microbreweries have difficulty achieving wide distribution of their products. The primary explanation for this difficulty is that the microbreweries are thinly capitalized businesses, while regional (let alone national) distribution networks are highly capital intensive.

Due to these distribution obstacles, the investor should be cautious about projecting a sustainable rapid revenue growth rate onto the microbrewers.

Nevertheless, there are a few strategies that a microbrewer can undertake to expand its distribution channels:

- Sometimes microbrewers will reciprocate with one another by distributing each other's beers.
- Some restaurant chains adopt a microbrew as a house specialty.
- Microbreweries benefit from participating in mail order beer clubs that promote various beers to customers all over the country. However, some states discourage mail order beer clubs from soliciting business in their states since it is difficult to collect related sales taxes. (Another challenge to the beer clubs may come from parents who believe that such clubs present an easy way to sell alcohol to minors.)

Distribution System

Most states require a three-tier system of distribution, which consists of the brewer, the distributor, and the retailer. Under the laws of most of these states, the brewer is allowed to own the distributor but distributors cannot own retailers. However, there are a number of inefficiencies built into this system. For instance, brewers load beer onto trucks just to have the distributors unload and reload the beer, which is in turn unloaded again at the retail level.

In recognition of these inherent inefficiencies, some states are considering reforming the three-tier distribution system. Contemplate the ramifications of such reforms on the major breweries and on the microbreweries. As a result of these pending reforms, many distributors will likely be squeezed out of business since the major breweries will deliver their beers directly to their large customers. Due to lower distribution costs, the major brewers will be able to sell their beers through mass merchants for lower retail prices, helping the major brands gain more market share.

On the other hand, the microbrews and specialty beers that rely on sales from bars and small retailers may be adversely impacted by reforms of the three-tier distribution system. The microbrewers will face challenges in moving their beers through the distribution process. For instance, microbrewers will not be able to afford to replace the distribution capabilities of the traditional distribution companies. Furthermore, sales of niche beers may decline as a result of bars' and small retailers' losing the credit terms, marketing support, and inventory management distributors have traditionally offered.

Excise Taxes

Similar to cigarette companies alcoholic-beverage producers are major collectors of excise taxes. Thus, the investor should be very careful to distinguish between the gross price and the net price of alcoholic beverages. When determining profit margins, use the net sales figure since this represents the proceeds to the company under review. Similarly, when calculating the price-to-sales ratio of the stock of a brewer or distiller, you should use the net sales figure because excise taxes (as well as returns and allowances) are such a large percentage of the retail price.

Interestingly, the excise taxes levied per gallon of an alcoholic beverage that uses citrus-based ingredients are much lower than the excise taxes levied on spirits composed of other ingredients. Thus, investors often search for distillers such as Florida-based Todhunter International that have a steady source of citrus ingredients. The downside to citrus-based wine, however, is that citrus does not travel well. In fact, it can only be shipped 1,000 miles before going bad.

Wines and Distilled Spirits

While tastes for beer are becoming more localized, distillers such as Seagrams enjoy worldwide cache. Thus, distillers can better achieve economies of scale since the same brand can be sold throughout the world. Also, while there is the threat of trading down in the beer industry, many liquor drinkers seek to trade up to the world-renowned brands of wines and spirits.

However, there are a few concerns regarding the outlook for the spirits industry:

- The demographics are very bad for Scotch in the United States since most Scotch drinkers are maturing. In fact, executives in the spirits industry are concerned that the entire domestic Scotch market could disappear in 25 years.

- There are political parties in Poland and Russia that, as one of their primary planks, promote beer drinking because it is less damaging to health than drinking vodka.

Analytical considerations for evaluating the wine and spirits distillers include the valuation of the dollar and the ease of mixing things with spirits. First, a weak dollar benefits the domestic wine industry since there is a great deal of international competition. (A weak dollar makes it more affordable for foreigners to buy American wines. At the same time, a weak dollar makes foreign wines more expensive for American consumers.) Second, it is easier and tastes better to mix something with a white spirit (gin, vodka, rum, tequila) than a brown spirit (bourbon, Canadian whiskey, blended whiskey, and scotch). Thus, brown spirits have a disadvantage relative to white spirits.

TOBACCO

Many investors are enamored with the cigarette manufacturers. These proponents perceive the following strengths of the tobacco industry:

1. Enormous brand loyalty (possibly even addiction), which generates repeat revenues, little competition from imports, and efficient manufacturing.

2. A high barrier to entry because the industry is capital-intensive.

3. The ability to use their huge cash flows to take advantage of the virtually unlimited overseas potential of American cigarettes.

However, prudent investors should challenge some of these traditional assumptions.

1. The demand for cigarettes in the United States should be scrutinized very seriously since such demand is supposed to fund growth abroad.

2. Neither the severity of antismoking ordinances nor the legal challenges that cigarette manufacturers face should be underestimated.

3. The challenges to selling cigarettes abroad should be given very close consideration.

Domestic Demand for Cigarettes

Analysts should not assume that all smokers are addicted to smoking. While regulators may argue that smoking cigarettes has addictive characteristics, the fact of the matter is that nearly 50 million Americans have quit smoking. Another way of looking at it is that roughly as many people in the United States have stopped smoking as currently smoke. Heightened smoking restrictions and social unacceptability toward smoking could encourage more smokers to try to kick their smoking habits.

Demographics, antismoking restrictions, and challenges to advertising should be analyzed since these factors could further reduce the demand for smoking.

As people age, their health usually deteriorates. Conscious of their deteriorating health, older people are more sensitive to the health risks associated with smoking. Therefore, older people are more likely to quit smoking.

On the other hand, the most likely new smokers are teenagers. The more teenagers, the more potential smokers there are since few people start smoking once they are 20 and older. Also, teenagers are virtually indifferent to the health risks associated with smoking since they generally have not yet encountered significant health problems.

However, analysts should also consider the relative ease or difficulty of attracting teenage smokers. When advertising restrictions on appealing to youngsters are tightened, the potential for attracting new smokers becomes more limited. Such advertising restrictions could include prohibiting cigarette advertising on billboards in close proximity to schools and playgrounds as well as discouraging the use of cartoons in cigarette advertising.

Another factor in determining whether teenagers will smoke is their interest in athletics. The more teenagers participate in athletics, the less likely they are to take up smoking due to the respiratory effects that smoking has.

Also, when the legal penalties for retailers selling cigarettes to underage minors are severe, cigarette sales to teenagers will be reduced because retailers will make greater efforts to comply with underage smoking prohibitions. Similarly, greater restrictions on placement of cigarette machines will result in less teenage smoking. Cigarette machines are an easy way for minors to obtain cigarettes since they do not need to present identification; however, fewer cigarette machines will make this means of obtaining cigarettes less convenient.

Antismoking Sentiment

In addition to prohibiting minors from smoking, local ordinances and actions taken by employers can make it more difficult for adults to smoke:

- In some cities smoking in restaurants and shopping malls is prohibited.
- Similarly, the United States Post Office has banned smoking in all of its facilities.
- Some auto makers' are even designing cars without ashtrays.
- Concern over greater employer responsibility for their employees' health care expenses is resulting in some major employers' trying to hire only nonsmokers.

However, it is difficult to define exactly what a smoker is. (Is someone who infrequently smokes a smoker?) These bans are also difficult to enforce. (How would an employer know if its employees smoke off the job without becoming too intrusive?) Nevertheless, there is some judicial precedent for trying to enforce bans on hiring smokers. For example, Florida's Supreme Court upheld North Miami's ban of smokers from government jobs.

Cigarette companies have traditionally had difficulty segmenting their markets with advertising. This is because advertising aimed at groups such as youngsters or minorities is opposed by their related advocacy groups.

Aside from these natural restrictions on marketing strategies, the tobacco companies are prohibited from advertising on television, and even some print media reject tobacco advertising. Moreover, cigarette manufacturers are terrified by the possibility that the government will disallow the tax deductibility for expenses related to tobacco advertising.

Further restrictions on marketing would have immediate adverse consequences for weaker brands of cigarettes and longer-term adverse consequences for stronger brands. Weak brands would have a harder time gaining market share. For instance, if there is a ban on self-service displays in stores many retailers would have to keep all of their cigarettes behind the counter. Since there would not be

T I P

☞ It is less damaging for cigarette companies when discount cigarettes proliferate than it is for food manufacturers when store brands proliferate. This is because the tobacco companies control the production of both the branded and generic cigarettes, and can thus better coordinate their pricing strategies over their entire product lines. (The introduction of store brands in grocery stores, on the other hand, causes food manufacturers to lose their pricing power.)

space for dozens of brands, only the best brands would get space. If the *branded* cigarettes could not advertise they would eventually have to compete on price since they would have no medium in which they could convince their customers of the merits of the premiums charged.

Responding to Antismoking Sentiment

One strategy that some cigarette companies have for trying to circumvent these advertising restrictions is to sponsor product giveaways. For instance, under some programs, smokers receive gifts based upon their accumulation of a number of proof of cigarette purchases. These giveaways not only boost sales but further benefit the tobacco companies when the logos on the awarded clothing and accessories are not required to carry warning labels from the Surgeon General.

Also, such giveaways make it possible for the cigarette companies to develop lists of smokers, thus allowing the cigarette companies to reach their customers through direct mail as well as target them for lobbying purposes. (These lists will be of extreme importance should cigarette advertising ever become non–tax deductible.) Finally, the development of lists is politically savvy since cigarette companies can legitimately claim that such efforts are intended to increase sales to existing smokers, not to attract new smokers.

However, there are problems with cigarette companies' developing databases of smokers. Some people do not want their names placed on these lists for fear of receiving too much junk mail, being charged higher insurance premiums, and facing a ban by potential employers.

Price Increases

Investors should not automatically take increasing prices as a sign of higher future profitability because a large percentage of the retail price of cigarettes actually consists of excise taxes. High excise taxes are problematic for the following reasons:

T R A P

⊘ There is so much sentiment against tobacco companies that pension-fund managers could be prohibited from buying tobacco stocks in much the same way many fund managers were restricted from buying shares of companies that conducted business in South Africa in the 1980s. In fact, in March 1996, New York State Comptroller H. Carl McCall asked the money managers of the $75 billion Common Retirement Fund (New York's pension fund) to put a moratorium on further purchases of tobacco stocks. Of course, moratoriums such as these will make it very difficult for tobacco stock prices to rise.

- They limit the room that cigarette companies have to raise their prices.
- They may force the retail price of cigarettes up so high that many people (particularly teenagers) may no longer be able to afford the cigarettes.
- They are one cause of cigarette companies' introducing discount cigarettes; it is problematic when cigarette companies sell more discount cigarettes (rather than premium-branded cigarettes) because profit margins on discount cigarettes are lower—after all, excise taxes still have to be paid on discount cigarettes.

Capital Intensity

Proponents of the cigarette stocks point out that the capital intensity of this industry creates a barrier to entry. While barriers to entry limit competition, the enormity of the growing capital intensity of this industry could result in tobacco companies' foreign expansion plans slowing and earnings growth stagnating. One factor causing growing capital demands in the tobacco industry is the apprehension on the part of cigarette suppliers to conduct business with tobacco companies; some cigarette suppliers are deciding to no longer do business with the tobacco companies for fear of liability, shareholder lawsuits, and bad publicity. For instance, some major paper companies are divesting their cigarette paper operations. Also, International Flavors & Fragrances Inc. announced that it will scale back or halt selling flavors that cigarette makers mix in their tobacco. Such reduced availability of supplies forces the cigarette companies to invest excessive amounts of capital in their infrastructure to replace lost vendors.

Exorbitant legal costs are still a significant barrier to entry. Thus, litigation expenses explain why there are no new cigarette companies. However, the prudent investor cannot stop his analysis here; rather he should determine whether the liabilities associated with tobacco companies' legal problems outweigh the barriers to entry presented by the defense of such claims.

The cigarette manufacturers have been extremely successful in winning court cases in which cigarettes have been accused of contributing to smokers' health problems. The tobacco companies' virtually unassailable record has discouraged many other people from filing such lawsuits. Smokers that still want to press their claims against the cigarette companies have traditionally had a very difficult time retaining competent counsel to present their case. This is because product liability litigators are retained on a contingency basis, and virtually no lawyer that is compensated on this basis wants to challenge the tobacco companies for the following reasons:

- The odds of winning are extremely small.

- The tobacco companies stretch out the case for as long as possible by employing such tactics as extending the discovery periods. Few lawyers can afford to litigate an all-consuming case that will likely last many years, and the longer these cases last, the harder it is for the plaintiff to win. (Witnesses' memories become increasingly blurred, or the witnesses relocate or even die.)

However, there is a way for plaintiffs' lawyers to overcome the benefits that tobacco companies' money can buy in the court room. In the mid-1990s, roughly 60 major law firms began pooling their money together to fight the cigarette companies in the Castano case. These law firms are organizing a class action lawsuit on behalf of smokers similar to the class action lawsuits that were filed against the manufacturers of silicon breast implants.

Thus, it may be instructive to consider what has happened to the makers of silicon breast implants. The basic principle of civil jurisprudence—that damages should be connected to harm—has been overwhelmed by the silicon breast-implant class-action suit. In fact, even though a 1990 survey by the American Society of Plastic and Reconstructive Surgeons found that 93 percent of women with implants were satisfied with the results, some 440,000 of these women joined the class-action settlement. The silicon breast implant manufacturers have apparently decided that, rather than contest the suits on the merits, they'll pay billions and hope the lawyers will look for new prey elsewhere. Should a similar litany of events unfold with regard to smokers' successfully suing tobacco companies, the cigarette companies would be severely adversely impacted.

TIP

It is more problematic for an industry to be besieged by regulators (e.g., the EPA or the FDA) rather than by politicians (e.g., members of Congress) because it is much easier to lobby a politician (or vote a congressman out of office) than it is to influence a bureaucrat (or remove him from office).

Another major concern regarding the vulnerability of litigation on the tobacco companies is that several states such as Mississippi, Minnesota, and Massachusetts are suing cigarette companies for the states' Medicaid expenditures associated with diseases caused by smoking. As do the pool of plaintiffs in class-action lawsuits, states have the resources to present a serious challenge to cigarette companies. Further, a few foreign governments are increasingly aggressive in suing tobacco companies. For instance, the British government has agreed to fund poor smokers seeking legal damages from cigarette manufacturers.

Any legal decision against the tobacco companies would have serious ramifications for these companies' earnings results. This is because cigarette companies do not have insurance nor have they taken reserves to fund such losses. Nevertheless, the mere fact that litigation is consuming so much of the tobacco companies' top executives' time and attention means that these executives cannot focus on pursuing growth opportunities for their companies. In other words, a tobacco executive cannot sign distribution agreements in New Delhi when he is being deposed in New Orleans.

New Threats

The cigarette manufacturers have recently been confronted with increasingly damaging accusations. For example, there are growing accusations that second-hand smoking causes cancer. Similarly, a number of civil court judges have ruled that second-hand smoke constitutes battery.

One of the major problems with the demonizing of second-hand smoke is that the alleged health risks of second-hand smoke to nonsmokers means that smoking is no longer just a privacy issue. The plethora of prohibitions against smoking in public and workplaces have been legitimized. For instance, the EPA's labeling second-hand smoke as a class A carcinogen has resulted in smoking bans throughout the country. Moreover, the classification of second-hand smoke as cancer causing means that cigarette companies cannot use the argument that smokers have the freedom to choose what to do with their own bodies since second-hand smoke is alleged to affect others.

Another problem is that the FDA has accused the cigarette manufacturers of spiking cigarettes with nicotine to induce addiction to smoking. If the FDA is successful in convincing Congress that cigarette companies keep their customers addicted by manipulating nicotine levels, Congress may then allow the FDA to regulate cigarettes as if they were drugs. If the FDA were to go to the extreme case of categorizing cigarettes as a drug, smokers could be required to obtain a prescription in order to buy cigarettes. Many people would not be able to obtain such prescriptions, and many other smokers would stop smoking due to the stigma associated with consuming a drug (cigarettes). Additionally, U.S. law sometimes prohibits the export of unapproved versions of a drug to less-advanced countries.

In attempting to blame the cigarette companies for addicting their customers, the FDA is shifting the debate from the smoker to the manufacturer. Again, this would mean that smokers would not be able to invoke their freedom to choose in the smoking debate.

Moreover, the tobacco companies' ability to lobby politicians has been reduced as a result of less employment in the tobacco industry. Thus, the argument that jobs will be lost if the tobacco industry is adversely impacted by legislation carries less water. The tobacco industry has attempted to enhance its lobbying power by forming alliances with gas stations, convenience stores, vending machine operators, and advertising agencies. The willingness of these entities to cooperate with tobacco companies can have a pivotal impact on the success of cigarette companies' lobbying efforts.

Foreign Opportunities

Cigarette companies are fond of pointing to the tremendous opportunity for growth of cigarette sales in foreign (especially developing) countries. The primary arguments are that these economies are growing rapidly, their populations are young, and smoking American cigarettes is chic. Also, there is little concern for health risks associated with smoking since nationals of these countries do not expect to live long enough to contract such diseases.

However, the prudent analyst must look beyond these foreign opportunities to determine the obstacles in achieving high volumes of cigarette sales:

1. The normal risks of doing business in developing countries exist, such as risks of expropriation, currency risks, and arbitrary rules regarding contract law.

2. It is extremely expensive to develop manufacturing facilities and distribution channels in such countries.

3. It is usually not possible to sell cigarettes at the full price in these poorer countries.

4. There are significant risks of bootlegging. For instance, the government of Thailand wants foreign cigarette makers to disclose all of the ingredients in their cigarettes; cigarette makers fear that such disclosure will lead to increased bootlegging.

5. Many developing countries oppose the expansion of cigarettes produced by foreign countries on their soil by instituting protectionist measures. The U.S. government cannot legitimately apply any pressure on these countries to import U.S. cigarettes since the U.S. government (the FDA and the Surgeon General) has determined that smoking is detrimental to one's health. Accordingly, it would be incredibly bad statesmanship for the U.S. government to try to pressure a foreign government to import a

product that the U.S. government believes would harm their citizens. Thus, foreign nations do not face any repercussions from blocking imports of U.S. cigarettes.

6. Some developing countries prohibit or restrict the advertising of American cigarettes. In such cases, consider how problematic such prohibitions or restrictions really are. In most cases, limits on advertising of American cigarettes are not problematic since demand for American cigarettes is so great that they do not have to be advertised.

RESTAURANTS

Restaurant Stocks

The stocks of restaurant operators are typically volatile because the restaurant industry is susceptible to boom and bust cycles. One reason for these cycles is that restaurant companies can easily be taken public since the restaurant business is readily understandable by the investment community. Also, since these companies pay little or no dividends, they reinvest most, if not all, of their earnings in future expansion, which further fuels their earnings. Moreover, these are small cap stocks and thus soar on limited buying power. Given these rising equity prices, investment bankers like to take additional restaurant operators public and to issue secondary offerings of publicly traded restaurants.

However, at the same time that these stocks are zooming ahead, the restaurant operators are drowning in new equity. The restaurant chains that sold their stock use the proceeds to compete against one another by

- Expanding their number of units. These additional units compete for a relatively fixed number of dollars that consumers are willing to spend on meals away from home.
- Purchasing prime real estate.

These higher costs reduce the industry's profitability, and since these declining earnings are concurrent with very high stock prices many money managers have a tendency to sell restaurant stocks on earnings disappointments. This is when the bust occurs.

However, the lower prices that result from the bust may present buying opportunities for savvy investors. This is because the restaurant industry is not homogenous. Rather restaurants can be segmented by price points, take-out or sit-down formats, levels of service, types of food served, and geographic regions served. Thus, when the market knocks down stocks of all the restaurant operators, knowledgeable investors should bottom fish for the types of restaurants that are best positioned to generate future earnings momentum.

Competition with Grocery Stores

While everyone must eat, nowhere is it said that anyone must eat in restaurants. Therefore, investors must factor in the competition that restaurants face from grocery stores. An initial step in this analysis is to monitor the trends in the percent of dollars spent for food consumed away from home. The higher this percentage is (also referred to as share of stomach), the better for the restaurant industry.

Restaurants are generally stronger relative to grocery stores when the economy is strong because people are better able to afford to pay higher prices. (Restaurants further benefit from people generally eating more when they eat out than when they are at home. The lack of health-food restaurant chains is testimony to the fact that people indulge when they eat out.)

Conversely, when the economy is weak, grocery stores become more competitive relative to the restaurants because people would rather avoid paying the costs that restaurants factor into their checks for preparing meals. Further, there have been times when there has been very little food inflation but considerable inflation throughout the rest of the economy. In these circumstances, the supermarkets should have the advantage because their food prices will remain constant while prices charged by restaurants will rise more dramatically due to inflated labor costs.

Restaurants should have a relative advantage over grocery stores when more women enter the workforce: Women still prepare more of their families' meals than men. When women work, they have less time to prepare homemade meals but more income that can be spent on ordering out from restaurants.

Casual Dining versus Fast Food

In the restaurant industry there is usually a trade-off between speed and service. The casual restaurants usually try to provide more attentive, rather than faster, service. Therefore, casual restaurants can never be as efficient as fast-food restaurants in terms of employee productivity. For instance, part of the casual-restaurant philosophy is that it is better to have waiters available to serve the customer rather than to have the customer wait for the waiter.

However, in the fast-food business, employee productivity can be much greater. For instance, some fast-food operators have installed cash registers that measure the average time it takes the cashier to serve a customer. Similarly, fast-food restaurants rely heavily on mystery shoppers who determine which employees are doing their routinized jobs the fastest. (In fact, when I was in high school, a friend of mine lost his job because a mystery shopper reported that he was not serving french fries fast enough.)

Many fast-food restaurant chains such as Sonic are trying to further speed the delivery of meals to customers by relying on drive-through service, and some restaurants are using cellular phones to enhance their already-existing drive-through service. Under one plan, the customer calls a dedicated number that connects them to the nearest outlet. Then the customer gets directions and picks up his food when he arrives. This eliminates the time that the customer would have otherwise spent waiting in the drive-through line.

Another difference between casual dining and fast food concerns the extent of the menus. The more extensive the menu, the more difficult the cook's job becomes; therefore, customers must wait longer for their meals. This is considered a fair trade-off in the casual-dining segment. Not only do their patrons demand a wide selection, but good chefs will leave the restaurant if their work is not challenging enough.

However, in the fast-food arena, speed is of paramount importance; therefore, the menu must be relatively limited. A limited menu is necessary to prevent the customers from deliberating their orders for excessive amounts of time. If customers spend too much time pondering their orders, some of the customers behind them will leave the restaurant without ordering. Also, a limited menu is necessary to market top-of-the-line awareness of the restaurant's trademark products. This awareness is important because fast food is largely impulse driven.

A fast-food restaurant is usually better served by offering "value meals" rather than enticing customers with coupons. Value meals offer combinations of entrees, side orders, and beverages for prices that are lower than it would cost to purchase each of these items separately. The expectation behind value meals is that the customer will appreciate the value that he is getting and will return. On the other hand, coupons indicate the deal will be short-lived and therefore limit motivation for returning. Another advantage of value meals is that by packaging these products together, value meals get customers to spend more than if they had neglected to purchase one of the items in a more segmented order.

Analysts should also consider how shifts in demographics will impact the various segments of the restaurant industry. For instance, as baby boomers mature, more money should be spent on sit-down dining. Also, older people do not eat much fast food.

Investors should realize that there is a direct correlation between the fragmentation of an industry sector and the growth opportunities for the large companies in that sector. Thus, the leading casual-dining chains may have better growth opportunities domestically than fast-food operators because the casual-dining chains have more market share to gain vis-a-vis the independent operators due to the casual segment's being more fragmented than the fast-food segment.

The outlook for upscale restaurants such as those owned by Ark Restaurants is much more impacted by changes in the tax deductibility of business meals: The greater the percentage of tax deductibility for business meals, the more money is likely to be spent on casual dining. Thus, the casual-dining companies should benefit much more in this case than the fast-food restaurants. Conversely, reduced deductibility for business meals should result in fewer business meals' being consumed in upscale restaurants, in which case it would be safer to hold fast-food-stocks. However, one exception to this rule is the fast-food restaurants that serve truckers could be adversely impacted by a lower deductable because truckers are usually allowed to deduct the costs of their business meals from their taxes.

Restaurant Sales

Since the price of restaurant stocks is often affected by news of sales trends, it is important to analyze the components of restaurants' sales. First, investors should consider *average table turnover* and *average ticket prices.* Average table turnover measures how many parties of patrons are served each day or each hour. Average table turnover is calculated by dividing the number of restaurant receipts by the number of tables in the restaurant. For example, if a restaurant generates 1,500 receipts each day and there are 50 tables in the restaurant, the average table turnover is 30 (1,500/50), which means that each table serves 30 customers each day. Furthermore, if the restaurant is open 15 hours each day, the average amount of time that each patron spends at the restaurant is a half an hour (15 hours divided by 30 table turns). In general, the faster the table turnover the better since higher table turnovers indicate that more patrons are being served at each table in the restaurant.

Investors should consider the average table turnover in conjunction with the restaurant's average ticket price. The average ticket price simply represents the average amount of money that each party of patrons spends in the restaurant, and it is determined by dividing the total dollar value of restaurant receipts by the number of receipts generated per day. Continuing our example, if the restaurant that serves 1,500 patrons each day takes in $22,000 daily, the average ticket price is $14.67 ($22,000/1,500). Generally, the higher the average ticket price the better since the fixed costs of the restaurant are better covered by these higher revenues. However, a low check average is helpful in generating repeat business. (On the other hand, a restaurant that does not depend on repeat business is able to average a higher check. For example, restaurants that are located on heavily traveled highways can charge higher prices since they are not dependent on repeat business.)

Interestingly, there is usually an inverse relationship between a restaurant's average table turnover and its average ticket price. The more money people spend in restaurants the higher the level of service they are entitled to expect. Thus, investors should seek those companies that generate the highest *product* of table turnovers and average ticket prices. For instance, the restaurant that has an average table turnover of 30 and an average ticket price of $14.67 generates $440.10 (30 × $14.67) in revenue for each table on a daily basis. Similarly, a restaurant that has an average table turnover of 25 but an average ticket price of $18.00 generates $450 ($18 × 25) a day in revenue for each table. Thus, the latter restaurant chain derives more revenue from each table.

Analyzing the two factors together makes it easy to compare restaurants that otherwise have many differences in terms of cuisine served, price points, levels of service, and geographic regions served. Keep in mind, however, the average-table-turnover ratio is usually most suitable for analyzing restaurant chains that exclusively offer sit-down service because fast food restaurants generate a large portion of their sales through other access modes such as takeout, delivery, and drive

T I P

When Wall Street dumps shares of restaurants that fail to post higher same-store sales growth, the prices of such shares often fall to very attractive levels. Since you now know that less favorable same-store comparisons are often a signal of a healthy restaurant chain, you can often safely purchase shares of growing restaurant chains when they fall out of Wall Street's favor.

through. Since patrons that purchase food through these alternatives do not consume their meals at the restaurant, the average-table-turnover calculation is rendered inoperative.

Same-Store Sales Growth

For reasons similar to those discussed in the Retail chapter, analysts are extremely concerned about the same-store sales growth of the restaurant operators that they follow. In other words, not only are the chains' entire sales supposed to increase but analysts expect each unit in the restaurant chain to reach higher and higher sales levels.

Wall Street expects that restaurant companies can post higher same-store sales growth indefinitely. However, in the real world this is impossible because restaurants can never be as efficient in feeding people as, say, factories are in manufacturing products. Since people like to eat at certain times of the day, restaurants cannot produce food evenly throughout the day. For instance, most people like to eat dinner between 5:00 PM and 8:00 PM; thus, there is little that restaurants can do to generate higher dinner traffic before 5:00 PM or after 8:00 PM. Also, because people do not like to spend a lot of time waiting for a table or for their orders, there are a limited number of patrons that can be served during peak times. A concrete example of this is that there was once a restaurant that was attracting so much drive-through traffic that the backlog of customers was blocking traffic in the city's main thoroughfare. The police demanded that fewer patrons be served so that the danger of so much congestion would be reduced.

Additionally, for the reasons that follow restaurants cannot easily generate higher same-store sales growth by enlarging their existing units:

1. Expanding an existing restaurant often causes the restaurant to lose its charm because larger restaurants are more difficult to manage thus compromising service.

2. Franchisors often impose very strict standards over the size of their franchisees' units.

3. Zoning restrictions sometimes make it impossible to expand existing stores.

As a result of not being able to indefinitely improve same-store sales results, restaurant operators take the logical step of capitalizing on their popular concept by opening additional units. The immediate affect of these additional units may be that same-store sales erode further; however, the longer-term effect is often that the chain's earnings improve

- The restaurant chain will be able to increase its revenues by serving more meals.

- The costs can be spread over a larger base. (For instance, advertising on a local radio station can lure patrons to a few restaurants instead of just one restaurant.)

- The restaurant operator will be able to demand larger rebates from its food suppliers because of its enhanced buying power.

Food Costs

In order to determine how food costs impact a restaurant's profitability, calculate the costs of food-to-revenue ratio. Analysts generally favor restaurant operators that are reducing this percentage; spending less money on food in terms of revenue means that the restaurant is either deriving bigger rebates from suppliers, reducing waste, or raising ticket prices. However, there is a limit as to how low the food-to-revenue ratio can fall. The customer must feel that he is getting good value or he will not return.

Further, food and labor costs should be considered together because this yields a clearer picture of the total costs associated with delivering a meal to a patron. Failure to consider food and labor costs together can result in distortion. For instance, had you not read *Bound for Growth,* you may have rated the ABC restaurant more favorably than the XYZ restaurant because ABC's cost of food-to-revenue ratio is 35 percent while XYZ's cost of food-to-revenue ratio is 50 percent. However, if ABC's labor-to-revenue ratio is 40 percent while XYZ's labor-to-food ratio is only 15 percent, XYZ will actually be the better investment. This is because XYZ will have a lower combined cost of labor and food-to-revenue ratio at 65 percent than ABC, whose combined ratio is 75 percent. An example of what might account for this discrepancy is that XYZ might buy premade salads, which are expensive but require little preparation. On the other hand, ABC might buy its own vegetables at wholesale but prepare the salads at its own expense.

Companies that feel they need to lower their combined food and labor-to-revenue ratios often try to increase their sales of alcohol. Alcohol is extremely profitable since it is purchased by the case and sold by the shot. Also, there is virtually no labor in serving alcoholic beverages. An alcoholic drink is just about the only product that can be produced (poured) and consumed in less than 30 seconds. (Compare this with the time required to produce and consume a salad.) However, one problem with alcohol is that it is very easy for bartenders to give away. Also, serving too much alcohol could hurt a restaurant's family image.

Labor Expenses

Since labor represents a huge expense for restaurants, you must monitor trends in labor costs very carefully. In particular, minimum wages and employers' responsibility for their employees' health care must be diligently scrutinized. First, consider minimum wages. There are both federal and state minimum wages. In many instances, the state minimum wages are higher than the federal minimum wages. Since companies must pay the higher of the two minimum wages, investors should search for restaurants that do business in states that have lower minimum wages than the federal minimum wages. Investors should also be wary of investing in restaurants that operate in states with liberal governors and legislatures. This is

T I P

Restaurants may not be as adversely impacted by any future mandatory health care coverage as you might think:

- The fine print in such reform bills might stipulate that employees must have worked at the restaurant for a minimum number of months before they are entitled to health care coverage; since turnover rates at restaurants are high, many employees may not be eligible for coverage.

- Coverage may not be extended to employees who work below a minimum number of hours a week.

- Restaurants may not have to cover those employees that are covered by their parents', spouses', or universities' medical insurance.

because liberal politicians are more likely to favor higher minimum wages than conservative politicians.

When you anticipate an increase in minimum wages, you should search for restaurants that have a low percentage of their employees earning the minimum wages. Similarly, you should try to invest in restaurant chains that have a large percent of their workers currently earning wages that will exceed the new minimums. This is because the higher minimum wages will only have to be paid to a small percentage of the workers.

For example, assume that the current minimum wage is $4.25 an hour but is scheduled to rise to $4.75 an hour. If 60 percent of restaurant ABC's workers earn $4.35 an hour and 60 percent of XYZ's workers earn $4.90 an hour, the XYZ restaurant chain will not be as immediately adversely impacted as ABC by the rise in the minimum wage. This is because ABC will be required to raise the wages it pays to 60 percent of its employees by at least $.40 an hour ($4.75 − $4.35). However, XYZ will not have to increase the wages that it pays to the majority of its workers because the current wages already exceed the forthcoming higher minimums.

Note that the above paragraph is counterintuitive; you've been advised to invest in the company that actually has the higher labor expenses currently. The rationale for this investment strategy is that the ABC restaurant will be more adversely impacted by the higher minimum wages compared with the XYZ chain.

Nevertheless, higher minimum wages often adversely affect companies that already have a high percentage of their employees earning above-minimum wages, as does XYZ, because seasoned employees rightfully expect to earn higher wages than entry-level workers. After all, experienced workers are usually more productive. Therefore, if a two-year veteran of a restaurant had been earning $2 above the previous minimum-wage level, or $6.25 ($4.25 + $2), she will expect to earn at least $6.90 an hour when the minimum wages rise to $4.90 an hour. These expectations are often met because above-minimum-wage pay is a powerful marketing tool for restaurants.

Analysts should also consider whether the geographic areas that restaurants serve are experiencing labor shortages. If the labor shortages are severe, wages for entry-level workers may exceed the minimum wages. There have been instances where some labor markets were so tight that restaurant operators actually had to bus their employees in from distant areas. These employees received full wages for the time that they spent traveling to and from work.

The threat of mandatory health care coverage could cause restaurant stocks to plunge. This is both because health care expenses are exorbitant and because this industry is so labor intensive. However, the route of restaurant stocks in reaction to the threat of mandatory health care coverage could be an opportunity in disguise for savvy investors.

One way to minimize your risk by investing in the restaurant industry during such upheavals is to invest in the shares of restaurant franchisors. Higher health care costs would hurt the entire restaurant industry. In response to higher costs, restaurant operators would have to raise their menu prices. These higher menu

T I P

The current ratio is one of the tenets of fundamental analysis that does not apply to restaurant stocks. It is perfectly acceptable for restaurant companies to have current ratios that are less than one to one. This is because restaurants receive cash from their customers immediately upon rendering their service. Also, inventory turnover is rapid because food is perishable. On the other side of the ledger, restaurants pay their vendors on credit. Thus, restaurants enjoy a lag between the time they receive payment and the time when they make payments.

prices would, in turn, result in fewer people eating at restaurants. Thus, the restaurant industry would be beset with higher costs but lower revenues. However, the independent operators would typically fare worse than the restaurant chains because the independents would neither be able to spread their higher costs over as large a revenue base. Therefore, more independent operators would go out of business. But the independents' woes are the chains' opportunities. With less competition from the independents, the franchisees would be able to increase their market shares and menu prices. Higher prices and more customers would result in greater revenue streams at the franchisee level. Even if the franchisees' profits do not increase, the franchisor's profits will rise as long as the franchisees' revenues rise. This is because the franchisor's profits are derived from collecting royalties that are based on franchisee revenue.

Other Expenses and Concerns

You should also factor in the other costs that restaurants are forced to bear.

- Higher paper prices will hurt the fast-food restaurants more than the casual-dining restaurants since a lot of fast food is wrapped or placed in paper bags.
- Restaurants that play music may be forced to pay royalties to the artists that produce the music because performance rights societies such as the American Society of Composers, Authors and Publishers are increasingly aggressive in collecting such fees.

- The costs of garbage collection, utilities, and taxes may affect restaurants' profitability. These expenses will be especially burdensome for a restaurant chain that is attempting to expand into large cities because these costs can be exponentially higher in large cities than in small towns.

- Restaurants will have to be increasingly careful of the claims that they make regarding the nutritional value of the food they serve; if the restaurants' menus are not in compliance with the FDA's rules governing issues such as what constitutes "light foods" and "low-fat foods," they will have to absorb the costs of reprinting their menus.

- Some cities are almost completely forbidding smoking in their restaurants which means that business will be lost if the bans are enforced or that fines will be levied if the smoking bans are *not* enforced.

Other restrictions that would be highly problematic for the restaurant industry include indoor air-quality standards and legislation requiring restaurants to actively reduce repetitive motion injuries.

Portability

Operators of publicly traded restaurants frequently introduce new dining concepts. Some managers are so optimistic about the potential of their new concepts that they lead investors to believe that these new concepts will be successful all over the country. However, you should realize that some concepts are not suited for every geographic region of the county. For instance, executives at one restaurant admitted to me that their Tex-Mex concept simply does not work above a certain line of latitude. Similarly, extremely high or low price points might not work in all markets.

In order to determine which concepts will succeed on a national basis, the analyst must consider the portability of the restaurant's concept. For example, a restaurant that has units in 30 markets throughout a region may have a portable concept while a restaurant that has 30 units in a given local market may not have a portable concept. This is because the chain that has units located in a multitude of markets will serve different demographics, climates, and tastes. If the chain can operate successfully in markets that serve these different groups, chances are that this chain will be more successful on a national basis than a chain that only serves a narrow cross-section of people in one local market.

Current Ratio

The current ratio is simply the current assets divided by current liabilities. Most analysts like to see the current ratio be at least 2:1 meaning the company under review has two dollars in current assets to meet each dollar of current liabilities.

Analysts like to review the current ratio because it provides an indication of the company's liquidity or its ability to pay off current liabilities if a serious business interruption occurred that caused fund inflows to dry up. This concern is not entirely academic in the restaurant industry. People will not patronize a restaurant when there is a health scare. For instance, business at Jack-in-the-Box® came to a virtual standstill after many people were sickend by undercooked hamburgers served by that chain.

Location

Restaurants should be operated in areas that have a great deal of traffic. Commonly, these units are placed in close proximity to shopping centers, movie theaters, sports facilities, and hospitals. One way to gauge how much traffic the restaurant is exposed to is to determine the average number of cars going past the front door each day. Also, to make it convenient to capitalize on this traffic, the restaurant should offer parking all around the building and have a multitude of entrances and exits.

Some restaurant chains such as McDonald's® are establishing satellite units and kiosks in areas where there are already large numbers of people. For instance, these satellites are being established within hospitals, universities, gas stations, and sports arenas. Since these stores are much smaller than the regular-sized stores, they are much cheaper to open and inexpensive to operate because they have less space to heat and cool. Additionally, these satellites allow the restaurant chain to leverage its existing infrastructure by using some of the nearby restaurants' employees and managerial talent. Similarly, the satellites can use the restaurants' kitchen facilities for preparing and heating some of their food. Finally, the satellites can use the restaurants for storing their equipment and supplies.

Strategic locations for establishing satellite restaurants include mass merchants and airports. Mass merchants are receptive to satellite units because they keep the customer in the store longer and because their employees will not have to travel during their lunch breaks—thus, the employees stay on location without the mass merchant having to establish an employee cafeteria. Also, satellite units at airports can be especially profitable when the airlines are cutting back on meals during flights.

However, there are some obstacles to rolling out satellites:

1. Franchisees do not like to compete against them.
2. Stadium workers have protested that it was unfair that large chains threatened their jobs.
3. Gas stations are not great places for satellite restaurants since gas fumes are present and the cars of food orderers may block those cars in need of fuel.

Franchises

One of the primary benefits of a restaurant chain operating as a franchisor is that the franchisees supply most of the capital for the chain's expansion. Thus, a franchise chain can grow much faster (and with less risk) than a chain that only grows by increasing the number of company-owned units.

However, the franchisor loses some of its control when it grants franchises. Another problem with having too many franchisees (in relation to company-owned stores) is that it becomes difficult to develop district and regional managers. Therefore, the franchisor must be very selective in deciding to whom franchises are granted so that the chain's reputation for standards is maintained. Indications of such selectivity follow:

- The franchisor only grants franchises to individuals involved in running their own units.
- Franchisees are required to finance their own units with a high percentage of nonborrowed assets.
- The franchisee is required to divest himself of all other business interests.
- The franchisees are required to periodically undergo training.

T I P

> One prudent strategy for building market share in foreign markets is to initially target the upper classes that can afford to pay the higher prices that will cover the cost of building the local infrastructure. The next step is to attract a broader base of customers so that economies of scale can be achieved and prices reduced.

In order to be granted a franchise, franchisees are usually required to pay large one-time franchise fees. These initiation fees boost the franchisor's sales. Further, these fees are highly profitable since there are no costs of goods sold to be deducted from these initiation fees. However, since these fees are nonrecurring, the investor should try to isolate these fees from the franchisor's performance; thus, you need to consider franchise initiation fees as a percentage of sales and pretax earnings. The more of a company's sales and pretax earnings that are in the form of one-time fees, the lower the quality of earnings are because these one-time fees are not nearly as predictable as royalty revenue. For example, if 25 percent of the ABC company's profits are derived from initiation fees while only 10 percent of the XYZ company's earnings are attributable to initiation fees, the XYZ company would have better earnings quality. Similarly, a company that sells many of its company-owned stores to franchisees (in order to receive the one-time franchise fees) should be viewed with extreme skepticism.

In another departure from fundamentalist theory, a large degree of insider ownership is not necessary for restaurants that operate as franchisors. Since franchisees usually invest a large part of their wealth in their franchise, they are committed to their franchise's profitability even if they do not hold stock in the franchisor. This does not mean that franchised restaurants cannot have large degrees of insider ownership. In fact, McDonald's is so proud of the level of its systemwide ownership (franchisees, employees, management, and vendors who own McDonald's stock) that it often highlights this percentage in its annual reports.

Despite the advantages of operating on a franchise basis, there are a number of potential problems with franchising of which you should be aware:

- Tensions are likely to arise between the franchisee and franchisor when the franchisee feels that the franchisor is selling new franchises too close to their existing units thus cannibalizing the sales of the existing units.

- Sometimes franchisees are required to purchase their supplies from commissaries that are owned by the parent company. However, some of these franchisees claim that the parent company is gouging them through the commissary.

- Franchisees are opposed to a typical provision in the franchise agreement that requires them to arbitrate in the parent's home state. Furthermore, franchisees are averse to not being allowed to abandon a system or sell their stores without the franchisor's approval. (If they do, they usually must forfeit all of their store's assets.)

- Because one poorly managed store can denigrate the image of all of the system's stores in a given region, franchisors want the right to buy out franchisees that are not meeting the parent's standards. However, this makes it more difficult for the franchisee to obtain loans (or loan guarantees) because under some legal interpretations they do not have full ownership rights.

- Franchisees can be more resistant to change than stores under company management. For instance, the franchisor may feel that it is imperative to introduce a line of Mexican meals to appeal to the growing Hispanic population. In order to produce such food, new equipment may have to be installed in each unit's kitchen. However, some franchisees may delay the rollout of Mexican food because they may be averse to making the necessary investment in the equipment. On the other hand, if the restaurant chain owned all of its units outright, there would be no delay. Store managers would not be opposed to installing the necessary equipment because they would not have to pay for it.

International Opportunities

American restaurant chains are extremely well positioned to capture international market share. In fact, there are virtually no foreign competitors for the international market. Further, foreigners often crave American restaurants. One reason is that American restaurants are an inexpensive way to get a taste of Americana, and eating at an American restaurant is a very visible way for foreigners to broadcast their chicness.

Moreover, American restaurants insist on high-quality food standards and enjoy a reputation for being cleaner and offering faster and friendlier service than their local competitors. Additionally, American restaurants are usually air-conditioned and smoke free.

You can use a formula to estimate how many restaurants a given chain can potentially build in a foreign market. The ratio is

$$\frac{\text{(population of the foreign country/number of people per store in the United States)}}{\text{(per capita income in foreign country/per capita income in the United States)}}$$

For instance, let us assume that McDonald's wanted to estimate how many of its restaurants China could absorb. In making this estimate, let us assume that the population of China is 1.2 billion; that there is one McDonald's for every 25,000 Americans; that the per-capita income in China is $1,000; and that the per-capita income in the United States is $25,000. Thus, the calculation would be [(1,200,000,000/25,000) ($1,000/$25,000)]. This formula would suggest, then, that China could absorb about 1,920 McDonald's restaurants. However, the formula does not take issues such as concentrations of wealth and eating habits into account.

Special Situations

One strategy that prudent companies sometimes implement is to position their restaurants in tourist areas. The logic is that travelers who stay in hotels do not have the facilities to prepare their own food but must eat nonetheless; therefore, travelers must patronize restaurants.

While this is often a sound strategy, there are a few concerns that should be addressed. First, tourist locations are almost always seasonal and the popularity of these locations is largely unpredictable. Thus, restaurants located in tourist areas will perform poorly in the off seasons; if the fixed costs are high, these slower periods will usually produce operating losses. Also, restaurants that are located in tourist areas are often required to pay an additional tax, which is used to fund the promotion of local tourism. This tourist tax is typically a sales tax added to the customers' bill. One problem with this tax is that it could raise the average ticket price to a level that is too high for the local patrons to pay thus magnifing the off-season losses.

Another prudent strategy is for restaurants to locate on highways where the distance between two towns is great. These restaurants will capture a lot of tourist traffic since these tourists have few alternative restaurants to choose from. However, these restaurants are dependent on favorable weather since inclement weather will result in less driving.

Other Analytical Considerations

When considering investing in a restaurant stock, you should be aware of the following:

- Renovation will not significantly boost a restaurant's traffic. Rather, renovation is a defensive tactic to keep existing customers coming, not an offensive ploy to improve the business.

- Restaurant seating capacity in a given market does not decrease significantly regardless of how bad the local economy gets. When one restaurant goes out of business it will usually be another restaurant that takes its place. This is because landlords are usually willing make concessions to lure another restaurant operator to rent their facilities because they do not want to go through the expense of removing the pre-equipped kitchen. Some landlords even grant the new tenant a rent-free period to obtain the required permits and open the unit.

- Restaurant companies that have a few different concepts often obtain leverage with property sellers and landlords. This is because the company can negotiate for more square footage at one site.

- The restaurant business is highly management intensive because managers deal with perishable foods and a labor force that is highly unreliable. Therefore, investors should consider the quality of store managers: One indication of a solid stable of skilled managers is a low turnover ratio; another is a high average number of years that the company's managers have worked at the given restaurant chain. Some chains try to increase this average by giving their managers a percentage stake in their unit in exchange for a given number of years of service. A further indication of solid management is a high number of applications received for each management position available. It is especially impressive when many of these applications come from managers that are affiliated with competing restaurants.

6

Leisure and Recreation

The leisure and recreation stocks are generally considered cyclicals. The stronger the economy becomes, the more money people can spend on their leisure and recreation. Conversely, when the economy appears poised for a downturn, people generally reduce their expenditures for these nonessential activities.

Another determinant of how these stocks trade is driven by changes in the marginal tax rate. (Marginal tax rates are the rates of tax that people pay on the last dollar of income earned.) The higher the marginal income tax rate rises, the more of a disincentive people have to work additional hours. Thus, higher marginal tax rates result in consumers' having more time to spend on leisurely activities, but when marginal income tax rates fall, people desire to work more hours (since they will retain more of the related income) and thus, have less time to engage in leisurely activities.

LODGING

Demand for Hotel Rooms

The lodging industry is somewhat cyclical. For instance, a healthier economy induces more travel than a deteriorating economy because, for example, businesses grant more generous travel allowances to their executives and people are more likely to vacation when they believe that their own finances are in order.

Conversely, both businesses and individuals are likely to scale down their travel itineraries when the economic outlook is grim.

While the hotel stocks have a significant cyclical component, there are many other considerations that you must take into account before investing in lodging stocks. These considerations include

- The degree of competition in the airline industry. Hotels benefit from fierce competition in this area. For instance, when there are air fare wars, more people can afford to travel. Also, when the penalties for failing to purchase airline tickets (14 or 21 days) in advance are lifted, people can be more spontaneous in their traveling, which benefits the hotels. Finally, the more days of each week that the cheapest air fares are offered, the more travel will be generated, which adds to the benefit of the hotel industry.

- Similar to air fares, the price of gasoline is an important determinant of demand for hotel rooms since many people travel by car. The lower the price of gasoline falls, the more people will be able to afford to travel and the more people will be able to travel further away from home, increasing the odds that they will need lodging facilities.

- Another consideration in determining the demand for (domestic) hotel rooms is the valuation of the American dollar. A weaker dollar is beneficial to U.S. hotels since a cheap dollar encourages foreigners to travel to the United States. Incidentally, the economy hotels such as La Quinta Inns or Sholodge are more affected by changes in the valuation of the dollar because they have a much higher percentage of their rooms in the United States than the more expensive chains (such as Hilton) with hotels worldwide.

  The hotels that appeal to foreigners coming from countries with more generous vacation policies will benefit from a longer average length of occupancy. Thus, the hotels that appeal to Europeans who have about 30 vacation days each year may represent more attractive investment opportunities than the hotels that appeal to the Japanese who only have about 10 vacation days a year.

- A more subtle determinant of demand for hotel rooms is demographics. Generally, the hotel industry benefits from growth in the number of senior citizens since traveling is a favorite pastime for seniors.

TIP

☞ There is an instance in which excessive competition in the airline industry can be detrimental to the hotel industry: when the airlines no longer require Saturday night stay-overs for their lowest fares.

- Another undercurrent that could benefit the hotel industry is that the nature of work is changing. People now travel more because of their jobs than in previous generations. For example, consultants travel more than factory workers.

Supply of Hotel Rooms

You should seek to invest in the hotel industry when the supply of hotel rooms is tightening because fewer hotel rooms will drive occupancy rates and room rates higher. Accordingly, the fewer hotels under construction, the better the prospects are for the hotel stocks. Some of the situations that result in a lack of hotel construction are

- When banks are unwilling to lend money to hotel developers. Such unwillingness often occurs shortly after banks take large charges for uncollectible loans previously extended to hotel developers.
- When the REIT (real estate investment trust) market is weak since REITs are major hotel developers.
- When there is an elimination of tax shelters associated with investing in hotels.
- When hotel rooms are converted into apartments (actually *reducing* the number of hotel rooms).

Profit Drivers

Investing in a hotel company when the hotel industry is benefiting from both greater demand for hotel rooms and slow growth in the number of hotel rooms under construction can be highly rewarding because hotel profits are driven higher by both higher occupancy rates and higher room rates.

Most investors do not sufficiently appreciate the leverage that occupancy rates and room rates contribute to a hotel's earnings power. When occupancy rates rise, roughly 90 percent of the differential falls to the company's bottom line. For example, when a hotel's occupancy rate rises from 65 to 75 percent, most of the revenues generated from accommodating the additional guests fall to the bottom line. This is because the hotel does not have to increase its production (as does a factory) when it rents more rooms. The rooms are already in place. Furthermore, the additional expenses associated with accommodating the extra guests are minimal—just a little bit more electricity, water, and room service is expended.

Moreover, when room rates rise, essentially 100 percent of the differential falls to the company's bottom line. For example, when a hotel raises its nightly rates for a particular room from $100 to $115, virtually all of the $15 difference is pure profit. This is because there are no added expenses when room rates rise. For a given room, all of the expenses are fixed regardless of the rates charged. The size of the room is the same, the amount of utilities used is the same, and the costs of

T I P

☞ The American Automobile Association takes a survey of the percentage of road travelers that plan to stay with relatives. The lower this percentage is, the better for the lodging industry.

room service are the same. Thus, when higher rates are charged, hotel profits soar. Additionally, when room rates rise, so do other hotel charges such as food, drink, and telephone charges.

(However, it is important to realize that the leverage occupancy rates and room rates offer can work in reverse. When occupancy rates fall, profits quickly diminish since the fixed costs are being borne by fewer occupied rooms. When fewer guests stay at a hotel, the hotelier still must pay the same marketing and administrative expenses and property taxes. Additionally, when room rates fall, profits deteriorate quickly since revenues plunge while both fixed and variable costs remain at the same levels.)

When you see that occupancy rates and room rates are rising, which kind of hotel should you invest in first? Extravagant hotels or plain hotels? The answer is inexpensive hotels because their operators are more leveraged to occupancy and room rates (than exquisite hotels such as the Ritz-Carlton), as most of their square footage is dedicated to rooms. Expensive hotels, on the other hand, have a larger percentage of their square footage dedicated to things other than rooms, such as fancy lobbies, swimming pools, and retail stores.

Incidentally, another problem with investing in premium hotels is that the respective management's culture is so geared to delivering exceptional service that the managers are not focused on their hotels' profitability. In fact, "Marriott chairman, J. Willard Marriott Jr., has said, 'There is only one reason to own a luxury hotel, and that's ego.'" [1]

Microeconomic Considerations

Hotel executives have often told me that in selecting hotel sites, microeconomic considerations are of even more importance than macroeconomic concerns. These executives have said that new hotels should be in close proximity to demand generators, including office parks, factory-outlet malls, hospitals, colleges, or even prisons. Moreover, it is imperative that the hotel is successful in generating local referrals since most people visit other cities because they have friends, family, or business associates there; it is these friends, family, and associates that often make

---

[1] Subrata N. Chakravarty and Seth Lubove, "Going for Gamblers", *Forbes* 157, no. 6 (March 25, 1996), pp. 106–11.

T I P

👉 While higher room rates are obviously preferable to lower room rates, there is one positive thing to be said for low room rates. Namely, low room rates discourage the building of more hotel rooms. Additionally, when room rates are low, some hotel operators are forced out of business. Thus, the stronger hotel operators that acquire such distressed properties can become extremely profitable when room rates rise since their acquisition costs were so low to begin with. It is particularly easy for healthy hotel operators to acquire hotel rooms when distressed hotels are owned by banks, insurance companies, or the Resolution Trust Company since these entities have no long-term interest in managing hotels.

the hotel reservations for their out-of-town guests. In order to generate local referrals, some hotels make a special effort to obtain local financing or allow locals to use their facilities (e.g., pool and workout rooms).

Other Investment Considerations

The hotel companies that own the real estate upon which their hotels are situated are sometimes the targets of takeover bids if investors believe that the value of such real estate is not adequately reflected in the company's stock. These takeover bids can result in the price of the hotel company's stock soaring immediately after such bids are revealed.

Oftentimes, the stocks of many hotel operators will soar once a takeover bid for one hotel operator is announced on the belief that other hotels' real estate is undervalued. However, be careful not to become caught up in this euphoria of rising hotel stock prices since not all hotel chains will receive takeover bids. For instance, the hotel companies that derive their income solely from managing other companies' hotels will not benefit from takeover offers based upon the value of their real estate since they do not own any real estate.

When reviewing a regional hotel chain, you should consider the strength of feeder cities. (In the hotel industry, a feeder city is a city from which many guests derive.) For instance, if you a reviewing a chain of hotels concentrated in the Pittsburgh area you should determine the strength of the economy in the Detroit area (since many auto executives may travel to Pittsburgh to meet with steel executives).

Higher minimum wages negatively affect hotel operators since the hotel business is labor intensive. Guests expect more than a room; they expect customer service. This customer service must be provided by people since technology cannot replace employees in such a service-dependent business. (Technology does not help make beds.)

Hotels located in close proximity to casinos are hindered when casinos expand the number of their hotel rooms since casinos often give away their rooms or use their rooms as loss leaders to attract more gamblers. In these circumstances, the stand-alone hotel companies must lower their room rates to compete against the low room rates (or free rooms) offered by casinos. On the other hand, hotels benefit when casinos spin off their hotels since these newly independent hotels will have to charge market rates (rather than subsidized rates), placing all of the hotels on equal footing.

There is a movement by corporate travel managers to force credit card companies to provide more thoroughly itemized bills of hotel charges. Hotels would be adversely affected if credit card companies provided travel managers with such detailed bills. The reason is that business people would not be able to spend as much money at the hotels. For instance, when hotel invoices are general, a businessman can use his corporate credit card to buy a souvenir for his wife at the gift shop; with a more detailed billing system, the businessman would not be able to charge the gift and may thus forgo such purchase.

CRUISES

Demand

Cruise operators may prove to be a source of sound long-term investment since cruises are popular with both passengers and travel agents. One reason that passengers are especially fond of cruises is that these packaged vacations are attractively priced. (Cruise operators can offer reasonable rates because they manage their costs well—for example, they may encourage early bookings by offering the lowest prices to the first registrants.) Passengers also like to go on cruises since roughly 85 percent of the cost of the vacation is spent up front. Thus, the uncertainty of the cost of the vacation is removed.

This predictability of passengers' expenses is one reason that cruise operators generate large degrees of repeat business. Some operators are trying to further capitalize on their repeat business by appealing to younger people. For instance, major cruise operators such as Carnival Corporation and Royal Caribbean Cruises are establishing gyms and discos on their ships as well as offering scuba diving lessons. Reducing the average age of passengers will benefit the cruise operators since more repeat business can be derived from younger passengers.

In addition to generating more repeat business, the cruise industry believes that it will benefit from attracting a larger share of the vacation market. Since only about 5 percent of the U.S. population has taken a cruise, cruise operators believe that they will prosper as a growing percentage of the population embarks on a cruise, and they have recently begun trying to attract this larger cross-section of the population by appealing to families via offering organized programs for children.

Travel agents like to book cruises because the commissions for such reservations are very lucrative. (They earn commissions on both the plane and cruise portions of the excursion.) Also, cruise operators do a good job of currying favor with travel agents by sponsoring special excursions for travel agents on their newest ships.

However, demand for all cruise ships can fall quite quickly due to a mishap on one ship. For instance, publicity surrounding outbreaks of legionnaires' disease or failure of a ship's plumbing system hurts the image of the entire industry. Problems such as these leave an indelible scar on cruise passengers' memories since the passengers, unable to leave the ship, are condemned to suffer through the duration of such problems. Also, uncooperative weather can result in the cruise operator's not being able to deliver the itinerary that was promised.

Capacity Considerations

Upon learning that the cruise companies are adding more ships, your initial reaction may be negative. You probably base this reaction on the theory that additional capacity will soften pricing. While this is a rational line of reasoning, there is a positive side to rising capacity in the cruise industry:

- Today's new ships, such as Royal Caribbean's 1,800-passenger Splendor of the Seas, tend to stimulate additional demand due to the excitement that surrounds the launching of these extravagant and massive vessels.

- Modern ships are so luxurious that they are usually able to charge higher rates.

- The dominant cruise operators can squeeze their smaller competitors out of business by introducing new ships since these ships are so ritzy that vacationers will not want to return to the smaller ships after they have been aboard a luxury liner.

- Bigger ships offer their operators economies of scale since they can better defray the costs of national advertising, reservations, legal compliance, and administration.

- The bigger ships also have more bargaining power over their vendors.

- The larger ships feature more cash-generating bars, boutiques, and casinos than their smaller competitors.

Regulations can act as another catalyst to consolidation in the cruise industry. For instance, the enactment of the Safety of Life at Sea (SOLAS) legislation required that all ships that dock at U.S. ports be equipped with sprinkler systems, special fire doors, and special lighting. Since regulations such as SOLAS are so expensive to comply with, some of the smaller cruise lines may not be able to

T I P

☞ Travel agents are especially willing to encourage their customers to take cruises when the airlines reduce the commissions that they pay travel agents.

afford to bring their ships up to standards. Thus, more stringent regulations may reduce capacity in the cruise industry, and be a positive development for the pricing of berths.

Cost Considerations

The labor and tax outlays for cruise ship operators are much lower than in most other industries. For instance, many cruise ships are staffed with crews from developing countries who are content to work for low wages. Also, many cruise operators are headquartered outside of the United States and are therefore not required to pay U.S. federal income taxes; they thus sport very wide net profit margins. Carnival Corporation, for example, averaged net profit margins of roughly 20 percent from 1990 to 1995, in part because its income tax rate rarely exceeded 3 percent.

From time to time the United States Congress considers imposing U.S. labor laws on foreign vessels that call on U.S. ports. Should such policy ever become law, cruise operators' labor costs would soar.

Also, the United States Congress occasionally debates prohibiting ships that were constructed abroad with foreign subsidies from docking in the United States. Since almost all cruise ships are constructed in foreign shipyards with the aid of subsidies, any such promulgation would be catastrophic for the cruise industry.

Other Investment Considerations

In analyzing a cruise operator, you should consider the level of advance bookings. The more people that book their cruises far in advance (e.g., six months), the fewer berths the cruise ship will have available closer to the time of departure. As a result, the cruise operator will be able to sell its remaining berths at premium prices. (One factor that helps the pricing of berths in the cruise industry is harsh winters in the northern part of the United States.)

Cruise operators receive large referral fees from the tourist destinations located where the cruises dock. However, the cruise ships are becoming so comfortable that people may not want to disembark. If too many passengers choose not to disembark, the cruise operator could lose not only its referral fees but also its docking rights in foreign ports of call.

It is more important for cruise ships (rather than hotels) to operate with very high occupancy rates since there is nothing a cruise can do to increase its occupancy rate once the ship leaves port. (In fact, cruise ships often operate with over 100-percent occupancy, with 100-percent occupancy being based on two beds in each berth. Occupancy rates above 100 percent are achieved by adding cots to berths.) Another benefit of operating with full capacity is that full ships generate more excitement—good for selling other things such as gambling.

GAMING

Trading Characteristics of Gambling Stocks

Similar to the restaurant stocks, gambling stocks are subject to speculative cycles. One reason that gambling stocks can rise so quickly in value is once gambling begins to proliferate it has a snowball effect. When one state legalizes gambling, neighboring states often follow suit since failure to do so would result in their residents spending their gambling dollars in a neighboring state. Also, when Indian reservations introduce gambling, the state in which such reservation is located will typically offer its own gambling alternatives in order not to lose all of its gambling revenue to the Indian reservations. Moreover, the small capitalization of these companies makes it easy for their shares to rapidly appreciate.

However, when the stock market believes that gambling companies are overexpanding, gambling stocks fall even faster in value. Thus, in order to protect your downside, you must determine when the gaming industry is overexpanding. In making this determination, you should look at the entire gambling landscape because one form of gambling competes with other gambling venues. For instance, companies that operate gambling in casinos, on Indian reservations, aboard riverboats, in dockside casinos, or over on-line services all compete with one another. Additionally, state lotteries compete with all of these forms of gambling. Excessive growth in one sector of the gambling industry can take away business from other gambling segments.

Since gambling depends upon discretionary dollars, the best time to accumulate shares in gambling companies is when consumers' balance sheets are strengthening and their disposable incomes are rising. The investor should also consider the percentage of disposable income that is spent on gambling. When this percentage is low but rising it means that the public is increasingly interested in gambling. Moreover, this would indicate that gambling has the potential to capture a larger percentage of dollars directed towards leisure. Conversely, when gambling represents a high but declining percentage of discretionary income, it is usually too late to invest in the gambling industry since gambling has already captured most of its potential discretionary dollars.

Legalization of Gambling

The stocks of many gambling companies trade on expectations of the company's moving into new and previously untapped markets. Often, investors become euphoric over the projected earnings that a gambling operator will make by serving customers in a market that had never before permitted gambling. Therefore, you should be aware of the arguments that could sway state legislatures in favor of (or against) the legalization of gambling in their jurisdictions.

There are a number of fundamental factors that can lead to increased legalization of gambling:

1. When states and municipalities have budget deficits of their own since it is politically easier to legalize gambling than it is to raise taxes.

2. When people are less sympathetic to traditional moral concerns.

3. When states have high rates of unemployment since casinos employ many people.

However, there are also several factors that reduce the odds of a jurisdiction approving gambling:

1. The perception of additional crime hurts. (This is especially true if the city already has a lot to lose because it depends on tourism.)

2. The fear that people will become addicted to gambling.

3. The fear that people will become compulsive gamblers.

4. The fear that legalized gambling leads to illegal gambling and that people (and companies) will not report winnings (and earnings).

While casinos are labor intensive, the opponents of gambling point out that this can actually be a double-edged sword. Gambling opponents point to examples of casinos' winning generous concessions from the local government by threatening to close. Most politicians favor granting casinos concessions such as tax abatements since the closing of casinos would be politically unpopular, as casinos hire so many people.

Also, various constituencies can lobby vigorously against the gaming referendums. For instance, other entertainment enterprises (such as theaters and ballets) often lobby against gambling since the introduction of gambling will siphon off money from more established forms of leisure. In fact, some existing restaurant and hotel operators have been successful in barring casinos from offering lodging or restaurant services. Further, it is often difficult to pass gambling referendums in areas that are heavily dominated by church-going people. Thus, it is said that a gambling referendum will have a greater chance of passing when it is held many days after Sunday or after Christian holidays since the clergy rally against gambling during their sermons.

Electronic Gambling

Currently, interstate on-line gambling is illegal. However, electronic gambling could still present competition for existing gambling venues such as lotteries, casinos, riverboats, racetracks, and Indian gambling parlors. This is because several companies are trying to establish on-line betting run from Caribbean islands. On-line gambling could prove to be popular with the young, affluent males who populate the Internet since they are also the most likely segment of the population to become avid gamblers. Also, electronic gambling could become highly profitable as the cost of managing and operating virtual casinos is almost nonexistent when compared with a real casino.

However, the success of on-line operators could be muted due to their credibility problems. For instance, the gambler does not know where the on-line casino exists; even if a gambler wins in cyberspace, the on-line casino may disappear. Finally, it would be difficult to ensure that electronic casinos are not rigged since regulation over them would be virtually impossible.

Casinos

It is said that the best odds in casinos belong to the house. (You probably have a better chance of making money by investing in the casino stocks than by betting in the casinos themselves.) Since casinos have the upper hand in all of the wagers that are made, there are basically two ways that casinos can increase their revenues:

1. By attracting the high rollers who make huge wagers.
2. By drawing huge numbers of small-time gamblers.

When analyzing casinos such as ITT Corporation's Sheraton Desert Inn that depend on high rollers, you should consider the source of the high rollers' wealth. When many of a casino's high rollers are Arabs or Texans, consider the direction of the price of oil; obviously, if the price of oil is rising, these high rollers will be able to gamble larger sums of money than if the price of oil is falling. Or if many of the casino's high rollers are Japanese, you consider the health of the Japanese economy. Investors should also consider the ability of casinos to sponsor the most highly visible boxing matches since these matches are one of the few sure ways to encourage high rollers to fly to the sponsoring casinos. Separately, another advantage of serving the high rollers is that they attract a lot of excitement in the casino.

Other casinos such as Circus-Circus have focused on attracting high volumes of small-time gamblers:

- With a view towards generating high levels of traffic, these casinos go to great lengths to foster comfort and excitement. For instance, these casinos are often liberal with their drinks, while lighting is carefully controlled so as not to induce drowsiness.

- They collectively provide over $1 billion a year in complimentary rooms, food, beverages, and coins.

- They are not terribly averse to the heavy regulations that are imposed on them since such regulation has helped change the image of casinos from mafia dens of vice to entertainment arcades. (Indeed, even the name of the industry has been changed from gambling to gaming.)

Many of the casinos in Las Vegas that strive to appeal to the small-time gambler have been trying to turn the image of Las Vegas into that of a multi-faceted entertainment city. Thus, shopping and entertainment has been empha-sized. Some casinos have encouraged gamblers to bring the entire family on the belief that a gambler will stay in Las Vegas longer if he is accompanied by his family.

However, executives of some of these casinos have begun to change their minds on the benefits of encouraging families to bring their children because

- Time is taken away from gambling. For example, the gambler may feel compelled to accompany his wife on shopping excursions or to spend time with his children at video arcades.

- Serious gamblers do not like to trip over children.

- The attractions that the casinos spent a fortune on for children (such as Mirage Resort's Treasure Island) are not popular because they pale in comparison to those offered at theme parks such as DisneyLand.

Challenges for Casinos

Despite the potential to make superb profits, casinos are presented with a number of challenges:

1. Even though casinos are large employers, states do not bestow largesse on casinos that locate in their states; casinos not only are required to pay heavy fees in return for a gambling license but must often offer to improve the infrastructure of the city in which the casino will be located in order to win the license. This is in contrast to states' competing with one another by offering incentives such as tax abatements and subsidized electricity to industrial companies (e.g., auto makers or steel mills) that locate in their state.

2. Casinos that locate in low-income areas often have difficulty recruiting and retaining qualified labor. Many casino applicants are alcoholics and illiterates. Sometimes casino operators must develop remedial training programs that teach the basics of holding down a job. Despite these efforts to train workers, many casino workers leave town after they receive their first paycheck; in fact, industry average turnover can be as high as 45 to 50 percent.

3. States may demand higher royalties when casinos' licenses are up for renewal. The states realize that casinos (together with their hotels and entertainment facilities) represent tremendous fixed costs. Therefore,

casino operators will often pay higher license fees as opposed to abandoning their investments.

Location of Casinos

Gamblers like to gamble where there are a lot of casinos nearby so they can go from one casino to the other if they think that doing so will increase their luck. Thus, the casinos that are located in Las Vegas and Atlantic City could benefit from new casinos opening up in those cities since it would make that city more of a gambling destination.

There are a number of factors that favor the casinos that are located in Las Vegas and enjoying more popularity than the casinos located in Atlantic City. Las Vegas is a good destination resort:

1. It has a large airport with flights to many U.S. cities, which is especially beneficial to these casinos when airfares are low.

2. The year-round warm weather is suitable for family vacations.

3. Casinos concentrated in Las Vegas (such as Primadonna Resorts) are beneficiaries of new venues of gambling; once people try gambling, they may want to try the ultimate gambling experience, which can only be had in Las Vegas. Thus, every new municipality that permits gambling could become a feeder city for Las Vegas.

However, casinos located in Las Vegas could actually be adversely impacted by overbuilding in that city. For example, there have been times when tourists

T R A P

⊘ Many gambling operators have casinos in both Nevada and Atlantic City. Since there are no income taxes in Nevada, these operators often finance their casinos in Atlantic City with heavy debt loads. The reason for such financing is that the related interest expense reduces the profitability (and therefore the income tax liabilities) of their Atlantic City-based casinos. However, when the economy slows or when the gambling industry overbuilds, the casino operators with facilities in both Atlantic City and Nevada face a greater risk of filing for bankruptcy than the casinos located solely in Nevada since the former casinos typically carry heavier debt loads. Furthermore, the casinos that operate solely in Atlantic City that do not file for bankruptcy protection may be hurt when their competitors benefit from bankruptcy protection.

have complained that all of the construction in Las Vegas makes it very difficult to navigate the city, and the Las Vegas airport has been so congested that travelers have been advised to arrive as much as three hours before their flights depart.

Another problem that the major casinos in Las Vegas face is the smaller casinos' practice of parasitic marekting. They allow the major casinos to conduct expensive national campaigns that bring people from all over the country to Las Vegas. Then, once the tourists arrive, the small casinos lure them in with unbeatable bargains such as giveaways or extremely inexpensive meals.

On the other hand, casinos such as Trump Hotels & Casinos that are concentrated in Atlantic City have a disadvantage in that Atlantic City is less accessible than Las Vegas to many parts of the country. Also, the cold New Jersey winters deter many gamblers from going to Atlantic City during that season. Finally, Atlantic City patrons are largely day-trippers who are lured there by the casinos' free handouts.

You should consider gaming policies adopted by the casinos' feeder cities. For instance, the Las Vegas casinos could be seriously adversely impacted if California legalized gambling since roughly 40 percent of Las Vegas's gamblers are Southern Californians. Similarly, the casinos in Atlantic City would be severely affected if Philadelphia legalized gambling as Atlantic City derives nearly 40 percent of its business from Philadelphians.

When considering investing in a small gambling operator that plans to move into a small gambling market, you should determine how prosperous casinos are in the same market. For instance, in the early 1990s, many people believed that New Orleans would become a major gambling center. Thus, the price of the shares of the gambling operators that were considering moving into the New Orleans market were rising very quickly. However, the existing casinos were not making very much (if any) money there. (One reason was that there is so much for tourists to do in New Orleans that most tourists have little time to gamble.) Thus, it would not have been wise to invest in a gambling company that was considering moving into the New Orleans market.

Slot Machines

Slot machines are extremely profitable for casinos because they attract masses of people who would not otherwise gamble. Also, no employees are needed to operate the slot machines. With mechanical slot machines there's no thinking, just pulling. Traditional slot machines have been rejuvenated by progressive slot machines, which are linked together via high-speed communications networks. These progressive slot machines are very popular because they offer more-frequent payoffs and bigger jackpots.

However, you should try to avoid investing in the casinos that operate in states that require them to install a high proportion of nickel slot machines. Since

T I P

☞ It is important that you detect overexpansion by riverboat operators before the broad stock market does.

these machines result in a steady downward trend in the amount of money wagered per bet, the profit potential of the casino is reduced.

Riverboat Gambling

Stocks of riverboat gambling companies are particularly susceptible to speculation. For example, President Casinos soared from $20 to $32 a share between March and May of 1993. However, less than three years later, in March 1996, the stock plummeted to less than $2 a share. One reason for the riverboat stocks' volatility is that riverboats can quickly earn high rates of return on their capital since so little capital is required to purchase a riverboat. Not only do riverboats themselves only cost a fraction of the cost of a casino, but very little infrastructure is needed to make the riverboat a viable gambling venue. While dockside casinos are usually attached to theaters and restaurants, riverboats obviously are not. Thus, low capital intensity and projections of swelling revenue streams often cause these stocks to soar; however, these low capital costs also lead to overexpanding by riverboat operators, sometimes causing plummeting stock prices.

One indication that riverboats may have overexpanded occurs when riverboats eliminate their entrance fees. Such action comes in response to increasing competition or in view of less demand for riverboat gambling. Moreover, the elimination of entrance fees is especially problematic for those riverboat operators that are required to pay a per-capita boarding fee to the licensing authority.

Another advantage associated with riverboats is that if a state's policy becomes unfavorable, the riverboat can simply be floated to a state with more favorable riverboat gambling laws. However, some states partially offset the benefits of riverboats' mobility by demanding high licensing fees. A riverboat company that pays a high licensing fee will be less likely to abandon its investment by moving to another state.

Some states such as Iowa only grant a set number of licenses, while other states such as Mississippi grant an unlimited number of riverboat licenses. It is generally advantageous for a riverboat to operate in a state that has a fixed number of licenses so that the operator will know who its competitors are. However, because of the predetermined number of licenses granted, limited-license states usually levy extremely high licensing fees.

While riverboats are relatively free to move into other jurisdictions, riverboats face a number of restrictions nonetheless:

1. The design of riverboats must be approved by the Coast Guard. Many riverboat operators complain that the Coast Guard requires the gambling space on riverboats to be too restrictive and overly compartmentalized, making it difficult for their patrons to move around and reducing the excitement on the boat.

2. Food and beverage service on riverboats is limited compared with such services offered in regular casinos.

3. Some states regulate the amount of time in which gambling is permitted on the cruise.

4. The amount of money that can be wagered per bet is sometimes regulated.

5. The amount of loss that a patron can suffer during a cruise is sometimes restricted.

Customers do not like these restrictions on riverboat gambling. If they are winning, they complain about being forced to leave when they are on a lucky streak, and conversely, if the gamblers have quickly reached their loss limits, they dislike remaining captive customers on the riverboat.

Consider also the state's docking requirements in which your riverboats operate. Riverboats that operate in states requiring their boats to leave the shore before gambling takes place can cause a number of problems for riverboats:

1. If the boat must be navigable, bad weather can result in the boat's being forbidden to leave the shore—consequently, gambling revenues are lost.

2. Late patrons will not be able to board the boats, which represents a loss of potential revenue.

3. Insurance is expensive to obtain for navigable riverboats since hundreds of gamblers, alcohol, water, and expensive equipment represent a risky combination for insurers.

4. Employees of navigable boats are covered under the Jones Act, a federal statute that allows for greater damage claims than laws covering harbor workers.

Investors who are seeking to invest in a less-regulated segment of the gaming industry may want to consider investing in companies such as Circus-Circus that operate dockside casinos. Since dockside casinos are stationary, they are not subject to states' docking regulations as the riverboat companies are. Also, dockside casinos can offer 24-hour gambling with far fewer restrictions than are imposed on riverboat operators. Moreover, dockside casinos offer spacious facilities (the design of which is not restricted by the Coast Guard) as well as full food and beverage services. The downside of this type of casino is that they are more expensive to establish than riverboats because hotels and restaurants are often attached to the gambling parlors, and unfavorable future legislation is more problematic for them (compared with riverboats) since they are not transportable.

Other Investment Considerations

Additionally, you should consider how demographics affect the gaming industry. Generally, growth in the number of older people is positive for the gambling industry since retirees have the time and resources to gamble. Also, older people enjoy gambling (as there are no children) and are inclined to gamble for long periods of time since it is not physically strenuous.

A separate concern is that drunk gamblers may not be liable for their losses. For example, Leonard Tose (a former owner of the Philadelphia Eagles) sued Sands Casinos for the losses that he suffered while gambling when he was drunk. More court rulings holding that drunk gamblers are not liable for their gambling losses would be catastrophic for the casinos.

It is a negative development when casinos spin off their hotels since casinos can no longer give away or subsidize their room rates as a ploy to attract more gamblers; and the new stand-alone hotels will have to charge market room rates, which may deter gamblers from traveling to such destinations.

When gambling operators are overexpanding, it still may be possible to successfully invest in the gambling industry. The best place to invest during such times is in companies such as International Game Technology that manufacture the gambling equipment (e.g., slot machines) that goes into all of the casinos.

7

Entertainment, Communications, and Information

Many investors have difficulty analyzing the industries that are being consumed by the information/entertainment revolution, one reason being the fluid nature of this sector of the economy. New products such as digital video disks threaten to displace older products such as videocassettes. Internet browser companies may make obsolete on-line service providers. Another reason for confusion surrounding the multimedia sector is the tremendous amount of convergence—computer companies are beginning to resemble communications companies while movie studios are morphing into television networks.

However, when analyzing any group of industries, it helps to consider the interplay among three components of the industries under review: content, context, and infrastructure. *Content* is the product that is being produced and sold. *Context* is the way in which the content is used, manipulated, or sold. *Infrastructure* is the system of channels by which the content is delivered to the context.

Before applying these terms to the Information Superhighway it may be easier to illustrate how they apply to the retail clothing industry. Factories produce the content (i.e., the clothing). The trucking companies, warehouses, and wholesalers provide the infrastructure through which the content travels. Finally, the context in which consumers purchase clothing ranges from department stores to catalogs to specialty boutiques.

These same factors are present in the industries that constitute the Information Superhighway. For instance, the infrastructure for the Information

Superhighway is being built by the telephone equipment manufacturers as well as the telephone and cable companies that are laying fiberoptic cable and broadband coaxial cables. The context is where the entertainment is viewed or where information is exchanged, including the movie theaters, television networks, newspapers, the Internet, and on-line services. Content is the actual information or entertainment that is viewed or exchanged, examples being raw data, telephonic conversations, and movies.

Premium on Content

In order to determine the value of the content providers, it is prudent to consider the demand for content relative to its supply. Demand for content will be great when the growth of the infrastructure is outpacing the growth of content. As you may know, the infrastructure of the Information Superhighway is growing explosively:

- Hundreds of miles of fiberoptic and cable lines are being laid every week.
- Memberships to on-line services are growing by the tens of thousands every month.
- Sales of direct-broadcast satellites are soaring.

Engineers continue to find ways to expand the capacity of the existing infrastructure. For instance, integrated services digital network (ISDN) lines expand the capacity of copper wires by 50 times. Also, by beaming infrared light frequencies through fiberoptic phone lines, fiber will have enough capacity to transmit three million high-definition television channels. Thus, the expansion of the infrastructure will result in a premium being placed on the content necessary to fill the growing infrastructure. (In other words, the builders of the Information Superhighway must procure content so that they have something for which tolls can be charged.)

MAJOR MOVIE STUDIOS

Copyright Ownership and Development

The major movie studios are perfectly positioned to supply and develop content for the rapidly growing infrastructure (e.g., more television channels due to cable and direct-broadcast satellites). First, the movie studios already own large libraries of movies. Unlike most industries (where a product's life exceeds its production time), it takes much longer to produce a film than to watch it. Thus, it is more expedient for the architects of the Information Superhighway to pay a premium for libraries of films as opposed to trying to build their own libraries from scratch. Indeed, large premiums were paid for Paramount Communications (by Viacom);

Castle Rock Entertainment (by Turner Broadcasting); and Miramax (by Disney) in recent years.

A second benefit of owning large libraries of movies is that movies never become obsolete. As *Forbes* magazine pointed out,

> Providing content is not capital intensive and is not subject to techno-logical obsolescence. On the other hand, hardware is capital intensive and quickly outmoded. Telephone and printing equipment and movie projectors from the 1930s became scrap long ago. However, *Gone with the Wind* is worth dozens of times what it cost nearly 60 years ago. [1]

Third, movie studios earn huge profits simply by copying their existing con-tent onto new platforms; the movies do not have to be rewritten, recast, or redi-rected. For example, the movie studios made vast sums of money when they copied their films onto videocassettes, and in the near future will be able to make a great deal of money by copying their libraries onto digital video disks (which are the same size as compact discs but offer exceptional audio and very crisp pictures).

Also of increasing value will be the studios' creative production capability. Since there are a growing number of outlets for programming, the demand for con-tent will continue to rise. Thus, the studios should be able to raise their licensing fees for the shows that they create.

More Difficult to Lose Money

Another attraction with investing in the major movie studios is that it will be more difficult for the studios to lose money. In the past, studios were completely depen-dent on box office sales. Due to the exorbitant cost of making movies, one expen-sive movie that turned out to be a box office bomb could bankrupt the studio.

Now, however, the proliferation of outlets (e.g., cable, video, pay-per-view) for movies is a source of residual demand. In other words, movie studios are able to derive some revenue from their movies that failed in theaters by licensing these movies to back-up outlets.

Second, Federal Communication Commission's (FCC) reforms make it harder for studios to lose money. For many years under the FCC's financial inter-est and syndication rules, networks were barred from taking an equity interest in the programs that were broadcast on their networks; thus the networks were very quick to pull new television series that did not achieve high ratings in the first few episodes. (In these situations, the movie studios lost much of their development costs. For example, a movie studio that produced 12 episodes of a television series could have had that series discontinued after the fourth episode.)

---

[1] Damon Darlin, "Movie Moguls Retreat." *Forbes,* February 27, 1995, p. 90.

Now that the FCC has repealed its financial interest and syndication rules, the networks are allowed to take an equity interest in the programming that they broadcast and will thus likely grant their shows a longer incubation period to attract viewers. Therefore, the movie studios will likely lose less money developing new programs.

T R A P

⊘ While American movies are popular abroad, be careful not to overestimate the potential of American *videos* abroad. For one thing, foreign ownership of video recorders is significantly less than in the United States. Also, while countries such as Japan have relatively high rates of video recorder ownership, their citizens use their video recorders almost exclusively for recording television shows. Finally, pirating and taxation of American videos reduces the appeal of selling videos in foreign markets.

Negative Factors

Studios' production expenses are likely to rise due to the increased demand for talent. As United Paramount, Warner Brothers, and the four major networks create more of their own programming, they will compete for scripts, actors, and directors, enabling these artists to demand heftier compensation packages.

Not only are top actors demanding more money, but they are also demanding more control over the production of their movies. This is problematic because these actors are often neither qualified to edit scripts nor to cast or direct their movies. For instance, one reason cited for the disastrous box office showing of MCA's *Waterworld* was that Kevin Costner usurped too many directing decisions.

Another problem that the studios face is that they may have fewer syndication opportunities: After a studio licenses its programs to networks, the studio often profits from syndicating its programs to independent stations and foreign markets; however, the addition of two new networks will absorb more affiliated stations, leaving fewer independents available for syndication.

Also, as the television networks develop more of their own content, they will be less reliant on studios. This dissipation of demand for films may result in the lowering of licensing fees (which networks pay to studios). Less licensing of studio productions by networks could hurt the studios in another significant way. Traditionally, the networks heavily promoted the programs that they licensed from the studios; when the networks advertised the studios' programs in commercials, the studios effectively received millions of dollars of free promotion. (The value that was created by such advertising benefited the studios because they owned the rights to the programming being promoted.) Now, however, studio shows may receive less free promotion, causing the value of their libraries to fall.

Nevertheless, even though networks are permitted to produce their own programming, they will still license shows from the studios due to the huge risks networks face when producing their own shows; if a network-produced show loses its ratings and stops being broadcast, the network will lose its development costs.

Analytical Concerns

Movie studios usually record movie production costs as assets on their balance sheets because they believe their movies will earn the studio profits into the future. Then the studios reduce the recorded asset values by annual amortization charges. In determining these amortization charges, studios divide a film's current revenues by the total revenues expected in future years and apply that fraction to the cost of the film. For example, suppose a movie cost $50 million to produce and the producer believes that it will ultimately generate $150 million in revenue. The first year the movie brings in $15 million, or 10 percent ($15 million/$150 million), of its potential. Thus, in the first year, the studio writes off 10 percent of the cost, or $5 million, leaving $45 million in unamortized assets. This process is repeated until the film's cost has been fully amortized.

You should be skeptical of very long (e.g., 30-year) amortization periods. First, it is impossible to accurately predict how much money a movie will generate over extended periods of time. Also, long amortization periods overstate current earnings since only small charges are taken each year. Similarly, low amortization charges overstate a studio's assets.

TELEVISION NETWORKS

Market Share

Many analysts have categorized the television networks as dinosaurs because they believe advertisers will be more interested in narrowly targeting their potential customers through cable stations and on-line services. While cable has indeed taken market share away from networks since the early 1980s, the following are factors that could allow networks to recapture market share in the future:

- The networks can afford to air the best programming because they generate the highest advertising rates (since they deliver the broadest audiences to national advertisers).

- Subscriber growth to cable networks could be a boon to the broadcasting networks since many people subscribe to cable just to receive better reception of broadcast network channels.

- Networks effectively use their rights to broadcast major events (e.g., the Olympics and Presidential debates) in order to showcase their program lineups to tens of millions of viewers.

T I P

> ☞ As far as the production of content goes, consider investing in com-
> panies that manufacture copyrights and distribute variations of their copy-
> rights through a multitude of distribution channels. In other words, you
> should search for prolific companies that are highly synergistic. For exam-
> ple, once The Walt Disney Company creates a new copyright (e.g., in the
> form of an animated movie such as *The Lion King*), Disney can profit from
> each of that copyright's permutations. Thus, Disney profits from inserting
> its characters in its Disney Channel, videocassettes, records, books, CD-
> ROMs, amusement parks, toy stores, Broadway Theater, and cruises. And
> on. And on. And on.

- The "water cooler" effect suggests that there is a natural tendency for
  people to want to have common frames of reference with their peers. Put
  another way, people want to be able to join conversations with their colleagues at the water cooler. Networks offer programming that is broad
  enough to appeal to most of one's contemporaries.

In-House Production

As a result of the FCC's liberalization of its financial interest and syndication rules
(discussed above), the networks are beginning to produce their own shows.
Accordingly, the networks are beginning to build their own libraries and will thus
eventually benefit from having libraries in much the same way that studios do.

While the networks do not have the skills in movie making that the studios
do, the value of the content that they create should rise quickly because they effectively spend tens of millions of dollars promoting their own programming.
Whenever you watch television, you see the networks advertising their own programs. All of this promotion adds to the value of the network's content. Thus, networks should be able to realize higher syndication fees for their programs.

Negative Factors

The networks will continue to face serious challenges from the proliferation of
television channels. Also, as discussed below, it is becoming increasingly expensive to acquire and affiliate with local television stations. Moreover, some politicians favor the auctioning off of the television spectrum that would be used for
advanced digital television broadcasting. According to some estimates, the networks could pay as much as $70 billion for this spectrum.

The proliferation of technology could allow people to become their own networks:

- The ubiquitous use of remote controls makes it effortless to change channels.

- As video-on-demand and time shifting (e.g., retrieval of previous broadcasts) become more common, the networks could lose their power to control audience flow; as networks lose control of their audiences, it becomes more difficult to develop reliable and consistent programming.

T R A P

⊘ During the up-front markets every spring, advertisers reserve time for their commercials in the next television season's prime-time schedule. Sometimes, impressive up-front sales growth is not as beneficial as it appears. For instance, when the networks do well in the up-front markets, they may not be able to take full advantage of demand in the scatter market. (The scatter market is when advertising time is sold for the television season already underway; time in the scatter market is usually sold at a higher price than in the up-front market.) Another advantage of scatter sales is that they generally do not come with audience-size guarantees whereas up-front sales usually do.

- As audience profiles become skewed, it becomes harder to appeal to advertisers since the demographics of the viewers are less well-defined.

Moreover, if too much time is sold in the up-front markets, and audience sizes delivered are below guarantees, the networks may not have enough time to allocate to make-goods. (Make-goods occur when networks give free time to sponsors to make up for shortfalls in audience projections.) If there is not enough make-good time available, the networks usually have to refund their advertisers.

FILM DISTRIBUTORS

Film distributors such as King World Productions make money by placing studios' films with movie theaters, networks, independent television stations, and foreign syndicated markets. These companies should benefit from the growing number of channels that need to secure programming.

However, film distributors could be hurt as more multimedia companies vertically integrate. For example, a company that produces its own sitcoms for its own network does not need a film distributor.

Another challenge for film distributors is that the FCC struck down its prime-time access rules. (These rules prohibited network stations in the 50 largest television markets from airing their own network-produced programming in the hour that preceded prime time.) The revocation of the prime-time access rules allows the networks to supply more of their own prime-time programming thus reducing the need for film distributors.

INDEPENDENT TELEVISION STATIONS

There should be more demand to affiliate with local television stations. One reason is that there are now six television networks (ABC, NBC, CBS, Fox, Paramount, and Warner Brothers), yet many markets only have four or five local television stations. Since demand by networks to affiliate with these stations exceeds supply of local stations in many markets, the networks will have to bid aggressively to affiliate with independent stations.

Before the Telecommunications Act of 1996, TV networks were allowed to own stations that reached 25 percent of the American viewers. Now, they can own stations that reach 35 percent of the population. Thus, more independent television stations such as those owned by companies like A.H. Belo or Tribune Company may be acquired by the networks. These acquisitions are more likely since independent stations are more important to networks than they were before.

Since networks are developing more of their own programming they are taking on both production and broadcasting risks. Thus, it is imperative that networks secure access to various geographic markets through ownership of more local television stations. Additionally, as one station is raided by a competing network in a given market, a ripple effect usually takes place, which means that the valuation of most of the stations in the given market rises.

T R A P

⊘ Unaffiliated independent television stations could be hurt by advertisers' growing attraction to sectionals. Sectionals are network ads that are broadcast nationally via satellite but carry messages tailored to audiences in different parts of the country. The risk to independent television stations is that sectionals make it much cheaper and more efficient for an advertiser to buy national air time as opposed to stitching together regional or local coverage in spot markets. Therefore, fewer advertisers will want to buy air time with unaffiliated stations.

RADIO STATIONS

The publicly traded radio station operators such as Emmis Broadcasting and Infinity Communications are worthy of investors' consideration. First, radios are pervasive. Ninety-nine percent of American households have at least one radio, and the average household has more than five radios. Moreover, the average American (over 12 years of age) listens to the radio for more than three hours a week, one reason being that radio is the medium that best allows its audience to do something else while listening. For example, you can exercise or wash your car when the radio is on but you cannot do these things as easily while reading a newspaper or watching a movie.

Advertising Advantages

In addition to people's listening to radio *frequently,* people tend to listen to their *favorite* radio stations *habitually.* Due to the local and loyal nature of radio listeners, radio stations reach very narrow demographics. This pinpointing of the audience is appealing to advertisers because they can reach their best prospects with few dollars.

There are other advantages for advertising on radio:

1. Since radio is audio, the commercials do not need video content; thus, radio commercials are much less expensive to create than television commercials and radio sponsors can spend more of their advertising budgets on actual air time rather than production costs.

2. The sponsors can be much more flexible in tailoring their messages to market changes. For example, assume that a mutual fund company is a sponsor of a business radio station. If the pharmaceutical stocks performed well on Monday, the fund company could quickly write a commercial touting its pharmaceutical fund. If the transportation stocks performed well on Tuesday, the fund operator could quickly write a script for a commercial touting its transportation fund. No other media offers this much flexibility.

3. Commercials are often read by the disk jockies or the talk-show hosts. Interestingly, advertisers usually pay more money per rating point for commercials on talk radio since they are convinced people actually listen to talk radio and to particular disk jockies rather than just play it in the background. Also, since talk shows more easily segue into commercials, they can accommodate more spots per hour.

Radio Economics

The Telecommunications Act of 1996 lifted the ownership rules for radio stations. Now a single company can own as many as eight radio stations in one market.

Previously radio companies were barred from owning more than two AM and two FM stations in the same market. The liberalization of ownership rules will allow for greater efficiency because fewer people will be needed in the administration, advertising, and compliance departments. The Telecom bill is also expected to

T R A P

🚫 There *are* challenges to newspapers' utility. For one thing, newspapers are perceived as being less timely since they recount yesterday's events, which readers saw on TV the night before.

result in higher advertising rates since there will be less competition due to rapid consolidation. (In fact, in just the first few months of 1996, more than 80 radio stations changed hands for a total of nearly $2 billion.)

Radio operators are also benefiting from the widespread use of syndication. Syndication occurs when one producer, such as Westwood One, develops a radio program that is digitally transmitted via satellite to radio stations all over the country. The syndicators are benefiting from the cheaper satellite technology that means that more stations can afford the satellite hookups. Therefore, distribution increases. Similarly, satellite technology allows the receiving stations to operate with far fewer disk jockeys.

NEWSPAPERS

The success of newspaper companies such as A.H. Belo and McClatchy Newspapers hinges on their circulation. While circulation alone does not bring in much revenue for newspapers, circulation determines the advertising rates that newspapers can charge.

Utility

While challenged by other media, the intrinsic value of newspapers ensures that they will not become obsolete. First, newspapers are extremely inexpensive and thus represent exceptional value. As a matter of fact, they may be one of the best bargains available today. Some daily newspapers contain more practical information than books that retail for over $20. And newspapers are timely. For no more than $0.75 (on a weekday), you can read about current events that have been gathered from all over the world.

Newspapers are valuable because the stories within them process huge amounts of information. Readers value the transformation of unmanageable amounts of information into easy-to-read articles. For instance, most people would

T R A P

⊘ Due to on-line services, every local newspaper now competes with heavy hitters such as the *New York Times.*

rather read an article that summarizes which groups of voters more heavily voted for a particular presidential candidate than analyze reams of pages of statistics that convey the same information.

Also, newspapers are completely portable. This absolute portability is one advantage that traditional newspapers will always have over new media such as on-line services.

Geographic Barriers

One advantage of newspapers is that the capital intensive nature of the business means that city newspapers are almost completely isolated from competition from other cities' newspapers. Thus, newspapers have a virtual lock on their readership simply by virtue of their location. As the legendary Warren Buffet said, "You're not going to sell a lot of Rochester newspapers in Buffalo. If you live in Buffalo, you are not going to change your views and want to read about Rochester, even if it's for a dime less."

Since there is little competition from newspapers serving other markets, there are almost never price wars between newspapers from different cities. Thus, newspaper companies can generate substantial cash flows when the local economy is strong. Prudent uses of this excess cash flow include debt reduction, stock buy-backs, and dividend increases. However, newspapers frequently use their excess cash flow to make acquisitions. There is generally less risk in making acquisitions of other newspapers than in investing in other forms of media. This is because newspaper companies already know the newspaper business. However, there is less opportunity (but more risk) in the newspaper business than in other forms of multimedia.

Circulation

While the newspaper industry is mature, you should search for newspapers that have growing circulations. A growing circulation indicates that the newspaper is increasingly popular. These newspapers will be able to charge higher advertising rates as their circulation grows, and a portion of these higher rates can be reinvested in the paper for things such as hiring better reporters and photographers. The remainder of the rate increase can fall to the bottom line or be paid to shareholders in the form of a dividend.

T I P

> 👉 Demographics affect newspapers' circulation. For instance, the graying of America should be positive for newspapers since senior citizens tend to read newspapers religiously. However, further into the future, the children that are now being reared on TV and video games should probably not be expected to be big newspaper readers.

Before investing in a newspaper stock you should make sure that the cities that the newspaper company serves are healthy. Cities that are in a state of decline represent a problematic chain of events for newspapers: First, deteriorating cities often experience brain drain. As the better-educated people flee to the suburbs, the big city newspaper will lose many of the readers that are most appealing to advertisers, thus triggering a fall in advertising rates. (Any surge in telecommuting would evoke the same consequences.)

Also consider a newspaper's circulation in terms of subscribers. The greater the percentage of subscribers (versus newsstand sales) the better, since subscribers demonstrate commitment to the newspaper. Also, circulation auditors can get a more accurate reading of the newspaper's circulation when its papers are sold on a subscription basis. This is comforting to advertisers whose rates are based on the number of readers their ads reach.

However, newsstands are an important tool in attracting new subscribers because they are a convenient way for readers to become acquainted with newspapers before committing to subscriptions. Also, newspapers derive revenue from their newsstand sales. Conversely, without newsstands, newspapers would have to expend much more money trying to attract subscribers by going through the process of buying mailing lists, making cold calls, and offering product giveaways as an inducement to subscriptions.

Advertising

You must pay very close attention to a newspaper's advertising trends because advertising is one of the main movers of newspapers' profitability. Basic considerations include advertising rates and the number of advertising pages sold. These figures should be compared with year-earlier results in much the same way that same-store sales comparisons are taken into account in the retail industry. Thus, the higher these growth rates, the better.

In addition to the number of pages of advertising sold, consider also the ratio of advertising space to total newspaper content. Generally, the higher this ratio is the better. However, it is unrealistic to expect that this ratio will progress indefinitely; no one will buy an established newspaper just to read the advertisements.

TRAP

Ø Over the short term, there is a crowding-out effect as far as advertising rates are concerned. High advertising rates can reduce the number of ad pages sold because most advertisers have fixed ad budgets. When advertising rates rise, the advertiser must reduce the number of ads placed.

Also, when you review the ratio of advertising space to total newspaper content, determine whether or not this ratio includes advertising for the newspaper itself. When comparing one paper's advertising ratio against that of another, the basis for such comparison must be equal. There is nothing wrong with a newspaper's promoting itself. In fact, it is prudent to try to convert casual readers into paying subscribers by placing subscription forms in the paper (as I have done).

In addition to the advertising rates and volume of advertising, you should appreciate the leverage that advertising has on newspapers' profitability. When more advertising pages are sold the additional variable costs (e.g., for newsprint and layout) are negligible, so most of the additional advertising revenue falls to the bottom line.

Also, as advertising rates rise, all of the rate increase falls to the bottom line since no additional costs or efforts are expended. For example, when the cost of inserting a quarter-page ad rises from $500 to $600, the entire $100 cost differential falls to the newspaper's bottom line because nothing on the cost side of the equation has changed; the salesperson gets paid the same amount, the cost of the newsprint is the same, and the cost of typesetting is the same.

However, you should also be aware that the advantages of advertising leverage can turn into disadvantages when advertising rates and numbers of advertising pages fall. When either of these events occurs, revenue falls but the newspaper's fixed costs remain high.

One tool that is useful in determining which newspapers have the most leeway in increasing advertising rates is the cost-per-thousand ratio. The cost-per-thousand ratio measures how much an advertiser spends to reach each 1,000 newspaper readers. When comparing two similar newspapers, the newspaper that has the lowest cost-per-thousand ratio is usually the more favorable. Let us suppose that the general interest newspaper in Houston is equal in every way to the general interest newspaper in Dallas. (For example, demographics reached, wealth of the readers, and journalistic quality are virtually the same.) Let us further suppose that the Houston paper has a circulation of 800,000 and charges $10,000 for a full-page ad. The Dallas paper has a circulation of 900,000 and charges $20,000 for a full page ad. The cost per thousand to advertise in Houston would be $12.50 [($10,000/800,000) × 1,000] while the cost per thousand to advertise in the Dallas paper would be $22.00 [($20,000/900,000) × 1,000]. Thus, if everything was materially the same between Houston and Dallas, we could safely assume that the Houston newspaper would be able to raise its rates.

However, the Houston newspaper would probably not be able to levy the entire differential immediately because doing this would risk losing advertisers who would experience sticker shock. Also, those newspapers that serve communities that are not very well diversified would have even more difficulty raising their rates quickly. Aggressively raising rates runs the risk of retaliation on the part of advertisers in the dominant segments of the economy when they have more leverage over the newspapers. These dominant businesses have more leverage when the economy slows down because they know that the newspaper has few other sources to turn to for advertising dollars.

Advertising Categories

The two major ad categories for newspapers are classified ads and retail ads. Classified ads primarily consist of help-wanted, real-estate and auto ads. Classified ads are very profitable on a per-line basis because the people that place such ads are generally infrequent advertisers who do not have the bargaining power to negotiate lower rates.

The importance of analyzing trends in classified rates and number of lines sold goes beyond the profits that classified advertising alone contributes to the newspaper companies. Classified ads are a good leading indicator of the local economy because classified advertising is very economically sensitive. For exam-

T R A P

⊘ It is sometimes difficult for a major newspaper operator to take an interest in an independent newspaper because some newspaper owners enjoy the power and prestige associated with owning a newspaper and do not wish to sell. Additionally, high capital-gains rates make it unattractive for many newspaper owners to sell. For instance, let us assume that a family purchased its newspaper 100 years ago for $50,000 and that the paper is now worth $50 million—almost the entire proceeds from such a sale would be subject to capital gains taxes.

ple, when the economy slows down companies stop hiring, so help-wanted ads dry up; people retain their cars longer, so advertising for used cars is halted; and fewer homes are placed on the market, resulting in the volume of real-estate ads plunging.

You can use classified advertising as an early warning signal for determining when to buy and sell newspaper stocks; when classified rates increase it may be time to buy newspaper stocks and vice versa.

TIP

One of the most serious challenges to classified ad sales are give-away magazines that exclusively advertise things like real estate, automobiles, employment opportunities and dating services. These giveaway magazines are well received since they are distributed free of charge. Also, since these magazines are so well targeted to a particular audience, their production runs can be minimized. Thus, advertisers can often achieve a lower cost-per-thousand ratio by advertising in the giveaway publication than by advertising in the classified section of the local newspaper.

You can further improve your performance by analyzing trends in classified advertising among the big city newspapers. Since big cities are more cyclical than rural towns, a change in the direction of the economy should first be felt by the newspapers that serve large urban markets. Therefore, upon detecting a rebounding economy, the first newspaper stocks that you should consider buying are the publishers of big city papers, such as the New York Times and Knight-Ridder, that are posting the most dramatic improvements in classified advertising. On the other hand, a deteriorating economy would hurt the publishers of small-town newspapers, such as Lee Enterprises and Gannet Company because small towns are less cyclical than big cities.

Newspapers are trying to increase their classified revenue by experimenting with new outlets such as telephones and on-line systems for their ads. For example, some newspapers operate voice mailboxes for personal ads. Other papers use voice-activation services to provide stock quotations, weather reports, and movie reviews via the telephone. Not only do callers pay for these services but these services, are often supported by advertising.

Of course, retail advertising is also very important for newspapers. Those newspapers that will generate the most growth in retail advertising revenue will be the ones that serve economically vibrant markets. On the other hand, advertising is a very visible expense. Thus, when a customer's revenues decrease, advertising is an easy place to look for cost-cutting opportunities.

Also, the paper's markets should be competitive. For example, a newspaper that publishes in a city that is a very important market for competing airlines will benefit from the advertising money that the various carriers spend promoting their best fares. On the other hand, if the city is the home of two department stores that announced that they will merge, department store advertising will fall since retail competition will be reduced.

Consider also how actions taken by local merchants will impact the newspaper industry. For instance, if retailers are adopting the every-day-low-pricing method for selling their merchandise, their ad budgets will fall because they are

TRAP

⊘ There are risks associated with newspapers trying to derive too much revenue from telephone services. For instance, some newspapers are beginning to sell movie tickets. This activity calls into question the newspaper's objectivity. If the newspaper profits by selling movie tickets, the readers may get the impression that the paper will silence its movie critics in order to maximize ticket sales. In other instances, newspapers are initiating airline ticket sales through the telephone; however, this kind of activity runs the risk of competing with the newspaper's own advertisers who are travel agents.

promoting less of their merchandise. You should also consider if grocers are using more coupons, shoppers or specialty direct mailers because these marketing pieces compete directly with newspaper advertising.

There are just a few other considerations as far as advertising goes:

- Consider if the newspaper has prohibitions against accepting ads from certain segments of the economy. For instance, some newspapers do not accept advertising from tobacco or alcohol companies or R-rated movies. Such prohibitions reduce potential advertising receipts.

- Consider what the local requirements are for running legal notices such as incorporations and bankruptcies in newspapers. Sometimes newspapers benefit from politicians' writing laws that increase the duration of these legal notices in order to gain favor with the newspapers.

Costs

Newspapers are expensive to operate because they are both capital and labor intensive: They require large office spaces, printing presses, computer systems, and fleets of delivery trucks, and they are heavily unionized. Even reporters, photographers, and advertising salespeople are often members of the Newspaper Guild—there are few industries that have such a high concentration of unionized professionals. Therefore, strikes can cripple newspapers while overtime merely maims them.

Also, newsprint can often be a major expense. Obviously, the more expensive newsprint becomes the more problematic the scenario for newspapers. However, there are methods to anticipate the direction of newsprint prices. For instance, the lower the number of days of newsprint supply, the higher prices are likely to rise because the lack of supply usually indicates that newspapers are having difficulty obtaining their requisite inventories. You can consider also the capacity utilization rates at newspaper mills. The higher such rates are, the higher newsprint prices will rise because this situation indicates that demand for paper exceeds supply. Another problem with higher newsprint costs is that newspaper companies often invest more capital in newspaper mills in order to be guaranteed a source of supply.

However, when newsprint prices fall, newspapers benefit from a double whammy: First, the variable newsprint costs fall. Second, newspaper companies often divest their interests in paper mills when they believe that the supply of newsprint is readily available. These divestitures provide cash windfalls to newspapers.

T I P

> Newspapers that serve cities with extensive public transportation systems have an advantage over other cities' newspapers because public transit passengers have more time to read newspapers than do drivers.

Other expenses associated with newsprint are the costs of recycling. You should consider to what length the newspaper must go to recycle and de-ink its newspapers. Similarly, some cities require newspapers to use a given percentage of recycled newsprint.

New Outlets

New technologies do not always replace older media. For instance, television did not replace radio any more than VCRs replaced movie theaters. Thus, it is not surprising that newspapers rarely cannibalize their hard-copy circulation when initiating on-line services because on-line services are largely complementary to traditional newspapers.

Newspapers derive the following benefits from placing their publications on on-line systems such as CompuServe:

- Usually the on-line company will pay large up-front fees to the newspaper in return for free advertising in the future. After these charges, the more time people spend reading newspapers on-line, the more revenue the newspaper receives.

- Computers do not have space constraints. For example, a newspaper may have just excerpts from a presidential speech but the computer user can retrieve the entire speech with just a few keystrokes.

- Interactivity allows computer readers to converse with reporters.

- The information can be saved in a much more accessible and manageable form.

- Subscribers can read their home-town newspaper when traveling.

- Newspapers can obtain a great deal of information about their readers because once a reader logs on, the on-line service can see the subscriber's every move and can feed that information to advertisers.

Despite these benefits, newspapers that go on-line must contend with the following drawbacks:

- Since some periodicals do not incorporate retail advertising into their on-line offerings, those people who read such magazines and newspapers on-line will not be exposed to the advertisements. Thus, on-line services risk infuriating advertisers since the highest-income readers will be siphoned off.

- On-line services also threaten a publication's big scoops. For instance, a monthly magazine may post an abbreviated version of a major story on-line a week before its hard copy issue is published. However, a reporter at a competing weekly magazine might read the abbreviated version of his competitor's story and decide to blow out a full story on the same topic in his magazine's next issue. Therefore, a copycat could actually beat the reporter with an original idea to the punch.

T R A P

> ⊘ You should not overstate the potential that CD-ROMs offer newspapers; many people never use their CD-ROMs. Additionally, many of the people who got bundled CD-ROM drives with their PCs do not buy additional software.

- On-line services require much more work from their reporters. For instance, electronic stories must be updated throughout the day.

- On-line services reinforce the notion that traditional newspapers are outdated when they are delivered. For example, a newspaper might post its on-line version Friday evenings when the hard copy reaches subscribers no earlier than Monday morning.

- Some newspapers publish their reporters' E-mail addresses under their bylines. Thus, reporters could end up spending more time sending E-mail back and forth to readers that do not even subscribe to the newspaper.

CD-ROMs

Another area in which newspapers are repackaging their content is CD-ROMs—5-inch software disks that offer perfect sound and picture quality and that cannot be copied. A single CD-ROM has a memory capacity equivalent to 250,000 pages of

T I P

Growing access to multiple forms of gaming (e.g., lotteries, casinos, riverboats) is resulting in people's becoming very impulsive. This is problematic for magazine advertising rates because many people would rather participate in a lottery (and quickly realize whether or not they won) than participate in a drawn-out sweepstakes sponsored by a stamp sheet agent such as Publisher's Clearing House. With fewer people subscribing to magazines through the stamp-sheet agents, magazine circulation contracts and their advertising rates erode. Another factor that results in fewer magazine subscriptions by way of stamp-sheet agents is lower mailings due to higher postage and paper costs.

text. Titling a CD-ROM with a well-known newspaper will help sell the CD-ROM. For instance, a financial CD-ROM that has *The Wall Street Journal* as part of its title should attract many buyers.

There are over four million CD-ROM drives in the United States, and the number of these drives is soaring due to falling prices and CD-ROMs' being "bundled" with personal computers. However, there are a number of obstacles to selling CD-ROMs including:

1. Bundling as many as 15 CD-ROM titles on a computer runs the risk of conditioning people to believe CD-ROMs can be had for free and therefore should not be paid for.

2. It is difficult to find shelf space in video game stores because the children who patronize such merchants will rarely choose CD-ROMs over video games.

3. Bookstores will also have to make a leap in making separate departments for selling CD-ROMs. Until they do this, it will not be worth their while to bother with stocking a few CD-ROMs. Moreover, the bookstores question how much demand there is for CD-ROMs since so many are given away (i.e., bundled with computers).

Retailers further complain that there is a lack of information available to buyers of CD-ROM titles. Video buyers have movie trailers and reviews; book buyers can simply turn pages or rely on the best seller lists in newspapers and magazines; music shoppers may have heard tracks from the album on the radio. However, there is nothing comparable for CD-ROM titles.[2]

---

[2] Richard A Shaffer, "Shelf Battle," *Forbes,* April 24, 1995, p. 178.

ADVERTISING AGENCIES

You may reap a number of advantages by considering investing in some of the publicly traded advertising agencies such as Omnicom Group and The Interpublic Group of Companies. First, the advertising agencies are an underfollowed segment of the stock market. Second, many of the analysts who follow the advertising agencies simply weigh the merits of these stocks based upon the cyclical nature of the economy. Thus, buy recommendations are routinely issued when the economy is strong, while many analysts advise their clients to sell the advertising agency stocks when the economy looks as though it will begin to slow.

However, when you simply consider cyclical factors you will be oblivious to the impact that secular developments can have on the advertising stocks. For instance, there can be fundamental shifts in the economy that render the advertising stocks attractive investments even when the economy is in a downturn. In an advertising agency industry conference that I chaired on behalf of the New York Society of Securities Analysts in early 1996, I laid out just how such events can transpire:

> Sure, it would be nice if the economy was stronger. But take a look at why corporate earnings are slowing. Companies cannot increase their profitability by raising prices since there is so much economic anxiety. Furthermore, companies cannot boost their profitability by slashing costs because they have already slashed their costs extremely aggressively over the past few years.
>
> Since companies generally cannot increase their profitability by raising prices or by slashing their costs, they must do one of two things. One strategy is to increase their market share while the other strategy is to introduce new products. The success of either of these strategies depends on convincing and enduring marketing campaigns. For instance, enticing customers away from the products that they habitually buy requires persistent marketing while rolling out a new consumer good on a national basis can easily cost $50 million.

Companies are increasingly pushing themselves to generate a high percentage of their revenues from products that have been launched in the past few years.

T I P

The issuance of patents and trademarks is a leading indicator of advertising spending because companies that spend money on research and development want to recoup their costs by selling their new inventions. (Since these new products do not have an existing customer base, their companies must make their products known through advertising.)

For example, Minnesota Mining and Manufacturing aims to generate at least 30 percent of its revenues from products brought to market within the past four years. In fact, some industry leaders such as Hewlett-Packard (which controls 60 percent of the personal-computer printer market) strive for self-obsolescence on the belief that if they do not improve their products, their competitors will.

Another favorable development for the advertising agencies lies in the main drivers of today's economy: information and entertainment.

Whereas the economy of yesterday was largely driven by industrial activities such as steel production and auto manufacturing, today's economy is driven by more intellectual endeavors such as software sales and the dispensing of pharmaceuticals.

However, the incremental costs of producing the products that are selling well today are much lower than the incremental costs of selling products that were the main drivers of yesterday's economy; the incremental costs needed to copy another piece of software are much lower than the incremental costs associated with producing another ton of steel. This is because the drivers of yesterday's economy required huge investments in plant and equipment and relied upon unionized labor. However, the goods and services that are growing rapidly today (e.g., research reports, videocassettes, and CD-ROMs) require neither large investments in plant and equipment nor unionized labor. In fact, virtually no labor at all is required to reproduce some products (e.g., research reports).

Thus, the gross margins on the products of the future are much higher than the gross margins on the products of the old economy. This disparity in margins allows the companies that produce today's leading-edged products the wherewithal to fund advertising.

Whereas the old way of boosting profits was to reduce costs (since incremental costs were so high), the new method of raising profits is to expand distribution through aggressive marketing campaigns. The old way of expanding was to open another steel mill. The way to expand today is to increase market share through advertising campaigns.

Aside from these macroeconomic shifts, let's consider how changes in the following industries will benefit the advertising agencies:

Health Care   The health care industry traditionally never advertised. Just a few years ago, advertising prescription drugs on television would have been unheard of. Now, however, many segments of the $800 billion health care industry are beginning to advertise.

First, pharmaceutical manufacturers are advertising the release of their over-the-counter drugs. New over-the-counter product launches can easily cost $100 million apiece. Similarly, pharmaceutical companies advertise their prescription drugs.

Second, health maintenance organizations (HMOs) are seeking to increase their memberships through consistent advertising. Also, hospitals are responding to overcapacity by trying to serve more patients by appealing to the public through advertising. Even some doctors (particularly plastic surgeons and dermatologists) are advertising.

Defense Contractors   The diversification of the defense industry should be a boon to the advertising agencies. Now the defense contractors are manufacturing an increasing number of products for the consumer sector. For instance, GM Hughes plans to spend about $150 million on advertising its direct-broadcast satellite systems in 1996. Moreover, the defense companies rely heavily on advertising agencies since they have had virtually no experience marketing in a competitive marketplace. On the contrary, their weapons systems have been procured by the federal government on a contract basis.

Telecommunications   Traditionally, the Baby Bells did not have to advertise since they enjoyed monopolies within their territories. Now, the telephone companies realize that they must advertise for both offensive and defensive reasons. On the one hand, they need to keep existing customers and markets. On the other hand, they must appeal to new customers and penetrate new markets.

Also, the telephone companies are no longer using advertising to compete solely with other telephone companies. Companies are also advertising to compete with competitors in other industries such as the cable and on-line service industries. This convergence introduces more dimensions to the competitive arena and thus results in more aggressive advertising.

Additionally, the telephone companies must maintain *aggressive* advertising campaigns since it is difficult to retain customers. This is because there are negative switching costs in the telephone industry—that is, the phone companies pay customers to switch carriers.

Electric Utilities   Eventually electric utilities may win the right to compete to sell power directly to end customers in new geographic regions. Thus, electricity could be marketed in much the same way that telephone service is marketed.

Aggressive advertising by the electric utility industry would have an enormous impact on advertising agencies. Even if the electric utility industry only spent 1 percent of its $200 billion annual revenue on advertising, expenditures on advertising would soar by another $2 billion. This is not as far-fetched as some may believe, as utility executives are already beginning to attend advertising conferences. In fact, UtiliCorp United of Kansas City has developed the EnergyOne brand name for the off-price power that it sells.

Retail   The domination of large retail chains is occurring in many segments of the retail industry including the drug store industry, the office supplies industry, and the home improvement industry. In fact, some retail chains are so dominant over independents that, in local markets such as Phoenix, there are essentially no independent drug stores remaining. The benefit to advertising agencies is that the large retail chains advertise aggressively, whereas the independent operators do very little advertising.

Also, there is more geographic overlap occurring among competing niche retail chains. For instance, major electronics retailers (e.g., Best Buy and Circuit City) home improvement retailers (e.g., Home Depot and Lowe's Companies) office-supply stores (e.g., Office Max, Office Depot, and Staples) and automotive after-market retailers (e.g., AutoZone and The Pep Boys—Manny, Moe and Jack) are moving into one another's markets. This overlap will result in increased competition and more vigorous advertising campaigns.

Another development in the retail sector that will benefit the advertising agencies is that product proliferation is placing a premium on retailers' shelf space. In fact, the number of new products that are introduced each year is roughly equal to the total number of products that the average store carries. Due to this imbalance, a common condition for a vendor being allotted shelf space is the vendor's commitment to a large and sustained advertising campaign.

This lack of shelf space has resulted in power shifting from the manufacturers to the retailers. One ramification of this power shift is that manufacturers no longer have the clout to push their goods through the retail channels. Rather manufacturers must pull their goods through the retail channels by generating genuine demand for their goods. The advertising agencies are crucial in generating this demand since it is they who create the marketing that is designed to appeal to the public.

Consumer Goods Manufacturers   The advertising agencies should benefit from the shift toward every day low pricing (EDLP) because the advertising agencies control more money under the EDLP method than under the promotional method. (see the grocery store chapter, pages 70–71) because much of the resources allocated under the promotional method are discounts, rebates, and the like. In fact, promotion allowances are so commonly employed in the beverage industry that they are viewed as price reductions rather than part of an advertising budget.

Technology   The technology sector is a source of great opportunity for advertising agencies:

1. This sector is just beginning to go mainstream. While personal computers and cellular phones have already reached the early adapters, these products are now being marketed to broad markets. Also, some high-tech areas that have just recently emerged are beginning to advertise. For instance, the on-line service industry emerged over the past five years or so and is beginning to advertise (e.g., America On-Line).

2. This sector of the economy is growing much faster than most other sectors.

3. The incredible importance of setting standards in the technology sector makes dominating market share crucial. For instance, there is only room for one standard with regard to videocassettes and digital video disks, and, of course, the garnering and retention of market share is primarily achieved through aggressive advertising campaigns. Therefore, even in the technology realm, marketing is more important than technological capability.

4. High-tech companies have short product life cycles, meaning new campaigns for new products have to be continually launched.

Restaurants   As restaurant franchisees' revenues rise, so too do the franchisors' advertising budgets. This is because franchisees are required to pay a portion of their revenues into a fund that is used to finance advertising campaigns.

There are a number of reasons that will cause revenues for the restaurant franchisees to rise:

- More meals are being consumed at restaurants versus being prepared at home.

- The large restaurant chains are adding more units. (For example, McDonald's added 1,100 new outlets in the United States in 1995 and plans to open as many as 3,200 eateries in 1996.)

Banking   Interstate banking will result in retention of more customers for the banks with initial client relationships. Thus, when people move to new locations, the banks that serve these locations will have to advertise more aggressively to win the customer over.

For instance, if someone moves from California to Oregon, it would traditionally have been assumed that the customer would sever his relationship with the California bank and initiate a relationship with the Oregon-based bank. However, due to interstate banking, the California bank may have a subsidiary bank in Oregon; the people that move from California to Oregon thus no longer have to switch banks.

Accordingly, banks located in Oregon, in this case, could not assume, nowadays that they would win the newcomer's account. They therefore would need to advertise more aggressively than before.

Major Motion Pictures   Movie studios are becoming bigger advertisers as they are now advertising the re-release of their movies in videocassette form. For instance, Disney spent about $100 million on the video release of *Toy Story*.

Aside from the changes occurring in the above industries, the trend of suppliers' branding their components and the rise in self-sufficiency will be a boon to the advertising agencies.

Suppliers Branding Components   It used to be that only the manufacturers of finished goods advertised. As a result, the consumer was unaware of the companies that produced the components in the end products. Consequently, these components were resigned to commodity status. Now, however, some manufacturers of components are beginning to brand their products. One of the most successful manufacturers of components to have branded its products is Intel, the leading computer chip manufacturer. This trend could be wildly positive for the advertising agencies because there are far more components than finished products.

Self-Sufficiency   Due to the prevalence of do-it-yourself books and videos (as well as more discretionary time), people are doing far more things (that they would traditionally have contracted out) themselves. Examples of this trend include people's remodeling their homes and selecting their own stocks. In the health care industry more people are medicating themselves by buying over-the-counter pharmaceuticals.

The advertising agencies will benefit from the trend towards self-sufficiency because more goods and services will have to be marketed to the public through mainstream channels. For instance, companies like Home Depot must market to the general public—not just to contractors. Also, over-the-counter pharmaceuticals must be marketed to millions of potential patients, not just to a few thousand health care providers.

Political Advertising   Advertising agencies and other media companies such as radio and television stations that depend on advertising revenue should benefit from the following secular political developments:

- It is now very difficult to lobby the executive and legislative branches of government. For instance, the House adopted a flat ban on gifts, while the Senate imposed a $50 limit on a single gift and a $100 annual gift limit from a single source. Thus, more money is being spent on advertising to appeal to the grass-roots level. For example, sugar farmers in Florida ran commercials against proposed taxes on their farms while Medicare cuts were opposed in an aggressive advertising campaign launched by the American Association of Retired Persons.
  Similarly, politicians and interest groups have broadcast commercials to support their policies. For example, President Clinton has run commercials in favor of gun control. Also, religious groups have been running commercials in favor of sexual abstinence.
- In stark contrast to the 1980s, it is now possible to defeat incumbent politicians. In fact, even the Speaker of the House was defeated in 1994—the first time that happened in at least a hundred years. Of course, more competition for political office results in more aggressive campaigning.

- Fewer incumbent politicians are even running for reelection. These open seats will generate much more advertising since the candidate from the incumbent's party must fight his way through his party's nomination process.

- The trend towards more voter initiatives is a boon to the media.

- Spending limits on political contributions may be eliminated, allowing for more aggressive campaigns. In fact, in early 1996, the Supreme Court agreed to decide whether political parties have a constitutional right to spend unlimited amounts of money to either support their candidates or urge the defeat of opposing candidates.

Advertising Agency Concerns

Advertising agencies should benefit from the following developments:

- Rising media costs. The more expensive media time becomes, the higher the advertising agencies' commissions rise. For instance, if an ad agency charges its clients 15 percent to place a commercial, its commissions will be higher if the media time rises from $200,000 to $300,000 per minute.

- The possible auctioning off of the television spectrum that would be used for advanced digital-TV broadcasting. If this spectrum were auctioned off, the networks would have to recoup these expenses by raising their ad rates. Since the advertising agencies charge their clients a percentage of ad expenses, the ad agencies' revenues would rise.

- Free trade agreements such as GATT and NAFTA. These segments spark competition that fuels advertising. Similarly, privatizations abroad lead to more competition.

- The growing number of media outlets. More outlets complicate the placement of advertisements. Thus, the ad agencies can charge higher rates for their placement services.

However, the following developments are adverse for the advertising agencies:

- Convergence among industries. Convergence presents conflict-of-interest problems: It used to be that when an advertising agency had one client in the computer industry and one client in the telephone industry no conflict of interest was presented since the clients competed in different industries. Now, the convergence in the information/communication/entertainment industries means that these two clients may compete against each other. Thus, one client may leave the agency.

- Mergers and acquisitions. The consolidation generated by mergers and acquisitions reduces competition. For example, if the two leading retailers in a city merge, the remaining retailer probably will not advertise as much as the two smaller retailers advertised previously since the large retailer will face less competition.

■ Greater competition from clients' internal advertising departments.

■ Greater on-line advertising. Nowadays clients can quickly determine which ads are effective in generating responses. The biggest thing advertising agencies have traditionally had going for them is that it was impossible to tell which ads were effective; as a result, clients could not determine how to reduce their advertising budgets. With interactivity, they will.

You should search for advertising agencies that

■ Are attracting high levels of net new business (new accounts plus new projects from existing accounts minus lost accounts and assignments). New business is important because while new accounts may have been announced, they are not immediately reflected in the ad agency's financials. Thus, future earnings should improve. Also, new business attracts more new business and better creative account executives.

■ Have broad geographic exposure. Advertising agencies must have the geographic reach to serve their clients that are conducting more of their business abroad.

■ Have a diversified business mix. That is, the advertising agency should not be too dependent on one industry.

■ Do not have excessive client concentrations. This means that the agency should not be overly dependent on a few clients.

■ Have clients with solid balance sheets to support large advertising campaigns.

■ Have prestigious clients. In the advertising business, image is everything. Thus, the leaders in one industry often migrate to the ad agencies that represent the best clients in other industries.

■ Have clients that are capitalizing their advertising costs. Capitalizing advertising costs often results in greater advertising expenditures since capitalizing such costs makes clients' earnings look better.

TRAP

⊘ Advertisers that specialize in direct mail, such as ADVO, Inc., face several challenges. First, telemarketing firms (the main competitor for direct mailers) are benefiting from falling communications costs while direct mailers are disadvantaged by rising paper and postage costs. Also, response rates are higher and faster for telemarketing.

- Have high levels of client retention. When fewer of an agency's accounts are put up for review, the agency undergoes the bidding process less frequently. The bidding process is very expensive since ad agencies have to develop prototype advertising campaigns with no assurance that their campaign will be accepted by the client. Thus, the more revenue derived from clients that have been represented by the agency for many years (e.g., 15), the better.

TIP

When you believe that there will be an increase in advertising, it may be best to look towards the electronic media first. This is because electronic media is more leveraged to the economy than the print media since the supply of time available for advertising is fixed. For example, when advertising volume soars, a radio station cannot increase the number of hours in a day. Thus, it can easily raise its rates. However, a magazine can insert more pages, which softens rates.

Also, there are generally more print outlets than electronic outlets for a given category. For instance, if a brokerage firm wishes to advertise, there are only two cable television stations that specialize in business news. However, there are at least a dozen national newspapers and magazines that focus on investing. These alternatives reduce the pricing power of each magazine.

- Have low defection rates of employees. Defections increase client turnover rates because clients follow their favorite account executives to new ad agencies.
- Win a high number of awards per billion dollars of billings.
- Do not annualize billings. Since a great deal of advertising is seasonal, annualizing billings can exaggerate an ad agency's earnings.
- Are making many presentations (solicitations). In general, the more presentations that it wins, the better. However, the terms must be favorable. Thus, too much of an agency's revenues in the form of incentive fees is problematic.

MOVIE THEATERS

Despite the growth of other forms of video delivery, movie theaters are unlikely to become obsolete for the following reasons:

TIP

👉 Extremely hot or cold weather can benefit movie theaters because people seek refuge from challenging elements.

- Movie theater chains such as Carmike Cinemas and Regal Cinemas are the prime beneficiaries of the millions of dollars that movie studios spend advertising their new releases. In fact, the movie studios pay for large percentages of movie theaters' advertising in local newspapers.
- People like the shared experience of seeing movies with other people. Similarly, people still consider going to the movies part of their entertainment experience.
- There are drawbacks to competing movie delivery systems. For example, pay-per-view is inconvenient since it is only aired at certain times. Also, the viewer cannot rewind a pay-per-view performance, which means that an interruption will cause him to miss part of the programming. Additionally, while high-definition television will offer pictures and sound quality that is superior to traditional analog television, the expense of those television sets will limit their adoption rates.

Movie theaters are generating higher revenue streams by showing more commercials. Advertisers like to place their commercials in movie theaters because the messages have a solid impact due to the theaters' large, high-resolution screens and superb sound systems.

Virtually all new movie theaters are being built in the multiplex format. There are a number of benefits associated with multiplex formats. Multiplexes allow for economies of scale since the operator needs fewer employees and less space. Second, some multiplex theaters offer so many movies that these theaters become entertainment destinations in and of themselves. Also, the theaters within multiplexes have less seating capacity than stand-alone theaters; thus, the spillover of patrons who choose other features because the most popular attraction sold

TIP

👉 Video stores have countered that studios selling their videos to end customers is not a major problem because sell-throughs are most effective for children's movies, which only account for a small part of the video rental business.

out raises the percentage of the entire multiplex's seats sold. (However, the spill-over phenomenon is jeopardized by companies such as Movie-Fone that allow people to buy their tickets in advance.)

VIDEO STORES

You should be aware of the challenges that video store operators such as Movie Gallery and Moovies face. As you probably know, video stores rely on video rentals for profits. However, video rentals are threatened by movie studios' selling a growing percentage of their videos through alternative distribution channels such as mass merchants and record stores. A second major threat to video stores comes from pay-per-view programs offered through direct-broadcast satellites (DBS). For prices that are competitive with video stores, DBS offers greater convenience than renting and returning videocassettes Thus, the rapid growth of DBS will become a growing problem for video stores.

T I P

> ☞ Higher paper prices adversely affect book publishers.

Finally, video stores have a tendency to overstate their earnings by taking insufficient depreciation charges. In the video business, depreciation charges should basically mirror capital investments because videocassettes have a brief shelf life. A video store may buy 40 copies of a new release; however, after a few weeks, demand for most of these videos will dissipate.

BOOK PUBLISHERS

While John Wiley & Sons and Thomas Nelson are among the few independent publicly traded book publishers, it is interesting to see how vertically integrated entertainment empires such as Viacom (through Simon & Schuster) benefit from having a captive book-publishing unit. Since it is far less expensive to publish a book than to produce a movie, books are an efficient form of testing ideas and stories. A media company may be able to withstand publishing 50 unsuccessful books if it has a few bestsellers and a strong backlist (of previously published books). However, the media company would unlikely be able to finance 50 unsuccessful movies.

Similarly, movie studios can leverage their copyrights of a popular fiction book by producing a related movie. When basing a movie on a fictional book, movie studios can better project how large a following the movie will attract.

These projections are helpful in budgeting. Similarly, movie studios can make additional money by publishing a book of a box-office hit, and publishers can make more money by turning books into CD-ROMs and "books on cassette." Other factors that affect demand for book sales include the following:

- Demographics. The prime age for Americans buying books is in the thirties.

- Self-sufficiency. The rise of self-sufficiency (as discussed in the Advertising Agency section on page 162) helps spur sales of do-it-yourself books.

- Technology. Technical books do well when many people who are employed in the professional and service industries need to stay abreast of the rapid technological changes that impact their industries. Similarly, sales of technical books do well when people are interested in things that rapidly change, such as computers and software.

- Education. The higher the percentage of the adult population that is educated, the better.

As you have surely noticed, the bookstore chains have been taking market share away from the independently owned bookstores. Now, at least 80 percent of the nation's bookstores are owned by a major chain. The consolidation of the bookstore industry is neutral for book publishers. On the negative side, the fewer

T R A P

⊘ You should never invest in content unless the infrastructure necessary to deliver that content has already been deployed. In the beginning of the 1990s, many entrepreneurs tried to raise money to create programming for cable networks. However, when the FCC reregulated cable rates in 1992, cash flows for cable operators fell; consequently, cable operators did not have sufficient cash flow to increase their broadband capacity. As a result, there was insufficient infrastructure to deliver additional cable channels, so many of those people who invested in new cable programming in the early 1990s lost money.

remaining bookstores have more market share and thus more buying power. Thus, chains such as Barnes & Noble and Books-a-Million are able to derive concessions from book publishers. (Book publishers have been offsetting this bargaining power with mergers of their own. For instance, Richard D. Irwin acquired Probus Publishing in 1995.)

However, the growth of bookstore chains has helped spur book sales since many of these stores are better managed than independent bookstores. Also, it is easier for the book publishers to deal with a fewer number of large bookstore chains than many independent bookstore operators.

CABLE OPERATORS

Cable operators such as Cablevision Systems and Comcast Corporation deliver multiple channels of television programming to subscribers who pay a monthly fee for the services they receive. Cable operators manage the delivery of television signals that are received over the air or via satellite delivery by antennas, microwave relay stations, and satellite earth stations. These signals are then modulated, amplified, and distributed over a cable operator's network of coaxial and fiberoptic cable to the subscribers' television sets.

Positive Developments

The Telecommunications Act of 1996 removes rate regulations for cable operators. However, for reasons of image, cable companies might not raise their rates. This bill also allows for outright cable mergers in small towns. Thus, some cable operators will benefit from higher rates and greater efficiencies resulting from consolidation.

      Another development that has been taking place in the mid-1990s is that the cable industry's customer service has been improving relative to the Baby Bells. Much of this improvement is attributable to the National Cable Television Association's embarking upon a program of service guarantees and refunds for late appointments. At the same time that these improvements are being made, the Baby Bells' customer service should worsen as a result of aggressive downsizings.

Offering Telephone Service

Many of the cable companies would like to offer telephone services. In fact, Time Warner already offers telephone service in Rochester while Cox Communications is preparing to offer telephone service in San Diego on a trial basis. One reason for cable's attraction to telephone service is that the local and long-distance market is huge, with a combined 1996 revenue of roughly $160 billion versus cable's $25 billion in revenue.

T I P

    Since coaxial wiring can handle broadband speeds right away, it is cheaper and technologically easier for cable companies to add voice than for phone companies to add video.

A second benefit of offering phone service is that customers would be less likely to cancel their cable television service, which would result in lower disconnection costs. Another benefit for cable companies offering phone services is that they are able to cherry-pick the best customers without being obligated to serve all customers in a territory.

Obstacles with Offering Telephony

Few cable operators can offer their customers telephone service since only about 8 percent of the nation's cable customers are served by systems with two-way communications capability. (That is, most cable service is one way—from the cable operator's network to the viewer.) To become interactive, cable companies must add switching capability. According to industry estimates, it will cost between $1,200 and $1,400 per subscriber to install the switching equipment necessary to deliver telephony. These costs are in addition to the costs of upgrading cable networks to provide greater channel capacity. Moreover, there are no assurances that these expenditures would be effective, as most technologies for delivering telephone services over cable networks are still untested.

Another problem with cable operators' offering phone service is that people are generally content with their basic phone service; thus, massive advertising campaigns would be needed. Such advertising campaigns would be a challenge because:

- Cable has no national brand identity.
- Cable companies entering telephony will not compete only against the incumbent phone companies but also against new entrants.

TRAP

⊘ Analyzing cable operators in terms of cash flow (which excludes interest expenses) is unwise because interest expense belongs to creditors rather than shareholders. Thus, excluding interest expenses overstates a cable operator's cash flow.

Further, cable companies will find it difficult to offer telephone service because cable operators are perceived as being less reliable than telephone providers. For instance, during the Blizzard of 1996 in the Northeast, customers received uninterrupted telephone service from Nynex and uninterrupted electricity from Consolidated Edison, but they received disrupted cable service from Time Warner. Additionally, reliability demands are much higher for telephone service

T R A P

🚫 One problem with the proliferation of television channels is obtaining reliable ratings. Some of the cable channels have such small audiences that the major ratings services cannot determine how many viewers they have. Without these ratings, it is hard to attract advertisers.

than for cable service. One reason is that telephone providers are responsible for lifeline services such as 911. Also, customers generally do not have confidence in the accuracy of cable's billing systems, which is imperative for companies wishing to offer telephone service.

Advantages in Video

Although the Telecommunications Act of 1996 allows the Baby Bells to offer cable services as soon as they wish, a number of reasons make it unlikely that they will present the cable operators with serious competition:

1. The Baby Bells are more likely to compete in long-distance telephone service rather than cable since the former is more predictable and economical to break into than cable television. Also, the long-distance market is nearly three times as large (estimated 1996 revenues of $70 billion) as the cable services industry (estimated 1996 revenues of $25 billion).

2. It would be very expensive for telephone companies to upgrade their infrastructure to facilitate cable. One reason is that telephone company employees are unionized and operate on a division of labor basis. Conversely, the cable companies have nonunionized workforces and do not experience such restrictive work rules. Thus, a telephone company may send more workers to lay coaxial cable than a cable company would have to deploy to add switches. In fact, Raymond Smith, the chairman and CEO of Bell Atlantic, said that it would take 2 1/2 to 4 years before the combined Nynex and Bell Atlantic will be able to offer interactive video in even six cities.[3]

3. Another disincentive is regulation. Regional telephone companies operate in large contiguous areas and are overseen by a few state regulatory authorities. On the other hand, cable companies are regulated by many municipal governmental bodies. Since cable operators usually serve

---

[3] Catherine Arnst with Joesph Weber, "For Whom the Baby Bells Toll," *Business Week,* May 6, 1996, p. 32.

many communities, local regulation presents high compliance costs and difficulty in strategic planning.

4. Cable companies have established relationships with program suppliers whereas most telephone companies do not. Also, the entertainment business is better managed by entrepreneurs (e.g., from the cable industry) than by executives that have managed heavily regulated monopolies (e.g., the Baby Bells).

Cable Modems

Cable modems may be the cable industry's trojan horse for offering residential telephone service. If cable modems prove to be reliable, people may become less hesitant to receive phone service from cable companies. Cable modems, up to 1,000 times faster than telephone lines, are sure to be highly popular due to the speed with which they allow their users to browse the Internet. In fact, cable modem users proved to be addicted to the instantaneous connections that offered during Continental Cablevision's test of cable modems at Boston College at the end of 1995.

However, there are a few obstacles to the widespread rollout of cable modems:

1. At roughly $500 per modem, these modems are prohibitively expensive for the mass market.

2 A lack of nationwide cable network standards complicates efforts to come up with a universal device for modems.

3. Unlike ISDN, cable modems can slow down when too many users are pulling down large files simultaneously.

4. Upstream paths (from the user to the cable network) are susceptible to electronic interference from household appliances, such as blow dryers and vacuum cleaners as well as from CB radios and Christmas lights.

Investment Considerations

You should search for cable operators with the following characteristics:

- High rates of subscriber growth. This will be harder to achieve since the early adapters already subscribe to cable.
- A high minimum channel capacity.
- The ability to aggressively upgrade their broadband capacity to offer more channels.
- Success in selling their customers premium channels as well as pay-per-view programming.

T R A P

⊘ Although most franchising authorities have granted only one franchise per area, substantially all cable television franchises are nonexclusive. Thus, cable operators could face greater competition in their own areas.

- Success in negotiating favorable programming agreements.

- Equity interests in companies that produce and distribute national and regional programming. These ownership interests ensure that the cable operator has access to content.

- The ability to pay their local government franchising authorities only low percentages of their total revenues for their franchising agreements. (Cable television systems typically are constructed and operated pursuant to nonexclusive franchises awarded by local governmental authorities for specified periods of time.)

- Long-term (e.g., 10- to 15-year) franchise agreements.

- A long history of renewing favorable franchise agreements.

- A high percentage of full-time installers. This is because independent contractors can often be surly to customers and do sloppy work.

- Operating presence in regions with very poor reception to broadcast television signals.

- Operating presence in regions with low rates of videocassette-recorder ownership. This is important because owners of videocassette recorders are able to rent many of the same movies, special events, and music videos that are available on certain premium services.

- Large net operating losses (NOLs) that can be carried over into the distant future. These NOLs shield future income from federal income taxation.

- Manageable debt levels. Interestingly, since cable companies typically carry heavy debt loads, they usually benefit from lower interest expenses resulting from lower interest rates.

- The ability to raise their advertising rates consistently and substantially.

- Superior customer service in terms of on-time performance, accuracy of billing, and responsiveness to customer complaints.

WIRELESS CABLE

Wireless cable is an interesting niche within the cable industry. Wireless cable operators use microwave technology to beam programming from a transmitter to antennas on customers' homes. These transmissions have traditionally carried up to 33 channels over a radius of 35 to 40 miles from each broadcast site. However, the technology on which wireless cable operates is being converted from analog to digital, which will quadruple the number of channels carried to over 120.

Aside from more channels, one of the advantages of wireless cable is that wireless operators can charge 25-percent less for their services compared with conventional cable since the cost structure associated with wireless is much cheaper. For instance, the costly cable infrastructure of coaxial cable and amplifiers is not needed. Another advantage of wireless cable is the existence of far less regulation over it. Moreover, since wireless cable spectrum is close to Personal Communications Services (PCS) spectrum, wireless companies may be able to offer paging and cellular services as well as Internet access.

Many phone companies appreciate the potential that wireless cable offers. For instance, Nynex and Bell Atlantic paid $100 million for warrants to buy as much as 45 percent of CAI Wireless Systems which has access to 11 million homes in cities such as Philadelphia and New York City. Also, Pacific Telesis

T I P

Advertising for DBS should accrue to the benefit of cable companies. This is because major broadcasters are loathe to accept advertising from cable networks but are amenable to broadcasting advertising for DBS operators. Thus, the programming that DBS commercials showcase (e.g., ESPN, CNN, CNBC) boosts demand for additional channels, which helps cable subscribers.

spent about $350 million on wireless cable licenses that cover 7 million homes in California.

Despite the advantages of wireless cable, you should be aware that wireless cable signals are sometimes compromised. This is particularly true in areas that are mountainous or populated with tall buildings. Sometimes even dense foliage can put a potential customer in a "shadow zone" that takes extra equipment and expense to cover. Similarly, rain can be a problem for wireless cable. And finally, wireless cable does not offer full interactivity.

DIRECT-BROADCAST SATELLITE SYSTEMS

Direct-broadcasting satellites (DBS) are a source of stiff competition for the cable operators. DBS certainly has wide appeal. While direct-broadcast satellites have only been on the market since 1994, more than 3 million dishes were sold by the beginning of 1996.

Perhaps the most attractive feature of DBS is that it typically offers more channels than cable operators. Moreover, since DBS operates on a national scale, it can profitably offer more narrowcasting than cable stations. For instance, assume that the local cable station in Kalamazoo (Michigan) does not have enough viewers in its area to profitably run a channel devoted to Italian cooking. However, there might be enough interest in Italian cooking throughout the nation for a satellite company to run a channel devoted to Italian cooking. Therefore, satellite systems are able to offer more diverse programming than cable operators.

Another competitive advantage that DBS operators enjoy is the enhanced clarity that their digital broadcast signals offer over cable's analog signals. (However, cable companies will be able to offer higher resolution pictures when they transmit digital signals via digital set-top boxes.) Additionally, satellites have a greater ability to deliver a variety of pay-per-view movies than cable. For example, some satellite operators can broadcast the same movie at 30-minute intervals, whereas most cable systems begin pay-per-view movies at two- to three-hour intervals.

DBS will become even more competitive with cable because major telecommunications players are becoming active in DBS. For instance, in early 1996, AT&T took a $137.5 million interest in DirecTV while MCI and News Corporation plan to spend $1.3 billion by the end of 1998 developing their own direct broadcast satellite network.

However, there are drawbacks to satellites:

1. Satellites are extremely expensive (roughly $1,000). (Satellites will become more affordable as satellite providers such as Echostar allow their customers to lease their satellites.)

2. Satellites cannot carry network-affiliated local stations, which still account for 60 percent of all TV viewing, in areas that already receive them.

3. Customers must buy additional decoders (at a cost of roughly $500 each) for each additional television set from which they wish to receive DBS programming.

4. There are zoning restrictions against satellite dishes in some communities. (However, 18-inch dishes are mitigating the obstacles presented by zoning restrictions.)

TELECOMMUNICATIONS

The telephone stocks were traditionally viewed as utilities—safe but slow growing. Now, with deregulation and convergence, telephone stocks offer much more growth potential but also more risk.

Another major development that is taking place all over the telecommunications industry is the rapid growth of data traffic. Telecommunications providers will continue to benefit from higher volumes of fax transmissions, E-mail messaging, and database downloads.

T R A P

⊘ Over the next several years, distributing inbound international traffic may become less lucrative if foreign governments privatize their state-run telephone monopolies.

LONG-DISTANCE CARRIERS

The long-distance carriers are positioned to benefit from growth in high-margin international calling resulting from the general increase in international business. Moreover, the long-distance carriers should fare well in the deregulatory era ahead.

International Traffic

You should seek to invest in the long-distance carriers that generate not only high volumes of international traffic, but also a high percentage of inbound (rather than outbound) traffic. Distributing inbound traffic from foreign countries is extremely profitable for long-distance operators. First, some background is in order: In most foreign countries international rates are very high in order to subsidize local calling, and there is generally less competition among phone companies in foreign countries. However, in the United States, outbound international calls are usually much cheaper since long-distance calls do not subsidize local calling. (AT&T® divested its regional bell operating companies in 1984.)

Given this background, the United States reciprocates with foreign carriers. For instance, suppose that there is an agreement between the United States and Germany whereby both nations agree that their long-distance operators will deliver calls made from the other's country for 40 percent of the revenue that the originating phone company charges. Since international calling is more expensive in Germany, suppose that Deutsche Telekom charges $4.00 for a five-minute call from Frankfurt to New York while AT&T charges only $2.00 for a five-minute call from New York to Frankfurt. Thus, AT&T would generate $1.20 ($2.00 × 60%) in revenue for handing a call to Deutsche Telekom. However, AT&T would generate $1.60 ($4.00 × 40%) in revenue for delivering Deutsche Telekom's inbound traffic. Moreover, incoming traffic is more profitable since there are no marketing or billing expenses associated with delivering it.

Operating Concerns

Another factor that is further widening profit margins is that long-distance companies are increasingly avoiding paying access fees. (Access fees are charges that the long-distance carriers traditionally paid to the Baby Bells for completing long-distance calls on the local carriers' networks.) For instance, MCI is building its local calling infrastructure in about 50 of the nation's largest cities. Also, Sprint is preparing to deliver phone calls through its partnerships with major cable operators such as Comcast Corporation and Cox Communication.

However, two of the challenges that confront the long-distance carriers are customer defections and greater competition from the Baby Bells. First, the long-distance carriers continue to spend enormous sums of money to attract customers who will leave as soon as a competing carrier offers a better incentive. In fact, roughly 15 percent of American households switch long-distance carriers once a year, while over 4 percent are bargain hunters (those who switch at least two times a year).

Second, while the long-distance carriers have many advantages over the Baby Bells on a national basis, the Baby Bells will challenge the long-distance carriers in their own regions. Already, about one-third of all long-distance calls are made in one Baby Bell's region (e.g., New York to Boston via Nynex or San Francisco to San Diego via Pacific Telesis). Thus, many analysts hold that the Baby Bells will be able to capture a large part of this in-region long-distance traffic. Accordingly, the Baby Bells should be able to capture even more in-region long-distance traffic resulting from contiguous mergers (e.g., Nynex and Bell Atlantic).

T I P

Second-tier long-distance telephone companies such as U.S. Long Distance and WorldCom, Inc., may be attractive acquisition targets for Baby Bells or cable companies that seek an expedient route into long-distance telephone service.

Regulatory Issues

The Telecommunications Act of 1996 allows the long-distance carriers to compete with the Baby Bells as soon as they wish. However, the long-distance carriers could most effectively compete if they received favorable regulatory rulings such as the following:

- "Number portability." This would allow customers to keep their same phone numbers if they switched to a long-distance company offering local service. Failure to achieve number portability would greatly hinder the long-distance companies from serving customers with local phone service because people do not like to change their phone numbers.

- "Dialing parity." This would eliminate the five-digit access codes now needed when callers use alternative local carriers.

The Internet Factor

Long-distance companies will face challenges from the Internet. This is because an Internet user only has to pay for a local phone call to speak to someone in another part of the world. Already, some businesses are using Internet calling to bypass high international tolls and cut costs of nonvoice traffic such as faxes. Going forward, leading net-browser companies such as Netscape Communications plan to incorporate Internet phoning in their programs.

T R A P

⊘ One problem with Bells' shifting from rate-of-return regulation to price regulation is that the Bells' credit ratings might deteriorate because regulators no longer ensure that the Bells will earn a stipulated rate of return.

However, there are some problems with using the Internet for long-distance communications:

- The other party has to be expecting the call.
- Both people need special software (provided by companies such as Vocaltec and Voxware) as well as a sound card and a microphone.
- Only one person can speak at a time.
- There can be delays in hearing the other person's voice of up to a minute.

Nevertheless, further into the future, Internet carriers are likely to increase their rates (and therefore become less competitive with long-distance carriers) when telephoning and video consume more Internet capacity.

REGIONAL BELL OPERATING COMPANIES (RBOCS OR "BABY BELLS")

Methods of Regulation

The two primary forms of regulation under which Baby Bells are governed are rate-of-return regulation and price regulation. Regulators typically used the rate-of-return method to cap the Bells' earnings. Under price regulation, the rates for basic services are frozen but not the profits that the companies are allowed to earn. Thus, price regulation allows the Bells to raise their profits by reducing their costs as aggressively as they wish. Furthermore, fees for enhanced services such as Caller ID are usually not capped under price regulation.

Interestingly, encouraging the Baby Bells to boost their earnings by reducing their costs is a double-edged sword. One of the drawbacks with the price method of regulation is that much of Baby Bells' expense reductions are being achieved by slashing payrolls. With lean workforces, the Baby Bells' customer service has deteriorated. However, state regulators will not tolerate inadequate telephone service. For instance, in January 1996, New York state ordered Nynex to refund five million of its customers a total of $50 million as a result of Nynex's record of slow repairs and installations. Similarly, in the spring of 1996, Washington state was considering forcing U S West to offer free cellular service to customers who were unable to obtain regular phone service in a timely manner.

Another drawback with the transition from rate-of-return regulation to price regulation is that the Baby Bells may be discouraged from making crucial investments in their infrastructure. As discussed below, if the Baby Bells do not modernize their infrastructure they will be passed by the cable companies and the long-distance telephone operators on the Information Superhighway.

New Competitors

Competitive access providers (CAPs) such as MFS Communications and IntelCom Group present the RBOCs with serious competition. These CAPs offer private-line traffic by connecting business customers to long-distance carriers, thus depriving the RBOCs of their access fees. The CAPs target the RBOCs' most lucrative customers which are usually large businesses. (Businesses generate lots of traffic and are the best prospects for high-speed data lines, videoconferencing, and consulting services.)

The CAPs (a.k.a. by-pass companies) have been able to attract business customers with low rates. They can offer these since they have not had to contribute to universal funds as the RBOCs have had to do. (The RBOCs pay about $20 billion annually into these universal funds which are used to subsidize services for the indigent, rural, and hearing-impaired customers as well as emergency calling.) Another reason why the by-pass companies have been able to underprice the RBOCs is that the RBOCs file their rates across state lines. Thus, if the RBOCs offered very low rates to their business customers they would have to offer all of their customers within a given state the same low rates. Also, of great concern to the RBOCs is that the long-distance carriers (and to a more limited extent, the cable companies) are beginning to emulate the CAPs by enticing the RBOCs' business customers with low rates.

As a result of the CAPs' cherry-picking the RBOCs' best customers, the RBOCs are left with providing service to their low-income and rural customers. These customers are expensive to serve. For instance, Nynex spends $1 million a month repairing vandalized pay phones. Also, some of the RBOCs must send bodyguards with their repairmen on calls to dangerous neighborhoods.

Impeding By-Pass Companies

However, the Baby Bells are trying to retain their near monopoly status by making it very difficult for the by-pass companies and others to use their local loops. Among the accusations leveled against the Baby Bells are the following:

- Charging high fees for equipment and the installation of that equipment.
- Charging high rental fees on the facilities that the by-pass companies use.
- Refusing to include by-pass customers in their directories.
- Refusing to give by-pass companies an adequate number of phone numbers to issue to their customers.
- Refusing to allow by-pass companies to offer enhanced services such as Caller-ID.
- Refusing to give the by-pass companies blueprints of the location of local lines, which is necessary for installing switches.
- Refusing to grant by-pass companies access to the Bells facilities when not specifically required to do so. (It is even rumored that a by-pass employee asked to use a Baby Bell's restroom but was denied the request because access to restrooms was not specifically mandated in the governing telecom regulations.)
- Running up high legal bills on litigation.
- Being most accommodative in connecting the by-pass companies with customers having poor histories of paying their phone bills.
- Arbitrarily disconnecting by-pass customers and then telling the customer that the by-pass company went out of business.
- AT&T has accused Ameritech of delaying the interconnection deals that AT&T needs to serve Chicago. Specifically, Ameritech has been accused of sending the wrong people to meetings and changing negotiators so as to begin discussions anew. Additionally, Ameritech persuaded almost one million of its customers to freeze their accounts allegedly on the belief that they would be protected against slamming (strong-arming a customer to switch phone carriers) by long-distance competitors. However, the main reason for freezing these accounts was to make it harder for a competitor to offer in-state calls and other local services.

Competing with Long Distance Operators

Enactment of the Telecommunications Act of 1996 will expose the Baby Bells to direct competition with the long-distance carriers in local as well as long-distance markets. This presents a number of serious challenges to the Baby Bells:

- Long-distance companies do not have to meet any regulatory approvals to compete in local markets.

- Baby Bells must allow competitors access to the last mile of their telephone lines into customers' homes. (On the other hand, Baby Bells cannot offer long-distance service until they demonstrate that competition exists in their local markets.)

Aside from the first mover advantages, the long-distance companies have the following advantages over the Baby Bells:

- Long-distance companies already have national reach. Thus, they can achieve economies of scale in marketing.

- Having operated in a competitive marketplace for many years, the long-distance carriers have competitive skills.

- Whereas the long-distance operators have already downsized, the Baby Bells have much more downsizing to do.

- The long-distance carriers enjoy tremendous brand identity. While everyone in the country knows the names of the three major long-distance carriers, few people are familiar with the names of even the regional Bells. Long-distance carriers have also been increasing their brand identity by offering credit cards. On the other hand, the Baby Bells have been *changing* their names. For example, over the past few years in New York, New York Telephone changed its name to Nynex and will again change its name to Bell Atlantic should that merger come to fruition.

- The Baby Bells will be hurt by AT&T's divestiture of Lucent Technologies (its equipment manufacturing arm). Before the spin-off, AT&T did not compete too aggressively with the Baby Bells for local service. This was because AT&T believed that if it posed too big of a threat to the Baby Bells, the Bells would not purchase AT&T's telephone equipment. Now that Lucent Technologies is a separate company, AT&T does not have to be concerned with losing telephone equipment orders.

- Deregulation is problematic for the Bells because they must expose their larger markets (with 1996 revenue of roughly $90 billion) to competition from the long-distance carriers while only being allowed to compete in the smaller long-distance market (with 1996 revenues of roughly $70 billion).

Antiquated Infrastructure

The Baby Bells have less-sophisticated phone lines than the long-distance carriers. This is because the Baby Bells deliver their traffic over copper wires, whereas the long-distance carriers transmit their signals over using fiberoptic cable (the width of a human hair), which boasts the following assets:

- It carries about a thousand times as much information as copper and does so with greater reliability and greater security; for instance, fiber is immune to interfering signals (unlike copper) such as neighboring wires, radio broadcasts and lightning bolts.
- Video signals do not fade nearly as much on fiber as on copper.
- Fiberoptics require far less maintenance than copper.

Separately, while all of the major long-distance companies' phone lines connect to digital switches, only about 70 percent of the Baby Bells' phone lines are connected to digital switches.

The Baby Bells' older infrastructure is problematic for two primary reasons. First, the disadvantages of copper relative to fiberoptics mean that the Baby Bells must invest heavily in the upgrading of their infrastructure. The problem is that the Bells cannot afford to replace all of their land lines without reducing their dividend payouts. (In fact, Pacific Telesis became the first Baby Bell to reduce its dividend by announcing that its payout will be slashed by 42 percent in the summer of 1996.) And of course, reduced dividend payouts make the stocks of the Bells much less appealing.

The second major problem with the Baby Bells' infrastructure becoming obsolete is that their earnings may be overstated. This is because regulators often require RBOCs to depreciate their assets over periods of time that exceed their

T I P

> The Baby Bells will benefit less from offering long-distance service within their regions than you may realize because they already receive access fees for these calls.

useful lives. Therefore, long depreciation schedules result in the RBOCs taking unjustifiably low annual depreciation charges, resulting in earnings appearing artificially high. (Regulators often use artificially high earnings as a justification to deny rate increases.)

Capacity Constraints

To a large extent, the Baby Bells and long-distance carriers will enter each other's business by leasing and reselling capacity from one another. This reselling is one area in which the Baby Bells have an advantage over the long-distance carriers because there is less capacity in the Bells' regions since there is only one carrier per region. However, there is much more excess capacity in the long-distance networks since there are three major long-distance companies. Thus, the regional carriers could lease long-distance capacity for reselling at discounts of around 30 to 60 percent. However, the long-distance carriers will only be able to lease capacity for reselling from the RBOCs at discounts of around 5 percent.

TIP

CAPs might be takeover targets for long-distance carriers because CAPs serve lucrative business customers and avoid paying access fees to Baby Bells.

In fact, AT&T is realizing the difficulty of trying to profit by reselling capacity with a very narrow spread between wholesale and retail prices. Frontier Corp.'s [Rochester, New York] wholesale price is only 5 percent less than its $12.96-a-month retail price for basic service, leaving AT&T a margin of just 65 cents a month per line to cover its marketing and billing costs.[4]

Other Sources of Profitability

In addition to benefiting from the disparity in capacity, the Baby Bells are trying to boost their earnings by undertaking a number of other measures:

1. The Bells are trying to sell more access lines per home for things such as fax machines, cable modems, and other family members. Similarly, the Bells are trying to sell related products such as ISDN lines, three-way calling, and Caller-ID.

2. As discussed previously, the Baby Bells will be somewhat successful in offering long-distance service within their regions.

3. Mergers among the Baby Bells are possible. In fact, Nynex and Bell Atlantic, as well as Pacific Telesis and SBC, have already announced mergers. (Notice how these mergers are in contiguous areas to facilitate long distance calls.) These mergers will allow the Bells to reduce advertising, administrative, and payroll costs.

4. Several of the Baby Bells are diversifying abroad. For instance, Nynex owns 19 percent of Thailand's telephone company and offers cable service in Britain. Also, SBC Communications owns 10 percent of Telefonos de Mexico, Mexico's dominant phone company.

---

[4] John R Hayes, "The Bundler," *Forbes* 157, no. 8 (April 22, 1996), pp. 82–88.

COMPETITIVE ACCESS PROVIDERS

In addition to the problems presented by the Baby Bells' obstinance (discussed previously), the CAPs are handicapped in several other ways.

- Only about half of the states allow CAPs to exist in any form.
- Some of the states that allow CAPs do not require number portability. The significant risk of lost business presented by changing a phone number deters many businesses from using a CAP. Also, businesses that change their phone numbers have to inform all of their clients, customers, and regulators as well as reorder stationery and business cards.
- Many customers that switch to a CAP complain of lower-quality connections and dialing.
- It is very expensive for the small CAPs to replicate even small parts of the Baby Bells' infrastructure.

CELLULAR PHONES

Many areas of the Information Superhighway are nothing more than technological capabilities in search of applications. However, cellular subscriber growth is spurred by the utility that cellular phones offer. Cellular service is practical for both the customers and for phone companies.

Utility for Customers

Cellular phones are an essential part of mobile offices for workers on the move and are a lifeline for people who need to stay in touch. Also, cellular phones can be marketed as a safety device. For instance, having a cellular phone in your car will allow you to call for help without leaving your car. Similarly, a cellular phone in the home means, intruders cannot sabotage home phone lines (there are no lines).

Another reason why cellular service is popular is that costs have been declining. Cellular operators subsidize the cost of the handset. Also, since cellular service lacks differentiation and since customers can easily switch carriers, cellular companies are competing on price. These lower costs, in turn, make cellular service more affordable for other potential customers. Thus, the more subscribers the cellular companies serve, the further they can reduce their costs.

Additionally, the functionality of cellular phones is improving. Some cellular providers offer features such as "call waiting" and "call return." Also, since cellular phones' dial tones are the same as land-line phones' dial tones, cellular phones can be used for modems, fax machines, and voice mail.

T I P

👉 It is more important that a cellular phone company increase its minutes of usage than the number of its subscribers. This is because there is less churn and lower marketing expenses associated with the former. In fact, when subscriber growth slows, margins usually expand since subscriber acquisition costs plunge.

Utility for Providers

There is also a great deal of utility in cellular service for phone companies because it is much more expedient to construct a few cellular towers every few miles than to lay hundreds of miles of telephone lines. Cellular phones are especially well suited for areas that have low subscriber density, such as Nevada, since long copper lines do not have to be laid. Similarly, cellular is a much more economical option than land-line service in mountainous regions such as Colorado, areas with many lakes such as Minnesota, and swamplands such as those in Louisiana. Cellular phones are also popular in developing countries since the deployment time needed to bring a city up on cellular can be as little as three months. Also, maintaining cellular infrastructure only costs a fraction of maintaining land-lines.

Moreover, partially due to lower maintenance costs, it may become cheaper for the Baby Bells to offer wireless service rather than wire-line service. Thus, even though the Baby Bells have over $300 billion (and over 65 million tons of copper) invested in their copper wire-lines, the Baby Bells could encourage their customers to use wireless service.

As fantastic as this scenario sounds, there is a paradigm for it; a similar scenario is currently being played out in the banking industry. Since it is cheaper for the banks to provide their services through ATMs and over the phone than at the teller windows, banks are beginning to charge their customers to use teller services. This is true even though the banks have much more invested in their branches than in ATM machines and telephone services.

Cellular Economics

By the mid-1990s, the cellular companies had pretty much saturated their prime prospects, the business customers. Consequently, the cellular operators began trying to attract more marginal users. Proponents of the cellular industry hold that declining average revenues per user (ARPUs) resulting from marginal customers are not problematic. Their argument goes that since the incremental costs (additional costs after fixed costs are covered) associated with providing cellular service

T I P

One niche of opportunity within the cellular phone industry are cellular companies such as Vanguard Cellular Systems 360° Communications—that serve rural markets:

- Rural markets are less vulnerable to fraud than higher-density markets.

- Rural markets derive a large portion of their profits from roaming fees (from other subscribers passing through their territory), which are high margined since there are no marketing or customer service costs associated with serving roamers.

- Since PCS transmitting towers have limited ranges, they must be situated closer together than cellular towers. Thus, PCS towers are prohibitively expensive to deploy in rural areas, and as a result, PCS companies may want to lease capacity on cellular transmitting facilities in rural areas.

are so low, cellular companies can maximize their profits by maximizing the usage of their cellular systems (by reducing prices) even if the average revenues per user are reduced.

However, analysts that are concerned with lower average revenue per user would counter the optimists' argument with the following joke. "A department store manager told the department store's president that he had both good news and bad news to report. The good news, the store manager said, is that sales volume is soaring. Merchandise is flying out of the door. The bad news is that we are losing a little bit of money on every sale."

All jokes aside, the cellular operators face the following challenges:

- To many people, cellular phones are an unnecessary novelty. Thus, the churn (cancellation) rate was 30 percent in 1995.

- Large telecommunications companies are bundling many of their services and are taking losses on the cellular portion. As a result of very low cellular rates charged by these bundlers, the pure cellular companies must lower their prices as well.

- Some residents try to block the installation of cellular towers and antennas with zoning laws based on the fear that electromagnetic fields are not safe. As a result, cellular companies' costs of building their infrastructure rises since they are pressured into camouflaging their infrastructure. For instance, if you looked at pictures of trees, highway signs, and light poles you would not be able to distinguish the authentic objects from the disguised cellular stations and antennas.

- The cellular telephone industry loses as much as $1 billion annually (or 7 percent of industry revenues) due to phone fraud. Cellular phone companies are trying to develop ways to reduce fraud and to ensure that cellular conversations will be kept private. However, the government is opposed to scrambling techniques that too effectively accomplish these goals since the government would not be able to wire tap these phones.

- Until the mid-1990s, there were only two wireless telephone operators in each region of the nation. However, these duopolies are being challenged with the addition of three PCS licensees in each region. In fact, Bell Atlantic reduced prices on its cellular service in Washington, D.C., shortly after Sprint established its PCS system there.

Analytical Considerations

Before investing in cellular phone companies such as United States Cellular Corporation or AirTouch Communications you should consider the following:

- The penetration rate (which is the number of subscribers divided by the population that the cellular operator serves) should be above the industry average.

- The company's operating cash flow margins (which is operating cash flow divided by revenues) should be rising.

- Subscriber acquisition costs (which consist of commissions and marketing expenses associated with attracting cellular subscribers as well as the cost of the cellular handsets) should be declining.

- Similarly, you should search for companies that recover their subscriber acquisition costs quickly. The ratio for making this determination is subscriber acquisition costs divided by average monthly revenue per user. The lower this ratio, the better.

- The spread between revenues per minute and interconnect charges (which cellular companies pay to wired telephone companies to connect phone calls) should be expanding.

- The company's market capitalization "per pop" ratio should be below the industry average. (POPs represent population, or points of presence, in the cellular operator's area.) This ratio indicates how richly the stock market values each of a cellular operator's potential subscribers. The lower the ratio, the more attractive the company is to a potential acquirer.

- The company should have substantial net operating losses to shield future income from future federal taxation.

- The company should have a manageable debt load.

PERSONAL COMMUNICATIONS SERVICES (PCS)

The promise of personal communication services (PCS) is that, in addition to using PCS for wireless phone services, subscribers will eventually be able to transmit data, paging, and video via personal digital assistants. Another benefit attributed to PCS (versus cellular) is that PCS has much more capacity because it operates at higher (1,800 megahertz) frequencies than does cellular (800 megahertz). Also, PCS operates on all digital technology versus cellular's analog technology. Due to the abundance of PCS capacity, PCS operators are able to offer rates low enough to entice many cellular subscribers.

Additionally, PCS towers are located closer together than cellular towers. Thus, PCS devices do not require as much battery power, meaning PCS handsets should be smaller, lighter, and therefore cheaper than cellular phones.

Because of these advantages over cellular, Australia has completely bypassed the cellular stage in adopting PCS. Also, PCS is much more popular than cellular in many parts of Asia.

Obstacles for PCS

It will be extremely expensive to roll out PCS nationwide:

- Companies wishing to offer PCS service such as Sprint and AT&T, spent roughly $7.7 billion when PCS spectrum was auctioned off, whereas the cellular companies did not have to pay anything for their spectrum.

- After paying for the right to use PCS spectrum, the auction winners will have to spend roughly $16 billion to build three PCS systems nationwide.

- Much of the PCS infrastructure will consist of as many as 80,000 more cell sites by the year 2000. However, it will be difficult to find enough locations for these cell sites—since these towers are as high as 150 feet, they are unsightly. Thus, community opposition and zoning restrictions could make securing enough leases difficult.

- Another expense related to establishing these cell sites is that the PCS providers will have to pay to clear parts of the radio-wave spectrum, which they won in the auctions. For example, PCS providers will have to move some utilities, railroads, and fire departments to new channels so that the spectrum to be devoted to PCS will be free from interference.

Another drawback with PCS relates to its higher frequencies, which for a given amount of power, will not travel as far as lower frequencies. Thus, PCS towers have to be placed closer together than cellular towers. Of course, wireless systems hand off calls from one transmitter to the next when users are on the move. If the transmitters are very close together and the caller is moving very fast, the PCS system might make the wrong guess about which of several adjacent cells the

T I P

☞ With all of the capacity in telecommunications, MCI Communications may have the best strategy. MCI is neither building its own cellular nor PCS infrastructure and will thus avoid paying for spectrum and building infrastructure. Rather, MCI intends to lease the excess capacity, for which its competitors paid so heavily, at deep discounts.

---

caller will enter next. Thus, the call could be switched in the wrong direction, and the connection would be lost.

Competing with Cellular

By the time PCS systems are up and running (probably by mid-1998), they will find competing against cellular very difficult. First, cellular will be entrenched, as tens of millions of Americans will subscribe to cellular services. These people will be most of the potential PCS subscribers. Thus, after spending billions of dollars on spectrum and infrastructure, PCS operators will have to spend millions of dollars annually on marketing to compete against cellular operators.

Also, cellular operators will become more competitive over the next few years. As they move from analog to digital technology, they will be able to provide much more reliable service at lower prices. In fact, the cellular operators are spending roughly $2 billion a year in making such upgrades, potentially increasing cellular capacity by between 3 and 15 times. Additionally, the digitization of cellular services will allow these companies to introduce higher-margined advanced services, will improve quality, reduce fraud, and help ensure privacy.

However, the lack of clear standards as to which digital technology the cellular industry will adopt is problematic, and the longer it takes the cellular industry to adopt a digital standard, the more of an advantage the PCS operators will have. There are three contending technologies for converting cellular systems from analog to digital technology:

1. Global Systems for Mobile communications (GSM) has already been adopted in 86 countries and accounted for about 88 percent of the world's digital cellular subscribers in early 1996.

2. Time Division Multiple Access (TDMA)—similary to GMS—is also already deployed in the United States.

3. Code Division Multiple Access (CDMA) offers the promise of superiority in terms of capacity, coverage area, security, and transmission quality and is supposed to eventually be able to transmit voice and data simultaneously. However, just as it took TDMA a few years to work out its

kinks, it will take CDMA companies such as Qualcomm, Inc., a while to work out its flaws. The risk with an unproven technology such as CDMA is that if it does not work customers will just go to another vendor. Thus, companies such as Sprint that prefer CDMA are taking an all-or-nothing gamble.

PAGERS

Many investors believe that the wide acceptance of wireless phones will result in pagers becoming obsolete. However, a closer review of the paging industry reveals that there are actually many growth opportunities for paging companies such as A Plus Network and Dial Page. In fact, the Personal Communications Industry Association has estimated that the number of subscribers to paging services will rise from 30 million in 1995 to 65 million in 2003.

Much of this growth will come as a result of penetrating more of the "mobile-professionals" market (25 million)—people who must stay in touch with their offices. Pagers are ideal for these people since their small size and light weight allows them to be used while the subscriber is on the move. Moreover, pagers have much longer battery lives and have better in-building penetration than cellular phones.

Also, pagers are inexpensive compared with other forms of wireless communication. They are so cheap, in fact, that many parents are buying them for their children. Similarly, some large restaurants are handing out pagers to their patrons waiting for tables so that they can quickly contact those on the waiting list when a table becomes available.

Image and Functionality

Pagers are becoming more popular because the image of pagers has been elevated from pagers being obtrusive to being fashionable for the following reasons: First, pagers are becoming less intrusive. Whereas pagers used to beep, they now vibrate. (Even the name of the industry has been dignified; pagers are hardly referred to as "beepers" anymore.)

Second, in 1994, Seiko introduced its Message Watch™ in a few U.S. markets. Their appeal could be another growth driver for the industry. The watch is worn like any other but also offers paging services, voice mail, and other information such as weather updates and stock market quotes. (Eventually these pagers will be able to transmit E-mail and banking information.) Also, wearing a pager in a watch form reduces the stigma some people feel when they wear traditional pagers. There is also less of a chance of losing the watch or leaving it behind.

More people will subscribe to paging services as the functionality of pagers improves:

- Some pagers are being equipped with acknowledgment features indicating that the intended recipient received the message.

- Motorola's VoiceNow™ pager alerts users that a message, which they can hear through the page, is available.

- Two-way paging allows paging subscribers to respond to incoming pages with a variety of canned phrases.

Serving Cellular Subscribers

The growth of cellular subscribers should not cannibalize paging subscribers. On the contrary, more cellular subscribers could *benefit* the paging industry; already, at least 30 percent of the people who subscribe to cellular phones also have pagers most likely because they dislike the charges incurred for receiving incoming calls on their cellular phones.

Moreover, people feel awkward receiving cellular phone calls in various situations (e.g., on a date or at a meeting), and they do not like to abruptly end cellular phone calls. Also, leaving cellular phones on standby to receive incoming calls consumes batteries quickly. Thus, many cellular users only give out their pager numbers so that they can screen calls and then return the less important calls with less expensive land-line telephones.

PAY PHONES

The publicly traded independent pay-phone companies such as Davel Communications and Peoples Telephone serve as an interesting investing niche. First, many state regulators are allowing pay phone rates to rise while their costs of leasing phone lines from the Baby Bells are falling. Since pay phones do not accept pennies, the rates increase by multiples of nickels. As rates rise to unusual rates such as $.35, some callers do not have exact change and therefore deposit too much money (e.g., two quarters), the remainder of which is pure profit. Also, more people are using pagers. Since not all of these people will have cellular phones, many of them will have to return calls from pay phones.

TRAP

⊘ It is important not to extrapolate U.S. telephone penetration rates on underdeveloped countries because these countries will not approach U.S. standards for many years to come. At the end of the last century, Lord Baden-Powell rhapsodized that the woolen industry would get an immense boost if only every African could be convinced to wear a suit. One hundred years later, Lord Baden-Powell's prediction has failed to materialize. Similarly, it is said that Brazil is the country with the most promise for the next 100 years—and it always will be.

Interestingly, the publicly traded pay phone operators have advantages over both the Baby Bells and smaller independents. First, independents have nonunionized workforces, whereas the Bells have high cost and inflexible unions. Thus, the Bells may have to send four different workers to repair, install, clean, and collect the coins from four pay phones that are on the same block. On the contrary, the independents can send one worker to service the same four phones.

Also, the host of convoluted rules and regulations are overwhelming for small independent pay-phone operators. Moreover, the small independents do not have economies of scale in installing, repairing, and collecting coins from pay phones. In some cases, workers for very small pay phone operators spend more time driving from one phone to another than servicing the phones along their routes.

Nevertheless, you should be aware of some of the drawbacks that pay phone operators face:

1. Pay phones are subject to high rates of vandalism and theft. In fact, some pay phones are literally cherry-bombed on the Fourth of July.

2. Outside phones are exposed to extreme temperatures.

3. Pay phones generate substantial toll fraud since the caller can simply walk away without being traced. Not only is no revenue generated from a fraudulent call, but the owner/operator must pay for the call.

TELEPHONE EQUIPMENT

Telephone equipment manufacturers such as Tellabs and DSC Communications should benefit from the creation of additional telephone infrastructure such as fiberoptic phone lines, coaxial cables, and PCS towers. Also, even though fully 94 percent of American households have telephones, Americans are still buying more phones per home as well as purchasing car phones and cellular personal phones. Moreover, there is tremendous potential for building telephone infrastructure in foreign countries. For instance, half of the world's population have yet to make their first phone call, fewer than 4 percent of the Chinese population have phones, and there are only about 12 phones for every 100 people in Brazil. These statistics pale in comparison with the 50 phones that exist for every 100 Americans.

TRAP

⊘ Due to the cooling in relations between the United States and China (as discussed in the chapter on the defense industry on pages 381–382), companies such as Motorola that are building wireless infrastructure in China may face a greater risk of expropriation than an opportunity to profit.

T R A P

⊘ You should avoid investing in equipment suppliers that enter into unfavorable contracts. For example, in early 1996, Sprint demanded that its vendors finance the construction, installation, and maintenance of its fledging personal communications service network. Sprint proposed to stretch out payments over 13 years and avoid any payments until at least three years after the start of the operations. Vendors that agreed to these terms would pay Sprint's imputed loan interest over many years.

Investor Concerns

Many investors believe that the promise of convergence in the telecommunications industry will be of benefit to the equipment companies. The theory is that equipment will be needed to facilitate everyone's getting into everyone else's business.

However, as discussed above, it is more likely that over the next few years, the long-distance carriers and Baby Bells will compete among themselves rather than enter the cable business. This is of less benefit to the equipment manufacturers because less equipment is needed.

A second concern is that independent telephone equipment manufacturers such as Andrew Corp. and ADC Telecommunications will be hurt by Lucent Technologies' (AT&T's former equipment unit) having been spun off from AT&T. Traditionally, the Baby Bells preferred to buy their equipment from the stand-alone suppliers rather than their nemesis, AT&T. Now that Lucent Technologies is no longer affiliated with AT&T, the Baby Bells will no longer be biased against dealing with Lucent.

A third concern revolves around the Baby Bells' shifting from a rate-of-return method of regulation to price regulation. Under the former method, the Bells had an incentive to invest as much as possible because the more money they invested, the more money they could earn. However, the reverse is true under price regulation. The fourth concern is that mergers among the Baby Bells will enhance the Bells' leverage relative to the equipment suppliers.

COMPUTER MANUFACTURERS

Personal computer (PC) shipments soared 25 percent, to 59.7 million units, worldwide in 1995. Much of this growth could be attributed to voracious demand in foreign countries. For instance, shipments surged 71 percent in Japan while advancing 30 percent in Europe. While the American PC market is more mature, shipments still increased an impressive 21 percent in the United States in 1995.

Reasons for the wide appeal and growth of personal computers include the following:

- *Exploding price performance.* Moore's Law (named after Gordon Moore, a cofounder of Intel Corporation) holds that computer chip companies will be able to double the number of transistors that they can place on semiconductors every 18 months, meaning the price performance of PCs doubles every 18 months. In other words, if you wait 18 months to buy a computer, you can either buy a comparable computer for half of today's cost or you can buy a computer with twice the power for the same price.

  To further illustrate how far computing power has come, consider that a 64-bit Nintendo game player that cost $250 in 1995 would have cost $14 million in 1985. Similarly, there is more processing power in singing greeting cards than existed in 1950.

  There is debate as to whether Moore's Law is sustainable. One reason for doubt is the exorbitant expense of building semiconductor plants (or fabs). The cost of each fab can easily run $1 billion and is rising quickly. In fact, there have been estimates that by 2006, Intel will have to spend its entire market capitalization to build one fab. Also, the circuitry in computer chips is becoming so small that the associated companies will soon have to begin splitting atoms, which can cause an atomic explosion. Also, miniature sub-micron circuit sizes throw off increasingly stronger electric fields that interfere with the chip's performance. Heat, too. Contemporary chips throw off as much as 10 times the heat as a comparable cookstove surface. Electrons start tunneling through the insulating walls, threatening to short the circuit.[5]

  However, other analysts believe that human ingenuity will continue to find the means to perpetuate Moore's Law. For instance, computer chip designers are trying to extend Moore's Law by using three-dimensional silicon chips instead of two-dimensional chips. Other chip designers are using multistate logic versus binary logic (i.e., 0,1,2,3,4 not 0 and 1). Additionally, some chipmakers believe that computing power can continue to rise by replacing silicon wafers with gallium arsenide or by developing biological computing.

- *PCs are consuming many functions that other electronic appliances have traditionally performed.* Thus, if you buy a PC with a CD-ROM, you can avoid buying a fax machine, telephone, answering machine, or even a stereo.

- *The replacement cycle for computers is very short.* Most people replace their computers every three to five years. For instance, when Microsoft released its Windows 95 operating system in August of 1995, many computer consultants advised their clients to replace their PCs if those PCs were over three years old rather than try to install the new operating system.

---

[5] Michael S Malone, "Chips Triumphant," *Forbes,* February 26, 1996, p. 82.

- *Computers are now extremely user friendly.* As recently as the early 1990s, one had to be a computer expert to operate a computer; now, PCs have evolved to plug-and-play usability.

- *The spread of capitalism should help foreign computer sales because computers are essential in enhancing efficiency.* Also, there are low penetration rates of personal computers in foreign countries, even developed countries.

Despite these growth drivers, the following are concerns that investors should have regarding the personal computer industry:

- Because more powerful versions are continually released, *PCs become obsolete very quickly*, and thus, the older versions must be sold at discounted prices.

- Largely as a result of Intel's "Intel Inside" advertising campaign, *PCs are increasingly being perceived as commodities.* Since Intel (and Microsoft) have convinced the public that it is their products that make computers run well, people are not as concerned about the casings in which Intel's chips and Microsoft's operating systems are delivered.

- Due to unrelenting price competition and commoditization, *PC manufacturers* such as Packard Bell *have been accused of placing used parts in computers that are marketed as new.* Such actions damage the image of PC manufacturers and risk action from the Justice Department.

- The *Japanese computer manufacturers are just beginning new offensives into the PC business.* Companies such as Sony that have a superb brand image will be particularly problematic for U.S. computer manufacturers.

- *The customer service that computer manufacturers offer* their customers after the purchase has been made *is an unrecorded liability.* With all of the training and other expenses involved in answering customers questions, each phone call costs at least $50 to handle. Worse for the computer companies is that some of the computer problems are actually caused by faulty components, but rather than calling the component manufacturers, PC owners often call the company whose name is on the box in which the computer was purchased.

- As computers are increasingly used to communicate, *regulators may decide that computer manufacturers must contribute to universal funds* (from which telephone services are subsidized). Moreover, regulators could make these subsidies more expensive by ruling that schools, libraries, and rural hospitals are also entitled to these subsidies.

- Another hidden liability for computer manufacturers is *the disposal of their computers.* "Some of the toxic substances in PCs include phosphorus that puts the color in computer displays, the lead baked into plastic casings, and the mercury in some switches."[6] If these computers are dumped in a regular landfill, the lead can leach into the water. Thus, municipalities could sue the computer manufacturers by tracing the released lead them.

- *It is more difficult to sell PCs in Europe and Asia.* One reason is that there are fewer major electronics stores in foreign countries. Moreover, fewer people are knowledgeable about computers in Europe and Asia, which means that potential customers have fewer sources to consult with when deliberating PC purchases. Finally, most PCs in emerging markets are local brand names that are made from imported components. Therefore, there may be more opportunity in emerging markets for component manufacturers such as Intel than assemblers such as Compaq Computer®.

Importance of Standards

Computers must be designed to operate on dominant operating systems. (Operating systems are where the integration of hardware and software takes place.) It is imperative that these operating systems maintain a large share of their markets. If manufacturers of operating systems lose market share, fewer software programmers would be willing to write software to run on that operating system. Also, consumers will not purchase computers with limited operating systems because there will not be a wide assortment of software available.

Another problem with having too little market share in the computer industry is that supplies may be hard to acquire, especially if the computer manufacturer relies on customized parts. An additional problem for these computer companies is that they cannot resell upgraded versions of their computers to their installed base of customers.

One way that developers of operating systems have quickly set industry standards is by licensing their technology to a wide array of computer manufacturers. Aside from quickly capturing market share, licensing results in the licensor collecting high-margin and recurring licensing fees. Interestingly, one of the ways that Microsoft's Windows™ operating system won dominance was that Microsoft's licensing agreements required the computer companies that used Windows to pay a royalty to Microsoft for each computer that they manufactured regardless of the operating system that they installed. Since it would not be profitable to pay a royalty to both Microsoft and another operating system designer, the computer companies relied solely on Windows. On the other hand, one of the greatest strategic mistakes that Apple® made was not licensing its technology soon enough.

---

[6] "Difficulties in Discarding Personal Computers." *Investor's Business Daily,* November 6, 1995, p. A6.

However, licensors can experience a couple of drawbacks to licensing their technology. First, licensing can result in the licensees capturing too much market share at the expense of the licensor. Also, research and development can consume a larger percentage of the licensor's sales since the licensor will share its revenues with its licensees.

Mail Order Computer Manufacturers

Mail order companies such as Dell Computer and Gateway 2000 are an interesting niche within the personal computer industry. The mail order manufacturers are more flexible than their competitors that sell through retail channels. Since mail order companies custom-design their PCs, they do not accumulate large inventories of finished systems and thus do not have the problems associated with obsolete inventory.

Another advantage that mail order PC manufacturers have is that (since they only manufacture custom-designed PCs) they carry very lean inventories of components, which is extremely important for manufacturers in rapidly changing industries. Low inventories allow manufacturers to quickly switch to suppliers of newer and more powerful components; thus, mail order companies can more efficiently deliver state-of-the-art computers than the mass producers. Speaking to every customer also helps mail order firms reduce their inventories of older components. For instance, a mail order representative could suggest that a casual computer user save money by purchasing a PC with a slightly slower microprocessor.

The mail order companies' highly efficient instantaneous mass-customization manufacturing process enables these firms to offer exceptional customer service. For example, when a customer places his order for a computer, the sales agent types the requirements into her computer. This information is simultaneously transmitted to the factory floor where the assembly of the computer begins in nearly real time. Then, the computer can be shipped to the customer by overnight delivery. Finally, mail order companies can undercut their competitors on price since they do not have to factor retailers' profits into the price of their PCs.

Internet-Application Devices

Many observers believe that today's PCs are powerful since most people use their PCs for just word processing, spreadsheets, and playing games, and do not need computers that are more powerful than the Federal Aviation Administration's entire air traffic control system. Moreover, more and more people wish to use their computers simply as a device to obtain information.

> As the computer becomes a device for communications instead of calculation, as the era of personal computing becomes that of personal communications, the power of our digital tools will reside less in their

processors than in the power of the processors to which they are connected; that is, their value will be in the information to which they
have access.[7]

Accordingly, there has been a great deal of talk about the development of
inexpensive (e.g., $500) Internet-application devices, designed to connect people
to the Internet. Already, Apple Computer has turned its Newton™ digital assistant
into a portable Internet terminal. Similarly, LSI Logic Corp. has developed a single
computer chip that will make the $500 Internet access device possible.

However, even Marc Andreesen, founder of Netscape Communications has
said that these devices will complement, rather than supplant traditional personal
computers. Since computing power is a sign of prestige, employees will be averse
to having their PCs replaced with inexpensive Internet-application devices.
Additionally, since computer files are personal, most people would like their files
stored on their own PCs, not in some distant server. If you want to author anything, you have to own your own PC.

Also, as video and sound grow more complex on the Internet, special video
and audio chips will be needed so users can download the material they find there.
These enhancements could boost the price to over $1,200. Since PC prices are
falling, many people would prefer just to pay a little bit more and get a PC.

Mainframe Computers

A few years ago, conventional wisdom was that computer networks would render
mainframe computers manufactured by companies such as IBM and Unisys obsolete. (The attraction of network servers produced by companies such as Cisco
Systems and Cabletron Systems is that many personal computers can be tied
together while sharing access to peripherals like printers.)

However, mainframe computers are proving to be resurgent. One reason is
that there are far fewer continuing costs associated with mainframes versus networks. For example, in a typical mainframe system, 80 percent of the lifetime cost
is in the one-time, up-front investment in hardware and software. The remaining
20 percent of the cost is in maintenance and management. With a distribution network, the ratio is just the reverse. Also, far more people are affected by computer
downtime with servers compared with mainframes.

Additionally, many mainframe computers are outliving their intended lives,
but this causes an interesting problem of its own: Most mainframes were originally
designed to see only the last two digits of the year because beginning in the 1950s,
computer programmers saved two bytes of precious memory by dropping "19"
from the continuous date function. This seemed like a prudent decision at the time
because memory was scarce and mainframes were built on the assumption that

---

[7] Richard A Shaffer, "Derivative Computers for the Mass Market," *Forbes* 156, no. 13 (December 4,
1995), p. 266.

T R A P

⊘ Software retailers such as NeoStar and Egghead will be threatened by falling software prices. For example, . . . in 1984, the bestselling Lotus 1-2-3 spreadsheet retailed for $495. Now you get Quattro Pro for $60. So a retailer who used to make $100 on each box sold now makes less than $15.[8]Another reason that software prices are falling is that people usually already know which software they want to buy before they enter the stores. (Unlike books, customers cannot browse through software to determine which is most suitable.) Thus, price is the sole criterion for purchasing software.

they would be replaced long before 2000. Unfortunately for the companies that depend on these mainframes, the first seconds of the year 2000 will wreak havoc. For instance, assume you make a long-distance phone call a few minutes before midnight on December 31, 1999. At midnight, the phone company's computer will jump to the year "00" and bill you for a 100-year phone call. Similarly, if you make a bank deposit on December 31, 1999, the bank might credit your account for 100 years' worth of interest by the next day. Thus, companies such as Viasoft or Analysts International that are capable of remedying this problem may benefit from lucrative contracts.

COMPUTER SOFTWARE

Software companies should benefit from the growth of the Internet and on-line services. These vehicles will make it convenient for software retailers and manufacturers to sell their programs. For instance, when software is sold over the Internet or over on-line services, real estate costs as well as logistics and inventory management problems are eliminated.

One of the most interesting niches to consider are the software companies (such as Cybercash) that can facilitate on-line commerce. Estimates from reputable sources indicate that there will be some $30 billion worth of on-line commerce in the year 2000. This should not be hard to believe because this represents just a small fraction of total commerce conducted annually.

Also, the fear of credit card fraud when transacting business on-line should dissipate for a number of reasons:

1. On-line transactions are no less secure than purchasing goods over the phone. In either case, you do not know to whom you are giving your credit card information.

---

[8] Damon Darlin, "Software Retails Survive on Minimal Margins," *Forbes* 156, no. 13 (December 4, 1995), pp. 262–64.

2. Even if there is on-line fraud, the credit card companies protect their customers against fraud after an initial (e.g., $50) deductible, some major telecommunications players will guarantee even this initial deductible. These measures almost completely insulate the customer from financial liabilities arising from on-line fraud.

3. Many people already conduct their brokerage and banking activities on-line. Thus, if people are not afraid to have much of their net worth exposed to on-line services, why should they be afraid to make a small purchase on-line?

Despite the benefits software companies will experience due to Internet growth, you should be aware of the following concerns before investing in a software company:

- Internet-surfing is an inexpensive alternative to buying software.

- The Cannibal Principle is at work in the software industry. The cannibal principle basically suggests that semiconductors absorb the functions of what were previously discrete software programs. Semiconductor manufacturers incorporate software into new computer chips and then basically give away the software programming for free on the next upgrade cycle.

- Software is being perceived more and more as merely a commodity: (1) Computer makers are bundling more software in "suites." These suites are often provided free with computer purchases. (2) More software is being pre-installed on computers.

- Even if sales of personal computers for home use rise, this does *not* mean software sales will rise at an equivalent rate because home users only buy about one-quarter as much software as business users in the year after the purchase.

- Software sales may slow as people buy fewer advanced versions of software, resulting from a slowing of the PC replacement cycle.

- Software is susceptible to counterfeiting since larger percentages of sales are coming from countries that are ineffective in countering the pirating of intellectual property. Also, more software is being copied since computer users are transmitting software over the Internet.

- American software companies depend greatly on foreign software programmers. However, many politicians dislike U.S. software companies' hiring foreigners at wages below those paid to Americans. Thus, there is a risk that Congress may require employers to pay 10 percent more for such labor or cut the number of foreign professionals allowed into the U.S. from 65,000 a year to 30,000 a year.

- Software companies are often the target of securities-fraud lawsuits. In fact, "more than half of the top 150 Silicon Valley firms have been hit with securities-fraud class actions after sudden stock drops."[9] Thus, the industry would benefit greatly from limits to the ways that securities-fraud suits can be brought in federal court.

SEMICONDUCTORS

A semiconductor is a collection of tiny interconnected switches that direct the flow of electronic currents in controlled patterns. Many people believe that semiconductors are solely purchased for installation in computers. However, semiconductors are becoming more common in virtually every aspect of our lives. Already, there are semiconductors in automobiles, telephones, VCRs, medical equipment such as pacemakers, and weapons systems. In the near future you could well find semiconductors in cartons (that open on demand); winter coats (that become warmer as temperatures fall), and light bulbs (that become brighter as it gets darker outside).

The semiconductor industry can be broken down into three roughly equal segments. One segment can be classified as "logic products." These products include microprocessors, programmable logic chips, and other specialty logic products for applications such as multimedia and communications. Within this sector, microprocessors make up the largest portion. Microprocessors, the brains of the PC, contain the logical elements for performing calculations carrying out stored instructions. While Intel dominates about 80 percent of the microprocessor market, companies that are challenging Intel include Advanced Micro Devices and National Semiconductor.

Another segment of the semiconductor market consists of memory products such as dynamic random access memory (DRAM) products that allow computers to store data. Companies, such as Micron Electronics, Inc. and Texas Instruments, that manufacture memory chips have benefited from software bloat—that is software programmers designed their programs to consume increasing amounts of memory. (This bloatware also benefited the computer manufacturers since consumers were on a perpetual upgrade treadmill; they had to buy new computers that had enough memory to handle increasingly bloated software.)

Now, memory producers are suffering from the reverse trend: As discussed previously computer users are beginning to realize that they do not need the most advanced computers or the most recent software releases. In fact, Microsoft reoffered its older Word 5.1 word processing software after customers complained that its Word 6.0 hogged too much memory and was too slow. As a result of software's becoming less bloated, less memory is required to operate such programs.

---

[9] G. Pascal Zachary and Jill Abramson, "Silicon Valley Firms Among the Biggest Beneficiaries of Tort Reforms," *The Wall Street Journal* CCXXVII, no. 49 (March 11, 1996), p. A1.

Finally, about one-third of the semiconductor market is composed of miniature integrated circuit devices including amplifiers, rectifiers, and other mechanisms.

The Book-to-Bill Ratio

Many investors rely upon the book-to-bill ratio to determine the health of the semiconductor industry. The book-to-bill ratio is simply the dollar amount of orders divided by the dollar amount of semiconductor shipments. For instance, a book-to-bill ratio of 122 indicates that $122 worth of semiconductors have been ordered for every $100 worth of semiconductors shipped. Investors generally like to see the book-to-bill ratio rise.

However, on closer inspection, you will see the following flaws with the book-to-bill ratio:

- The ratio can become overstated if customers inflate their orders in order to be sure that they will obtain their necessary supplies of semiconductors. Conversely, sharply higher monthly billings (shipments) could force the book-to-bill ratio lower even though improved shipments bode well. Thus, it is important to consider the sales and order numbers separately.

- Because the book-to-bill ratio measures revenue instead of volume, a drop in semiconductor prices would reduce the value of industry orders. Thus, the declining numerator would cause the entire ratio to fall. However, this scenario could disguise a strong semiconductor industry. For instance, volumes could be rising while prices are falling.

- Shorter lead times will result in lower orders. Similarly, semiconductor companies whose orders are for two years hence are in worse financial condition than those whose orders are for two months hence.

- Since the book-to-bill ratio is actually a three-month moving average, current trends are disguised. For instance, if March is a particularly strong month for orders while January and February were extremely weak, buoyant sales in March would be diluted by the two previous months.

T I P

When there is a glut of semiconductor manufacturing capacity, it is best to invest in semiconductor companies that do not own fabs. Rather, companies such as Xilinx and Altera rely on outside contractors for their production, and will be able to take advantage of excess capacity in negotiating manufacturing contracts.

Niches of Opportunity

In my opinion, the following are among the most interesting areas of the semiconductor industry:

- *Nonvolatile memory chips.* These chips, manufactured by companies such as Atmel Corp., retain information even when their power supply is turned off.

- *Flash memory.* Companies such as Intel manufacture flash memory chips, which are primarily used for portable products.

- *Encoders* are chips that compress video for entertainment and transmission purposes. Companies like C-Cube Microsystems are designing the chips that are necessary to operate digital video disk players and digital video cameras.

- *Programmable logic* is a technology that allows customers to program a logic chip for a specific function, rather than ordering a chip preprogrammed. Programmable chips, designed by companies such as Xilinx Inc. and Altera Corp., can be programmed in one day whereas other chips have to be ordered six months ahead of time.

- Since fabs become obsolete within two or three years, semiconductor companies have insatiable demand for *the equipment that is used to manufacture semiconductors.* Thus, companies such as Applied Materials (a producer of wafer fabrication equipment) and Watkins-Johnson (a producer of chemical vapor-deposition equipment) should benefit from this demand. Moreover, much of the same equipment can be used to make both silicon chips and the much-heralded flat-panel (e.g., television) displays. In fact, firms that make machines for etching or cleaning semiconductors are now offering lines of flat-panel display products.

ON-LINE SERVICES

On-line service providers have been growing at torrential rates in the 1990s. Up from essentially no subscribers in 1991, on-line services had roughly 11 million subscribers at the end of 1995. Moreover, in April 1996, *Business Week* reported that America Online was attracting 75,000 subscribers every week.[10]

Despite this tremendous growth, you should be aware of the following potential dangers of investing in on-line service providers:

- To many people, on-line services are a mere novelty that soon wears off. Thus, you should be aware that on-line companies such as America

---

[10] Amy Cortese, "The Online World of Steve Case," Business Week, April 15, 1996, p. 78.

Online and CompuServe have extremely high churn rates—a measure of the number of customers that cancel their service within one year of subscribing. Moreover, since on-line services are so new, it is difficult to calculate the churn rate; many customers have been on-line subscribers for less than a year.

- Many people interested in cyberspace will simply go directly to the World Wide Web.

- Some on-line service providers capitalize (rather than expense) the costs associated with acquiring new users. When such costs are capitalized, profits may often be overstated. For instance, *Business Week* reported that America Online's losses would have increased from $33.6 million to $84.4 million in 1995 if America Online expensed (rather than capitalized) its subscriber acquisition costs.[11]

- Cable can present serious competition for the on-line services. As cable increasingly narrowcasts, such programming will appeal to people who may have otherwise used on-line services for entertainment or informational purposes. For example, individual investors can more easily obtain information from CNBC than by subscribing to on-line services. Also, watching television is much cheaper than paying per-hour fees to on-line service companies.

- On-line services are sometimes responsible for the content of their subscribers' electronic messages. This presents a number of problems for the on-line operators: (1) It is impossible to monitor the millions of messages that are transmitted on on-line systems; (2) even if it were possible to monitor so many messages, subscribers would be opposed to such censorship; (3) on-line services could be sued for copyright infringement committed by their members; and (4) on-line services could be sued for worse crimes. For example, if one on-line user told another user how to make a bomb, the on-line service could be sued for the damage that such bomb caused.

---

[11] Ibid., p. 81.

8

Financial Services

Most stocks in the financial services industry normally trade at below market P/E multiples. One reason for this is that banks have traditionally been low-growth stocks because they must be cautious in their primary business, which is making loans. Similarly, the property and casualty insurers trade at low multiples because their conservative underwriting and investment cultures result in these companies' growing slowly. The brokerage stocks traditionally trade at low multiples because their future prosperity could be jeopardized by a sudden drop in the stock market. Also, the stocks of brokerage firms that are heavily engaged in trading for their own account (a.k.a. principal transactions) typically trade at even lower multiples since they bear even more risk than stocks of brokerage firms that do *not* trade for their own accounts. Therefore, you should not assume that stocks of financial service companies are undervalued just because they are trading at below market P/E multiples.

BANKS

Economic Sensitivity

The banking industry is economically sensitive. Since banks face less demand for credit when their local economies are weak, they may lower their lending standards in hopes of boosting loan originations. Also, a sluggish economy is bad for banks because it becomes more difficult for borrowers to repay their loans. The result of deteriorating loan portfolios is greater provisions for loan losses. Since these provisions are direct charges against earnings, earnings growth will naturally be restrained when banks' loan portfolios deteriorate.

TIP

Even though a vibrant economy makes it easier for borrowers to repay their loans, it is best to avoid investing in bank stocks at the height of economic prosperity. Since the economy is cyclical, peaks are followed by troughs.

Net Interest Income

Net interest income is the largest contributor to banks' earnings. Thus, it is imperative to review the components of net interest income. Net interest income is simply total interest income minus total interest expense. In our example on page 210, net interest income is $33, the difference between total interest income ($100) and total interest expense ($67).

Total interest income consists of interest earned by banks on the loans that it has outstanding as well as interest earned on its bond portfolio. Factors that affect a bank's total interest income include the following:

- *Competition among lenders.* When there is little competition among lenders, banks can price their loans higher, producing more interest income.

- *Competition from nontraditional sources.* This can reduce banks' loan originations and thus their interest income. These sources include credit card issuers, automakers' financing arms, and mortgage banks. Also, banks' corporate customers can reduce their demand for bank debt by issuing their own commercial paper. In fact, many of the country's corporations are finding it cheaper and more expedient to issue commercial paper than to assume commercial loans since some corporations' credit ratings are higher than their banks' credit ratings.

- *Insufficient demand for loans.* This can reduce interest income; for instance, when corporations' cash flows rise (e.g., due to aggressive downsizing and streamlining), they may not need to borrow money. Thus, banks may price loans lower to encourage borrowing.

- *The maturity of the banks' portfolio.* Bonds of shorter maturities have lower yields than longer-term securities.

Total interest expense is the aggregate of interest paid to depositors, interest paid to holders of certificates of deposit (CDs), interest paid on short-term borrowings (e.g., discount borrowings from the Federal Reserve), and interest paid on the bank's long-term debt.

The following are among the ratios that you can use to determine how effectively the bank has been generating net interest income:

- *Interest income-to-earning assets.* This ratio simply divides total interest income (e.g., from bonds and loans) by earning assets (such as loans and securities). The higher this ratio, the better. In our example on page 210, this ratio is 6 percent ($100/$1,658).

- *Interest expenses-to-earning assets.* This ratio simply divides total interest expense (e.g., interest paid to depositors) by earning assets. The lower this ratio, the better. In our example, this ratio is 4 percent ($67/$1,658).

- *Net interest income-to-earning assets.* This ratio simply divides net interest income (total interest income minus total interest expense) by earning assets. The higher this ratio, the better. In our example, this ratio is 2 percent ($33/$1,658).

- *Earning assets-to-total assets.* This ratio illustrates the percentage of a bank's assets that are earning interest and yield-related fee income. The higher this ratio, the better. In our example, this ratio is 90.5 percent ($1,658/$1,833).

- *Core deposits-to-total deposits.* The more core deposits a bank has relative to its total deposits, the less risk there is in a bank's losing its customers to competing banks that offer higher interest rates.

- *Loan-to-deposit.* The higher this ratio rises, the less liquid the bank becomes. When banks become illiquid, they have to resort to wholesale borrowing in order to increase their loan originations. Wholesale borrowing is generally more expensive than retail borrowing. Another disadvantage of wholesale borrowing is that there is no chance of selling other products (e.g., insurance and mutual funds) as is the case with retail deposits. Thus, it is wise to find a bank with a loan-to-deposit ratio that is lower than the average in its market. Then, the bank under review will have the capacity to make further loans from its deposits while competing banks will be forced to fund their loans from wholesale borrowings. In our example, the loan-to-deposit ratio is 87.9 percent ($1,400/$1,592).

- *Equity-to-assets* This ratio should not be too low (roughly below 4) because it will indicate that the bank does not have the capacity to make loans. On the other hand, if this ratio is too high (generally above 9) it might result in the bank's making too many loans or imprudent loans in order to make use of its excess equity. However, prudent managers can use high equity-to-asset ratios to repurchase stock or to increase dividend payments.

Loan Portfolio

Since loans are banks' largest category of assets and since loans usually produce most of banks' interest income, it is extremely important to monitor the quality of banks' loan portfolios. Indications of banks' adopting more liberal loan origination policies include requiring fewer guarantees on personal loans to closely held businesses, enforcing fewer meaningful covenants, and granting longer maturities on loan repayments. Also, a decline in borrowers' debt-service coverage ratio (the number of times that pretax income exceeds total interest expense) in the loan covenants indicates that banks' loan policies are becoming more liberal.

Among the financial ratios that are useful in assessing the quality of a bank's loan portfolio are those presented below:

- *Loan application rejection rate.* This ratio divides the number of loan applications received by the number of loan applications rejected; lower ratios indicate that the bank is highly selective in making loans.

- *Collateral-to-loan value.* This ratio indicates the percentage of a loan that is backed by collateral. For example, if a bank makes a loan for $100,000 and that loan is secured by a piece of property appraised at $90,000, the collateral-to-loan value would be 90 percent ($90,000/$100,000). The higher this ratio, the more conservative the bank's lending policies are. Consider also at what collateral-to-loan value the bank requires its borrowers to obtain insurance. The lower these triggering points are, the more conservative the bank is in its lending policies.

- *Nonperforming loans-to-total loans.* This ratio simply measures the percentage of a bank's loan portfolio that is nonaccruing or has been restructured. Of course, the lower this ratio, the better. However, it is most important for analysts to obtain an accurate reading of the bank's nonperforming loans. In our example, this ratio is 5.4 percent ($75/$1,400).

- *Reserves-to-nonperforming assets.* This ratio indicates the degree to which reserves are covered by reserves for loan losses. Generally, the higher this ratio, the better. In fact, if nonperforming assets are overstated, the excess reserves can flow back into earnings. In our example, the reserve to nonperforming assets ratio declined from 30.7 percent ($23/$75) in the beginning of the year to 21.3 percent ($16/$75) at the end of the year. This decreasing coverage should be of concern to investors.

- *Loan loss reserves-to-gross loans.* This ratio measures the extent to which reserves have been taken to cover gross loans. The more conservative the bank's lending standards are, the lower this ratio needs be. In our example, this ratio declined from 1.6 percent ($23/$1,400) in the beginning of the year to 1.1 percent ($16/$1,400).

- *Net charge-offs-to-loans.* Ideally, a bank will not have to charge off much of its loans. A high net charge-off-to-loan ratio may mean that the bank's lending policies are too liberal and that its collection policies are too lax. However, some banks that are turning around take large charge-offs just to position themselves to make a fresh start. In our example, this ratio is 0.7 percent ($10/$1,400).

- *Long-term debt-to-debt plus equity.* This ratio illustrates the capacity that a bank has to make further loans. The lower this ratio, the more capacity the bank has to make loans. Conversely, the higher this ratio, the less capacity the bank has to make additional loans. Further, it is preferable to invest in banks whose long-term debt-to-equity ratios are lower than its competitors. In this situation, the bank under review will be able to originate more loans than its competitors. In our example, this ratio is 41 percent ($58/$141).

- *Loans-to-total assets.* This ratio illustrates the capacity that a bank has to make further loans. The lower this ratio, the more capacity the bank has to make loans. Conversely, the higher this ratio, the less capacity the bank has to make additional loans. Further, it is preferable to invest in banks whose loan-to-asset ratios are lower than its competitors. In this situation, the bank under review will be able to originate more loans while its competitors will not. In our example, this ratio is 76.4 percent ($1,400/$1,833).

Another problem with deteriorating loan portfolios is that collection and workout costs soar. For instance, each time a loan payment is past due 30 or 60 days, the offending company consumes as much as 10 hours of a relationship manager's or a workout specialist's month. This represents a major expense in terms of the professional's salary and related expenses. Moreover, the bank must absorb another opportunity cost in the form of that manager's being unable to call on profitable customers or to cross-sell other products to the borrower.

T I P

Many banks, such as KeyCorp, are securitizing large percentages of their loan portfolios. Essentially, securitization occurs when a bank sells its loans to another party while retaining the right to service such loans. The effect of securitization is that loan assets are removed from the bank's balance sheet while the bank maintains income from those relationships. Accordingly, securitization converts loan interest income into fee income. Since this fee income does not put the bank's capital at risk, no capital reserve is required; therefore a bank's capital ratios are increased. A further consequence of securitization is that less pressure is placed on deposit rates.

T I P

Banks would be major beneficiaries of bankruptcy reforms that would result in it becoming more difficult for borrowers to accumulate debts before declaring bankruptcy. Similarly, banks would benefit from reforms that result in less dissipation of corporate assets on legal fees.

The XYZ Bank

Income Statement

Total interest income	$ 100
Total interest expense	(67)
Net interest income	33
Provision from loan losses	(3)
Noninterest income	3
Noninterest expense	(7)
Pretax income	26
Income tax	(8)
Net operating income	$ 18

Reserve for Loan Losses

Balance, beginning of year	23
Provision for loan losses	3
Charge-offs	(13)
Recoveries	3
Net charge-offs	$ (10)
Balance, end of year	$ 16

Nonperforming Loans	$ 75

Balance Sheet

Assets		Liabilities and Shareholders's Equity	
Cash	$ 8	Deposit	$1,592
Temporary Investments	33	Short-term borrowings	100
Investment securities	225	Long-term debt	58
Loans	1,400	Total Liabilities	$1,750
Reserve for loans	(16)	Shareholders' equity	83
Building and equipment	183		
Total assets	$1,833	Total Liabilities and shareholders' equity	$1,833

Noninterest Income

Among the sources from which banks have traditionally derived noninterest income are checking account fees, ATM fees, and trust services. Noninterest income has been increasingly important to banks as banks have been very aggressive in raising these fees. For instance, according to the U.S. Public Interest Research Group, between April 1993 and April 1995, the annual cost of maintaining an interest-bearing checking account climbed an average of 11 percent; maintenance fees on saving accounts climbed 9 percent; and the average monthly balance needed to avoid checking-account fees rose 30 percent, to an average of $1,242.

In addition, banks such as Mellon Bank Corporation (through its 1994 acquisition of Dreyfus mutual funds) and Salt Lake City–based First Security Corporation are making major efforts to sell other financial products such as mutual funds and insurance.

One advantage that banks have in offering these traditionally nonbank products is their extensive customer knowledge which can be used to determine which products are most suitable for their customers. Also, banks have deep and trusting relationships with their customers since customers constantly interact with their banks.

Despite these advantages, banks face a number of obstacles in selling traditionally nonbank products:

- The availability of almost all of these products elsewhere.
- Long learning curves.
- A possible additional layer of regulation.
- Chilling head-to-head competition from the established companies in each of these arenas.

Competing with Brokerage Firms

Banks will find it very difficult competing against the brokerage industry. In comparison, banks have no proprietary products, antiquated distribution systems, and no sales culture. Securities firms have a much more aggressive sales culture than do banks. For example, stock brokers spend four times as much time making calls to customers as do bankers. Due to better compensation and prestige, securities firms generally attract more talented and ambitious people than commercial banks; Many bank tellers only work part-time and the motivation of career bankers has often been considered limited. Stock brokers deserve more compensation since they sell more individual stocks and bonds, while banks focus on selling mutual funds and annuities. Thus, banks cannot generate nearly as much repeat business nor do they benefit from impulse buying. Additionally, most investment products are most effectively sold through full-commissioned brokerages. However, most banks are disadvantaged by their use of discount brokers as their initial vehicle for

T I P

> In determining the effectiveness of a bank's sales force, you should consider the bank's cross-sell ratio, which is the average number of financial products that the bank's customers have purchased. Of course, the higher the cross-sell ratio, the better because high cross-sell ratios indicate that the customer is so integrated with his bank he will not likely defect.

entering the trading business. The main reason for their choosing discount brokers is that it is less expensive to establish a discount brokerage than a full-service brokerage because, for example, discount brokers do not have to be members of as many exchanges or provide research to their customers.

This comparative disadvantage can already be observed when reviewing mutual fund sales. To put things in perspective, banks sold 4 percent of all mutual fund dollars in 1994, while Fidelity Investments alone sold almost 10 percent. Moreover, much of the banks' mutual fund sales has come from mergers between banks, banks buying mutual fund companies, and the restructuring of existing trust assets.

Going forward, banks will clearly have difficulty improving their mutual fund sales performance:

- Banks must take numerous measures to convince the public that mutual funds are not federally insured as are deposits.

- It will be very difficult for banks to gain name recognition for their proprietary funds as there are now more mutual funds than stocks that trade on the New York Stock Exchange.

- Banks entering the mutual fund business do not have long records of investment performance, which are extremely helpful in selling funds to investors.

Brokerage Accounts

In addition to being formidable competitors with banks in mutual funds and other traditionally nonbank products, brokerage firms will become increasingly competitive with banks for deposits. For instance, some brokerage accounts, such as Merrill Lynch's Cash Management Account (CMA), combine stock and bond trading with access to money funds. These accounts pay market-related interest rates on cash balances and provide standard checking-account features (such as unlimited check writing) as well as debit cards that can be used to withdraw cash from ATMs.

Moreover, by using investments as collateral, account holders can borrow against a portion of the market value of their stocks, bonds, and other securities at reasonable rates. Finally, the account holder also benefits from having up to $500,000 worth of insurance on these accounts.

Acquiring Brokerage Firms

In view of the advantages that brokerage firms have in selling financial products, many observers believe that the eventual repeal of Glass-Steagall (the federal law requiring a separation of banks and brokerage firms) will result in banks' aggressively acquiring brokerage firms. Indeed, Canada's Toronto Dominion announced that it would acquire New York City–based Waterhouse Securities in April 1996. However, you should be advised that banks are often not successful in integrating brokerage firms. In fact, many key S.G. Warburg employees resigned from that British investment bank after their firm was acquired by Swiss Bank Corporation

One of the main challenges in the merging of investment banks with commercial banks, is the integration of two very different cultures. Commercial bankers are very conservative and are prone to make decisions in committees; investment banks are more risk tolerant and innovative, even encouraging their employees to develop exotic derivative products and new trading strategies by offering generous bonuses as incentives. The attraction of these bonuses results in investment bankers' behaving very independently and competitively, even among their own colleagues.

A further cultural difference between commercial banks and investment banks is that bankers for the latter are compensated far more generously than commercial bankers. It is not unheard of for a 25-year-old stock broker to earn more money than a 25-year veteran commercial banker.

Another difference is that commercial banks are savage cost cutters. Staffing at most branches has been reduced to skeleton crews, while employees often have to pool their money to keep coffee stocked in the pantry. Most pens at teller windows are chained down. Investment bankers and stock brokers, however, are lavished with expense accounts, posh offices, and country club memberships, making it impossible for banks to launch a cost-reduction campaign. To wit, morale among the rank-and-file employees would be severely dampened if they made a concerted effort over a few months to save a few hundred dollars by using less paper only to have a stock broker blow even more money by taking a few clients out to lunch. Conversely, investment bankers and stock brokers recoil when their perks are threatened or when their business practices are micromanaged by commercial bankers.

Not only do the cultures sometimes not mesh but views on the economy might not be consistent as they should be. For instance, the commercial bank may be more cautious (so as not to encourage overextending credit), while the brokerage firm may have a more optimistic view, which makes it easier to sell stocks.

Regulatory Concerns

Regulators have serious concerns about banks' becoming more active in the brokerage business. Many of these concerns center on whether a bank's brokerage unit should be a subsidiary or a holding company. Most proposed banking legislation envisions banks' brokerage units as separate holding companies for a couple of reasons:

1. Losses incurred by a cavalier securities unit would remain with the holding company rather than be consolidated in the parent's income statement. Thus, the holding company would act as a buffer against a run taking place on the parent bank due to losses at the brokerage unit.

2. Many legislators oppose allowing banks to run their securities business through subsidiaries because such activity would be essentially covered by federal deposit insurance.

Reasons for Consolidation

In addition to trying to increase noninterest revenues, banks have been trying to reduce noninterest expenses. Accordingly, recent years have witnessed a flurry of banking mergers and acquisitions. For instance, there were at least 500 bank mergers in 1994. Further, the combined value of all financial institutional mergers in the first half of 1995 was $59 billion—nearly twice the $32 billion in deals negotiated in the first half of 1994.

The following are among the reasons for the flurry of consolidation witnessed by the banking industry in the mid-1990s:

- With roughly 10,200 banks and 2,000 savings and loans, the United States is simply overbanked. Even though the number of banks is down significantly from an all-time high of 14,496 in 1984, the United States still has far more banks (even adjusting for population) than any other country in the world.

- Lackluster revenue growth is spurring mergers.

- After years of aggressive cost cutting, there are few cost-cutting opportunities remaining outside of consolidation.

- Technology is raising the cost of remaining competitive. In other words, since banks cannot afford to buy sophisticated mainframe computers or establish telebanking facilities independently, they are forced to combine their resources with other banks to offer such services.

- Mergers often create a chain reaction because few small banks are eager to compete with a behemoth in the same market.

- Some mergers are defensive meaning the acquiror is afraid another bank will acquire its preferred target. In fact, some analysts have opined that Chase Manhattan Corporation and Chemical Banking Corporation merged because neither bank wanted an outside bank to acquire the other.

- The media has widely reported the phenomenon of mergers in the banking industry. This attention attracts shareholders that are more inclined to vote for a merger if a premium bid surfaces.

- The heightened merger and acquisition activity may lower the psychological barrier for other bankers to agree to mergers and acquisitions.

- Bank holding companies were allowed to acquire banks anywhere in the nation as of September 1995. By June 1997, banks will be able to convert all of their banks into branches of a single interstate bank. Interestingly, it is preferable for a bank to expand through branches rather than through holding companies since holding companies require more infrastructure. For instance, holding companies are required to have separate Boards of Directors, must be separately capitalized, and must file regulatory papers separate from the parent company.

- Despite so many mergers (and so many large mergers), there has been little concern over antitrust issues. In fact, of the 2,300 bank mergers that the Department of Justice examined in 1994, only four banks were required to restructure their deals. This is because most markets are still served by several banks, and the blending of financial institutions (e.g., brokerage firms into commercial banks) has injected more competition into the entire financial services industry.

T I P

You should consider a bank's full-time employees-to-part-time employees ratio. The lower this ratio is, the easier it is to dismiss employees. A low ratio is particularly helpful in laying off employees during times of consolidations.

Benefits of Consolidation

Benefits of consolidation include less competition for deposits and the opportunity to sell more of the bank's products to a larger customer base. Consolidation also allows for expense reduction through reducing headcount, consolidating operations (e.g., check clearing), and closing underperforming branches. Interestingly, consolidation in the banking industry is facilitated by natural attrition, which relieves banks from taking large charges against earnings to eliminate positions.

Mergers versus Acquisitions

Shareholders of smaller banks usually fare better when that bank is acquired rather than merged into a larger bank because the acquirer typically pays a premium price for the stock.

TIP

There is a greater chance that earnings disappointments will occur in mergers in which the goal is revenue growth rather than in mergers in which the goal is cost reduction; it is much easier to predict expense reduction than revenue growth since bank officials can control the former but not the latter.

However, for the new bank, mergers are sometimes preferable to acquisitions because, since no premium was paid, they are cheaper. Thus, there is usually neither new debt assumed nor goodwill created, which would later be written off against earnings.

Nevertheless, the lack of a premium poses problems of its own for the surviving bank:

- Without a clearly dominant buyer, the bank boards often bicker over where the new entity will be based, whose culture will dominate, and who will fill the top posts.

- Shareholders who are unhappy that they did not receive a premium for their investment may oppose this kind of deal.

- Some people are tempted to sell recently awarded shares of stock soon after they are received.

Obstacles to Consolidation

The following are among the obstacles to further consolidation in the banking industry:

- Fear by institutional investors that acquirers are overpaying for acquisitions. For example, some of PNC Bank Corporation's largest institutional shareholders raised objections to the bank's $2.84 billion stock acquisition of Midlantic Corporation saying it was expensive and dilutive. Similarly, NBD Bancorp's debt was downgraded after its merger with First Chicago Corporation was announced because there was doubt about synergies and cultures and because NBD agreed to acquire a weaker-rated bank.

- Opposition by officers. Mergers and acquisitions often face opposition from top bank executives because these events can ruin their careers. CEOs of banks typically work their way to the top by being good company men over periods of as long as 25 years. Thus, they see the CEO's spot as an entitlement and are therefore reluctant to subject themselves to the wishes of an alien management.

- Opposition by communities. City officials may oppose mergers because losing a bank often results in less funding for the community; this is because the top bank executives are often highly integrated into the community's philanthropic and cultural scene.

- Opposition by regulators. Local regulators may oppose mergers for political reasons. For example, officials in Connecticut urged the Federal Reserve Board not to approve a merger between Fleet Financial Group, Inc., and Shawmut National Corporation until those banks guaranteed that the move would benefit the state's economy.

   Separately, regulators may oppose some of the largest mergers because the consequences of missing signals of problems (e.g., faulty loans) become much bigger when the banks under review are enormous.

- Stocks of potential acquirers often trade at lower levels because analysts believe that these banks will make dilutive acquisitions. Since the market devalues the acquirers' stock, the affected bank is less capable of financing an acquisition with its stock.

Expense of Branches

It is obvious that banks can benefit enormously by eliminating branches through consolidation or by replacing branches with ATM machines. One reason is that banks must pay between $15,000 to $20,000 per year for each teller that staffs these branches. Also, the capital investment required to build a full-service branch

T I P

From an investor's perspective, the higher the percentage of institutional ownership in the acquiring bank, the better. This is because institutional investors are more discriminating regarding overpaying (diluting) for acquisitions.

can average $800,000 to $1,500,000 versus $12,000 to $14,000 for a cash dispenser or $25,000 to $40,000 for a more traditional ATM. Moreover, Barnett Bank calculated that a retail withdrawal or deposit transaction processed through the use of a live teller costs $1.85, compared with only $0.79 when done via the telephone, and just $0.19 when done via ATM.

   However, branches still have a useful role to play:

- Branches are needed to establish relationships with customers. People need a place to go when they open a bank account.

TIP

☞ You should avoid banks whose management is averse to being acquired because there are few hostile takeovers in the banking industry. One reason is that regulatory procedures necessary to complete acquisitions commonly take as long as six months due to the difficulty of conducting due diligence. This period of time is long enough for key customers and executives to flee to competitors. Another reason why there are few hostile takeovers in the banking industry is that there are many white knights (i.e., other banks by whom the target bank would prefer to be acquired).

- Many customers (particularly those over 50 years old) feel more comfortable doing their banking in branches.
- It is very difficult to market sophisticated financial products without face-to-face banking. Indeed, the mutual fund industry has discovered the value of branches: Mutual funds had tremendous cost advantages over banks because banks had to have a massive presence—in cities, for instance, there were banks on almost every block, whereas mutual funds could be located in remote parts of the country. However, Fidelity Investments is an example of a mutual fund company that has been very aggressive in opening new offices to get close to the customer.
- Banks can use their bricks and mortar to sublet to other financial service providers (e.g., discount brokers). By doing this, the bank actually receives rental income while giving their customers the impression that the bank is a full-service financial provider under one roof.
- It is often politically difficult to close branches because regulators may claim that such closures would reduce customers' access to their money.
- When banks close a branch, they must write off the cost of that branch.

Regulation

Government regulation of the banking industry is so great that all consumer transactions are controlled in some manner by law. Regulation becomes more complicated in terms of documentation and reporting requirements as consolidation results in more interstate transactions. For example, the laws of the lender's state control issues such as usury, the laws of the borrower's state control issues such as disclosure requirements, and the laws of the state in which the collateral is located control the documentation required to perfect liens.

TIP

☞ In order to determine the efficiency of a bank's delivery system, you should consider the bank's efficiency ratio, which is overhead costs divided by revenues. Generally, the lower this ratio is, the better. However, if this ratio falls too far (roughly below 55%), it means that the bank may not be investing enough money in technology and in the training of its personnel.

The Community Reinvestment Act (CRA)

The CRA, originally promulgated in order to ensure that banks make credit available to all qualified applicants regardless of minority status or place of residence, is probably the most hated body of regulation in the banking industry. The CRA is the object of many bankers' scorn for the following reasons:

- At over $2 billion a year, the CRA accounts for at least 20 percent of banks' compliance costs. Moreover, the CRA reduces banks' capital. Under the Basel Agreement, lenders must maintain capital equal to 8 percent of their business loans. Thus, each dollar of capital spent on CRA-related compliance reduces between $8 to $12 in banks' lending capacity.

- The CRA is also unfair in that it is not applied to nonbank lenders.

- One of the biggest problems with the CRA is that anyone can claim that a bank is not in compliance with the CRA. For example, in 1995, the International Brotherhood of Teamsters pressured the Justice Department into investigating NationsBank's lending practices. The Teamsters were angered that NationsBank used Pony Express to transport canceled checks to the Federal Reserve since the Teamsters failed to organize a union at Pony Express. Additionally, in the fall of 1995, it was reported that Jesse Jackson threatened to bring CRA charges against Chase Manhattan for its intended merger with Chemical Bank.

- Another major problem with the CRA is that claims of noncompliance can destroy a bank's strategy. Community groups are especially effective in coercing banks to invest in minority areas during acquisitions. For example, when Dime Savings Bank wanted to acquire Apple Savings Bank, Dime agreed to expand its presence in the Bronx, which was not part of its growth strategy.

  However, some Republican legislators have endorsed legislation that would provide banks with top CRA records with a safe harbor against community group protests.

- Yet another drawback to the CRA is that it is so liberally written that regulators can determine that almost any bank has violated the law. For example, in September of 1992, federal regulators fined Decatur Federal Savings & Loan $1 million for a pattern of discrimination based on the thrift's market share in heavily minority areas. This case did not involve a single case of specific discrimination.

T R A P

⊘ Despite the hype surrounding electronic banking, some aspects of electronic banking could be disconcerting to users, the government, and banks. Take the case of using digital cash on an on-line computer system or over the Internet. If your computer crashes your electronic bank account could be lost forever.

Also, the government has legitimate concerns about digital money on computer systems. First, since electronic commerce would be very hard to monitor, tax evasion would be easy. Second, since digital money could easily cross borders, money laundering would be difficult to detect. Third, counterfeit digital cash would be virtually impossible to detect. After all, one string of 1s and 0s looks just like any other.

Finally, the emergence of electronic banking will introduce banks to a whole new panorama of competitors such as software and on-line companies. As Citicorp's Chairman John Reed said, "software will allow people to transact within the marketplace, and there won't be much need for (financial) intermediaries."

- Finally, bankers argue that there is little need for the CRA since banks have very impressive records of nondiscrimination. For instance, according to the Equal Employment Opportunity Commission (EEOC), the number of discrimination complaints against banks fell by more than 10 percent between 1990 and 1995, while the number of complaints in all other industries increased by 50 percent during this same period.

Other Investor Considerations

You should search for banks that dominate the geographic markets (in terms of deposits among all deposit-taking institutions) in which they serve. Also, you should search for banks that are increasing their

- Return on assets. ROA is simply net income divided by average assets. In our example, the ROA is 1.00 percent ($18/$1,833). While an ROA of 1 percent is unacceptable in most other industries, an ROA of 1.0 percent or higher is quite satisfactory for a banking concern.

- Return on equity. ROE is simply net income divided by shareholders' equity. In our example, the ROE is 21.7 percent ($18/$83), which is very impressive.

Competition from Credit Unions

In analyzing community banks (generally those banks with assets up to $15 billion with a strategic focus on the consumer and small business markets in a defined geographic region) for several years, I have neither read one analysts report nor heard one analyst speak about the competition that community banks face from credit unions. However, it is perilous to invest in a community bank without determining its competitive position vis-a-vis local credit unions.

In fact, research has indicated that a high percentage of the nation's community bankers believe that credit unions represent their greatest competitive threat. The following are among the reasons that credit unions are problematic for community banks:

- Credit unions enjoy very high levels of customer loyalty since their members almost always have more of an affinity with their credit unions than depositors do with their banks.

- Credit unions often offer higher yields on deposits and lower servicing fees than do banks since their cost structure is lower than that of banks. (They do not pay federal income tax because they are nonprofit, and they keep their costs down because they are staffed by volunteers, from the Board of Directors down to the tellers.)

- Credit unions can offer their members almost as many products as banks can offer their customers.

- Credit unions offer low loan rates since they can originate loans less expensively than banks. One reason is that credit unions do not have to comply with the Community Reinvestment Act.

- Some credit unions are expanding their reach by liberalizing the criteria regarding who can join a credit union. For instance, some credit unions

T I P

Since credit unions are so competitive vis-a-vis banks and since they are growing at a brisk rate, it is prudent to invest in the community banks that are the least exposed to competition from credit unions. Thus, the sparsely populated states have lower concentrations of credit unions while credit unions are concentrated on the two coasts and in industrial states such as Pennsylvania and Texas.

are open to anyone living in a given county or within a given number of miles of any one of its branches. In fact, National Credit Union Administration expansion grants added more than a million potential members to credit unions in the first nine months of 1995.

MORTGAGE BANKS

One of the most important determinations to make when analyzing a mortgage bank is the percentage of the bank's business that derives from loan originations versus loan servicing. Then, the next determination that you should make is the future direction of interest rates. When interest rates decline, mortgage banks such as Green Tree Financial Corporation that are heavily exposed to originations will benefit from the resulting high volumes and favorable margins. Further, independent mortgage banks have an advantage over community banks in offering mortgages since the former's capital requirements are less stringent than the latter's.

However, the mortgage banks that are more active in servicing mortgages will benefit when interest rates rise. Servicing activities include collecting and remitting loan payments, accounting for principal and interest, impounding funds for payment of property taxes and hazard insurance, making any physical inspections of the property, contacting delinquent mortgagees and supervising foreclosures and property dispositions in the event of unremedied defaults. In high-interest-rate environments, the servicing sector excels because prepayment activity declines, resulting in greater earnings from the servicing investment.

Conversely, in low-interest-rate environments, prepayments rise, leaving the mortgage bank with fewer mortgages to service. This servicing run-off is problematic since mortgage banks generally receive servicing fees based on the declining principal balance of the loans in their portfolio. Thus, the lower the principal balance of mortgages serviced, the lower the servicing fees.

Other Investment Considerations

For mortgage banks that are primarily involved with originating loans, you should search for mortgage banks that

- Securitize a large percentage of their mortgages since doing so reduces exposure to defaults. However, mortgage banks have difficulty both selling their mortgages into the secondary market and complying with

T I P

☞ Mortgage banks such as Countrywide Credit Industries that have both originating and servicing units are countercyclical.

increasingly onerous "fair lending" initiatives. In order to sell loans into the secondary market, the loans must fit rigid formulas. For instance, a car repossession or the filing for bankruptcy may automatically be rejected by Fannie Mae.

However, exceptions to these hard and fast rules must be made in order to meet requirements for serving low-income people. Some of the provisions of these fair lending guidelines include lower down-payment requirements, more liberal guidelines in areas such as credit and employment history, less income required and no cash reserve requirements at the date of funding.

- Have low and declining delinquency and foreclosure rates.

- Operate in areas of the country with improving home affordability.

- Require downpayments that are at least 10 percent of the cost of the home.

- Operate in areas of the country with little competition from savings and loans.

You should also realize that mortgage banks that are heavily exposed to originations are generally subject to seasonal trends. These trends reflect the general pattern of sales and resales of homes. Sales and resales of homes typically peak during the spring and summer seasons and decline to lower levels from mid-November through February.

When analyzing mortgage banks that primarily service loans, you should consider the percentage of the value of the mortgages that the mortgage bank receives for servicing such mortgages—the higher, the better. Also, the bank should operate in states that allow prepayment penalties so that servicing run-off will be reduced. Finally, the quality of loans serviced should be high since servicing a loan in foreclosure can raise servicing costs as much as sixfold.

THRIFTS/SAVINGS AND LOANS

Thrifts were originally created to insure a source of money for home mortgages. However, while thrifts have largely outlived their mandate due to the popularity of mortgage banks, they nevertheless enjoy the following benefits:

- Thrifts have traditionally been freer than banks to engage in other financial activities such as selling insurance and affiliating with industrial companies. In fact, thrifts can make direct investments in real estate, sell title insurance, and engage in real estate management. Currently, banks can only engage in these activities through a holding company and with the permission of the Federal Reserve. Thrifts are already allowed to operate interstate branches under one entity and with one Board of Directors, whereas these powers will not be granted to banks until 1997.

■ Thrifts enjoy close relationships with their customers because these customers maintain their most private banking accounts such as checking and savings accounts (rather than credit cards), at thrifts. Also, homeowners often remain loyal to the institution from which they obtain their first mortgage, which is often a thrift.

TIP

The price-to-book value ratio is generally a telling indicator in the thrift industry. One reason is that thrift assets are mainly liquid mortgages and securities (whereas industrial companies' assets are of much less certain value because they are less marketable). Also, the liability side of a thrift's balance sheet is composed almost entirely of customer deposits. There is no difference between the book-value and fair market value of these deposits. Thus, a thrift's net worth is a relatively certain value.

■ Banks are also attracted to the fact that thrifts are usually cheaper to purchase than other banks in terms of their price-to-book value ratios. In fact, the banking industry has acquired about 7 percent of the thrift industry annually over the 1990–1995 period.

Despite these advantages, you should be aware of the following obstacles that thrifts are presented with:

■ Thrifts lost most of their advantage over banks when Congress in the late 1970s scrapped regulations that had required banks to pay depositors an interest rate a quarter of a percentage point below the rates offered by savings institutions.

■ Thrifts' customer bases offer limited opportunity for cross-selling. This is because thrifts have traditionally appealed to low-income people as well as those who are risk averse (e.g., immigrants and senior citizens).

■ Thrifts' technology is inferior to that of banks.

■ Thrifts are at a disadvantage versus the mortgage banks since thrift loan officers are generally salaried while the loan officers at the mortgage banks usually work on a commission basis.

■ Increased competition with mortgage banks has resulted in mortgages' becoming commoditized, low-margin products. Similarly, most thrifts lack the huge economies of scale that are necessary to make acceptable margins on the servicing side of the equation.

■ Since, at the end of 1995, the Savings Association Insurance Fund (SAIF) was undercapitalized, savings and loans are paying as much as $.31 in insurance premiums for every $100 of deposits. In comparison, since the Bank Insurance Fund (BIF) has already been recapitalized, banks' insurance premiums have fallen to an average of $.04 for every $100 of deposits. However, this tremendous disparity in insurance premiums may be reconciled by merging the thrift industry into the banking industry.

CONSUMER FINANCE COMPANIES

Small-loan consumer finance companies such as World Acceptance Corporation prosper by making uncollateralized loans to individuals of up to $1,000 with maturities of one year or less. This business is insulated from competition, originates secure loans, and enjoys a large customer base.

Competition

Banks generally make loans of more than $1,000 with maturities greater than one year. Also, banks have more stringent credit requirements and demand that property be pledged as collateral. Thus, banks willingly cede people who do not meet these criteria to the consumer finance companies.

At the other extreme, pawn shops make smaller loans with shorter maturities than consumer finance companies. Pawn shops extend loans based exclusively on the assessed value of the collateral. Pawn shops experience much higher default rates than small-loan consumer finance companies and therefore derive a large portion of their revenue from the sale of forfeited collateral.

T I P

An investment opportunity may lie in the fact that not all thrift deposits are SAIF insured. In fact, some thrift assets are BIF insured. (Most of these thrifts are located in the northeast part of the country.)

Thus, if the stocks of thrifts plunge as a result of investor apprehension over thrifts' being assessed for recapitalization, the shares of those BIF-insured thrifts will not be adversely impacted and thus present a buying opportunity.

Default Rates and Potential

Consumer finance companies generally experience low default rates since these companies typically generate the vast majority of loans from refinancings of outstanding loans and the origination of new loans to previous customers. Credit, life, accident, and property insurance are commonly sold in connection with such loans, which cover the borrower in the event of death, unemployment or the destruction of collateral.

Most customers of consumer finance companies are low-income individuals who lack access to other forms of credit. The potential market for such services is huge, as 25 percent of American adults do not have a checking account—a standard prerequisite to obtaining other forms of credit.

PROPERTY AND CASUALTY INSURERS

Property and casualty insurers, such as The Chubb Corporation and The St. Paul Companies, try to make money by underwriting property and casualty insurance policies that they expect will yield greater premiums than payouts. Property insurance protects individuals and businesses from financial risks associated with the ownership and operation of property. Casualty insurance protects policyholders against liabilities arising from harm caused to others. The second primary source of income for property and casualty insurers is investment income.

Underwriting

Premium revenue is determined by the volume of policies underwritten as well as by the pricing that is realized on such policies. However, due to the potential for huge claims, it is more important that an insurer exercises selectivity in the policies that it underwrites than tries to aggressively increase its market share.

T I P

It is best to invest in an insurer that has a great deal of underwriting capacity in times in which the rest of the insurance industry has little underwriting capacity. To illustrate, assume that the property and casualty insurance industry writes $150 million in premiums in 1996 and that the leverage ratio (the number of times by which premiums can exceed policyholders' surplus) is 3:1. The required policyholders' surplus would be $50 million ($150 million ÷ 3). If the insurance industry had $52 million in actual surplus, the industry as a whole would be able to write an additional $6 million in premiums ($156 million – $150 million).

Further assume that the company under review wrote $15 million in premiums. The required surplus would be $5 million. But suppose that this company had an actual policyholders' surplus of $7 million. This company would be able to write $21 million in premiums ($7 million × 3) or an additional $6 million ($21 million – $15 million) worth of insurance. Thus, this would be the only company in the industry that could write additional policies.

T I P

☞ When there is excess underwriting capacity, the outlook for pricing could be better than initially perceived. Situations that would result in better pricing include the industry's being underreserved; the industry's suffering from higher catastrophe or investment losses; the bond market's deteriorating; or a lack of reinsurance.

There are a number of factors that affect the volume of property and casualty insurance underwriting. On the positive side of the equation, inflation usually helps the P&C industry since the value of assets that should be insured rises. Also, the adoption of just-in-time inventory management means that the overall value of existing factories increases giving rise to the need for greater insurance coverage.

On the negative side of the equation, underwriting volumes are adversely affected by self-insurance. Some of the factors that lead to a rise in self-insurance include corporations' being averse to

- Subsidizing their catastrophe-prone competitors by paying premiums in excess of the risk that they assume.
- Paying large deductibles after a catastrophe.
- Rising premiums in the aftermath of a claim.

Also, some businesses claim that they can better forecast their own risks than insurers. Finally, self-insurance allows companies to avoid expensive litigation costs associated with insurers disputing their clients' claims.

However, there are a number of drawbacks to self-insurance:

1. When a company self-insures, its insurance premiums are no longer tax-deductible.
2. A heavily indebted company will lose access to capital if it has to pay out a large claim by itself.
3. Shareholders of self-insured companies could be more likely to file lawsuits against the companies that cannot relegate some of their claims to outside insurers.

Additionally, underwriting capacity in the market affects the volume of policies that can be written. Insurance commissioners generally allow insurance companies to write policies worth between $2 and $3 for every dollar of policyholders' surplus. When the ratio of net premiums written to policyholders' surplus is low (e.g., 1:1), there is excess capacity, which means that more insurance policies may be underwritten.

Premium Pricing

The following factors affect the pricing that insurance companies charge for the policies that they underwrite:

- Excess underwriting capacity, as discussed previously, can cause pricing to deteriorate.

- Higher interest rates (e.g., bond yields) attract competition because they allow insurers to generate more investment income. Heightened competition then weakens the pricing of premiums charged, which reduces underwriting profits.

- Traditionally, it had been easy for insurers to raise their premiums after a disaster occurred. Insurance commissioners wanted the P&C companies to remain solvent; therefore, higher premiums were sanctioned so that insurers could meet their claims. Thus, it used to be that insurance stocks would rise after a disaster occurred.

    Today, the situation has changed. Many politically ambitious state insurance commissioners use their power to reject higher insurance premiums as proof of their consumer advocacy. Thus, higher premiums less frequently follow catastrophes.

TIP

The property and casualty insurance industry typically fares better when Republicans set the legislative agenda than when Democrats do so. First, Republicans are generally in favor of reduced capital gains taxes, which would bolster insurers' investment income. Second, Republicans are generally in favor of tort reform, which would result in smaller jury awards. Third, Republicans generally favor reforming the Superfund legislation, which would reduce insurers' exposure to environmental remediation expenses. In fact, in the beginning of 1996, Representative Michael Oxley (R-OH) proposed a bill that would virtually eliminate liability for hazardous waste cleanup. One caveat to Republican rule, however, is that state regulation (which Republicans often prefer over federal regulation) causes confusion, as 50 different rules and regulations create enormous difficulties in selling insurance and settling claims across state lines.

Underwriting Mix

It is often preferable to invest in insurance companies that write more casualty lines than property lines. Casualty insurers have longer tails. (A tail is the length of time it takes an insurer to pay losses arising from policies that it sold.) Since these

T R A P

> ⊘ One drawback to casualty policies is that, since they are often not set-
> tled for many years, inflation raises settlement costs.

long tails make it difficult to estimate losses, casualty lines require larger loss reserves—which are a source of investment funds for the insurer. Thus, the greater the company's loss reserves, the more of its clients' money the company can invest.

Conversely, since insurers that write more property lines pay out a higher percentage of their premium dollars in the form of loss settlements, they have fewer reserves to invest.

Also, regulators tend to give shorter-tail property insurers more leeway in surplus leverage than casualty insurers because of the relatively greater predictability of underwriting performance in the former. However, this greater leverage increases capacity which often leads to a deteriorating pricing environment.

Claims

The greatest risk that property and casualty insurers face is that they will have to make good on the policies that they underwrite. The very nature of insurance subjects property and casualty insurers to adverse selection, which means that those more vulnerable to risk are more likely to buy insurance. Similarly, insurers must factor moral hazard (policyholders behaving more recklessly knowing that insurers will indemnify them) into their policies.

These risks have recently been compounded by a greater incidence of natural catastrophes. In fact, of the 20 largest insured catastrophes in American history, 16 have occurred since 1989. Similarly, the average annual cost of disasters (in 1993 dollars) was less than $1 billion in the 1960s; in 1990–1993, it was almost $12 billion. Also, humans are increasingly destructive. Until 1987, humanity had never caused a catastrophe that wrecked over $1 billion in damage. Since then, however, humans have caused numerous such disasters (e.g., the Exxon Valdez oil spill, the Los Angeles riots, and the Chicago River's breaking).

Additionally, insurers face enormous potential asbestos and other environmental claims. For instance, past and future asbestos claims could eventually cost the industry as much as $40 billion while American and foreign insurers could end up paying as much as $1.5 trillion through the year 2020.

You should also be advised that insurers will likely pay higher claims when the incidence of public adjusters rises. (Public adjusters represent claimants against the private adjusters employed by insurance companies. Since the public adjusters work on a contingency basis they have huge incentives to obtain the highest payouts from insurance companies.) These public adjusters are often successful since they work against private adjusters, who work on a salaried basis and are paid to close cases.

You should also be aware that insurers normally reduce their risk by selling a portion of their policies to reinsurers. However, when reinsurers buy fewer policies, the primary insurers must expose more of their own capital to risk.

You should calculate the following ratios when assessing an insurers underwriting skills:

- *The combined ratio,* which is
$$\frac{\text{claims, expenses + dividends}}{\text{premiums}}$$

  When this ratio is below 100 percent, policies are profitably being written; when the combined ratio exceeds 100 percent, the insurer is taking losses on its underwriting.

- *The loss ratio,* which is
$$\frac{\text{claim losses + related expenses}}{\text{earned premiums}}$$

  The lower this ratio, the better.

- *The expense ratio,* which is
$$\frac{\text{underwriting expenses}}{\text{net premiums}}$$

  The lower the expense ratio, the better.

Investment Income

Insurance companies can be profitable, even when their underwriting is unprofitable. This is because insurance companies' investment income can exceed underwriting losses. Thus, it is extremely important to analyze insurance companies' investment performance.

Insurers derive funds for investment from three primary sources:

1. *Loss reserves,* which are funds set aside to pay claims whether or not such claims are reported, filed, or adjusted. However, insurers have difficulty setting aside large reserves for potential claims for fear that such action could be used against them as an admission of guilt in court. Also, the IRS opposes insurers' taking reserves since reserves are pretax earnings and reduce tax liability.

2. *Unearned premium reserves,* which are liabilities for that portion of a written premium applicable to the unexpired, or unearned, part of the period for which the premium has been charged. For instance, a company may make a three-month premium payment in January. The unearned premium reserve would be the premiums received for February and March.

3. *Policyholder surplus,* which is a measure of an insurer's claims-paying ability and is similar to shareholders' equity. Policyholders' surplus is increased by retained earnings (reduced by losses), increased by unrealized gains (diminished by unrealized losses), and increased by additions to investors' capital.

To illustrate the accounting involved with determining changes in policyholders' surplus, consider the following:

Policyholders' surplus beginning of year	200
Operating income	25
Realized capital gains	8
Income taxes	(11)
Net after-tax income	22
Unrealized capital gains (loss)	(8)
Stockholders' dividends	(3)
Change in policyholders' surplus	11
Policyholders' surplus end of year	211

When analyzing an insurer's ability to generate investment income, remember:

- Higher effective tax rates that corporations pay on dividend income hurt insurance companies since insurers hold large amounts of common and preferred stock.
- Rising interest rates could erode the value of insurers' bond portfolios.
- Disporportionately large capital gains may not be sustainable.
- The higher the insurers' yield on average invested assets, the better.
- The higher the junk bond-to-surplus ratio—the percentage of an insurer's capital invested in below-investment-grade bonds based on policyholders' surplus—the lower the quality of the insurer's bond portfolio.
- The higher the survival ratio—reserves divided by average annual claims, indicating the number of years it would take to exhaust reserves based on the present rate of claims—the better.

Other Investment Considerations

Making the following calculations will give you additional insight into property and casualty insurers:

- *Amount of investments in affiliates' surplus.* This illustrates the amount of an insurer's surplus invested in the bonds, preferred stock, and common stock of affiliated companies. The concern with insurers' having high levels of investments in their affiliates is that these investments are typically illiquid. Additionally, it is usually difficult to move capital between the insurer and its affiliates.

- *Reinsurance recovery ratio.* This measures an insurer's exposure to credit risk from reinsurance recoverables. The higher the reinsurance recovery ratio rises, the more dependent the insurer becomes on the financial condition of its reinsurers.

- *Risk-based capital ratio.* This measures an insurer's total adjusted capital to the minimum capital level required by regulators. A ratio over 100 percent indicates that a company has capital in excess of the requirement, while a company with a ratio of less than 100 percent is subject to regulatory action and will find it extremely difficult to underwrite new business.

T I P

Companies buy property and casualty policies that will provide them with coverage for very long periods of time. Thus, they use only insurers that have the resources to remain in business for many years. Accordingly, invest only measures in insurers that have very strong balance sheets and very high credit ratings.

- *Return on surplus.* The higher an insurer's net income rises as a percentage of policyholders' surplus, the better.

- *Loss-development ratio.* This measures the estimated losses and loss expenses incurred as a percentage of surplus. A rising loss-development ratio may indicate that the prior year's reserves were too low, while a declining number may indicate that there were adequate reserves.

Investment Niches

Aside from these general factors, you should consider developments in the specific lines of business that insurers in your portfolio underwrite. For instance, malpractice reforms could make companies like Frontier Insurance Group more profitable, while crackdowns on workers' compensation fraud would be a boon to insurers such as Orion Capital Corporation. Also, auto insurers such as Allstate Corporation could be adversely affected by higher speed limits, airbags, and antilock brakes, resulting in people's driving more carelessly.

Finally, losses suffered on derivative investments by municipalities such as Orange County (California) could be helpful in selling municipal bond insurance since losses remind city and county commissioners that such insurance does have value. (Municipal bond insurers such as MBIA, Inc., and AMBAC Inc. agree to

T R A P

⊘ Despite the above advantages that reinsurers enjoy, the following story relates a major risk that reinsurers face. Electric Mutual Liability Insurance Co. started out as a mutual insurer which was owned by its policyholders with GE being the largest. At GE's behest, this insurer split into two companies in Massachusetts. After this split-up, Electric Mutual had all of the environmental and asbestos liabilities and moved to Bermuda. Shortly after moving to Bermuda, Electric Mutual filed for liquidation, the equivalent of a bankruptcy filing for an insurance company. Under Bermuda law, policyholders have significant control over a liquidation which is detrimental to reinsurers.

While the state insurance commissioner usually oversees insolvencies in the United States, creditors in Bermuda generally have a say in appointing the liquidator. So, for example, as the only creditor of Electric Mutual, GE may help select and oversee the liquidator.

Moreover, GE could have a key role in how the insurance tab is calculated. For instance, in Bermuda, liquidators can estimate all future claims, generating early payments to policyholders, and therefore early bills to reinsurers for those claims. That means policyholders may collect, and reinsurers may be asked to pay, on claims that haven't materialized yet. In Massachusetts, regulators liquidating an insurance company typically pay claims and bill insurers only as claims are brought. So while liquidations in the United States can take more than 20 years to finish, the Bermuda approach has resolved liquidations in half of that time. Unless reinsurers are able to block that process, GE could get its claims money sooner.

However, one possible downside to this scheme is that the next time that Electric Insurance, the surviving Massachusetts company, needs backup reinsurance coverage, some reinsurers could well run the other way.

Amy Barrett with Tim Smart, "GE Sails into a White Squall," *Business Week,* February 19, 1996, pp. 60–64.

pay the principal and interest in the event that a municipality defaults on its bonds. This raises the credit rating of the bond, thus reducing the issuer's interest costs.)

REINSURANCE

Reinsurance companies, such as National Re Corporation and Transatlantic Holdings Inc., assume some of the risks that primary insurers write. Reinsurers are worthy of consideration for the following reasons:

- Facultative reinsurance (when the reinsurer assumes the insurance company's risk on a case-by-case basis) is safer than primary insurance because both the primary insurers and reinsurers review the policies. However, treaty reinsurance (when the reinsurer agrees to accept a fixed percentage of risk on all of a primary insurer's deals) bears more risk than facultative reinsurance.

- Unlike regular residential insurance rates, which are controlled by state regulators, reinsurance rates are free to float with supply and demand.

- Foreign insurers contribute to the domestic insurers' claims since such policies are purchased by reinsurers all over the world.

- Reinsurers generally protect themselves by laying off business among retrocessionary companies.

- Since reinsurers have long tails they must keep higher loss reserves than primary insurers. Thus, reinsurers can earn investment income on these tax-free reserves for many years. Some reinsurers even overestimate their losses in order to create larger reserves to shelter even more of the compounding assets.

- There is a barrier to entry since no one wants to buy reinsurance from a start-up that may not be around in a few decades when the claims actually come due.

BROKERAGE HOUSES AND INVESTMENT BANKS

Fundamentalists do not include a forecast of the overall health of the stock market in their stock-picking regimen. However, even they would agree that the strength of the stock market is an important factor in assessing the health of brokerage stocks. One reason is that brokerage firms derive a large part of their revenue from commissions which are based on the volume of trades that are executed. In fact, in 1995, commissions accounted for 60 percent of A.G. Edwards' revenue, 45 percent of Quick & Reilly's revenue, and 24 percent of PaineWebber Group's revenues. Of course, commission revenue is dependent upon a rising stock market because investor confidence is highest when the market is rising and is an important determinant in the level of trading activity. When investors are extremely confident, they often trade on margins, which results in more trading power (and usually more trading volume) since investors are leveraging their portfolios.

T I P

☞ The greater the average daily trading volume on the American stock markets, the better.

T I P

[icon] The stronger the market, the better the outlook is for the brokerage stocks.

Commission revenue also rises in lockstep with the ascent of the stock market because most commission schedules charge investors more to trade high-priced stocks than to trade low-priced stocks. Similarly, more companies are likely to split their stocks when their stock prices climb steadily. As a result, investors have more shares to trade, increasing total volumes.

On the other hand, bear markets result in lower commission revenue because trading activity is reduced. Moreover, falling stock prices result in lower commissions because most commission schedules charge less for executing trades of lower-priced stocks.

Some novice investors say that a stock market crash would not hurt the brokerage industry because brokerage houses generate commissions when their clients sell stocks just as they do when they execute buy orders. True, a lot of commissions are generated on the day of stock market crashes. However, during the remainder of the ensuing bear market, fewer people will trade stocks.

Aside from cyclical challenges to commissions, full-service brokerage firms face secular challenges to their commission revenues. Among those challenges are the following:

- As investors are becoming increasingly educated they are less reliant on research from full-service firms. Along with the rise in independent research comes the belief that these should not have to pay high commission rates; thus, a growing number of individuals are trading through discount brokerage houses. As the discounters continue to increase their market share, they are putting pressure on the full-service firms' commission schedules.

- Program trading reduces commission revenue since the automatic nature of these trades provides little justification for charging high rates.

- Dividend reinvestment plans (DRIPs) and direct-purchase stock plans (buying shares directly through a company) lower commission revenues for brokerage houses. Incidentally, direct-purchase stock plans are becoming more popular as larger companies such as Wal-Mart and Amoco Corporation are instituting them and thus making them legitimate.

- When investors execute their own trades over the phone, on on-line services or through software programs like Quicken™, financial products are turned into commodities for which high commissions cannot be charged.

- Commission rates might fall if mutual funds are required to report the average commissions per share that they pay.

- Reporting aggregate commissions on customer statements would be devastating for full-commission brokerage firms. This is because investors would realize the high cost of full-service commissions.

- Greater popularity of index mutual funds and the like results in lower commission for brokers since money managers simply hold the stocks that constitute broad market averages (e.g., the S&P 500).

Estimates of Inheritance

In 1993, two Cornell University professors conducted a study that concluded that the baby boomers stood to inherit $10.4 trillion. Many analysts irresponsibly extrapolated this alleged huge inheritance onto the brokerage industry. The following should make you skeptical of such wishful thinking:

- Even if baby boomers were really going to inherit so much money, not all of this money would be new money to the brokerage industry since much of it is already parked there. In other words, since the parents of baby boomers already have brokerage accounts, their bequeaths will not all be new money to the brokerage industry.

- This inheritance would occur over a very extended period of time.

- Not all bequeaths are made to one's children; many are made to charities and foundations. Also, of growing popularity is "painless giving" in which the title to assets is signed over to a charity, but the donor receives an income stream from these assets during his life. Many beneficiaries wrongfully assume that just because their parents derive income from their assets that they will eventually inherit such assets.

- More seniors are buying annuities, which disappear on the death of their owners. (Annuities are income flows that last only as long as the owner survives.)

- Greater acceptance of reverse mortgages and home-equity loans is reducing much of the equity that people have in their homes.

- Accurate estimates of such large inheritances are nearly impossible to make. For instance, there is an enormous difference between wealth near death and wealth at the time of death. Unfortunately, the former is much larger than the latter since a huge amount of money is spent during the last few months of life—on funerals and estate taxes.

- Older people are not as self-sacrificing as they used to be. Many older people are spending their savings on travel, and many are remarrying. Thus, older people will have less savings to pass on to their children.

■ Savings rates may be lower in anticipation of such expectations.

On the other hand, you should not automatically accept reports brokerage firms issue indicating that Americans are completely unprepared for retirement. Some of these reports may be issued as a means to scare people into consulting with brokerage houses.

Stock Brokers' Productivity

Investors are often concerned about the productivity of stock brokers. You can begin to determine how productive a sales force is by calculating the firm's average annual gross commissions (total commissions/number of salespeople). Of course, the higher the better. You can also consider the brokerage firm's average account size. The greater the average account size, the better since fixed costs are more completely covered by large accounts. For instance, on a percentage basis, the costs of processing a client's account statement are lower for large accounts than small accounts. Similarly, you should seek those firms that have the highest average net worth of brokerage clients.

There are, however, a number of factors that could reduce stock brokers' productivity. First, the Securities and Exchange Commission (SEC) is opposed to sales contests. The reasoning is that brokers will simply try to make as many sales as possible regardless of the suitability of the stocks that they are selling to their clients.

Second, due to such opposition from the SEC and the cyclical nature of commission revenue, some brokerage firms such as Merrill Lynch are trying to become asset gatherers. One product that is aimed at keeping more assets at the given brokerage house is "wrap accounts." These accounts provide customers with money management services and allow an unlimited number of trades for a predetermined annual fee. One attraction with wrap accounts is that customers may feel comforted in knowing that the brokerage firm has no interest in churning their account.

The downside for firms that take an asset-gatherer approach is that they will naturally have lower productivity ratios since they have less interest in generating commissions. However, asset gatherers will usually present better investment opportunities when the market is weak because they will still collect their annual fees while other brokerage houses will suffer from plummeting commission revenue.

Investment Banking Fees

Underwriting initial and secondary offerings as well as consulting on mergers and acquisitions is another source of profit for investment banks. For example, Alex Brown derived over 36 percent of its revenues from investment banking fees in 1995.

T I P

☞ Deregulation and convergence among industries benefit the investment banks because companies restructure, merge, do spin-offs, and form partnerships during those times.

You should be aware that there is often an inverse relationship between underwriting fees received and mergers and acquisitions fees generated by investment banks. Companies might not want to issue stock when the market is weak because such actions would be dilutive. However, a weak stock market might present a good opportunity to acquire companies that are trading at attractive quotations, thus, when the stock market is strong it is usually best to invest in those investment banks that are more exposed to underwriting than consulting on mergers and acquisitions.

U.S. investment banks are positioned to benefit from privatizations and deregulation worldwide. Since these stock issuances are so large, foreign countries must list some of their newly issued shares on other countries' stock exchanges because such issuances would overwhelm local exchanges. There are a number of advantages for foreign companies listing their shares on U.S. exchanges:

1. Having shares traded on an American exchange lends more credibility to a company's shares in its own market.

2. The U.S. financial markets are very sophisticated, having been deregulated since 1975.

3. The U.S. has more financial analysts than any other country, which is important in publishing research on listed companies' developments.

4. The U.S. markets are the most liquid.

You should be aware of a few of the secular threats to investment banking fees:

■ When the corporate sector has a solid balance sheet, mergers are less complicated, and since less complicated financing is required, investment banks cannot charge high fees.

■ Chief financial officers (CFOs) compete with investment bankers for investment banking services. A very talented CFO does not need to heavily rely upon investment bankers for advice. For example, when The Walt Disney Company acquired Cap Cities/ABC, Steve Bollenbach (Disney's CFO) did so without the help of a single securities firm. Similarly, some companies have made so many acquisitions that they have developed internal acquisitions departments.

TIP

🖑 It is more lucrative for an investment bank to represent the seller in an acquisition; the seller is less sensitive to investment banking fees since the buyer ends up absorbing the acquisition costs.

- Legal restrictions are making it more difficult for investment bankers to make political contributions to state officials in hopes of winning municipal finance business.

In determining an investment bank's underwriting and consulting performance, you should consider the underwriting fees as a percentage of the face value of the underwriting. Similarly, you should consider average fees charged on mergers and acquisitions work as a percentage of the transaction value. The higher these percentages, the better.

Competition from Banks

Commercial banks will present investment banks with greater competition for underwriting assignments, which will consequently result in lower fees. However, underwriting will probably be very complicated for banks. For example, a separate subsidiary might have to be established in a separate location and the directors might have to be different. Also, most companies prefer to retain investment banks to lead their underwriting since the investment banks have strong sales forces to place their securities with investors as well as research analysts to follow the companies.

The emergence of commercial banks into investment banking will increase compensation costs by increasing competition for investment bankers. Another factor that raises costs for the securities industry is the poaching of analysts. Defection of analysts usually results in a chain reaction because brokerage firms have shallow industry coverage. For example, if one brokerage firm loses its coal analyst it will often try to hire another firm's coal analyst.

Separately, the disallowance of deduction for compensation that exceeds $1 million a year is problematic for brokerage firms since many brokers and investment bankers earn more than $1 million a year.

Interest Income

Brokerage firms can generate a surprising amount of revenue from interest income. For instance, in 1995, Merrill Lynch derived 57 percent of its revenue from interest income. Much of this interest income is derived from interest payments received on the firm's bond portfolio. The brokerage industry especially benefits when the yield curve is wide since brokers can finance their securities inventory at low short-term rates while earning interest at higher long-term rates. Investment banks also derive interest income by making bridge loans, which are used to help their clients finance acquisitions.

Short selling is another interest generator because money is received on the initial sale. Brokerage firms also generate interest from lending securities to other brokerage houses for purposes of short selling.

Moreover, brokerage firms earn interest income on the margin loans they extend to their customers. Finally, some brokerage firms are slow to sweep their customers' interest and dividend payments into money market funds. This use of resources represents a source of interest income to brokerage firms.

T I P

☞ Securities firms are often named as codefendants in lawsuits brought against their clients. Thus, securities firms would benefit from tort reform that limits their financial liability for fraud committed by their corporate clients.

Legal Issues

The Supreme Court in 1987 allowed the securities industry to force nearly all clients to arbitrate any claims against it. Brokerage firms derive numerous benefits from arbitration. First, since the securities industry sets the rules and picks the pool of arbitrators, arbitration awards are usually less than court awards. Second, brokerage houses are sometimes able to state no punitive damages clauses in contracts. Third, arbitration cases do not have broad precedential value. Fourth, agreements settling disputes between brokerage firms and their clients have confidentiality clauses, which usually include a bar against publicly disclosing the terms of the settlement.

DISCOUNT BROKERAGE FIRMS

Discount brokerage firms such as The Charles Schwab Corporation are more cyclical than full-service firms because they have a higher percent of fixed costs. For instance, their sales force is usually salaried while the full-service firms' sales force is compensated on a commission basis. Therefore, in a bear market, the discount firms' earnings fall faster since the discount broker is saddled with its fixed costs of maintaining a sales force, whereas the full-service firms' earnings are less adversely impacted because their costs fall in lockstep with reduced commission revenues.

Payment for Order Flow

Of course, one of the main attractions of discount brokers is their low commission rates. Discount houses can still be profitable while offering very low commission by being paid for their order flow. Payment for order flow occurs when dealers on the floor of the NASDAQ exchange pay brokerage firms to direct orders their way. For instance, a dealer may offer to sell a share of stock to an investor at $16 while only bidding (offering to buy) the stock at $15 a share. Thus, the dealer makes a $1 profit for each share traded. The payment for this order flow occurs when the floor dealer pays the brokerage firm (let's say 10 cents a share) for orders the brokerage firm sends him.

The SEC frowns upon payment for order flow because it gives brokerage firms an incentive to trade through a floor broker with the highest payments rather than through a dealer that offers the customer the best price. Accordingly, brokers must disclose whether they receive payment for order flow on trade confirmations and annual account statements as well as when a client opens a brokerage account. In conclusion, further crackdowns on payment for order flow would be adverse to discount brokerage firms since this is a major source of their profitability.

Other concerns with investing in discount brokerage firms are that (1) they may lose customers to on-line trading and (2) they are more exposed (than full-service firms) to banks' entering the brokerage industry since most banks do so through discount operations.

Trade Settlement Times

In June of 1995, trade settlement times were reduced from five business days to three. Larger discount brokerage firms should benefit from shorter trade settlement times while the smallest ones should be *adversely* affected. Shorter settlement times mean that investors will not be able to wait to receive their trade confirmations in the mail before sending cash or securities to settle their trades. Many small brokerage firms do not have money market accounts from which cash can quickly be transferred. Thus, investors will shift their accounts to larger firms that have the capability to quickly transfer assets from cash accounts to stock accounts.

Second, shorter settlement times may squeeze out the marginal brokers because brokers will only be able to use their clients' money for three days as opposed to five.

T I P

Since discount brokerage firms do not recommend stocks to their customers, they are exposed to far fewer arbitration cases than full-service brokers.

MUTUAL FUND COMPANIES

Nothing succeeds like success. In the mutual fund industry nothing attracts money to mutual fund companies better than a rising stock market. Other factors that lead to higher net inflows of cash include the following:

- A rising number of households that own mutual fund shares. Once a household begins to invest in mutual funds, it is likely to increase its mutual fund holdings in the future.

- More employers establishing defined-contribution pension plans. Under these pension plans, individual employees generally decide how their retirement funds are invested.

- More investors who have seen nothing but bull markets. People that have never experienced a bear market are less apprehensive about investing in the stock market through mutual funds.

- The SEC's allowing mutual funds to send prospective investors a so-called profile prospectus. These profile prospectuses are more appealing since they are much shorter than the standard prospectuses which are laden with impenetrable boilerplate.

- Additional certification for selling mutual funds. For instance, brokers can already become a Certified Fund Specialist while the Investment Company Institute is developing a "Chartered Fund Counselor" program. These titles credentialize brokers and financial advisers that sell mutual funds.

- More people nearing retirement age. The closer people come to retiring, the more important investing becomes.

T I P

You should invest in mutual funds that demonstrate rising net cash inflows—a better gauge of a mutual fund company's growth than assets under management because the latter includes higher equity prices.

- Social Security reforms that allow individuals to divert some or all of their Social Security payroll taxes into private accounts, which they would manage themselves.

The economics of the mutual fund business is very attractive. For instance, fund operators usually do not pass along savings from economies of scale to their account holders. In fact, fees often rise as funds grow—and of fees, there are many: Mutual funds charge their customers management fees, custodial fees, transfer-agency fees, 12b-1 fees, shareholder servicing fees, accounting fees, administrative fees, legal and audit fees, reporting fees, insurance fees, and print-ing and postage fees.

On the cost side of the equation, the money management business has low fixed costs and low reinvestment costs. Yet, the mutual fund business is perhaps the only industry in which rising compensation costs detract from the quality of the product sold. Mutual funds sell a return on investment, and the higher their com-pensation costs rise, the lower their return on investment becomes. In comparison, even if Hershey Foods doubled all of its employees' salaries, Hershey's® chocolate bars would still taste just as good.

No-Transaction-Fee Mutual Fund Networks

You should be aware of the effect that mutual fund networks such as Charles Schwab's OneSource™ program has on mutual funds. First, some background: OneSource allows Schwab customers to trade hundreds of no-load mutual funds free of charge. This program is appealing to investors because investors like to trade funds from different groups without having to make multiple phone calls, fill out many forms and wait for money to be sent from one group to another. They also like receiving a single monthly statement encompassing all of their fund hold-ings, rather than separate fund statements from each group.

Under this system, funds rebate part of their management fees to sellers of the funds. Typically, mutual funds on the no-transaction-fee networks pay 25 to 35 cents a year for each $100 in assets sold by the discount broker. In return, the dis-count broker handles most of the phone calls as well as various back-office tasks such as mailing out monthly statements.

Schwab's OneSource is problematic for large mutual fund companies. First, the no-fee nature encourages trading in and out of funds. This results in less loy-alty for families of funds. For example, assume that an investor initially held Fidelity's Gold Fund. When this investor wants to switch to an energy fund he can just as easily choose a different company's energy mutual fund.

However, mutual fund networks reduce marketing costs for small mutual funds. Also, these networks benefit mutual funds with a limited variety of funds since investors of these funds will have access to many more funds from other families of funds. Thus, the proximity to other mutual funds benefits small mutual fund operators because they attract investors who would not otherwise invest in a fund operator with few alternative funds.

When investing in a publicly traded mutual fund company, such as Eaton Vance, search for companies that

- Attract a large percentage of their funds from 401(k) plans, Keogh accounts, and other retirement accounts. Retirement money is a steady business in that there is little switching between mutual funds because the investor has such a long-term perspective. Also, the regular inflow of 401(k) money provides a steady source of management fees.

- Have a low stock turnover ratio. (This is calculated by taking the fund's aggregate purchases or sales and dividing this amount into the fund's average assets.) The lower the turnover ratio, the better since long-term capital gains are taxed at lower rates than short-term capital gains. Also, high portfolio turnovers result in higher commission costs.

- Have fund managers with impressive track records at the same fund. For instance, fund managers should have high Morningstar ratings. (Morningstar is a leading mutual fund rating service.)

- Fund managers should manage the same fund for a high average number of years. This is especially important for those funds whose sales depend on financial advisors because financial advisors must base their decisions on such statistics.

   On the other hand, problems for funds that frequently switch managers include the following:

1. The new manager may not be as talented as his predecessor.

2. A change in direction results in duplication. Assume that the first fund manager favored defensive stocks while the second manager favored growth stocks and that you have long held a growth mutual fund. As a result of the change in fund managers, your financial advisor may advise you to redeem your shares in this fund since you already own a similar growth fund.

3. Such shifts in strategic direction result in excessive trading costs as well as taking losses prematurely.

CREDIT CARDS

Credit card transaction volume has consistently increased by roughly 15 percent annually since the mid-1980s. There are several reasons for this growth. First, more nontraditional merchants such as fast-food outlets and grocery stores are accepting credit cards. Second, reward programs (e.g., free travel miles) and rebates effectively motivate customers to boost their credit card usage.

   Third, corporate purchasing cards are growing very rapidly. These cards are aimed at minor and unanticipated purchases that offices and factories make (e.g., duplicate keys, staplers, hammers). Corporate purchasing cards are suitable for

T I P

☞ Credit card processors such as Total Systems Services and Verifone benefit from higher processing volume but do not bear credit risks.

these purchases because such transactions are too small for national contracts, yet accounting for them would cost a fortune in paperwork. These cards incorporate codes that set credit limits and restrict where they can be used. For example, a secretary might carry a card limited to the local office supply store.

GLOSSARY OF SELECTED BANKING TERMS

accrual basis accounting   Accounting method whereby income and expense items are recognized as they are earned or incurred, even though they may not have been received or actually paid in cash.

adjustable rate mortgage   (ARM) Mortgage agreements stipulating predetermined adjustments of the interest rate at specified intervals. The mortgage payments are tied to some index outside of the control of the bank or savings and loan institution.

bank holding company   Company that owns or controls two or more banks or other bank holding companies.

basis point   A unit of measure for interest yields and rates equivalent to one one-hundredth of one percent. One hundred basis points equals one percent.

book value per common share   The value of a share of common stock determined by dividing total common stockholders' equity at the end of a period by the total number of common shares outstanding at the end of the same period.

core deposits   Deposits that are not interest-rate sensitive. Examples include cash in checking accounts and cash that is used to secure a credit card. The greater the percentage of core deposits a bank has (in terms of total deposits), the better.

credit card securitization   An off–balance sheet funding technique which transforms credit card receivables into marketable securities. The receivables are transferred to a trust and interests in the trust are sold to investors for cash. In this transaction, the net of interest income, fee income, charge-offs, and the investors' coupon payments becomes servicing fees.

cross-sell ratio   This ratio measures the average number of a bank's products sold to each of its customers. The higher this ratio, the better.

demand deposits   Account balances that without prior notice to the bank, can be drawn on by check, cash withdrawal from an ATM, or by transfer to other accounts using the telephone or home computers.

discount rate   Interest rate that the Federal Reserve charges member banks for loans, using government securities as collateral.

earning assets   Assets that generate interest income and yield-related fee income, such as securities available for sale, investment securities, and loans.

efficiency ratio   Noninterest expenses divided by the sum of net interest income (on a fully-taxable equivalent basis) plus noninterest income.

federal funds rate   Interest rate charged by banks with excess reserves at a Federal Reserve district bank to banks needing overnight loans to meet reserve requirements.

fully taxable equivalent (FTE)   An adjustment made to interest income to facilitate comparison of interest income earned on tax-exempt or tax-favored loans, leases, and securities with interest earned subject to full taxation.

full-time equivalent   A measurement equivalent to one full-time employee working on a standard day and based on the number of hours worked in a given month.

gap   An asset/liability management term. Gap assigns each interest-earning asset and interest-bearing liability to a time frame reflecting its next repricing or maturity date. The difference between total interest-sensitive assets and total liabilities at each time interval represents the interest-sensitivity "gap" for that period.

intangible assets   Goodwill, purchased mortgage servicing rights, deposit-based intangibles, and insurance intangibles.

interest-bearing liabilities   Liabilities upon which interest is paid for the use of funds such as deposit accounts (except demand deposits), short-term borrowings, and long-term borrowings.

interest-rate risk   The risk that changes in interest rates will impact net interest income.

interest-sensitivity gap   The amount by which interest-rate sensitive assets exceed interest-rate sensitive liabilities, and vice versa, for a designated time period. An excess of assets is referred to as a net asset position; an excess of liabilities is referred to as a net liability position.

interest-rate sensitive assets/liabilities   Assets and liabilities whose yields or rates can change within a designated time period, due either to their maturity during this period or to the contractual ability of the institution to change the yield/rate during this period.

leverage ratio   Tier I capital divided by the current quarter's total average assets less goodwill and other disallowed intangibles.

managed credit card portfolio   The total of credit card loans, credit card loans held for sale and securitized credit card loans.

net charge-offs   The amount of loans written off as uncollectible, net of any recoveries on loans previously written off as uncollectible.

net interest income   The difference between total interest income and total interest expense.

net interest spread   The difference between the yield on interest-earning assets (on a taxable equivalent basis) and the rate paid on interest-bearing liabilities.

net yield margin   A measurement of how effectively an institution utilizes its earning assets in relationship to the interest cost of funding them. It is computed by dividing net interest income (on a taxable-equivalent basis) by average interest-earning assets.

nonaccrual loans   Loans on which interest accruals have been discontinued due to the borrower's financial difficulties.

nonperforming assets   The total of nonperforming loans and foreclosed properties.

nonperforming loans   The total of nonaccrual and restructured loans.

OREO   Other real estate owned plus other foreclosed assets.

potential problem loans   As defined by the SEC: performing loans that have characteristics that cause management to have serious doubts about the borrower's ability to comply with the present loan repayment terms. These loans are less than 90 days past due and are accruing interest.

problem assets   Nonperforming assets plus accruing loans past due 90 days or more.

productivity ratio   Noninterest expenses divided by average total assets.

provision for loan losses   A charge against income made to adjust the reserve for loan losses to a desired level to cover potential future loan losses.

purchased deposits   The total of large denomination certificates and foreign deposits.

reserve for loan losses   An adjustment made to loans to recognize possible future loan charge-offs. All loan losses are charged against this reserve as they become probable and subject to reasonable estimation. Recoveries of amounts previously charged off are credited to this reserve. It is adjusted by means of the provision for loan losses.

reserve requirement   The Federal Reserve system rule mandating the financial assets that member banks must keep in the form of cash and other liquid assets as a percentage of demand deposits and time deposits. This money must be kept in the bank's own vaults or on deposit with the nearest regional Federal Reserve Bank.

restructured loans   A loan is considered restructured when an institution for economic or legal reasons related to the debtor's financial difficulties grants a concession to the debtor that it would not otherwise consider.

return on assets (ROA)   A measure of profitability that indicates how effectively an institution utilized its assets. It is calculated by dividing net income by total average assets.

return on equity (ROE)   A measure of profitability that indicates what an institution earned on its stockholders' investment. It is calculated by dividing net income attributable to common shares by total average common shareholders' equity.

slippage   This is the money that is left on travelers checks and prepaid cards that never gets used.

supplementary capital (or Tier II)   Capital that consists of an institution's subordinated debt instruments, redeemable preferred stock, and a limited amount of the allowance for loan losses.

tangible common equity ratio   Common stockholders' equity minus intangible assets, divided by the sum of total assets minus intangible assets.

taxable equivalent income   Tax exempt interest income that, for comparative purposes, has been increased by an amount equivalent to the federal income taxes which would have been paid if this income were fully taxable at the federal statutory rate.

Tier I capital (or core capital)   Consists of an institution's common stockholders' equity plus qualifying perpetual preferred stock less goodwill.

time deposits   Savings accounts or certificates of deposits held in a financial institution for a fixed term or with the understanding that the depositor can withdraw only by giving notice.

total capital   The total of Tier I capital and supplementary capital (Tier II).

9

Health Care

Until the early 1990s, it was relatively easy for health care providers to consistently increase their prices because there was both price insensitivity and a lack of accountability throughout the U.S. health care system. First, price insensitivity: Whenever people are sick, they want the best treatment regardless of the cost. Also, medical providers, trained to deliver the best health care possible, generally did not take the cost of care into account. Even if doctors wanted to reduce inflation in the health care sector, there was little that they could do. For instance, since pharmaceuticals were sold to individual doctors, these doctors had no buying power.

As for accountability, patients were not concerned with health care inflation since their insurers paid their medical costs. Additionally, insurers were not price sensitive because they simply passed the high costs of health care onto employers in the form of higher premiums.

However, by the early 1990s, private health care payors and the government simply could not continue paying for health care costs that were rising three times as fast as overall inflation. Moreover, these payors felt compelled to act to reduce runaway health care costs before the aging baby boomers threatened to force health care costs to spiral further out of control.

These concerns gave rise to managed care providers such as health maintenance organizations (HMOs). One of the methods HMOs have used to squeeze costs out of the system is through capitation, under which the HMOs accept fixed monthly fees for each of their enrollees. In return, HMOs agree to pay medical providers and medical facility operators a fixed monthly fee regardless of the extent to which the HMOs' enrollees use those providers or facilities. Similarly, the government's Medicare program shifted from reimbursing medical facilities for reasonable costs to fixed rates per diagnosis.

Also, the early years of the Clinton Administration scarred the health care industry (especially the drug companies) into reducing its prices. In fact, some of the pharmaceutical companies committed to voluntarily pegging their price increases to a minimal premium over the general inflation rate.

T I P

> Stocks of companies in the health care sector are usually defensive plays (i.e., safe places to park money during times of economic uncertainty or economic sluggishness) because health care companies serve people that are relatively price insensitive. When you need medical attention, you find a way to pay for it.

BRANDED PHARMACEUTICALS

The efforts by third-party payors to contain health care costs (as discussed previously) will make it difficult for drug companies to raise their prices. However, the pharmaceutical companies should be able to increase their volumes for the following reasons:

- Third-party payors (including the government) realize that pharmaceuticals are often the most cost-effective method of treatment. While pharmaceuticals only account for less than 10 percent of the nation's health care expenditures, they save hordes of money by keeping people away from exorbitantly expensive hospitals and doctors. Also, in many situations, symptoms treated early enough with medicine will not become more severe. Thus, it is prudent for the major third-party payors to make drugs more accessible to people.

- The populations of developed countries such as the United States, Japan, and Europe are aging. This is beneficial for drug makers because people over 65 years old consume up to three times the amount of drugs that younger people consume.

- Pharmaceutical companies are becoming more active in disease management—drug companies' assistance in guiding patients' overall care by encouraging patients to take their drugs more regularly.

- Pharmaceutical companies are now increasing demand by advertising their prescription and over-the-counter (OTC) drugs.

T I P

> ☞ It is problematic when pharmaceutical companies agree to limit their price increases to inflation as a way to avoid political pressure. However, during these situations European drug companies, such as Novartis or Glaxo Wellcome, may fare the best because they are more accustomed to price controls.

- Some pharmaceutical companies are forcing the health plans to earn their discounts from drug makers by delivering market-share gains.
- A low dollar helps this industry because pharmaceutical companies derive a great deal of their revenue abroad.

Despite these growth drivers for pharmaceuticals, you should be aware of some of the factors that could impede the volume of pharmaceuticals dispensed. First, advances in medicine can render some drugs obsolete. For instance, a drug that cures an ailment in two weeks will reduce total drug sales if the previous drug took three months to do the same. Second, political pressure on the Food and Drug Administration (FDA) to accelerate its approval time runs the risk of undermining the medical community's confidence in prescribing drugs.

The FDA Approval Process

Unlike most other companies, pharmaceutical firms cannot sell their products as soon as they are discovered. Rather, their products (drugs) must be approved by the FDA—an extremely expensive and time-consuming process. Congress's Office of Technology Assessment reported that the cost to get a new drug approved reached $359 million in 1994, and according to Tufts University, it takes an average of 12 years to bring a new drug to market.

A quick review of the FDA's approval process is in order:

- A pharmaceutical company discovers a new compound and immediately files for patent protection.
- The company spends an average of about 3½ years conducting laboratory and animal studies to determine the drug's side effects and efficacy.
- The company files an Investigational New Drug (IND) application, informing the FDA that human studies will commence in 30 days unless the FDA objects.
- These human studies take roughly six years and consist of three phases.

     In the first phase,

     1. The drug is given to a small number of healthy people to test its safety; the dosage is slowly increased to determine its safety at higher levels.

2. The drug is then administered to patients suffering from the relevant disease.

3. Finally, the largest group of ill patients is tested against placebos in order to ascertain the drug's safety, effectiveness, and dosage regimens.

- When the basic research has been completed, the manufacturer submits a New Drug Application (NDA) to the FDA. (The NDA includes research obtained from all of the phases as well as information regarding the drug's formula, production, labeling and intended use.) While this review process has been accelerated, there are proposals that would result in faster approval times still.

Regardless of when drugs are approved, such approvals are no guarantee of commercial success. Even though only about 5 percent of the drugs that seek approval eventually achieve it, even some of these can be recalled. In fact, some adverse side effects that result in a drug's recall only surface after widespread use of the drug has been established.

T I P

In January of 1996, 13 major drug manufacturers tentatively settled a lawsuit in which independent pharmacies charged these drug makers of conspiring to overcharge them for drugs. While this settlement could cost these manufacturers as much as $600 million, it could be wildly positive for the pharmaceutical industry because the drug companies could use this settlement as an excuse to stop giving large HMOs big discounts.

Faster Approvals

One policy that shortened drug approval times was the Prescription Drug User Fee Act of 1992. This act requires pharmaceutical companies to pay to the FDA (for each drug submitted) a fee covering the cost of hiring more reviewers and thus accelerating the drug review process. Because of this act, approval times for new molecular compounds fell from a mean time of 23 months in 1993 to 14.8 months in 1995.

Encouraged by this success, other proposals to shorten approval times have followed:

- Senator Nancy Kassebaum (R-KS) proposed to force the FDA to reach a decision within four months of receiving an NDA—a policy that could backfire since the FDA may not feel that it has enough time to properly review an NDA and could simply decide to play it safe by rejecting the application.

- It has been proposed that some product reviews be farmed out to outside experts. (This is already done in Europe.) The drawback to this policy, however, is that confidentiality could be compromised. For example, an oversight board reviewing an NDA from the ABC Company could have a reviewer with ties to the XYZ Company. This reviewer could reject ABC Company's proposal and then submit the data to the XYZ Company for development.

T I P

A long review process gives the major pharmaceutical companies an unfair advantage over the smaller companies. Many small biotech companies cannot afford to undergo a long approval process alone; they often partner with a dominant company. Faster approval times, then, could make the biotechs less dependent on the major drug companies. Also, the long review process provides a barrier to entry into the pharmaceutical industry.

Among the other developments and proposals that may result in the pharmaceutical companies' being able to sell their drugs sooner are the following:

- In early 1996, the FDA announced that it will accept evidence of a cancer drug's effectiveness from 26 other countries rather than requiring lengthy testing in the United States. Thus, drugs approved in these 26 countries could become widely available in the United States before companies submit applications for FDA approval.

- Usually drug approval is based on patients' survival time and quality of life—both of which require very long periods of evaluation. However, the FDA may approve some drugs based on "partial responses" or "surrogate markers," such as a therapy's effectiveness in shrinking tumors.

- The FDA may allow the export of some drugs and devices not approved for sale in the United States.

- Drug companies would benefit from being free to distribute scientific literature on unapproved drug uses. Physicians already are permitted to prescribe many drugs for unapproved uses, but the FDA has traditionally enforced regulations against drug-company promotion of such uses.

- The FDA may approve drugs that are either safe *or* effective, but not necessarily safe *and* effective. Similarly, the FDA may allow the sale of unapproved drugs if they state that they are not FDA approved. (Moribund patients have lobbied for such drugs.)

- Drug companies may be allowed to make new products more readily available when they offer substantial promise and when no alternative therapies exist prior to an FDA decision.

Patent Life

If patent protection is granted shortly after the discovery of a new compound, it is now in force for 20 years from the date of filing, yet an NDA may not be granted until many years later. Thus, by the time that a pharmaceutical company is able to sell its discovery, much of its patent protection has expired. And though under the Hatch-Waxman Act of 1984 up to five years of a patent can be restored, there can never be more than 14 years of patent protection from the granting of the NDA.

The branded pharmaceutical companies will benefit from GATT's extending the patent life of branded drugs from 17 years from the date of issuance to 20 years from the filing date. For instance, assume that a drug company discovered a new compound on January 1, 1985, and filed for patent protection on the same day. Then assume that the patent was issued one year later, on January 1, 1986. Under the old patent system, the company would have patent protection until January 1, 2003 (17 years from the date of issuance). However, due to GATT, that same company would enjoy patent protection until January 1, 2005 (20 years from the date of filing). Due to this provision of GATT, Glaxo Wellcome is able to sell its ulcer remedy, Zantac, originally due to lapse in 1995, until July 1997.

Operating Concerns

The pharmaceutical companies were a major beneficiary of physicians' insensitivity to the cost of medicine. However, the growing influence of managed care

TRAP

Ø It is imperative that you understand that patent expirations are potentially devastating for more than just the company whose popular drugs are about to lose their patent protection—rather, an entire class of medication becomes vulnerable in that situation because generic drugs will take market share away from all of the branded drugs in the given category. For example, assume that both company ABC and company XYZ produce branded antidepressants and that the ABC drug will lose *its* protection in 1998 while the XYZ drug will not lose its patent protection until 2008. Even though the XYZ drug has 10 more years of patent life, it will face a barrage of generic competition in 1998.

providers has taken much of these physicians' prescription power away. Rather than doctors' being able to prescribe whichever medicines they choose, more doctors are now part of larger medical groups that have formularies—lists of preapproved medicines from which doctors must write their prescriptions. With use of formularies on the rise, the drug makers must sell their drugs at competitive prices to win places on them.

Despite managed care providers' taking pricing power away from the drug companies, the growth of managed care has proved to be a catalyst for pharmaceutical companies' cost reduction efforts: Drug companies historically relied upon well-paid sales forces to convince doctors all over the country to prescribe their drugs; Now that most of their drugs are sold to relatively few managed care organizations, most of their very expensive sales forces can be eliminated.

Also, the pharmaceutical industry had traditionally been disinterested in manufacturing costs since these costs were almost insignificant compared with the price of their drugs. When each pill was sold for $2, who would care if the costs to produce that pill were two cents, ten cents or twenty cents? Now that there is price pressure on the pharmaceutical industry, the drug companies are making efforts to reduce their manufacturing costs. One method of reducing manufacturing costs is to eliminate excess capacity by merging. For instance, management of the newly merged Pharmacia & Upjohn's believes that it can reduce its cost by $300 million a year by closing 40 percent of its 56 drug-manufacturing facilities.

Proponents of mergers further point out that, in the drug industry, the largest expenses for pharmaceutical companies are the operating expenses (not cost of goods sold). In addition to mergers' allowing drug companies to rationalize their manufacturing, drug makers can further reduce their sales, marketing, administrative, and research expenses. (For instance, American Home Products' 1994 acquisition of American Cyanamid is expected to result in a $650 million cost savings by 1997.) Moreover, merging often creates greater clout for these companies with managed care providers.

However, top-ranking executives at companies such as Pfizer claim that mergers and acquisitions are unwise because drug companies need a large number of R&D projects since one blockbuster drug has to pay for the development costs of dozens of drugs that die in development; the merging of companies jeopardizes the companies' futures by eliminating research projects.

Additionally, Merck, SmithKline Beecham, and Eli Lilly have paid about $13 billion for pharmacy-benefit managers since 1993. However, as discussed below, it is unclear whether these companies will derive any benefits from their acquisitions. This lack of previous success in mergers is another reason why drug companies should be cautious when considering a merger.

Investor Considerations

Before investing in a pharmaceutical company, you should consider the following:

- The company should not be reducing its R&D in terms of its total revenues. Similarly, the company should have many products in late stages of development.

- There should only be a few drugs that cannot be used in conjunction with a company's new approvals. Moreover, the population of patients that cannot use both drugs should be small.

- New approvals should not cause many serious side effects. For instance, on March 25, 1996, Merck's market capitalization lost $1.2 billion when Wall Street learned that Merck wrote to 150,000 doctors and 50,000 pharmacies about side effects suffered by users of its Fosamax osteoporosis drug.

- The company's product lines should be diverse but not so far flung that the company will not benefit from the cross-fertilization of drugs.

- The company's drugs should prove efficacious in initial trials. If too many trials are conducted for a given drug, the FDA could claim that if something is tried 20 times, it will usually succeed at least twice.

- Pharmaceutical companies derive a number of benefits from selling their drugs over-the-counter (OTC). First, branded drugs are awarded three years of exclusivity when the FDA allows a branded drug to sell over-the-counter. Thus, for three years no other company can make a cheaper OTC copy. Second, drug companies can charge as much as the market will bear for OTC drugs. Third, managed care providers are in favor of self-medication because people who do so can avoid going to doctors, thus reducing total health care expenditures. Finally, most third-party payors do not reimburse the purchases of OTC drugs.

GENERIC DRUGS

Generic drugs continue to take market share away from the branded drugs. For instance, the percentage of prescribed drugs filled in the generic form rose from 9 to 50% between 1980 and 1985. By the year 2000, generics should account for about two-thirds of the nation's prescriptions.

The primary reason for such growth is that generic drugs are much cheaper than branded drugs (in early 1996, Bristol-Myers' Capoten™ heart drug was selling for $57 for 100 tablets while generic versions were selling for $3 for 100 tablets) because there is far less research and development associated with the former; generic manufacturers only seek to copy successful drugs, not the compounds that the branded companies failed to bring to market. While it can cost as much as $359 million to bring a branded drug to the market, a generic drug can cost as little as $500,000 to bring to the market.

In addition to the previously discussed factors fueling demand for pharmaceuticals, the following are some of the drivers of demand for generics:

- The major third-party payors (e.g., HMOs and insurance companies) are highly price sensitive. As these third-party payors continue to grow, so too should their reliance on generics to reduce their costs.

- Doctors are less afraid of legal liabilities associated with prescribing generics since the generic drug scandals of 1989 are further behind.

- Popular branded drugs are losing their patent protection. For example, 14 of the biggest selling drugs (which generated annual sales of $10 billion in 1994) will lose their patent protections by the end of 1996.

- Generic drug makers benefit from the liberalization of the terms under which generic drugs are prescribed: It used to be that third-party payors advocated the use of generic drugs only if the active ingredients in those generics were identical to the active ingredients in the branded drugs. Now third-party payors advocate the use of generic drugs as long as the therapeutic effect is the same as the effect of the branded drug, even if the active ingredients are different.

- The Financial Accounting Standards Board's (FASB) rule number 106 requires corporations to report their post-retiree benefits as a liability on their balance sheets. Since drug costs can account for as much as 35 percent of total health care costs among post-retirees, corporations are buying more generics in order to report stronger balance sheets.

- Since the wholesale costs of generics are so low, pharmacies often make more money selling generic drugs than branded drugs. Thus, some drug stores pay their pharmacists bonuses based on their generic fill rates. These bonuses often result in generic substitution—replacing a doctor-prescribed branded drug with a cheaper alternative.

- Some pharmacies have automatic adjudication systems that monitor third-party payors' maximum reimbursable costs. This system tells the pharmacist that there is a fixed reimbursement for all drugs that are available generically. These reimbursement levels are set below the cost of the branded drug. Thus, if the pharmacist dispenses the branded drug, he will either lose money on the prescription or will need to collect additional funds from the patient. Similarly, some HMOs require patients to pay the difference between a branded drug and a generic substitute.

- Since most European countries have nationalized health care systems, their governments are very sensitive to health care costs. Thus, there is tremendous pressure in Europe to use generics whenever possible.

Despite the many drivers of the growth of generics, the following are among the impediments to generics' profitability:

- Generic drug companies face competition from branded companies who are buying or setting up their own generics units. These branded drug companies often begin selling generic versions of their drugs before the branded drug's patent expires, thus allowing the company to secure contracts, establish distribution channels, and begin manufacturing the generic drug before a competing generic company can spring into action. (However, the Federal Trade Commission disavows this behavior as unfairly perpetuating patents.)

- Branded drug companies often enjoy the right of first refusal. Thus, when a branded drug loses its patent protection, the drug purchaser must allow the branded company to counter other companies' offers for the production of the generic version of the drug.

- Generic drugs will still face price pressures from third-party payors. Thus, the fewer the number of competitors for a given line of generic drugs, the better.

- It is important to be first in the generics business. This is because drug stores usually buy the first low-cost alternative and then rarely switch. Also, the first generic drug to steal business from a branded drug (as the latter's patent expires) is usually introduced at around 70 percent of the price of the branded drug. Afterwards, as many more generic drugs enter the market, the price of the drug can be as little as 10 percent of the branded price.

- Drugs that serve small patient bases are not suitable for generics because generic drugs must be produced in high volumes in order to achieve the economies of scale that are necessary to keep costs low. Similarly, since complex drugs involve many steps, they have high learning curves and are expensive to produce.

- Sometimes the supply of compounds for generics is difficult to obtain.

- GATT is problematic for the generic drug companies because it extends the branded companies' patents.

- Capitation reduces the appeal of generic drugs. For instance, if a hospital has access to a pharmaceutical's drugs for a set monthly fee, the hospital may choose to use branded drugs over generic drugs since there is no cost differential.

- Ivax CEO and founder, Phillip Frost, discussed problems with quarterly earnings. "In the generics business, the intense competition and high level of secrecy makes it nearly impossible to preplan earnings. You have no clue when a key approval will come from the FDA. You do not know how many competitors will be in your market or, as a result, how deeply you should discount your product until it's launched." [1]

---

[1] Jennifer Reingold, "Short-Term Jitters at Ivax," *Financial World* 165, no. 4 (March 11, 1996), pp. 24–26.

BIOTECHNOLOGY

Biotech drugs manipulate organisms at the molecular level to produce new products from naturally occurring substances within the body. In other words, biotech drugs treat ailments by repairing abnormal genes. Biotech researchers use gene sequencing to determine how genes make the human body function. Similarly, some biotech companies are working on signal-transduction blocking technology, which will produce drugs that keep cells from malfunctioning by blocking the message that causes them to misbehave. This technology may stop allergies, rheumatoid arthritis, osteoporosis, and transplanted-organ rejection.

Biotech drugs are considered more innovative than traditional chemical-based pharmaceuticals. For instance, from 1991 to 1994, traditional pharmaceutical companies only had 81 truly new drug approvals while 998 new medications were variations of existing drugs. Also, Bristol-Myers Squibb (one of the world's largest cancer research companies) failed to discover Neupogen (a widely popular anticancer drug), which was instead produced by Amgen, a leading biotech company.

Biotech drugs are often more effective in treating previously untreatable ailments. Thus, demand for many biotech drugs is enormous. For example, Chiron's BetaSeron (a treatment for multiple sclerosis) was so popular that a lottery system was used to help decide who the first 20,000 patients would be.

Another advantage of producing break-through drugs is that these drugs move through the FDA approval process faster than "me-too" drugs. Also, since many biotech drugs are relatively new, they will benefit from relatively long-lasting patent protection.

Gene Sequencing

Companies such as Human Genome Sciences use gene sequencing to determine the probability that people with given gene sequences will develop certain diseases. These companies claim that such information is crucial in determining which genes must be altered in order to avert diseases. While this may be true, you should be aware of the following drawbacks associated with gene sequencing:

- There are terrible psychological consequences associated with knowing that you have a high probability of contracting a serious ailment. What 18-year-old wants to know that she has a 92 percent chance of contracting brain cancer by the time she reaches 26? Moreover, while this teenager may be part of the 8 percent of the population with the given gene sequence that will *not* contract brain cancer, the psychological effects of the odds' being against her could produce physiological problems that are even worse than the diagnosis.

- Results of gene sequencing are currently publicly available, producing many problems for people with a serious diagnosis resulting from such tests: it could be harder to obtain health care coverage because such diagnosis would qualify for pre-existing conditions; it could be more difficult for that person to adopt a child, and it could cause one's fiance to cancel the wedding.

- If human genes are too easy to find and sequence, the courts may deem the information "obvious" and thus unpatentable. (Similar rulings were issued with regard to multimedia software and plant genetic engineering.) Or if gene sequencing patents are deemed so broad, the Patent Office may eventually withdraw them, devastating the biotech companies who need these patents to raise capital; these patents ensure that the company is able to earn a profit from its research.

- Many companies that have patented human DNA sequences do not have any related products. For instance, Japan's Takeda Chemical Industries Ltd. had 63 patents but had not developed any gene-related drugs in the spring of 1996.

Company Innovations

It is helpful to assess how innovative a company is. Of course, the more patents and patent applications that a company has the better. However, *Business Week* takes this assessment further by calculating a "patent scoreboard," which has the following three major components:

- *The current-impact index* measures how important a company's patents are based on how often they are cited in other patents. This shows how frequently such patents are used as the foundation for other inventions. The higher a company's Current Impact Index, the better.

- *Technological strength* is a measure of the number patents that a company has times the current-impact index. Again, the higher, the better.

- *Technology cycle time* is the median age of the U.S. patent references cited in the company's new patents. The lower the number, the more quickly the company is replacing one generation of inventions with another.

Investment Considerations

You should consider the following issues before investing in the biotechnology sector:

- It generally takes between 7 to 10 years and between $100 million to $150 million to bring a new biotech drug to market. Since the biotech companies usually have small market capitalizations, they must have access to outside capital in order to be able to continue their product development. Thus,

1. The venture capital business should be strong. Moreover, the venture capitalists' perception of biotechnology should be positive.

2. The stock market should be strong so that biotech companies can raise cash by making secondary offerings.

3. Large pharmaceutical concerns should be receptive to forming partnerships with biotech companies. Interestingly, the large drug companies' buying power increases when biotech companies become desperate. Thus, the majors often delay their deals until the biotechs become *extremely* desperate.

- Biotech drugs should serve large markets (e.g., annual revenues of over $200 million).

- Biotech drugs should generate repeat sales by offering chronic relief as opposed to a one-time fix such as would a vaccine.

- Biotech drugs should be able to be taken orally, not solely by injection.

- The company's management team should be experienced in the private sector (not academia) in order to raise financing and shepherd drugs through the FDA's approval process. The board of directors should consist of an accountant, a venture capitalist, someone with regulatory experience, and someone with connections to the large drug companies.

- The biotech company should have alliances with large pharmaceutical companies. Aside from benefiting from such financing, these alliances indicate that other scientists are confident in the biotech company's research capabilities. The higher the value of these deals in terms of the biotech's market capitalization, the better. Similarly, the more partnerships the biotech has with major drug makers, the better. The greater the premiums that the majors pay over the biotech's stock price, the more confidence the majors have in the biotech's product pipeline. Finally, it is promising when there is competition among the majors for alliances with the biotech company.

T I P

☞ Since these companies usually cannot be analyzed using traditional fundamental tools (because they do not have revenues or earnings), news announcements of drug trials and Wall Street comments greatly affect biotech stocks. For instance, on June 12, 1995, Cephalon announced that its Myotrophin drug could slow the advance of Lou Gehrig's disease. Consequently, on that day alone, Cephalon's stock soared 75 percent.

T R A P

🚫 Since most biotech companies are poorly capitalized and have no earnings, they often compensate their top executives and researchers with stock options. However, biotech companies' earnings per share would be diluted if the FASB required companies to account for the granting of stock options in such a way that shares outstanding would increase.

- If there are many initial public offerings (IPOs) of biotech companies, this sector could become speculative. The earlier the average phase of the IPOs' trials, the more speculation there is in the biotech sector.

Opposition to Biotechnology

There are many opponents to biotechnology. First, politicians such as Senator David Pryor (D-ARK) have accused the biotech companies of price gouging. Indeed biotech regimens can be quite expensive. For instance, BetaSeron can cost $10,000 per year per patient. However, any legislation to cap biotech prices would be catastrophic for the biotech companies because they must earn a return of roughly 25 percent to attract investors. Also, biotech companies must charge high prices because their small product lines serve small patient bases.

Second, many religious leaders are opposed to the patenting of human genes, saying this violates the sanctity of human life and reduces the "blueprint of humanity" to marketable commodities. These opponents are particularly averse to breeding children through eugenetics. The fear is that a mad dictator could use biotechnology to clone himself, thus populating the world with many a Saddam Hussein or Muamar Khaddafy. Additionally, it is feared that overly imaginative combinations of animals could be cross-bred.

DRUG STORES

Publicly traded drug store chains such as Longs Drug Stores and Rite-Aid should benefit from greater demand for prescription drugs, as previously discussed, since most drugs are dispensed at pharmacies. Additionally, drug stores will be a major beneficiary of the trend toward self-medication. More people may actually buy drugs if they are over-the-counter because they can do so without the inconvenience and cost of obtaining a prescription. Similarly, greater use of home care would be of benefit to the drug stores since people would have to procure their own medical supplies.

Large Chains Dominate

Drug store chains should continue to take market share away from the independent drug stores because the big third-party payors find it easier to contract with a few large drug store chains as opposed to many independent operators.

Aside from losing at the prescription counter the independents are losing out in their shopping aisles as well. For instance, independent drug stores' smaller store formats accommodate fewer stockkeeping units. These smaller formats are less convenient places to shop—a major drawback for older people. The independents also have less money to spend on marketing, advertising, and remodeling. Similarly, few of the independents can afford to invest in technology such as scanning equipment, which allows for faster check-outs and better inventory keeping. As a result of these disadvantages, bankers are reducing credit availability for the independents. Moreover, the independent drug stores are hurt more than the drug store chains by the competition that the entire industry faces.

T I P

The higher the percent of prescriptions that a drug store chain fills for people that are covered by managed care or PBMs, the worse. This is, of course, because third-party payors are aggressively reducing their prices. However, some of the largest drug store chains have leverage over PBMs.

Industry Competition

Drug stores face competition from mass merchants. Drug stores complain that because their volumes are lower, they do not get the low prices that are available to the mass merchants and thus, must charge more. However, if more people just pay small co-payments for their prescriptions, then the emphasis will be on convenience instead of price which will benefit drug stores, not mass merchants.

Traditional drug stores also face competition from mail order drug suppliers, such as Bindley Western. These mail order firms are often able to undercut the drug stores on price. One reason is that drug stores must stock everything or they will disappoint customers. Since they buy less of each drug than the mail order houses (since they serve customers locally rather than nationally), their prices are higher. Also, mail order firms can more efficiently utilize their pharmacists, which is important since pharmacists are well paid.

However, the following are some of the factors that will mute the competitive threat from the mail order firms:

- Some drug stores are establishing their own mail order services.

- The prescription shopper is among the most loyal in retailing because these customers depend upon advice from their pharmacists.

- Mail order is only suited for dispensing drugs for chronic relief, not drugs for acute needs. (When you are in severe pain you want immediate relief cannot wait for even the few days it may take to receive drugs from a mail order house.)

- There is some concern about theft of mail order drugs.

- One of the attractions of mail order firms is that they can efficiently dispense large prescriptions. However, large prescriptions (e.g., a 90-day supply) of some drugs such as sleeping pills and antidepressants make it easy for the recipient to commit suicide.

- Some states discourage mail order drugs by requiring the pharmacist that dispenses the drugs to also be licensed in the receiving state.

PRESCRIPTION BENEFIT MANAGERS (PBMS)

PBMs are essentially middlemen between pharmaceutical manufacturers and large drug purchasers. PBMs assemble pharmacy networks with discounted prescription prices for health insurers, health maintenance organizations, and self-insured companies. In addition, PBMs provide claims processing, utilization management, physician monitoring, and education.

In the mid-1990s, PBMs were popular takeover candidates because large pharmaceutical companies believed that acquiring a PBM would ensure distribution to the large third party payors. The prevailing theory was that having a captive PBM would allow the drug company to place its drugs (and exclude its competitors' drugs) on the increasingly important formularies. Thus, Merck acquired Medco Containment Services in 1993 and SmithKline Beecham acquired Diversified Pharmaceutical Services a short time later.

However, these acquisitions are proving to be unrewarding. For instance, the Federal Trade Commission has forced PBM units of large drug makers to handle drugs from all drug makers. Accordingly, the selection of drugs for formularies

TRAP

⊘ Drug stores have been sued for things for which you may not feel they are responsible. For instance, drug stores have been sued for patients' accidentally overdosing on a prescribed drug; for failing to realize that a new drug might interact badly with other medications; and for failing to catch a physician's mistake.

must be based strictly on price and quality considerations. Also, the FTC has blocked PBM units from sharing data with their parent companies about rivals' prices and marketing strategies.

Additionally, third-party purchasers are reluctant to retain PBMs that are affiliated with large drug makers to help establish their formularies. These managed care providers are concerned that such alliances represent a conflict of interest and that they will not provide the lowest prices possible. Thus, it has been rewarding to invest in the PBMs that are not affiliated with drug makers. In fact, shares of Express Scripts soared over 90 percent in seven months.

MEDICAL FACILITIES

The managed care providers have been trying to shift their enrollees away from hospitals, which are extremely expensive, and toward less-expensive facilities such as nursing homes and outpatient surgery centers. Hospitals have accounted for over 40 percent of all health care expenditures, which is more than Americans spend on doctors, dentists, and prescription drugs combined. Moreover, many patients can be effectively treated in lower-cost settings.

The following are among the reasons that it has been so expensive for hospitals to deliver care:

- Hospital charges have traditionally been covered by third-party payors. Thus, doctors and patients were insensitive to costs.

- People genuinely want to be cared for in the most reputable (expensive) hospitals, even when the necessary care can be delivered equally well in many other settings. As one doctor told me, "if a hospital has a good reputation, people will want their toenails extracted there."

- Hospitals provide many services to uninsured and indigent patients who have no means to pay for their treatment. Much of this care is rendered in the emergency room where costs are the highest. Thus, hospitals have large uncollectible receivables.

- Hospitals must be fully staffed around the clock. Similarly, since hospitals must be prepared to treat a vast array of diagnoses, they do not benefit from economies of scale.

- Many hospital employees are unionized.

- Hospitals were traditionally pressured to acquire the most expensive medical equipment, whether or not it was needed, just to be able to retain the best doctors.

HOSPITALS

Since the emphasis throughout the health care industry is to minimize the time people spend in hospitals, it is very difficult for hospitals to raise their revenues.

For instance, the HMOs are problematic for hospitals because they require their enrollees to receive prior authorization before hospital admissions and to obtain mandatory second opinions before surgery. Also, in the early 1980s, the government shifted from reimbursing hospitals for "all reasonable costs" to a fixed schedule of fees based on some 470 diagnostic related groups (DRGs); if hospitals cannot treat an illness for less than the stipulated fees, the hospitals lose money. Similarly, many HMOs contract with hospitals on a capitated basis. Thus, the name of the game in the hospital industry is to aggressively reduce costs.

One way that publicly traded hospital chains such as Columbia/HCA and Tenet Healthcare have been able to reduce costs is to consolidate local markets through mergers and acquisitions. Sometimes these companies buy hospitals and then immediately close them in order to reduce local capacity, thus increasing hospitals' leverage over third-party payors. (In these situations, HMOs cannot extract price breaks by playing one hospital against another.)

There are other advantages of consolidation as well:

1. Consolidation allows hospitals to cut costs by reducing duplication.
2. Mergers yield hospitals greater buying power over medical suppliers.
3. Combining hospitals provides the affected hospitals with the resources to purchase the technology that will increase efficiency.
4. Consolidated hospital operators can often refinance the hospitals' high coupon debt with investment-grade securities.

Investment Considerations

Ideally, the hospital operators in your portfolio should demonstrate the following:

- Rising same-hospital admissions trends.
- A relatively small percentage of fixed-priced patients.
- A declining discharge-to-bill time.
- Rising DRG rates (reimbursement rates) versus changes in the costs of goods and services purchased by the hospital to treat such diagnosis.
- Locations in areas with growing populations.

T I P

It is often wise for hospitals to establish a strategy of co-ownership with physicians. Physicians who have an ownership interest in a facility take a more active role in recruiting other physicians and in improving efficiency by containing costs and making more rational capital expenditure decisions.

- Service to populations with heavy incidences of senior citizens. People over 65 years old typically stay 4.5 times longer in hospitals than do younger people. However, Medicare will continue to vigorously reduce its health care expenses by limiting access and reimbursement to hospitals.
- A rising average length of hospital stays.
- Reducing capacity. However, technology can exacerbate hospitals' excess capacity. For instance, more surgical procedures can be conducted on an outpatient basis. In fact, cataract surgeries used to require a two-week hospital stay but are now performed in doctors' offices on an outpatient basis. Similarly, the growing popularity of minimally invasive treatments increases capacity since patients are discharged sooner.

SUB-ACUTE CENTERS

Dedicated surgical care centers are a prime beneficiary of the trend toward outpatient care. Surgical care centers such as National Surgery Centers are designed, equipped, and staffed for the performance of surgical procedures that do not require overnight hospitalization.

Third-party payors prefer to send their enrollees to surgical care centers because they can perform procedures less expensively than hospitals; surgery centers achieve economies of scale since they perform a high volume of a narrow array of procedures. Since the operations performed there are relatively simple, cases can be scheduled close together, yielding high turnover in operating rooms.

Also, advances in technology broaden the scope of surgeries performed in outpatient facilities. For example, the development of minimally invasive surgical techniques has enabled physicians to perform highly sophisticated procedures on an outpatient basis.

REHABILITATION CENTERS

Rehabilitation providers such as RehabCare Group and GranCare are an interesting niche within the health care industry. First, rehabilitation is extremely cost-effective. Once someone is rehabilitated, they demand fewer continuing treatment costs. In fact, every dollar spent on rehabilitation saves at least $7 in continuing treatment costs. Further, third-party payors appreciate the long-term benefits of rehabilitation. Thus, market share gains by these payors should help the rehabilitation industry.

Second, there are a number of factors fueling demand for rehabilitation service providers. For instance, the aging population is of significant benefit because many older people have the misfortune of deteriorating health and of injuring themselves. Thus, they turn to rehabilitation in order to preserve their self-sufficiency. Also, medical advances are improving the survival rates following illness and trauma, which necessitates rehabilitation. Additionally, sports and recreation are becoming more risky, making it more likely that participants in sports and recreational activities will injure themselves.

T I P

☞ It is preferable for rehabilitation providers to operate in states whose workers' compensation laws encourage workers to use rehabilitation services in order to return to their jobs sooner.

Furthermore, the large, publicly-traded rehabilitation operators have several major advantages over the independent providers. First, due to so much demand for rehabilitative services, the only constraint that rehab companies have upon growth is their ability to attract and retain certified therapists. The larger companies are more successful in this regard because they can afford to offer the most lucrative compensation packages.

Also, rehabilitation is best administered in the facilities that reflect the severity of the patient's problems. As a patient progresses through his rehabilitative course, the ideal setting changes. For instance, a patient that lost his legs in an accident may begin his rehabilitative course with the fitting of prosthetics. The next stages may entail the delivery of rehabilitation in a hospital, in a stand-alone rehabilitation center, on an outpatient basis, and then at home. The larger companies such as Novacare can offer this continuum of care, which is favorable to managed care organizations such as HMOs because it is easier for these payors to contract with one rehabilitation provider that offers a continuum of care rather than a series of rehabilitation providers that offer only one part of the patient's rehabilitation program.

NURSING HOMES

Nursing home operators such as Beverly Enterprises and Healthcare and Retirement stand to benefit from rising demand for their services and diminishing capacity (i.e., supply of nursing home beds). While nursing homes' revenues are largely determined by Medicare and Medicaid reimbursement policies, the significant favorable imbalance between supply and demand should allow these companies to attract a larger percentage of private-paying patients.

One factor fueling demand is demographics. As people age, their deteriorating health often makes it necessary for them to have daily medical supervision. Nursing homes are often the ideal setting because they are less expensive to operate than hospitals. Also, it is more efficient to treat patients that are not self-sufficient in nursing homes than at home. (In nursing homes, there may be 100 patients within walking distance. However, if these patients were treated at home, health care providers would spend more time driving between patients' homes.)

On the supply side of the picture, it is very difficult for nursing homes to expand. In many states, nursing home operators wanting to build new facilities, or even to establish more nursing beds in an existing facility, must apply for a Certificate of Need with the state authorities, who realize that because there is so much demand for nursing home beds, more beds will lead to more nursing home patients. The problem for the states is that most of these patients will pay for their nursing home services with their Medicare benefits, and since most states do not want their Medicare liabilities to rise, they simply reject the nursing homes' Certificate of Need applications.

Interestingly, many nursing homes are raising their per-diem charges by upgrading the level of service that they offer. For instance, nursing homes are expanding into sub-acute care and rehabilitation, thus generating more revenues through the same asset base.

HOME CARE

Home care providers, such as RoTech Medical and Lincare Holdings, should benefit from the growth in home health care. According to the Health Care Financing Administration, total spending on home-based care rose from $3.8 billion in 1985 to $16 billion in 1993. Going forward, total spending is projected to reach $30 billion by the year 2000.

T R A P

> ⊘ Since home care is lightly regulated, there are many allegations of abuse and kickbacks to discharge planners. However, home care cannot be monitored too aggressively due to its being provided in the privacy of the patient's home.

The third-party payors favor their self-sufficient enrollees being treated at home since home care is much less expensive than care delivered in other medical facilities. One explanation for home care's being relatively inexpensive to deliver is its lack of capital intensity; for instance, there are no real estate, building, or maintenance costs. Also, as one chief financial officer of a leading home health care provider told me, "The home health care industry is not capital intensive. If you know a discharge planner and can lease a wheelchair, you can be a player in home care. Even hospitals cannot discharge 100 percent of their patients to home care companies that they own since doing so would violate antitrust rules."

Of course, the aging population is a boon to this industry because roughly 70 percent of the patients on home care are 65 years of age and older. Moreover, minimally invasive surgical procedures and outpatient surgeries have increased the incidence and length of recovery at home. Similarly, advances in technology have dramatically increased the number of diseases that can be treated with home infusion therapy. Finally, clarified regulatory reimbursement guidelines that expand eligibility and heighten payor awareness of the potential cost savings will benefit the home care industry.

TIP

☞ It is preferable to invest in those home care providers that offer home medical equipment (which includes beds, wheelchairs, and walkers) to home care patients because they can profit from the product markups.

HEALTH MAINTENANCE ORGANIZATIONS (HMOs)

HMOs, such as PacifiCare Health and Oxford Health Plans, provide comprehensive health care services to their enrollees for a fixed monthly premium that does not vary with the frequency, value, or type of services provided. These prepaid health plans cover preventative services, checkups, and serious illness. HMOs usually include supervisory features such as mandatory second opinions before surgery, prior authorization before admission to a hospital, and access to specialists only if referred to by the primary care physician. HMOs save money in administrative overhead by not requiring the completion and submission of claims forms. However, HMO enrollees do not enjoy complete freedom in choosing their own doctors.

Enrollment

It is extremely important that HMOs have large and growing enrollments because it is difficult for them to achieve premium increases and because large enrollments provide them with leverage against doctors and hospitals.

HMOs have traditionally expanded their enrollments by managing health care services for employees of large corporations. This was because it was less expensive to market health care plans to employees of large corporations than to welfare recipients or to employees of small companies. However, now that HMOs have penetrated much of the corporate market, they are trying to attract other groups of people, such as Medicare recipients. However, there are constraints as to how fast the HMOs can capture the Medicare market, one reason being older people's frequent resistance to joining HMOs because they prefer to remain with their own doctors.

Since HMOs are primarily regional in nature, you should seek to invest in those that operate in healthy regions of the country. It is especially important that employment growth is growing steadily in the region under review. You should also seek to invest in HMOs that serve underpenetrated regions of the country. Interestingly, it becomes much easier for HMOs to expand once HMO penetration rates in the given region reach between 20 percent and 25 percent because word spreads that HMOs can deliver quality care and because doctors begin to realize that it is incumbent upon them to become affiliated with HMOs.

Competing with Insurance Companies

You should be aware that HMOs often compete with health insurance companies in offering health care coverage. Thus, it is problematic when insurers lower their rates. Also, some insurance companies like CIGNA Healthcare are basically turning themselves into national HMOs.

However, HMOs can make a great deal of money by acquiring indemnity insurers because the insurance company's policyholders pay much more to obtain their coverage. Also, some of the insured will naturally end up visiting doctors and hospitals with which the HMO already has contracts. Thus, it is not surprising that earnings per share of United Healthcare (which acquired The MetraHealth Companies in October 1995) should soar from $2.12 in 1995 to $3.35 in 1997. Additionally, acquiring insurance companies allows HMOs to quickly expand their geographic reach.

Nevertheless, there are risks associated with HMOs' acquiring insurance companies. First, the newly merged company may trade at the insurers' lower multiples since the combined company's exposure to medical costs is higher. Second, there is limited opportunity when the insurer's contracts are for self-insurance. Under these policies, the client takes the risk and uses the insurer only for administrative purposes. This limits the company's upside, since even if it can convert clients from fee-for-service to the more profitable managed-care plans, it still earns only the administrative fee.

Other Investment Considerations

You should consider the following before investing in the HMOs:

- The loss ratio (medical costs/premiums) should be in the range of 77 to 82 percent. While HMOs should strive to lower their loss ratios, there are limits as to how low these ratios can fall. For instance, HMOs may be better off if their expenses rise in the near term so that ailments can be remedied before they become more severe and cost much more. Also, HMOs should make investments in their information systems. Moreover, there is some public sentiment against HMOs' aggressive cost cutting. For example, New York Governor George Pataki signed a bill into law forcing HMOs to pay for hospitals' allowing new mothers to remain there at least 48 hours after giving birth.

- The HMO should have a low disenrollment rate.

- The HMO's patient bed days-per-thousand ratio should be below the industry average. (This ratio measures the number of days that a HMO's enrollees spend in hospitals.)

- Many contracts between HMOs and their networks stipulate that the HMOs will pass along to their networks any premium increase that the HMOs obtain from their customers. Since these stipulations make it difficult for HMOs to expand their profit margins, it is preferable to invest in HMOs that do not have these stipulations.

- The average age of the HMO's members should be below the industry average since younger people generally need less medical attention.

- The HMO should have below-industry-average Medicare complaint rates.

- The HMO should score well on reports by the National Committee for Quality Assurance (NCQA). The NCQA ranks HMOs on at least 50 plan activities related to quality management and improvement, credentialing, rights of members, preventative health services, medical records, utilization management, and enrollee satisfaction measures. High NCQA ratings are crucial for winning new contracts.

- Medicare reimbursement rates are set on a county-by-county basis. Thus, it is preferable to invest in those HMOs that operate in counties with rising Medicare reimbursement rates.

- It is best to avoid investing in the HMOs that operate in the states that have "any willing provider" legislation. Any willing provider legislation requires HMOs to include any doctor or hospital in its network as long as they are willing to accept the HMO's prevailing rate. HMOs prefer to limit the number of doctors that they include in their systems, thus allowing them to negotiate lower fees in return for promising large physician groups the exclusive rights to a high volume of business. With any willing provider legislation, large doctor groups are less willing to give up-front discounts in the hope of getting increased volume. This is because the doctors would know that any other provider in the community could get into the network by matching the early bidder's rate.

- It is preferable to avoid investing in HMOs that operate in states requiring them to disclose any financial incentives they offer participating physicians to hold down medical expenses.

- HMOs that have shares trading at low market capitalization-to-enrollee ratios may be takeover targets. For instance, assume that there were a few HMO takeovers within the past three months and that the average

T R A P

⃠ A large part of the profits that many physician practice management companies generate come from hefty markups on the prices of drugs that they dispense. Since these markups are a target for HMOs and government programs such as Medicare and Medicaid, the profits of many PPMs could plunge.

valuation of the acquirees' enrollees was $1,000. Thus, if you have discovered an HMO whose market capitalization-to-enrollee ratio is $600, this HMO may be an attractive investment because it could become an acquisition target.

PHYSICIAN PRACTICE MANAGEMENT COMPANIES (PPMS)

Physicians are extremely powerful players in the health care sector. Doctors control patient admissions to hospitals and play a part in determining which medicines are prescribed as well as which equipment their hospitals purchase. In fact, physicians indirectly control about 80 percent of the nation's total health care expenditures.

In 1965 only 10 percent of U.S. physicians were part of medical groups. However, reimbursement pressures from managed care providers, greater administrative burdens, greater competition from a glut of doctors, and rising malpractice insurance costs have made it increasingly difficult for doctors, to maintain private practices. In fact, by the year 2000, 60 percent of America's physicians should be part of groups.

Thus, many doctors are joining physician practice management companies (PPMs) such as Phycor and Coastal Physician Group. PPMs allow doctors to focus more on treating their patients by undertaking all of the office management work including billing, scheduling, staffing, recruiting, and other paperwork. PPMs also help negotiate volume contracts with other health care providers like hospitals, malpractice insurers, and medical device suppliers. Additionally, PPMs provide doctors with access to capital that is necessary to install information systems and state-of-the-art technologies.

AMBULANCE OPERATORS

The publicly traded ambulance operators, such as American Medical Response and Rural Metro, are an interesting niche for investors to consider. First, independent operators are being squeezed out. This is because the ambulance business is capital intensive since computers, satellite time, emergency medical technicians, and ambulances are needed. Interestingly, these communications systems are vital since ambulances must be the first on the scene.

Second, earlier discharged patients need ambulances to go home or to return for treatment. Similarly, hospitals are discontinuing unprofitable specialties, which results in more patients being transported by ambulance to and from the remaining facilities. Also, some HMOs demand that their patients be transferred in ambulances from emergency rooms to their preferred hospitals.

Interestingly, hospital transfer patients and other nonemergency cases are more profitable than emergency cases because they allow the ambulance service to reject the uninsured, which cannot be done when responding to emergency calls. On the other hand, since these companies *are* obliged to pick up all emergency victims, about 40 percent of ambulance companies' bills go uncollected.

Third, many uninsured people are treated at home by paramedics and many politicians are calling for increased reimbursement for such care. Also, more curbside medicine may be delivered by emergency medical technicians. For instance, ambulances may be used to go to poor neighborhoods to administer vaccinations and to perform checkups.

Fourth, paramedics hired by the private ambulance companies are much less expensive than firemen because they are less extensively trained. Thus, there is

TIP

It is most expensive for hospitals to treat patients in their emergency rooms. Therefore, PPMs such as Inphynet Medical Management that specialize in emergency department physician services could benefit from greater outsourcing of emergency room functions.

some growth potential as cities and counties are considering privatizing their ambulance services in order to reduce their budget deficits.

MEDICAL DEVICE MANUFACTURERS

Medical device manufacturers, such as Becton, Dickinson and Stryker, face a number of challenges in the years ahead. First, outright restrictions by managed care companies on certain procedures will have a negative impact on sales of medical devices. Similarly, the fact that HMOs are taking decision-making power away from doctors and are restricting access to specialists will result in fewer procedures.

T R A P

⊘ It is difficult for private ambulance operators to compete against government ambulances since the latter pay neither taxes nor rent.

Second, hospitals traditionally relied upon their surgeons to decide which medical devices they should buy. Since doctors were paid by procedure, they wanted the most innovative medical devices (regardless of the cost) so that their procedures would be very smooth. Now, more doctors are being compensated on a salary and bonus basis. Since these bonuses are often tied to their groups' profitability, doctors will be more selective in the devices that they recommend their hospitals to buy.

Third, consolidation in the hospital industry will hurt the medical device manufacturers because there will be fewer potential purchasers and because the remaining purchasers will have more bargaining power. For example, Columbia/HCA does not allow suppliers to send commissioned sales people to its premises. These sales people can only explain the usage medical devices, not try to increase volume of their sales. For similar reasons, the consolidation of doctors' offices will hurt the medical device industry.

Fourth, advances in medicine reduce the demand for medical devices. For example, there are fewer thyroid procedures since doctors have learned that most thyroids are not malignant. Also, there are fewer gastrectomies since related problems can be treated with drugs such as Tagamet™ and Zantac™.

Fifth, it used to be that the fear of malpractice lawsuits encouraged doctors to run many tests in order to insulate themselves from malpractice claims. However, recent malpractice reforms reduce the demand for laboratory testing and therefore less equipment is needed. For example, in California, trial lawyers and doctors have agreed to just one year of discovery as well as structured settlements. (An example of a structured settlement is when payouts are made annually rather than up front. Such settlements are easier to finance and can be much lower if the recipient dies before receiving the entire settlement.) Also, some states have placed limits on pain and suffering awards resulting from malpractice.

MEDICAL DISTRIBUTORS

Similar to the medical device companies, medical distributors, such as Baxter International and Owens & Minor have a number of obstacles to contend with. First, distributors' sales and earnings may be adversely impacted because the relative inability of medical device manufacturers to raise their prices will limit markups at the wholesale level. Second, distributors may be adversely impacted by sophisticated buyers purchasing generic drugs directly from the manufacturers so as to avoid the wholesalers' markups. Third, since hospitals are heavily bureaucratic, medical distributors' receivables are often outstanding for long periods of time.

CLINICAL INFORMATION

Health care providers are relying on state-of-the-art information systems to better serve patients and payors. Thus, companies that are proficient in collecting, processing, and interpreting data related to the effective provision of health care have been very popular investment themes in the mid-1990s. For example, Cerner

T I P

Manufacturers of minimally invasive devices such as Boston Scientific should benefit from the warm reception that the medical community has demonstrated toward these cost-saving devices.

Corporation's shares soared from less than $12 in 1994 to $36 in 1995. Also, HBO & Company's shares surged from less than $33 in 1995 to over $121 by early 1996.

The following are among the reasons for the growing importance of clinical data:

- The delivery of health care is becoming increasingly integrated. Thus, the larger entities can only serve their growing patient loads if they are able to share and access information quickly and easily.

- Health care payors rely on outcomes data in selecting their health care providers.

- The methods of paying for health care are shifting from fee-for-service to capitated arrangements. Since medical care providers are no longer reimbursed for each procedure, they are now required to have a much better understanding of the actual costs associated with providing health care products and services. Similarly, the provision of health care to indigent people makes it more important for health care providers to try to reduce their expenses.

10

Cyclical Industries

As the category implies, the performance of cyclical companies is largely contingent upon the health of the economy. Thus, when the economy is booming, cyclical companies are likely to experience strong revenue growth. However, what many investors do not adequately appreciate is that, a strong economy puts pressure on the cost structure of many cyclical companies. For instance, when the steel mills are generating very healthy profits, the United Steelworkers union often threatens to strike for higher wages. Also, when cyclical companies such as the forestry producers are making solid profits, they are tempted to expand their capacity which causes pricing to deteriorate. Thus, the best time to invest in a cyclical industry is not when the economy is at its peak but rather when the economy is beginning to rebound from a downturn. During this recovery phase, revenues expand while cost pressures remain benign.

INTEGRATED STEEL MANUFACTURERS

Integrated steelmakers are highly capital intensive and highly cyclical. They are highly capital intensive because their factories require exorbitantly expensive blast furnaces, basic oxygen furnaces, and rolling mills. Also, most integrated steel mills are reliant on unionized labor.

They are highly cyclical because their largest end markets—the transportation industry, the construction industry and the capital goods industry—are highly cyclical. Moreover, steel operators are interest-rate sensitive (and interest rates are a main driver of economic cycles) because they typically carry heavy debt loads.

Manufacturing Processes

Integrated steel mills undertake every step of the steel making process. The integrated manufacturing process typically began with the conversion of mixtures of iron ore, limestone, and coke (made from coal) into molten iron using a blast furnace. Historically, this resulting molten iron was refined into raw steel in a basic oxygen furnace. This steel was then cast into ingots, from which the resulting steel was later shaped into slabs, billets, or blooms of steel. However, this ingot teaming method was inefficient since molten metal was cast in ingots only to be removed from those ingots once they solidified.

Now, most integrated mills have replaced this method with continuous casting, under which molten iron is directly converted to rolls, plates, bars, tubes and other marketable products in rolling mills. Thus, continuous casting allows steelmakers to bypass the production of ingots and the casting of billets, slabs, and blooms, and it is less complicated and yields a product of superior quality.

Efficiency Measurements and Gains

Virtually all of the U.S. steelmakers have enhanced their productivity by shifting to continuous casting. However, you should search for those steel companies that constantly strive to increase their efficiency, indications of which include

- A decline in the number of man-hours required to produce a ton of steel.
- A rise in the number of tons of steel produced per employee.
- A rise in operating profits per ton of steel produced.
- A decline in the company's rejection rates from both its internal inspections and from its customers. The company's rejection rates should also be below the industry average.
- Very high capacity utilization rates. Making the greatest use of its facilities most effectively leverages the company's fixed costs.
- A relatively low yield. (Yield is the ratio of raw steel to shipped steel. The difference between raw steel and shipped steel is scrap steel.) When a steel mill becomes extremely efficient, little scrap steel will result. However, not having enough scrap steel can force the steel company to buy scrap steel on the open market.
- Their being located in places with good access to transportation since low transportation costs and reliability are important factors in steel mills' winning contracts. Thus, you should try to avoid investing in the steel companies that could be adversely impacted by railroad track reductions resulting from consolidation in the railroad industry.

- Improvement in existing facilities as opposed to a closing down of the most wasteful operations.

- No loss of tonnage (even of low-grade steel) to the minimills. (Losing tonnage is problematic because the integrateds need to maintain high operating rates to maintain reasonable average production costs.)

Worker Relations

You should consider the degree of unionization in the steel industry. One of the best indications of the degree of the steel industry's unionization is the percentage of steel that is produced by unionization labor. It is preferable when this percentage is declining.

You should also consider trends in steel companies' relations with their unionized workers. First, the longer the period of time that union contracts cover, the more trust there is between the steel mill and its workers. Second, steel mills benefit when they are not required to hire new workers for retired workers. (However, guaranteeing jobs is not so bad for steel companies if many of their workers are older since many of them will retire in the near future anyway.) Other favorable clauses in union contracts include swapping equity for wage concessions, allowing the cross-training of workers, and having fewer job classifications. Finally, you should refer to the discussion regarding strike funds in the automobile chapter on page 312.

Aside from union relations, you should consider the number of recordable lost-day incidents and injuries that the steel company under review experiences. Similarly, you should search for companies with low and declining absentee rates. Also, you should be aware that integrated mills typically have high legacy costs, which include obligations to pay pension and health care benefits to retirees. The integrated mills have had severely underfunded pensions, it is thus preferable to invest in a steel operator that has a young labor force since this results in lower medical costs and lower pension expenses.

You should search for steel companies that are not top heavy. Thus, the steel companies in your portfolio should have a high ratio of tons shipped to salaried employees. For instance, it is better to invest in a company that has 50 salaried

T I P

To gauge the efficiency of a company's workers, it is important to measure the output in units (not revenue) that each worker produces. The flaw with measuring worker productivity in terms of revenues per worker is that rising prices can account for the rising revenues.

employees and ships five million tons (100,000 tons per salaried employee) than a company that has 65 salaried employees and ships six million tons (92,308 tons shipped per salaried employee).

Steel Processing Plants

A great deal of steel produced by integrated mills is further processed at separate steel processing plants such as those operated by Pittsburgh Des Moines. These processing plants do not manufacture steel. Rather they cut and shape the steel and give it the precise qualities the end customers request.

Since processing centers cater to the end buyers of steel, the processors are very sensitive to changes in customer demand for steel. Thus, it is extremely important to monitor changes in these processing centers' steel inventories. When these inventories are very high (in terms of the number of average weeks it would

T R A P

There are instances where factory capacity can be overstated, resulting in capacity utilization being understated. For instance, in the early 1990s, some steel mills had capacity that could not be used because doing so would have violated environmental regulations. However, some of these steel companies could not reduce their stated capacity because they lacked the equity to write off their noneffective capacity. Thus, these companies' capacity utilization was understated. Therefore, it is important that you consider a steel mill's *effective* capacity.

normally take customer orders to deplete such inventory), the outlook becomes bearish for steelmakers because the steel processors will be able to use their inventories (rather than buy more steel) to meet their customers' orders. Conversely, low inventory levels at the steel-processor level are bullish for the integrated steel companies since the steel processors will be forced to meet a rise in customer orders by buying more product from the integrated mills.

In order to determine the demand for steel, you must consider the strength of the end markets for steel. The largest markets for steel are construction, transportation, and capital goods.

Transportation

The transportation sector is a major consumer of steel as there is a great deal of steel in automobiles and other segments of the transportation industry. For example, railroad tracks are composed of steel, as are locomotives, freight cars, and

T R A P

⊘ Often, steel unions threaten to strike during a presidential election. Usually when this happens the candidates promise to intervene on the unions' behalf. The reason is that steel making represents a chokepoint for the U.S. economy since up to 61 times as many people work for industries that are dependent on steel than the number of people that work directly for the steel mills.

loading cranes. Also, parts of freight containers used by trucks, railroads, and barges are composed of steel. Thus, the steel industry benefits when more containers and railroads are manufactured or when railroad tracks are added or replaced.

You should consider the number of pounds of steel in automobiles. Of course, the greater the trend in the number of pounds of steel used in automobiles, the better for steelmakers. However, the steelmakers face serious challenges from aluminum and plastics producers.

There are a number of benefits for automakers replacing steel with aluminum:

1. Aluminum is easier to form into shapes, making it more efficient to produce automotive parts; for instance, aluminum can be extruded while steel must be stamped.

2. Since aluminum is lighter than steel, vehicles with aluminum can use smaller engines, which yields better fuel economy and less pollution.

3. It takes less energy to recycle scrap aluminum than to recycle scrap steel.

4. Aluminum is corrosion resistant.

However, aluminum producers face a number of obstacles in serving the auto industry:

1. Aluminum prices are more volatile than those of steel since aluminum trades as a commodity whereas steel is purchased pursuant to long-term contracts.

2. Automakers would need to invest billions of dollars in machinery to form and bond aluminum at high volumes, and aluminum is more expensive on a total production basis. (In fact, according to a study by the Massachusetts Institute of Technology, for each dollar car makers save by substituting aluminum for steel, they spend $1.50 in added raw materials and manufacturing costs.)

3. Since steel is sturdier than aluminum, steel cars hold up better in crashes. Similarly, there is less liability for automakers manufacturing cars out of

steel since there are nearly 100 years' experience and crash data from cars made from steel, while there is comparatively little testing of how aluminum cars hold up in crashes.

4. Steelmakers are trying to reduce the weight of steel and have already designed a steel car body weighing as much as 35 percent less than the typical body for a five-passenger sedan.

One advantage that *plastic* has over steel is cost.

Plastic auto parts are generally less expensive since tooling costs are much lower and because one plastic part can take the place of several steel parts that must be welded or bolted together. The use of plastics in automaking results in labor and weight savings, as well as enhanced aerodynamic properties. Thus, plastics have replaced steel in such applications as dashboards, fenders, and inner panels.[1]

TRAP

⊘ Overly aggressive accumulation of semi-finished steel by steel processors may be a signal to sell integrated steel stocks because such accumulations may mean that these processors believe that supply from integrated producers may be interrupted (e.g., as a result of strikes).

However, plastic materials are not well suited in applications where resistance to high temperatures is necessary, and plastics used for automaking are extremely difficult to recycle because cars contain about 25 chemically incompatible kinds of plastics, which cannot be melted together and reused. The impracticality of recycling plastics is extremely problematic since 95 percent of the 10 million cars and trucks that are retired each year go to recyclers.

Construction

The construction industry is a major destination for steel. There is a lot of steel in homes, office buildings, and civil works. For example, there are nails, joists, beams, plumbing, and air conditioning in new homes. Thus, rising housing starts are a boon for the steel industry. Also, the steel industry benefits from increased spending on civil works (where steel is used in bridges, dams, and tunnels), which occurs when the nation's infrastructure is being repaired as well as from pork barrel funding for those programs. For further discussion on the construction industry, you should refer to page 288.

---

[1] Standard & Poors Industry Surveys, February 16, 1995.

The growing popularity of constructing homes with steel frames could be highly beneficial to the steel industry. There are numerous advantages of steel framed housing:

- Steel-framed housing is sturdier than wood-framed housing. Similarly, steel does not burn, warp, rot, or attract termites as does wood. Thus, fire insurance premiums are lower for steel-framed housing than for wood-framed housing.

- Steel responds to capacity better than wood: A ton of steel can be produced in only four man-hours; it can take as long as 80 years to wait for a tree to grow.

- There is less waste in manufacturing steel-framed housing compared with wood-framed housing.

T I P

Stocks of steel companies often fall when steel prices deteriorate. However, the steel processors, which acquire semi-finished steel to use as their raw material, benefit from lower steel prices. (Other times, steel processors do not buy steel. Instead, they enter into trolling agreements with their customers; under trolling, the steel processors treat the steel for a fee.) Thus, you may be able to bottom fish for stocks of steel processors such as Worthington Industries or Gibraltar Steel when both the price of steel and steel stocks are low.

However, there are several significant obstacles to using steel frames in houses. For instance, steel is more conducive than wood, meaning that steel frames cool faster and thus require more insulation—an added expense for the home buyer. Similarly, steel can burn workers' hands, and most homebuilders are inexperienced in cutting and joining steel. Furthermore, homebuilders are concerned that steel will not conform to housing codes; many builders fear having to pay for additional engineering to have their houses certified as safe. Finally, environmentalists are not whole-heartedly in favor of steel since the production of it is energy intensive and comes from a nonrenewable source.

Capital Goods

You should refer to the discussion of capital goods on page 301, for determining how the outlook for capital goods manufacturers will impact the steelmakers.

Foreign Considerations

In analyzing the domestic steelmakers, you must consider foreign competition. Many foreign governments (even Western European governments) substantially control their steel industries through heavy subsidization. These governments manage their steel industries, not to make money or to manufacture steel efficiently, but as a means to employ people. As a result, these countries produce large volumes of steel. However, as these countries face growing budget deficits of their own and become parties to international trade agreements, they will have to reduce their money-losing social programs and should accordingly reduce their output of steel.

You should consider the rate at which foreigners are reducing their steel capacity. Less foreign capacity should mean less competition for U.S. steel companies. Reduced steelmaking capacity on a worldwide basis will also mean that there will be fewer imports and therefore higher domestic prices.

Greater demand for steel in developing countries will help the U.S. companies in two significant ways. First, increased foreign demand will keep foreign steelmakers out of the United States. For instance, rising demand for steel in Eastern Europe will result in Western European steel producers shifting some of their U.S.-bound exports to Eastern Europe. Second, the U.S. steel companies will win some of the new business.

Valuation

You should consider the market capitalization of a steel company in terms of the tons of capacity that it is capable of producing on an annual basis. If this ratio is lower than the amount of money that it would take to replace that capacity, the company would be undervalued in terms of its replacement costs. For example, assume that the market capitalization of the steelmaker under review is $750 million and that the steelmaker can produce three million tons of steel annually.

T R A P

⊘ Announcements of steel companies increasing their prices is not always positive. First, these price increases do not always stick. Second, the steel companies could have previously agreed to sell a large percent of their steel at lower prices. For instance, in January 1996, U.S. Steel and LTV announced a February 4, 1996, price increase. However, these companies' large customers (e.g., automakers and household appliances) had already obtained supply contracts for 1996 at lower prices.

Under this set of facts, each ton of capacity is valued at $250 ($750m/3m). Then, if you learned that another steel company was planning to spend $2 billion on a steel mill that would ultimately produce four million tons of steel annually, each ton of this new mill's capacity would be valued at $500 ($2b/4m). Thus, the steel company with the older mills would be an attractive takeover candidate since its capacity is valued lower than its replacement costs.

TIP

☞ Another boon to steelmakers is when more of the foreign vehicles sold in the United States are manufactured domestically as opposed to being manufactured abroad (with foreign steel) and then shipped to the United States.

MINIMILLS

Minimills like Nucor Corporation are steel companies that have lower cost structures than integrated mills because they incorporate fewer steps into their manufacturing processes. They typically begin their manufacturing by melting scrap iron or steel in electric arc furnaces, which is much less expensive than converting iron ore, coking coal, and limestone in blast and oxygen furnaces. Then, the resulting steel is continuously cast into blooms and billets.

The steel that minimills produced was historically of a lower quality than the steel that the integrateds produced. However, the minimills have taken over 40 percent of the domestic steel market from the integrateds because their costs are lower and because they have been making increasingly higher grades of steel.

Aside from the less-complicated manufacturing process, minimills such as Oregon Steel Mills and Birmingham Steel enjoy the following cost advantages over integrated steel companies:

- Minimills do not have to locate near supplies of raw materials. Thus, they can go to a large number of states and seek out the lowest-cost electric power whereas the integrated companies are hostage to regions that produce coking coal to fuel their blast furnaces. As a result, minimills are able to operate closer to their customers, which reduces their transportation costs. However, it is important for minimills to locate close to their sources of scrap steel.

- Many minimills are located in the southern and midwestern part of the United States and benefit from less-expensive, nonunion labor. Thus, minimills' employee compensation costs are often linked to production and profits, not union contracts, and their employees are more flexible and present lighter retiree obligations than do the integrated steel mills' employees.

- Since minimills are generally newer than the integrated mills, their facilities and technology are generally more sophisticated.

- Minimills have an environmental cost advantage over the integrateds since minimills are naturally cleaner. Integrateds must face the problem of coking coal emissions, which are highly toxic. In fact, coke oven emissions represent the most expensive problem posed by the Clean Air Act.

Scrap steel (which is generated as a by-product of the integrated steel-making process as well as derived from retired automobiles, household appliances, railroad tracks, and the like) is the main input for minimills. Thus, minimills can be severely adversely impacted by higher scrap prices. The following factors can cause the price of scrap steel to rise:

- Rapid expansion by the minimills.

- A boost in the internal use of scrap steel by integrated steelmakers.

- The adoption of continuous casting. This process reduces the amount of revert (or home scrap) that is a by-product of the integrated steel making process, forcing the integrateds to buy scrap on the open market, thereby pushing scrap prices higher.

- It is important that minimills (especially those that wish to produce steel for finished products) use low residual ferrous scrap. In other words, scrap cannot contain too much nonferrous elements such as copper, zinc, plastic, and other materials. Problems with residuals include the compromise of surface quality and a decline in the resulting steel's ability to bend without cracking.

Another concern is that the minimills are expanding their capacity too quickly. For example, domestic minimill capacity will probably be 40 percent higher in 1997 than in 1995. Aside from this capacity reducing the pricing structure in the minimill industry, too much capacity encourages minimill executives to start their own minimills, which further exacerbates the capacity problem. Additionally, the existing minimills may lose the managerial depth necessary to compete against the integrateds.

TIP

👉 Rising steel imports do not necessarily mean that foreigners are becoming more competitive than domestic producers. Indeed, there have been times when domestic demand was so strong that American steel producers could not satisfy all of the domestic demand.

TIP

☞ When foreign steel producers invest heavily in joint ventures with U.S. producers, these foreign steel producers usually will not aggressively try to export to the United States since this would be competing against themselves under these circumstances, U.S. steel stocks should benefit as American steel producers will face less foreign competition.

CONSTRUCTION INDUSTRY

Since the construction industry is highly cyclical it is difficult for these companies to consistently post rising earnings. For instance, all of the major publicly traded homebuilders posted lower earnings-per-share results in the bottom of the recession of 1990 than in 1989. In fact, some of this earnings deterioration was dramatic. For instance, Hovnanian Enterprises earned $1.05 a share in 1989 but lost $.74 a share in 1990 while The Ryland Group's earnings per share plunged from $3.25 in 1989 to $1.53 in 1990. Moreover, general contractors usually experience similar earnings deterioration in recessions. For instance, Perini Corporation's earnings per share slid from $3.11 in 1989 to a loss of $1.20 in 1990.

Due to this cyclicality, many investors view construction stocks more as trading vehicles than long-term investments. If you decide to trade the construction stocks, you must stay ahead of earnings releases. Thus, you should consider purchasing these stocks on announcements of housing starts or the receipt of large commercial or civil works contracts, rather than waiting for earnings announcements. Likewise, you should be prepared to sell these stocks on indications of deteriorating economic conditions such as rising interest rates or rising inventories of unsold homes.

HOMEBUILDING

Demand Factors

As you probably have already realized, the homebuilding industry is very interest-rate sensitive. Of course, this is because people rely on mortgages to finance the purchase of their homes. Thus, low interest rates and declining mortgage rates are bullish for the homebuilding industry.

One indication of the future direction of adjustable mortgage rates is the strength of the bond market. Since bond yields move in reverse direction to bond prices, the higher bond prices rise, the lower the bond yields (and consequently adjustable mortgage rates) fall. Therefore, when the bond market is strong, declining mortgage rates are likely to make homes more affordable.

When mortgage rates fall, mortgage applications should rise, an early indicator of housing starts. Also, increased competition in the mortgage banking industry should result in higher levels of mortgage originations. Interestingly, mortgage refinancings are a leading indicator of mortgages for home purchases. This is because mortgage banks make less money when mortgages are repaid sooner, so they become more aggressive in originating new mortgages in order to counter this problem. Also, it is beneficial to homebuilders when government regulators pressure banks and other mortgage market players to enlarge their low-income and minority lending.

However, if homeowners' insurance or earthquake insurance is limited, banks will not provide for mortgages. Similarly, you should consider if the government cracks down on its federal relief efforts and instead forces people to buy disaster insurance in disaster-prone areas. Such policies would hurt the homebuilders since the true cost of living in such areas would be increased.

You should also consider the direction of home affordability indexes in various geographic regions of the country. For example, Fannie Mae's affordability index relates the principal and interest payments on a median-priced home (assuming a 30-year mortgage and a 20-percent down-payment) to the median family income. For instance, a reading of 23 means the median family would have to spend 23 percent of its income on principal and interest payments on a new median-priced home. Of course, the homebuilders that serve the regions with the lowest Fannie Mae home-affordability readings stand to benefit the most from rising orders.

Other opportunity indexes relate the percentage of families in a given area that can afford to buy a home at the median price in the given locality. The homebuilders that serve the localities with the highest opportunity index readings face the most promising futures.

A strong resale market is important for homebuilders. Regions of the country that are experiencing rising prices for existing homes better allow people to finance the purchase of their new homes. Also, robust sales of existing and new homes reduces backlogs. Thus, the fewer the number of months of supply of newly built homes and existing homes that a region has, the better the outlook becomes for that region's homebuilders.

You should consider home-ownership rates in a given region of the country in conjunction with savings rates in the same region. While lower-than-average home-ownership rates may indicate that there is upward potential for home ownership, people in that region will typically not be able to buy a home unless they have sufficient savings to make a down payment. (It is important to consider savings rates/levels rather than income because virtually everyone has to save to make a down payment.) Thus, suppose the home-ownership rate is only 55 percent in California but the savings rate there is only 3 percent of income, while the home-ownership rate in Florida is 65 percent and the savings rate there is 7 percent of income; the homebuilders in Florida may have more upward potential because the higher savings rate indicates that there is greater home affordability in Florida.

Vacation Homes

One profitable niche in the homebuilding industry includes the contractors that build vacation/secondary homes. First, high prices do not intimidate the wealthy as these people are not terribly sensitive to cyclical weaknesses in the economy. Second, prices of vacation homes are less subject to erosion than primary residences. One reason is that sellers are rarely under pressure to sell or to enroll their children in school by September.

Third, there are usually few hotels in exclusive areas. Thus, rental incomes generated by owners of vacation homes can cause the prices of vacation homes to rise. (You can consider the percentage of a home's capital value that a renter pays to use during peak seasons. The higher, the better.) Finally, many vacation-home owners do not use mortgages and would therefore be less impacted by reduced tax deductibility of mortgage payments, perhaps resulting from flat-tax initiatives.

T I P

Vibrant home sales are beneficial to the home improvement retailers such as Home Depot, Hechinger, and Lowe's. This is because sellers often remodel their homes to make them more appealing. Similarly, people often remodel parts of their homes within two years of moving in. Other factors that benefit home improvement retailers include an aging housing stock, harsh weather, and a strong home-improvement work ethic.

Demographics

Demographics play an important role in household formation, which is a major driver of demand for housing. One of your first demographic considerations should be the pool of 25-year-old men. The reason is that 25 is the median age for men marrying for the first time which is when young people typically form their first households. The more men that are 25 years of age, the better.

The greater the percentage of families that have children, the more optimistic the outlook becomes for homebuilders because most families with children prefer to live in houses as opposed to apartments.

Another demographic consideration is the divorce rate. Actually, higher divorce rates are positive since one divorcee needs a new home. To illustrate, according to my own unscientific surveys, 48 percent of America's husbands kiss their wives goodbye when they leave their homes but virtually 100 percent of America's husbands kiss their homes goodbye when they leave their wives.

Also, rising levels of immigration result in higher demand for homes. However, it is important to realize that it takes about 10 years for immigrants to be able to afford homes. Due to the wide disparities in home-ownership rates among immigrants it is important to consider the countries from which these immigrants come. Homebuilders that serve areas that have higher levels of oriental or Western European immigrants benefit more than homebuilders that serve areas predominated by Latin American immigrants. This is because, according to Harvard University's Joint Center for Housing Studies, 82.8 percent of Chinese/Taiwanese immigrants who came to the United States between 1970–1979 and were between 35–44 years of age in 1990 owned homes in 1990. The home-ownership rates for other ethnic groups of the same age range were as follows: Western Europe—71.1 percent; Korea—66.2 percent; Mexico—43.2 percent; and Central America—29.3 percent.

The final positive demographic factor that will be discussed here is the legalization in some states of homosexual marriages. The homebuilders that operate in the states that legalize gay marriages could experience greater demand for housing than homebuilders that operate in comparable states that do not legalize gay marriages. This is because homosexuals may feel that their relationships will be more enduring if they have legal sanction, and as a result of a greater sense of permanence, the two partners may feel more comfortable buying a house together.

Of course, some demographic shifts can be negative for the homebuilding industry. For instance, more adult-age children returning to live with their parents reduces household formation and demand for housing. Also, greater numbers of single mothers are problematic for homebuilders because it is extremely difficult for the typical single mother to save enough money to make a down-payment on a house.

Geographic Variances

Due to the high capital intensity and great variations in building codes, homebuilding is a highly regional industry. Thus, you should attempt to invest in the homebuilders that are active in the fastest-growing regions.

When trying to determine which geographic regions are positioned to experience the most growth, you should consider the following factors that attract businesses and people:

- The cost of doing business. These costs include the region's tax policy, energy costs (in terms of average costs per kilowatt-hour), and labor costs (in terms of personal income per dollar of output). Of course, the lower these costs are, the more attractive the region is for business.

- The strength of regions from which migrants derive. For instance, the Florida economy will greatly benefit when the real estate market in the northeast is very strong since these migrants will bring the proceeds from their home sales to Florida. On the other hand, the Salt Lake City economy will benefit less when the California real estate market is weak since

Californians may delay their moves until the California economy improves.

- The costs of housing in the region under consideration. The lower the median cost of such housing, the better.

- The cost of living, which takes into account things such as health care, food, utilities, and public transportation.

- The level of education. Businesses are generally inclined to move to areas that have a high percentage of college-educated (graduates) people. Similarly, you can use average SAT and ACT scores as measures of the region's quality of primary education which is important to parents.

- The computer literacy of a region's workforce. To determine this, you can obtain the percentage of households with PCs and the percentage of adults that currently use PCs in their work. Of course, the greater the region's computer literacy, the more appealing the region becomes for prospective businesses.

- The degree of litigiousness in a region. You can determine this by calculating the ratio of lawyers to the population as well as the number of tort cases filed per capita. You should also determine the ratio of punitive damages to compensatory damages. The higher these ratios are, the less appealing the region is for employers.

- The degree to which a region's airports are equipped to accommodate rising levels of traffic.

- The region's quality of life. This subjective category includes the quality of health care, transportation, level of crime, arts, recreation, and climate.

- The level of entrepreneurial spirit. For instance, the region should have many successful start-up companies, access to venture capital, and banks that are willing to lend money to new businesses. Additionally, the region

T R A P

⊘ Activist shareholders can be problematic for cyclical companies such as homebuilders. It is usually prudent for a homebuilder to accumulate cash in the profitable years so that it will be able to buy property when prices are low. However, an activist shareholder could pressure a homebuilder to deplete its accumulated capital by increasing its dividend payout or by repurchasing its stock. Undertaking either of these measures would be problematic since the homebuilder would no longer have the resources to accumulate land when land prices become attractive.

should have a high number of registered businesses per every one hundred inhabitants.

- The degree to which the region attracts immigrants since immigrants are generally hard working and entrepreneurial.
- The degree to which the region is experiencing out-migration or even moves within the region. (It is preferable when this kind of movement is *minimal.*) When people move less frequently, they will generally take better care of their homes, which enhances property values. Of course, higher property values benefit homebuilders since they can charge higher prices for their newly constructed homes.

Risk Factors

In assessing the risk profile of a homebuilder, you should make the following determinations:

1. The number of months' worth of lots owned by homebuilders that are cleared for development. When the region under review is strong, it is preferable to find a homebuilder with many lots ready to develop. However, when the region under review is beginning to deteriorate, it is best to avoid homebuilders with large inventories of cleared lots since the homebuilder will usually not be able to profit from them.

2. Whether the homebuilder purchases options on land upon which it plans to build homes or purchases the land outright. The benefit of options is that it is possible to obtain the approvals before acquisition of the land. These approvals enhance the value of the land. On the other hand, if approvals are denied the homebuilder loses less when it only paid for the options, as opposed to the underlying land.

3. Whether the homebuilder builds homes on speculation or only commences construction after a contract has been signed and a deposit has been made. Of course, the fewer homes that a homebuilder builds on speculation, the less inventory risk it faces after completions are made. However, when homes are built according to predetermined contracts, there is less upside for the contractor. For instance, if a contractor agrees to build a home for $100,000 and the local economy booms while the home is being built, the homebuilder would suffer an opportunity cost (of $50,000) if that home had a market value of $150,000 at the end of completion. Thus, it is best to invest in those homebuilders that are building homes on speculation in markets where homes are appreciating. However, it is preferable for homebuilders to build homes pursuant to predetermined contracts when the local economy is weakening.

4. Whether the contractor subcontracts on a fixed-price or a cost-plus basis. It is usually preferable for the homebuilder to subcontract on a fixed-price basis since doing so insulates the homebuilder from rising materials' prices. Also, knowing its costs makes it easier for the homebuilder to deliver homes in accordance with contracts while maintaining its profit margins.

5. The percentage of closings financed through a company's own mortgage division. Having a captive mortgage unit facilitates the closure of contracts since the buyer's mortgage can be arranged while the buyer is still interested in the home. Also, when a homebuilder has its own financing unit, the mortgage payments account for a larger part of its earnings stream. This annuity-like payment reduces the volatility of the company's earnings, which often results in the stock's being awarded a higher multiple.

   However, there is a risk that a homebuilder will become too aggressive in arranging mortgages. For instance, there have been times when homebuilders allowed new home buyers to close mortgages through their captive mortgage units without making any down payment. Thus, you should consider the percentage of downpayments that are required by the company's captive financing unit. The more a homebuilder's captive mortgage unit's policies are in keeping with independent mortgage banks', the better.

6. It is unfavorable when homebuilders sign more contracts by aggressively offering price incentives and waiving closing fees. Also, it is problematic when a homebuilder continues to make housing starts when there are already high levels of unsold inventories in that homebuilders' region. This situation could force the homebuilder to discount the homes after their completion.

Competitive Factors

Ideally, the homebuilder that you are considering investing in will have rising new orders of homes, rising value of new orders, and a rising average price of the new

T R A P

⊘ You should not invest in a homebuilder that is concentrated in markets that have been growing rapidly for many years because too much growth can lead to no growth initiatives. Also, the related stocks will likely be trading at very high multiples.

homes. Second, the homebuilder will have a solid history of deliveries. These deliveries should also have appreciating values and increasing average prices. Additionally, it is preferable when new orders exceed deliveries since backlogs will result.

Consider the following data for a hypothetical homebuilder:

	'94	'93	'92	'91
Deliveries	*1,583.00*	*1,324.00*	*1,019.00*	*676.00*
Value ($ in millions)	91.00	73.00	50.00	32.50
Avg. price (#)	304,000.00	288,000.00	263,000.00	261,000.00
New orders	*1,716.00*	*1,595.00*	*1,202.00*	*863.00*
Value ($ in millions)	191.00	151.00	107.00	87.00
Avg. price ($)	331,000.00	302,000.00	288,000.00	260,000.00
Backlog	*1,025.00*	*892.00*	*621.00*	*438.00*
Value ($ in millions)	370.00	278.00	187.00	114.00
Avg. price ($)	332,000.00	306,500.00	289,000.00	271,000.00

In this example, all of the trends are positive. New orders have risen consistently as have the value of such orders. Also, since new orders have been in excess of deliveries, backlogs have been rising. To calculate a given year's backlog, take the difference of new orders minus deliveries then add this number to the previous year's backlog. For instance, in determining 1994's backlog, you add 133 (1,716 – 1,583) to 892 to get 1,025.

Labor Costs

It is important to consider labor costs since the homebuilding industry is labor intensive. However, rising labor costs are not always problematic. One reason is that in rapidly growing markets, the only way that homebuilders can deliver their orders is to attract construction workers from other regions by increasing the pay. Also, greater incidence of unionized workers should not always be construed to be a negative development since the skill of these workers is often worth higher pay.

Aside from hourly wages or salaries, consider workers' compensation insurance premiums in terms of the number of dollars that the homebuilder pays per $100 of payroll. (The homebuilder should have a premium/payroll ratio below the national average.) Also, the homebuilder's premium/payroll ratio should be declining. Additionally, you should consider the percentage of times that lawyers get involved in workers' compensation claims. It is especially problematic when states allow lawyers and doctors to solicit business by advertising or by buying lists of laid-off workers. Moreover, the homebuilder is particularly disadvantaged when the states in which it operates allow workers to collect for stress.

Similarly, you should consider disability insurance rates as well as the disability claim frequency in terms of claims filed for every 10,000 workers. Of course, the lower disability rates are and the lower the claims frequency, the better for homebuilders.

Commercial Construction

One of the most telling indications of new commercial (e.g., office) construction is the vacancy rate. The lower this rate falls, the more commercial building will likely take place because low vacancies (or high occupancies) indicate that demand for commercial space is catching up with supply of space. Also, the accompanying rising rents will encourage property owners to reinvest their profits in future buildings.

Conversely, high vacancy rates (or low occupancy rates) are an indication of little future construction. In addition, landlords granting free months' rent indicate that conditions are not favorable for future building. Similarly, when rents per square foot are declining, little construction can be expected in the future.

Other demand indicators for new commercial construction include the difference between annualized rent receipts and replacement costs. The higher this ratio rises, the more likely construction will commence. Also, a strong market for real-estate investment trusts (REITs) leads to more building. Other signs of future construction are when the age of buildings is rising as well as when the condition of their amenities, heating, ventilation, and electronics deteriorates.

As far as competition among contractors goes, the publicly traded contractors will benefit from fewer mandatory set-asides because the large contractors will be able to bid for more contracts on an equal footing. These contractors will also find it easier to subcontract with the most-qualified subcontractors.

T I P

☞ For the nation's largest publicly held homebuilding firms, overly cautious banks do not necessarily inhibit these homebuilders' growth since these companies can go directly to the debt market to obtain capital. Thus, the larger homebuilders have an advantage over the smaller homebuilders because the latter arc dependent on bank loans for future development.

Industrial and Municipal Construction

Industrial and municipal construction usually lags residential construction because more infrastructure (e.g., streets, sidewalks, and sewers) is needed to serve newly built residential neighborhoods.

T I P

☞ When a development occurs that is generally assumed to be adverse to the entire homebuilding industry (e.g., higher interest rates) most home-building stocks will fall. However, those homebuilders that have the largest backlogs will be hurt the least since they will not be very dependent on new orders. For instance, a homebuilder that has a two-year backlog will be able to withstand a two-year economic downturn better than a homebuilder that only has a six-month backlog.

Another major driver of industrial construction is the replacement of the nation's aging infrastructure including roads, bridges, and tunnels. A final element of industrial construction is pork-barrel politics. Sometimes the government spends money on unnecessary infrastructure projects. For example, I believe that it was completely unnecessary to build a subway system in downtown Pittsburgh since the downtown area in Pittsburgh is so small.

MANUFACTURED HOUSING

Companies such as Champion Enterprises and Clayton Homes that deliver manu-factured housing have a number of natural advantages over the traditional home-builders. First, manufactured homes are priced between 20- and 40-percent below a comparably sized site-built house with similar features.

Second, the fact that factory-built homes are constructed in controlled envi-ronments helps ensure that the homes meet quality standards. In fact, manufac-tured homes must conform to national building codes (in terms of durability, energy efficiency, and fire resistance) that are often more stringent than many local codes for site-built housing. Third, since factory-built homes are manufactured faster than site-built homes, the customer has less exposure to rising materials prices, which, in the case of site-built homes, are often passed on to the customer.

Moreover, the manufactured-housing industry has been benefiting from an industrywide effort to improve the quality and perception of manufactured housing:

- The reduction of the perceived quality gap between site- and factory-built homes has been reduced due to advertising the benefits of manufactured housing.
- Increased customization helps the image of this industry.
- More manufactured homes are being placed on private plots of land, a positive trend since private land owners are usually more diligent land-scapers, which allows them to realize higher property values. These

TOOL

> Vacancy rates must be considered on *very* localized levels. For example, in New York City, contractors compare vacancy rates among the uptown, midtown, and downtown areas as well as between the upper West and the upper East sides of Central Park to determine where the best building opportunities lie.

higher property values, in turn, lead to lower mortgage rates for private land owners since the loan is collateralized with land.

Investor Considerations

Before investing in the manufactured housing-industry, you should consider the following:

- It is best when the populations of first-time homebuyers and empty nesters (e.g., parents whose children have moved away) are growing rapidly.

- Strong sales of existing homes make manufactured housing more affordable.

- The manufactured-housing industry is very sensitive to apartment rents. The higher apartment rents rise, the better for the manufactured-housing industry, and vice versa. Thus, tax legislation that spurs low-income apartment construction and/or the growth of real-estate investment trusts (REITs) that fuel construction of apartments are negative developments for the manufactured-housing industry.

- Growth for the manufactured homebuilders will be constrained if there is not sufficient space in rental parks.

- Manufactured homebuilders that have captive finance subsidiaries enjoy flexibility. For instance, they can extend the term of the loan if the price becomes prohibitive. (Similarly, they can do away with accessories such as costly drapes or a built-in stereo system to make the home more affordable.)

Manufactured-/Mobile-Home Park Operators

Operators of manufactured-/mobile-home parks such as Oakwood Homes and Manufactured Home Communities are an interesting niche of investment opportunity. First, it is relatively easy for these operators to make timely collection of rents because monthly payments on manufactured/mobile homes are relatively low (even including lease payment for a site at a park). Also, park turnover rates average between 10 and 15 percent annually, far below the 50 percent in apartment buildings. One reason for this low turnover is that it can cost $3,000 to move a double-wide home to another park's site.

Another advantage for these operators is that, unlike in other real estate businesses, they do not have to spend much money on improvements to attract tenants; only the common areas must be maintained.

CAPITAL GOODS

A capital good is a good that is used to populate a factory with things that will allow it to produce a machine. In other words, capital goods makers, such as Acme-Cleveland and Giddings & Lewis, manufacture equipment and machinery that is used in factories to manufacture other hard goods.

As you can imagine, capital goods are extremely expensive. Thus, the optimum time to invest in a capital goods manufacturer is when the following conditions are met:

- The economy is very strong. When the economy is strong, corporate balance sheets usually strengthen and the stock market generally rises. This is important since the exorbitant cost of capital goods requires most companies to finance the purchase of such capital by borrowing or issuing stock. Also, when the economy is vibrant, corporate cash flows rise and capital budgets (a key consideration in analyzing the capital goods sector) expand.

- Orders of capital goods are above their customers' depreciation levels.

- Long-term interest rates are low or appear to be positioned to decline. Most of this equipment is financed which means that financing costs are a major component of the acquisition cost. Also, low interest rates makes equipment upgrades more affordable, which shortens the life of the existing equipment. Finally, capital goods companies benefit from low interest rates because they typically carry heavy debt loads.

- Financing for capital goods purchases is readily available. It's best to invest in a capital goods manufacturer when equipment leasing companies are highly competitive.

- The market for used equipment and machinery is strong. Rising demand for used equipment and machinery in developing countries such as those in Latin America and Eastern Europe will result in higher prices for used capital goods. Thus, greater proceeds from sales of used equipment will make it more affordable for factories in developed countries to afford new capital goods.

- Capacity utilization in the industrial and manufacturing sectors is very high. When factories are using nearly all of their available capacity, they will likely have to invest in additional equipment and machinery to fill more orders.

- There is a trend of more new factories' being built. This is a particularly telling indicator of rising capital goods orders in the future since equipment and machinery must be installed in such factories. More foreign transplants are good for capital goods manufacturers since these foreign manufacturers will install equipment and machinery in their U.S. plants.

- The dollar is weak. American capital goods manufacturers since American equipment and machinery will thus become more affordable to foreign manufacturers.

- There is greater competition among capital goods buyers. Events that could spur fiercer competition in the United States include industry convergence (e.g., telecommunications) and industry deregulation (e.g., of the utilities). In fact, even the *possibility* of deregulation often spurs capital spending. Looking abroad, privatization in foreign countries helps capital goods since these privatizations raise a great deal of capital, which can be used to make more capital investments.

- The cost of labor rises. Manufacturers are more prone to invest in equipment and machinery when workers' compensation rises because they believe they will be able to replace some of their workers with better equipment and machinery. Rising discrimination and sexual harassment charges will also deter hiring. So, too, will legislation that requires employers to give their employees advanced notices of eventual dismissals (thus reducing employers' flexibility).

  Additionally, employers will be more willing to replace workers with equipment and machinery when demographics indicate that the pool of potential workers is shrinking.

- Customers of capital goods manufacturers are planning a flurry of new product launches. New equipment is often needed to produce these new models. For example, automakers often must invest in new equipment and machinery to manufacture new vehicle models.

- Customers of capital goods buyers are raising standards on their suppliers. For example, it used to be that automakers would accept returning 5 to 10 percent of steel to the steelmaker. But now they only accept 1 percent substandard steel; thus, steel mills feel compelled to improve their manufacturing processes by investing in new equipment and machinery.

- Consolidation occurs among capital goods companies' customers. Since capital goods are so expensive that only the largest companies can afford them, consolidation makes these purchases feasible.

- Customers of capital goods companies are demanding deliveries of products shortly after their orders are placed. Capital goods customers must invest in the equipment and machinery necessary to meet their own customers' rising expectations of vendor delivery.

- The stocks of capital goods companies' customers are trading at high multiples. This occurs when it becomes cheaper for them to build the equipment and machines than to obtain it through purchasing a competitor.

Performance of Capital Goods

It is usually most prudent to invest in those capital goods manufacturers whose equipment and machinery can demonstrate the following:

- Few defects in early hours of equipment usage.

- Few parts in equipment. (The fewer the parts, the lower the risk of malfunctions.)

- High fuel economy ratings compared with those of the replaced equipment.

- Few repairs per number of hours the equipment and machinery is operated.

- Ability to manufacture products that are worth a large number of dollars per man-hour.

FORESTRY PRODUCERS

The forestry industry is extremely difficult to manage. One reason is that, as a producer of commodities, one company is beholden to every other forestry companies' decisions. As it is said, a CEO of a commodity producer can only be as smart as his dumbest competitor.

Second, the very long periods that are required for trees to grow make planning for harvesting nearly impossible. For example, it can take as long as 80 years for a tree to become completely grown. And the older the tree, the more valuable its timber. Thus, a dilemma arises: Is it better to cut a tree in its 50th year when prices are particularly strong? Or is it better to wait until the tree fully ages? It is nearly impossible to determine how strong the demand will be 30 years in the future.

Third, it is difficult for forestry executives to determine how far apart trees should be planted from one another. Planting trees too far apart (or excessive thinning by controlled forest fires) can result in young trees not getting sufficient shading; excess sunlight causes trees to grow excessive branches, reducing the strength of their trunks. In addition, when trees are planted further apart, the forest owner can lose the use of much of his land for the better part of a century.

Fourth, forestry companies are beset with a serious dilemma in the implementation of mutable environmental regulations. A company like Union Camp Corporation can take a highly compliant strategy whereby it expends all of the money necessary to meet all environmental regulations. This strategy may earn the company goodwill with its local community and environmentalists and should ensure that the company will face few fines for regulatory noncompliance.

Or, a forestry company can use the strategy of delaying implementation of environmental regulations for as long as possible. This may result in the company's incurring fines and ill-will among the environmentally sensitive populace. However, these delaying tactics could save the company hundreds of millions of dollars in unnecessary capital expenditures if the environmental regulations were either repealed or made more favorable. For example, according to the American Forestry & Paper Association, expected 1996 changes to 1993 rules on air and water emissions were estimated to cut the costs of compliance for American forestry companies from $14 billion to below $5 billion.

Commoditization

Even though there are many different grades of paper (e.g., containerboard, newsprint, coated paper, and tissue) and lumber (e.g., plywood, lumber, particleboard and oriented strandboard), forestry producers still compete in a commodity business. To illustrate, paper companies' customers demand uniformity in their office paper because office machines have narrow tolerances for variances in quality. (Even a minor flaw in a single sheet of paper can cause a photocopier to jam, for example.)

The commoditization of the forestry business is accentuated by there being few new ideas introduced into the forestry products industry. One reason is that many of the top executives of these companies tend to be single-company people who rose through the ranks over a few decades. In fact, many decedents of the forestry companies' founders hold top jobs. For example, George H. Weyerhaeuser is the President and CEO of Weyerhaeuser Company while Peter T. Pope is the chairman and CEO of Pope & Talbot, Inc. It is also said that these executives tend to surround themselves with people who generally agree with them.

Capacity Considerations

When any industry produces products that are as commoditized as those that the forestry industry produces, it is imperative to consider changes in production capacity on an industrywide basis. The higher the production capacity rises, the more output will result, forcing producers to lower their prices since there is virtually no other way to differentiate one company's given grade of paper versus that of another company. Additionally, higher factory capacity is detrimental to this

T I P

👉 When analyzing a manufacturer of heavy goods, give their backlogs a close look. Generally, high levels of backlogged orders are positive since they will insulate the manufacturer from a downturn in number of orders. Also, it is usually acceptable for capital goods manufacturers to have backlogs since capital goods are not impulse items.

However, backlogs can also be an albatross around the neck of manufacturers because a company with large backlogs will have to devote its resources to working down its backlogs instead of developing more sophisticated products, whereas a competing supplier (that does not have large backlogs) can bring innovative products to the market since it does not have to manufacture older products.

Of course, backlogs are not acceptable when the manufacturers' customers operate on a just-in-time inventory basis. Finally, backlogs resulting from manufacturing problems are always a negative sign.

industry since the capital-intensive nature of timber cutting and sawmilling means that these facilities must be heavily utilized.

Of course, it is better to invest in the forestry industry when capacity is moderating as opposed to expanding. Even though it takes a few years to bring new capacity on line, forestry stocks usually act poorly on announcements of new capacity. The following factors can affect capacity in the forestry industry:

- Rising profitability among the forestry companies can lead to capacity expansion, while low levels of profitability inhibit capacity.

- It is preferable when forestry producers acquire mills through mergers and acquisitions as opposed to building mills. Buying capacity means that the paper mills are not building more capacity.

- Low operating rates provide paper mills little incentive to expand.

- Technological improvements in sawmilling add to capacity.

- When permits to use new machines are difficult to obtain, capacity is being limited—a plus for investors. (Such restrictions also cause operating rates to rise which causes prices to rise.)

- Increasingly stringent environmental regulations are not all bad for the timber industry. Even though compliance with these regulations is extremely expensive, the mere fact that so much money is directed toward environmental compliance means that forestry producers have less money to spend on capacity expansion. Thus, you should consider the percentage of the industry's capital expenditures that are directed to the compliance of environmental regulations. The higher this percentage is, the less resources the paper companies will have to spend on expansion; less expansion is favorable for high paper prices.

- When more acres of timberlands are deemed to occupy the habitat of endangered species, less timber harvesting will result because environmentalists can cause timber-cutting restrictions to be imposed on these lands which is good for paper prices. In fact, out of concern for the spotted owl, the Clinton administration was successful in reducing timber harvesting on federal lands in the Northwest from 5 billion board feet a year throughout the 1980s to no more than an annual 1.1 billion board feet.

Forest fires reduce the supply of timber to a greater extent than may be immediately realized. For instance, in the summer of 1994 forest fires destroyed four million acres of prime federal forests. This amount of acreage may not have seemed significant compared with the 489 million acres of total (federal, state, and private) forest acreage. However, since trees in the Northwest can take up to 80 years to grow, the total number of acres that had trees that were ready to be harvested was much smaller. Thus, the four million acres of destroyed trees reduced the nation's supply of harvestable trees significantly.

Recycled Paper Producers

The U.S. paper industry already recycles about 40 percent of the paper it uses and aims to recycle 50 percent by the year 2000. Paper companies such as Chesapeake Corp. and Mosinee Paper Corporation that produce quality paper with some recycled content will have a marketing advantage.

However, with these marketing advantages come manufacturing challenges. First, recycled paper costs between 10- and 15-percent more to process. Since the fibers in recycled material have already been squeezed at least once by the rollers of a paper machine, they are inherently weaker than fibers that come from virgin pulp. (In fact, wood fiber can only be broken down between three and five times before it turns to sludge—fiber so small that it will not hold together.) Thus, existing machines must be retrofitted to accept wastepaper and do not run as efficiently. Also, recycled paper makers must make huge investments in de-inking facilities.

A second concern is that recycling presents challenges to paper quality. This is because pulp variability becomes increasingly problematic as the proportion of recycled fiber content rises. For example, in tissue, the increased use of recycled fiber introduced the need for softening agents. Also, in higher-grade papers, recycled fiber introduces impurities and is resistant to bleaching.

Other Analytical Considerations

From a broader perspective, the forestry products industry should provide a sound investment opportunity over the long run. As Third World countries develop, their citizens consume more paper as they become more literate and increase their exports, thereby boosting demand for corrugated boxes. Also, as populous nations such as China and India prosper, hundreds of millions of their citizens build homes, increasing the demand for lumber. Additionally, as countries develop, they deplete their own timberlands.

However, on a more microeconomic level, you should consider the following before investing in the forestry industry:

- Paper is a world commodity since it is used and produced in many countries. Thus, paper stocks are vulnerable to news of price cuts or a new mill from anywhere in the world.

- Higher paper or lumber prices will not enhance the valuation of a company's forests unless its trees are at least 14 years of age.

- Mergers, such as the Federal Paper Board and International Paper merger announced in 1996 create investor interest in forestry groups.

- Due to the onerous environmental restrictions in the United States, the timber companies in your portfolio should have timber-cutting rights in foreign countries.

- Due to international competition, a stronger dollar is negative for U.S. forestry companies. Similarly, devaluations of a competing paper/timber producer's currency (particularly the Canadian dollar) is detrimental.

T I P

There are many variations of paper. Thus, when the prices of a particular grade of paper are rising, you should consider investing in those producers that are most leveraged to producing that grade. For example, when newsprint prices soar, as they did in the mid-1990s, consider investing in Bowater. Also, when considering investing in a lumber producer such as Louisiana-Pacific, you take into account the strength of the homebuilding industry.

- Restrictions on paper and lumber imports from Canada benefit American producers. A primary reason why such restrictions are occasionally imposed is that the Canadian government subsidizes its forestry industry by allocating timber rights rather than promoting bidding as is done in the United States.

- A timber company's property must be located in accessible places.

- You should search for forestry companies with below-industry-average fatality and injury rates.

- Some tree farmers are using genetics to improve their yields. One benefit of genetic cloning is that superior fiber is produced. This fiber also produces more uniform pulp.

- Some tree farmers have been trying to replace diverse natural forests with tree plantations, using one species of fast-growing trees. However, there are some drawbacks to such methods. First, the wood is usually less dense and less strong than that of the slower-growing trees. Second, wood from tree plantations is more likely to have excessive knots, making it more prone to twisting and splitting. Third, such lumber may be more difficult to sell to builders who have a perception of inferior quality of wood from such plantations.

- Forestry companies often have undervalued balance sheets because their forests were recorded at the prices that these companies paid many years ago. For example, St. Joe Paper Company acquired its land before 1940. Then, St. Joe made a $50 million (pretax) gain on the sale of its forestry division in 1996.

11

CHAPTER

Transportation

AUTOMAKERS

Demand for automakers' shares rises in lockstep with demand for automobiles. In estimating the demand for new vehicles, you should consider both the replacement cycle of automobiles as well as consumers' ability to afford new vehicles. Of course, the shorter the replacement cycle and the greater consumers' ability to buy new cars, the brighter the outlook becomes for auto manufacturers.

Replacement Cycle

In estimating the replacement cycle for new cars, consider these factors for vehicles in use: average age, the average number of total miles driven as well as the average number of miles driven annually. The higher these averages rise, the sooner automobiles will wear out and the sooner auto owners will have to replace their vehicles.

However, you should factor trends in durability into your estimates of replacement cycles because increasingly durable cars are likely to slow the replacement cycle. Additionally, when trucks are winning market share at the expense of cars, the replacement cycle of vehicles on the road will be lengthened since trucks usually last longer than cars.

Another indication of auto replacement is provided by the scrappage ratio. The scrappage ratio is the number of vehicles turned in for conversion to scrap metal as a percentage of the number of automobiles in operation. Of course, the higher the scrappage ratio rises, the brighter the outlook is for car sales.

Yet another indication of shorter replacement cycles for vehicles is increasingly stringent auto inspections. More stringent auto inspections (e.g., in terms of safety standards, fuel efficiency, and emissions levels) will result in fewer older vehicles being classified as road-worthy; vehicles that fail these auto inspections will have to be replaced.

Ability to Buy

There are many factors that lead to changes in consumers' ability to purchase new automobiles. Of course, the strength of the economy is a major factor. Obviously, the stronger consumers' balance sheets are the more affordable automobiles become, even the more expensive vehicles; thus, an increasingly healthy economy benefits the automakers.

In addition to considering the state of the overall economy (as discussed in the retail chapter beginning on page 37), you should consider a number of other factors when estimating the demand for automobiles:

1. The greater the number of weeks of median income necessary to purchase a car selling for the average price, the more problematic for the auto industry. For instance, it took 18.8 weeks of the average workers' wages to pay for a new car in 1978. By 1994 it took 25.9 weeks. This was because in November of 1994, the average cost of a new car was $19,500, up 85 percent from 1978 when the average price was $10,500, and median incomes had only risen 40 percent over the same period of time. Thus, the increase in the number of weeks of work necessary to afford a new car indicates that cars are becoming less affordable.

    Similarly, another troubling sign occurs when car makers stretch out the payment terms of their car loans. For instance, the average car loan rose from 48 months in 1984 to 54 months in 1994. These longer payment periods are another indication that consumers are having difficulty meeting their monthly payments.

2. Since most new vehicles are partially financed with credit, the availability of credit is an important determinant. Thus, improving consumer credit ratings (and lower consumer default rates) is positive for auto sales since more consumers will qualify for financing. Also, competition among banks', credit unions', and automakers' financing units is positive for auto sales since such competition is likely to result in lower financing rates.

3. New cars become more affordable as demand for used cars rises. Higher demand for used cars raises the price for used cars, which is important

since people frequently use their trade-ins to finance the purchase of new cars.

Similarly, you should determine the percentage of new-car sales that are actually leased. While leased cars are counted as car sales, excessive leasing may indicate that few people can afford to buy new cars. Thus, too many leased cars (as a percentage of cars leased and sold) may signal deteriorating affordability for new cars.

4. When estimating consumers' ability to purchase new cars, consider the other costs associated with owning a car, including insurance costs, registration fees, gasoline prices, and taxes on gasoline. Of course, the lower these costs are, the better the outlook for new-car sales since the total costs of owning a car are reduced.

TRAP

🚫 There are scenarios under which rising used-car sales represent problems ahead. In order to determine when such scenarios are likely to arise, you should scrutinize total (new- and used-) car sales. When the ratio of used-car sales to total car sales rises too rapidly, it may mean that people that otherwise would have purchased new cars are buying used cars.

Other Demand Factors for Automobiles

Changes in the utility of owning a car will impact demand for new cars. For example, chronic congestion in major cities, excessive car theft and a well-run mass transit system are a convincing combination to discourage urban car purchases. Similarly, legislation designed to protect the environment can restrict car owners' freedom to drive. For example, under the Clean Air Act, large businesses located in the most polluted American cities were required to instruct their employees to use alternative means of transportation. Thus, legislation can reduce the utility of owning an automobile.

Especially when analyzing a domestic car maker, you should consider the valuation of currencies. A weak dollar is generally beneficial to American automakers making foreign cars more expensive for American buyers while making U.S.-produced cars more affordable to foreign buyers. Thus, a weak dollar may also give American manufacturers an umbrella for lifting prices since imported cars become more expensive when the dollar loses value. However, foreign car makers might mitigate their disadvantages caused by a depreciating dollar by manufacturing more of their cars in the United States.

Interestingly, you can use developments in factory production as indications of the level of demand for vehicles. For instance, the more machine tools that the automakers are ordering, the brighter the long-term outlook is for car demand. (The automakers would not likely have ordered more machine tools unless they believed that they would be increasing their production.)

On the other hand, the more assembly plants that car makers idle (for reasons other than strikes, retooling, or unavailability of parts) and the longer these plans are idled, the weaker demand is for new cars.

Consider also which automakers will be more affected by the shutdowns. When car plants account for a disproportionate amount of the downtime, those automakers that produce more cars than trucks will be more severely impacted than those vehicle producers that manufacture more trucks than cars.

T I P

Consider inventories of cars on dealer lots in terms of the number of days of supply at current selling rates. Typically, a 60- to 65-day supply is considered ideal. Thus, rising inventories at car dealers' lots indicates that demand is soft, usually resulting in a reduction in the dealers' orders to the automakers, which in turn often results in the shutdowns of assembly lines.

Changes in the Car Buying Process

In the future, fewer cars will be sold in dealers' showrooms and more cars will be sold in superstores, through (mass merchants' and employers') referral services, and through on-line services and the Internet. In fact, the number of dealerships has already plunged from 47,500 in 1951 to 22,400 in early 1996, while superstores such as Carmax and AutoNation USA and on-line brokers such as Autobytel are growing very briskly. This growth is being fueled in part by a genuine preference on the part of car buyers to purchase their vehicles with the least possible amount of haggling with commissioned salespeople. Also, consumers benefit from lower prices that result from the greater efficiency that these delivery systems offer and the absence of commissions that would normally be directed to a dealer's sales force.

While this trend is potentially devastating for the nation's auto dealers, the impact on the car makers is likely to be mixed. On the positive side, the lower prices that consumers pay could encourage them to purchase more expensive models. Also, the more accommodating atmosphere that the superstores offer enhances the car-buying experience.

However, having a weakened commissioned sales force at the dealerships will make it more difficult for the car makers to dispose of their less-popular models. Also, as these supercenters sell more multiple brands at the same locations, the ease of comparing the merits of competing vehicles could result in greater price pressures. Finally, if these superstores become too powerful they could dictate terms to the automakers in much the same way that Wal-Mart instructs its suppliers to meet its policies.

Company-Specific Considerations

When deciding which automaker to invest in, you should

- Consider the product mix that each manufacturer has in various segments of the automotive industry including cars, jeeps, trucks, and minivans. The most favorable company is the one that derives the greatest percentage of its business from the sector that is experiencing the most rapid growth. (In other words, if minivans are selling like gangbusters, invest in the company that derives most of its revenues from minivans.) Additionally, it is particularly favorable when that growth is coming from trucks and minivans since these larger vehicles usually carry the widest profit margins.

- Be advised that it is problematic when auto companies too heavily discount their vehicles or offer excessively generous rebates. This is because the profit margins on each vehicle sold will be diminished and the public will become conditioned to waiting until cars are promoted on a discount or rebate basis before they enter showrooms.

- Consider how much the automaker spends per vehicle on warranties. The less, the better. Similarly, consider the number of warranty repairs per 100 vehicles. In general, the lower an automaker's warranty costs the better. Automakers seeking to reduce warranty expenses should try to recover more funds from suppliers of defective goods and improve quality to reduce overall defects.

   However, it is acceptable for an automaker to have high and rising warranty expenses if it can demonstrate that its warranty policy results in greater customer retention. Thus, some auto companies have become increasingly generous with their warranties. For example, new warranty policies often automatically cover new-vehicle owners; offer roadside assistance and loaner vehicles; and offer longer periods of coverage.

Production

You should seek to invest in automakers with short product cycle times (i.e., from concept to rollout). "Not only do faster development times cut costs by saving overhead and using engineering and production resources more efficiently, they make it possible for auto makers to market new cars before trends and customer tastes change. " [1]

Product cycle times can be accelerated by placing various car models on similar platforms and using computers in the design process. "However, comparing the development times is perilous, because companies define starting points differently, complex models require more time, and no one independently verifies each auto makers' claims." [2]

Similarly, you should consider the number of hours it takes automakers to manufacture their cars. Of course, the fewer hours necessary to assemble a car (of a comparable level of complexity), the more efficient the automaker is. Productivity gains can result from more outsourcing, adoption of just-in-time inventory management and better relations with the United Auto Workers (UAW) union.

Labor Relations

Consider also automakers' relations with their workforces, especially their unions. The UAW is not afraid to flex its muscles when it believes that it can win concessions from the automakers. Moreover, it is known to strategically strike those factories that can most readily cause bottlenecks for the automaker; while these strikes may only affect a small portion of the automakers' workforce, they can result in a work stoppage throughout a disproportionate percentage of the automakers' production facilities. In fact, a March 1996 strike by 3,000 UAW workers at two Dayton, OH, brake plants caused General Motors to close a total of 26 plants with about 121,000 hourly workers.

Thus, examine the number of strikes experienced by the automaker in recent years and consider the amount of working time lost to strikes. Of course, the lower the incidence (and the shorter the duration) of strikes, the better for the automaker.

Even if an automaker has a problematic history with strikes, try to determine if such experiences will change in the future by considering the depth of strike funds. (A percentage of union dues are directed to strike funds, which are used to compensate union members during strikes.) The lower these strike funds are, the less time workers are likely to be able to afford to strike. Other factors that indicate that unions are becoming less influential include declining membership, lower union dues, political battles within a given union, and competition among unions wishing to represent the same workers.

When unions appear poised to lose power, auto companies could benefit from a number of factors. First, there would be fewer strikes. Second, unions

---

[1] Valerie Reitman and Robert L.Simison, "Automakers Race for New Models," *The Wall Street Journal* CCXXVI, no. 126, (December 29, 1995), p. B1.

[2] Ibid.

T R A P

⊘ Even when a union's strike funds are low, unions can still launch strategic strikes. For instance, most of the 118,000 workers (121,000 total – 3,000 strikers) that were idled as a result of a strike at GM's brake plants qualified for a combination of state unemployment insurance and supplemental unemployment benefits, which have together usually amounted to roughly 95 percent of the workers' normal pay. Moreover, these payments do not reduce the UAW's strike funds.

would win fewer concessions from automakers merely by threatening to strike. Third, redundant safety measures could be eliminated.

However, strikes are not always terrible for the automaker. For example, an automaker that does not cave in to union demands may avoid increasing its workers' compensation and benefits. Also, unions may become more hesitant to strike an automaker again that has withstood a strike already. On the other hand, quickly meeting union demands just to bring about a swift end to a strike may encourage unions to organize further strikes.

In fact, sometimes a car company wants to be the first target of a strike. The first company that risks a strike can influence the direction of the negotiations that the UAW will try to apply to the other car makers. Since the car makers are no longer homogeneous, the targeted company's competitors could be hurt when the unions try to force the other manufacturers to accept the same measures that the target company accepted, which is to the benefit of the targeted company. For instance, many observers believe that Chrysler would benefit if it was the first domestic automaker targeted by the UAW in its contract renegotiations in the summer of 1996. Chrysler already buys most of its parts from outside companies and may be willing to agree to freeze further outsourcing, in exchange for other concessions. Then, the UAW would demand that Ford Motor Company and General Motors accept identical arrangements. This series of events would benefit Chrysler since Ford and GM (both of which make more of their own parts than Chrysler) would not be able to enjoy the benefits of outsourcing.

Also, a greater incidence of strikes can confirm that the prospects for automakers are bright because unions typically strike when they are confident that the targeted companies can afford to provide workers with better compensation and benefits.

Other Operating Considerations

You should search for automakers that have a low average number of defects per vehicle since automakers generally strive to improve the quality of their vehicles by reducing this number of defects per vehicle. Fewer defects results in greater customer satisfaction, as well as higher ratings on surveys such as those conducted by *Consumer Reports*. Thus, higher market share often follows a reduction in defects.

However, too much devotion to eliminating defects may result in the automaker's losing its creativity. For example, Honda has very low defect rates but has been criticized for having unexciting product offerings.

Automakers are burdened with heavy costs that are not explicit in their costs of goods sold. For instance, the auto industry has huge medical expenses. In fact, General Motors was the largest private purchaser of health care in the United States in 1992. During that same year, GM spent $929 per vehicle on health care coverage for its employees. Thus, the auto industry would be a major beneficiary of any health care reforms that reduce employers' responsibilities for their employees' health care coverage.

T I P

You should monitor the amount of money (per vehicle produced) that automakers spend on their employees' health-care. Of course, the further this amount falls, the better the profit picture becomes for the automaker.

Similarly, American automakers are frequently targets of product liability suits. In fact, in 1992, there were over 1,000 cases filed against automakers in the United States whereas Ford only faced one product liability suit in Europe that year. Also, American juries side with the plaintiffs in about half of these cases, and the punitive damages awarded to these plaintiffs have been soaring. For instance, awards in auto-related product liability suits rose nearly 300 percent between 1983 and 1993. Thus, the automakers would tremendously benefit from liability reforms.

Separately, automakers have historically had underfunded pensions. Thus, you should take a close look at the level of pension deficits (the differences between pension assets and pension liabilities) when evaluating an automaker's total debt levels. Also, shareholders should not anticipate that an automaker with severely underfunded pensions will be able to take measures aimed at enhancing shareholder value (e.g., stock repurchases or greater dividend payouts) even when earnings are rapidly rising.

Rising interest rates can be particularly problematic for automakers with underfunded pensions when that company's pension assets are heavily invested in common stocks. This is because stocks often lose value during times of rising interest rates. Thus, higher interest rates can reduce pension assets, increasing pensions deficits.

T I P

Rising interest rates can be beneficial to domestic automakers if they occur during times of surging demand for automobiles. This is because higher interest rates will dampen near-term demand for cars, preventing customers from going to foreign car makers if domestic manufacturers cannot meet current demand.

Electric Cars

By 1998, 2 percent of all cars for sale in California must be "zero-emission vehicles." This percentage rises to 5 percent in 2001 and 10 percent in 2003. This rule applies to all car makers selling more than 35,000 vehicles a year in the state. Car makers that fail to sell the required number of electric cars face a $5,000 fine for each car under the threshold. At least a dozen other states have adopted, or are considering adopting, similar measures.

You should be aware of the host of problems that electric cars present for automakers. First, electric cars will be a hard sell since they are genuinely unpopular with consumers for a number of reasons including their being much more expensive than gas-powered vehicles due to high development costs and low production runs.

Also, battery-powered cars are less reliable since they have limited driving ranges (between 60 and 150 miles), and recharging batteries is highly inconvenient since there is very little infrastructure for doing so. Even when recharging stations become accessible it will take hours to recharge batteries. Further, drivers of electric cars will likely face higher electric bills when they recharge their batteries.

Replacing batteries is expensive as they must be replaced about every three years and cost between $1,500 and $3,000. Moreover, there is a disposal problem for batteries. Finally, electric cars cannot carry much cargo and perform poorly in cold weather.

A second major problem presented by electric cars for automakers is that the car makers may decide to recoup part of their losses on electric cars by raising prices on their gas-powered vehicles. If this subsidization were to occur, fewer people would be able to afford gas-powered cars.

However, environmentalists claim that the price of electric cars will decline as demand and production rises. They further argue that much of the recharging would occur at night when there is an excess of electricity, thus obviating the need for additional electricity generation. Furthermore, the California Air Resources Board has reported that there are neither tune-ups, oil changes, smog checks, nor moving parts to break down with electric cars.

Leasing

Leasing has been growing increasingly popular with customers since customers lease new cars for short periods of time and thus have few maintenance concerns associated with their new vehicles. Also, leasing relieves customers of depreciation risks.

However, there are both pros and cons of leasing for the automakers. First, leasing can be positive for automakers since they can profit by selling a car to a dealer and then by financing the lease payments through their financing arms.

Second, leasing allows car makers to build more-expensive vehicles. Since it is cheaper to lease a new car than to purchase a new car, customers can afford to drive more-expensive leased cars than they could normally afford to buy. It is cheaper to lease a new car because the lessee only pays for the portion of the car that he uses during the lease agreement. For instance, if a customer leases a $40,000 vehicle that has a residual value of $28,000 at the end of the two-year lease, the monthly lease payments would be $500 (the $12,000 value that he would use divided by 24 months).

Third, leasing allows automakers to smooth out their production runs since they can better determine when their customers will be looking for new automobiles. (When a lease expires, the lessee usually wants a new car.) Fourth, due to the low maintenance required, drivers that lease cars for short periods of time are happier with their cars than people who own their cars for extended periods of time. Thus, leasing engenders loyalty, which makes it easier for the dealer to sell or lease another car when the customer returns his leased vehicle. Fifth, the automaker and the dealer can derive ancillary fees from their leasing programs. Such leasing fees include "excess wear and damage" charges, disposition fees (which are charges for transporting and selling the car) and excess-mile charges.

A fundamental problem with leasing is that a surge in leasing may indicate that consumers cannot afford to buy new cars. Thus, leasing may just be a mechanism to get people to avoid looking at the price of new cars.

Second, too much leasing may force used-car prices down. This is because leased cars are placed on the used-car market once their leases expire, and a flood of leased cars hitting the used-car market could dampen the prices of used cars. Lower used-car prices will, in turn result in higher lease payments in the future (since the residual values on newly leased cars will be lower), which could dampen the demand for leases.

A similar factor that could lower used-car prices (and consequently result in higher lease payments) is greater fleet sales. Fleet cars can be relegated to the used-car market after as little as six months of use. Thus, excessive fleet sales could jeopardize a car maker's leasing program. Additionally, these almost new cars from fleets present stiff competition for new-car sales.

Foreign Opportunities

You should be very careful about the way that you estimate demand for vehicles in foreign markets. Some analysts simply determine the penetration of cars in the United States versus the penetration of cars in foreign countries. Under this reasoning, the analyst would argue that since there is one car for every 2 people in the United States and only one car for every 652 people in China then there is tremendous dormant demand for vehicles in China. However, this logic is too simplistic even when it is adjusted for a country's wealth.

Regarding foreign sales potential, population may not be such a good indicator of future demand because the distribution of wealth is sometimes severely skewed in developing countries. Since rapidly rising national wealth may not be felt by the masses in developing countries, car sales should not be expected to soar when an emerging country displays rapid economic development.

Another impediment to there being greater demand for automobiles is that many developing countries do not have adequate roads, and people will not buy cars (even when they can afford to do so) if the infrastructure necessary to drive is not in place. Thus, *the ratio of vehicles per thousand miles of paved road is a good indicator of demand.* (The larger the ratio, the better.) Additionally, in attempts to reduce pollution, underdeveloped countries often have restrictive laws on driving, making owning a car less attractive even for those people that can easily afford to do so.

AUTO PARTS SUPPLIERS

To a large extent, the auto parts suppliers' stocks trade as cyclicals. When the economy is strong, more cars are manufactured and sold. Thus, more parts are ordered by the original equipment manufacturers (OEMs). On the other hand, a deteriorating economy will result in fewer auto sales and thus the automakers will reduce orders to suppliers.

However, no serious investor will stop his analysis of the auto parts suppliers here. Rather you must contemplate the secular developments that could affect the outlook for the auto parts suppliers.

T R A P

⊘ Naturally, unions militantly oppose outsourcing. Thus, suppliers that generate a large portion of their business from OEMs whose unions are becoming increasingly strident risk losing part of their business. This could happen when an OEM's management reduces its outsourcing programs in order to placate its unions.

Favorable Secular Developments

It is best to invest in auto parts suppliers when the Big Three and transplants favor outsourcing. A leading reason for these OEMs to favor outsourcing is that heavy unionization results in a labor force that is expensive, inflexible, and prone to strike. By shifting more work to their suppliers, the OEMs believe they can avoid these problems.

Similarly, the dominant auto parts suppliers benefit when the OEMs streamline their purchases; when the OEMs aim to reduce their purchasing staffs and infrastructure, they contracting with fewer suppliers. Thus, the suppliers that win contracts gain much larger pieces of the OEMs' business.

Also, suppliers benefit when the automakers are buying more component systems instead of individual parts. Since the production of components requires engineering, designing, prototyping, and testing of whole assemblies, automakers buying components will likely execute long-term contracts. This allows the auto parts suppliers to do a better job of planning and thus smooth out their earnings, which analysts like to see.

The dominant auto parts suppliers can benefit from increasingly stringent environmental regulations (e.g., regarding auto emissions as well as fuel-efficiency and safety standards) since the quality of auto parts must be improved. These improvements allow the auto parts suppliers to charge higher prices and therefore generate wider profit margins. Furthermore, the domestic automakers that comply with these environmental standards will benefit as the Europeans (and others) adopt environmental regulations similar to those in the United States. When this happens, the leading U.S. companies will face little competition since foreign suppliers do not have much experience in this field.

A brutally demanding OEM purchasing chief can make the entire U.S. auto parts supplier industry more competitive against foreign rivals. For instance, Jose Ignacio Lopez de Arriortua, General Motors' former purchasing chief, was so aggressive in forcing GM's suppliers to reduce their prices that the latter soon became extremely efficient.

TIP

Weak auto sales in foreign markets can present a buying opportunity for the shares of auto parts suppliers. When foreign auto markets are weak, investors have a tendency to sell all of their auto-related stocks, forcing the prices of these stocks down. However, since the auto parts suppliers usually have much less international exposure than the Big Three, shares of auto parts suppliers may become oversold in such circumstances, presenting investors with a buying opportunity.

Auto parts suppliers benefit from transplants because they have more potential customers to sell to when more foreign automakers manufacture their vehicles in the United States. On the other hand, when the auto parts suppliers' only customers are the Big Three, the domestic automakers have a great deal of buying power.

T I P

A major U.S. trade deficit in automobiles can be to the domestic auto parts suppliers' advantage if the country with which the United States has the deficit agrees to alleviate its surplus by importing more American auto supplies. For instance, under terms of a U.S.–Japan trade agreement executed in the summer of 1995, Japanese car makers agreed to import an additional $2 billion more worth of U.S.-made parts.

U.S. auto parts suppliers also benefit from a weak dollar since foreign automakers often take advantage of a weak dollar by buying American-made auto components for installation on vehicles produced in their home country.

Also, foreign trade agreements that include domestic content provisions can benefit the U.S. auto parts suppliers. For example, under NAFTA, if a foreign (e.g., Japanese) automaker wants to assemble a car in Mexico and export it to the United States for sale with the lowest tariffs possible, 62.5 percent of such cars must consist of North American–made parts. Since most North American auto parts suppliers are American, such domestic content provisions are beneficial to the U.S. suppliers.

Once you have decided to invest in the auto parts supplier industry, you should search for those auto parts suppliers whose parts are placed on a rising number of cars and who can claim a rising dollar value of these parts.

Another potential benefit to investing in this sector is that this is a relatively small cap sector. While there are hundreds of auto parts suppliers, only a few dozen have publicly traded stocks. Thus, positive developments could result in the rapid appreciation of these stocks.

AUTOMOTIVE AFTERMARKET

The automotive aftermarket industry is countercyclical. When the economy is weak, fewer people purchase new cars. Thus, they will spend more money on maintaining their aging cars. As a result, the stocks of automotive aftermarket retailers, such as Autozone and The Pep Boys—Manny, Moe, and Jack, often outperform the automobile manufacturers when car sales are sluggish.

T R A P

Ⓧ Interestingly, the automotive aftermarket is one segment of the retail industry for which consumer confidence readings may not be accurate. While women are more heavily polled (than men) for consumer confidence surveys (since women account for a disproportionate amount of retail purchases), men purchase far more automotive aftermarket merchandise than women. Thus, while deteriorating consumer confidence surveys are negative for the retail industry as a whole, such gloomy surveys of consumer confidence may not have any impact on the automotive aftermarket retailers.

One secular trend in car buying that is problematic for the automotive aftermarket is leasing. Leasing is a problem since lessees experience very few maintenance problems (and those problems that they do encounter are often remedied by the car dealer). Thus, there is little need for individuals to shop at automotive aftermarket retailers when they lease cars.

Also, the stocks of those automotive aftermarket retailers that operate on the EDLP method of merchandising may perform better than those of retailers using the promotional method because customers buy parts for their car when they are needed not when they are on sale.

Additionally, the automotive aftermarket retailers that you invest in need not be overly concerned with maintaining optimum inventory levels. In other words, it is better to have too much inventory than not enough because people are extremely dependent on their cars and thus will not tolerate automotive aftermarket stockouts. (They will rather go to a competing automotive aftermarket retailer to obtain the necessary item.)

RAILROADS

The railroads have traditionally traded as cyclical stocks because the railroad business mirrors the economy. Since railroads are used to transport raw materials to factories and to deliver finished products to warehouses, the profitability of railroad operators usually improves when the economy begins to rebound and there is a greater need for transportation services.

Competing with the Trucking Industry

Since the railroads compete not only with one another but also with the trucking companies, it is important to determine the relative competitiveness that the railroads have with the trucking industry by considering the share of intercity freight

TIP

> Railroads stand to benefit from consolidation in the industrial and manufacturing sectors. For instance, assume Chrysler has manufacturing plants in Denver, Detroit, and Pittsburgh. Then suppose Chrysler consolidates its manufacturing operations by closing its plant in Detroit. The result will be that the distance between the remaining plants (in Denver and Pittsburgh) will be longer, giving the railroads an advantage over the trucking companies.

ton-miles that railroads control. Of course, when the railroads are capturing a greater portion of intercity freight ton-miles, they are becoming more competitive relative to the trucking companies.

The diligent analyst will attempt to determine the trends in the relative competitiveness of railroads before statistics on intercity freight ton-miles are released. In order to make this determination, you will have to weigh the advantages and disadvantages that railroads have versus the trucking companies.

One of the biggest advantages that railroads have is their ability to transport the same amount of freight with just a fraction of the workers that are required by trucking concerns. For example, a train can haul 300 containers of freight with just two workers. However, a trucking company would have to hire 300 truck drivers to haul the same amount of freight. Thus, railroad service is much less expensive than trucking service, especially over long distances.

However, railroads have a number of disadvantages versus the trucking industry. First, customers often prefer to contract with truckers because trucking companies are generally more reliable than railroads. Railroads' relative unreliability is in great part attributable to the time variability that exists because incremental demand is not predictable in the railroad industry. For instance, a coal company may not know how much coal one of its utility customers wants until a few hours before the railroad is scheduled to leave the coal mine's loading area. As a consequence, the right number of railcars are often not in the right place to haul the customers' shipments, and waiting for a few more railcars holds up the entire train. On the other hand, individual trucks can depart once each truck is loaded with freight.

This problem of time variability is compounded when railcars are taken out of service to reduce capital costs, making it even more difficult to quickly dispatch railcars where needed on short notice. Also, time variability is further aggravated by interline shipping, which causes delays due to the time that is required to switch the freight. (Interline shipping occurs when a customer's goods are handled by two or more railroad companies.)

A second disadvantage that railroads have relative to trucking companies is

T I P

☞ One indication that a railroad's reliability might improve occurs when its interline shipments (as a percentage of its total freight ton-miles) are declining.

You should try to invest in those railroads that have achieved above-industry-average on-time performance ratings, especially for their biggest customers. Having high levels of on-time performance is particularly important for railroads whose freight consists of merchandise traffic as opposed to commodity freight such as coal. Similarly, on-time performance is especially important for railroads that serve customers operating on the just-in-time inventory method (under which small units of inventory are delivered just before they are needed).

Another reason why customer service is so important is that poor customer service can impede a railroad's merger. This is because the Surface Transportation Board (the successor to the Interstate Commerce Commission) seeks comments from shippers when reviewing potential mergers. Unfavorable comments from shippers can result in the denial of merger applications.

that train operators must build and maintain their own infrastructure including their tracks, rights-of-way, bridges, and signals, whereas trucking companies benefit from the government's building and maintaining the nation's highways. This disadvantage is made strikingly evident in the aftermath of national disasters. As you may have realized, following the 1993 floods in the Midwest, the railroads had to rebuild the hundreds of miles of track that were lost to flooding. Trucking companies, on the other hand, did not have to rebuild the freeways that were damaged as a result of the Northridge, CA, earthquake in January of 1994 since the government financed such repairs.

However, one mitigating factor to the railroads' having to pay their own way is that Congress and the executive branch of the federal government are aware of this disadvantage. Washington further appreciates the self-financing nature of railroads in light of the government's being in favor of improving the nation's infrastructure without adequate finances to do so. Therefore, during times of standoffs between railroads' management and labor, the federal government often sides with management. For example, the Presidential Emergency Board of 1991 allowed the railroads to reduce their redundancies. As a result of this government intervention, the second brakeman and fireman positions were eliminated.

Intermodal Shipping

Railroads do not always compete with truck operators. In fact, railroads and trucking companies have been increasingly cooperating through intermodal shipping arrangements—when a shipment is transported by railroad in a trailer or container that originates and terminates with either a motor carrier or an ocean shipping line. Railroads benefit from intermodal shipping because they can leverage off of trucking companies' warmer relationships with customers since the truckers' service is more dependable.

One of the most innovative containers in intermodal shipping is the Roadrailer—a trailer equipped with both highway and rail wheels, and thus pulled by either a locomotive or truck cab. The Roadrailer also reduces freight handling since overhead cranes are not needed for placing the trailer on flatcars. However, implementing intermodal transportation will face some obstacles. For example, the shortage of connector highways (highways that truckers can use to deliver and receive containers in close proximity to railyards) creates bottlenecks.

Competition with Barges

Barges offer shippers numerous advantages over railroads. Since barges are twice as fuel efficient as railroads and carry more freight, it is no surprise that barge rates can be as little as half as much as railroad rates. Another reason that barge rates are so low is that barges do not have to invest nearly as much capital in their infrastructure as do the railroads.

However, shippers cannot rely too heavily on barges: When rivers are frozen, barge traffic is suspended, and when waterways are too shallow, barges must reduce the weight of their cargo by limiting the freight they carry.

End Markets

When trying to determine the future prosperity of a given railroad, you must consider the geographical regions that the railroad serves as well as the railroad's end markets. For example, those companies (e.g., Burlington Northern Santa Fe) serving coal-producing regions are typically dependent on coal; the rails (e.g., Conrail) in the midwest may be dependent on automobile production; while those trains (e.g., CSX Corp.) serving the Gulf of Mexico may be beholden to grain exports. Thus, greater coal usage by electric utilities may warrant investor attention in those railroads serving the coal-producing regions since those railroads will benefit from rising revenue ton-miles. Also, the idling of automotive factories (or strikes at such factories) may be a warning to sell shares of those railroads that are dependent on transporting automobiles. Similarly, rapid inventory depletions by chemical users and rising grain exports can benefit the railroads that transport chemicals and grains.

You should also search for those railroads that are transporting increasingly expensive merchandise. When prices of transported merchandise are rising, transportation will account for a smaller percent of the total delivered cost and customers will thus be less sensitive to rail costs.

Impact of Consolidation

The last few years have witnessed a number of mergers in the railroad industry. For example, Southern Pacific agreed to merge into Union Pacific, which had previously acquired Chicago and North Western Transportation. Also, Burlington Northern acquired the Achison and Topeka lines from Santa Fe Railway.

One result of consolidation in the railroad industry is that the larger railroads will be less exposed to particular geographic regions and to particular end markets. This is simply because large railroads will serve more markets and contract with more suppliers. Therefore, a railroad that had traditionally been heavily dependent on transporting automobiles will be less exposed to the trends in auto sales after it merges with other railroads. This greater diversification of revenues resulting from industry consolidation means that individual railroads will profit less when the industry upon which they were formerly dependent experiences a great deal of growth.

However, there are a number of benefits associated with consolidation in the railroad industry:

1. Railroads serving different geographic areas can bring stability to revenue streams and earnings results. For example, weakness in one geographic region can be offset with strength in another geographic region that the railroad under review serves. Similarly, a larger railroad can haul a more diverse array of freight. Therefore, a reduction in demand for transportation services by any particular end market will be less problematic since such category of freight will represent a smaller proportion of the railroad's revenues.

2. Railroads resulting from mergers benefit from deriving more business from existing customers since the railroads can offer their services over a greater geographic region.

3. Mergers allow railroads to increase the distance of their shipments without incurring the expense of switching freight among different carriers. Thus, reduced switching may permit the closure of rail yards, thereby reducing labor costs. Another benefit of closing rail yards is that the railroad operator can sell real estate, thus freeing up additional capital. Also, spending less time in rail yards reduces the incidence of vandalism.

4. Consolidation makes intermodal shipments more reliable by reducing interlining. Also, long-haul, single-system routes enable the carrier to offer long-term contracts, which is better than interlining (whereby

differing interests among the participants can bring negotiations to a stalemate).

Disposition of Track

As a result of consolidation in the railroad industry, merged railroads often find that they have excessive track. There are a few different courses of action that such railroads can take with regard to excessive track. One avenue is *abandonment of track* which means that the railroad obtains regulatory approval to liquidate (sell) its track, usually preferable to the discontinuance of service by railroad operators since the operators can derive revenue from their unused track. *Discontinuance of service* of a given route means that the railroad must maintain its track in serviceable condition for future sale. Thus, when service is merely discontinued, the track owner must expend funds to maintain its unused tracks.

A second avenue is to spin off the extra tracks to short-line operators, which benefits the seller if the short-line operator becomes more efficient. As a result of greater efficiency, the short-line operator can lower its fees, which generates more business. Thus, more volume is fed into the long-distance railroad.

T I P

Sometimes there are two prospective buyers for a given railroad. In many cases, the two railroads that agree to merge will grant the losing acquirer trackage rights in order to avoid antitrust concerns. (Trackage rights allow the losing acquirer to haul its own cars over the merged company's tracks.)

Thus, the stock of the losing acquirer may be penalized since it will not benefit from the consolidation. However, this may nonetheless present a buying opportunity for the stock of the company that won the trackage rights. This is because the losing acquirer will not have to pay for the use of additional track. (At least no significant amount.) On the other hand, the winning acquirer was likely to have paid significantly for the acquired company, partly because of the competition between the two bidders. Also, the losing acquirer will be able to generate new revenues from the trackage rights that it was awarded.

Analytics

You should generally search for railroads that have rising revenue-ton-miles. (Revenue-ton-miles of freight traffic is the weight in tons of freight carried for hire times distance in miles.) Rising revenue-ton-miles indicates that the railroad is winning new contracts and transporting such freight over longer distances.

One telling gauge of railroad productivity is revenue-ton-miles per employee. The higher this ratio is, the more efficient the railroad operator is. For example, if railroad ABC generates ten million revenue-ton-miles with 25 employees, ABC's revenue-ton-miles per employee would be 400,000 revenue-ton-miles (10 million/25).

Moreover, the railroad stocks in your portfolio should demonstrate rising revenues per ton-mile. Revenues per ton-mile is net freight revenue divided by revenue-ton-miles of freight traffic. This ratio is extremely revealing because it measures the amount of revenue derived from transporting freight each mile. For instance, assume that railroad ABC generates $20 million a year from delivering freight and delivered forty million revenue-ton-miles of freight. Thus, ABC's revenues per ton-mile would be $.50 ($20 million/40 million).

You should search for railroads that have decreasing gallons per ton-mile, which is the amount of fuel required to move one ton of freight one mile; when the gallons per ton-mile are decreasing it indicates that the railroad under review is becoming more fuel efficient.

T I P

Railroads are not always adversely affected when their fuel costs rise. This is because railroad operators often have acceleration (or escalation) clauses in their contracts with shippers. Under these acceleration clauses, shippers pay for higher rail-fuel costs. However, these acceleration clauses do not always take effect immediately after the railroads' fuel costs rise. Thus, you should search for those railroads whose acceleration clauses kick in soon after prices rise since the railroad will not be exposed to rising fuel costs for very long.

Other Investment Considerations

Consider the age of a railroad's tracks. The newer the tracks are, the better. More modern tracks allow for greater reliability and improve ride quality, resulting in fewer damages claimed. It is also important to note that those railroads that have much of their tracks located in areas of harsh winters often suffer from snow clogging their rail yards, frozen switches, and generally slower delivery times.

Since railroads are in the transportation business, their equipment must keep moving. Thus, you should consider the average movement per railcar per day. The more hours that each railcar is moving per day (as opposed to being loaded or repaired) the better. Similarly, you should search for railroads that have a low percentage of their locomotives out of service.

Railroad crews are paid by the number of miles traveled rather than by the hour. Thus, in order to determine who is gaining leverage (managers or the workers) you should consider how many miles a crew member must travel before he is eligible to receive overtime pay. Railroads' earnings are boosted when the number of miles is rising. For instance, it would be a bullish trend if workers had to travel 130 miles in 1992 before receiving overtime but, in 1995, had to travel 160 miles before earning overtime pay.

TRUCKING

Similar to the railroad industry, the trucking industry transports raw materials to factories and delivers finished products to warehouses. Thus, the trucking industry's *revenues* are largely a function of the health of the economy. However, a buoyant economy is not completely positive for the *earnings* of trucking companies because a very strong economy forces truck operators to raise their compensation levels to recruit and retain qualified truck drivers.

Secular Considerations

While trucking is a cyclical business, there are a number of factors besides the strength of the economy that you should consider when deciding whether or not to invest in the trucking industry:

1. Free trade helps truckers since more exports and imports are transported to and from the nation's ports. Since these ports are located in the coastal regions of the country, these exports and imports are transported to the furthest reaches of the continental United States. Free trade is particularly beneficial to truckers when it results in more trade with Mexico and Canada because freight deliveries to these nations can be made solely with trucks rather than by ship.

2. Population shifts to the suburbs and the decentralization of industry helps the trucking industry since the suburbs are more accessible to trucks than railroads. The trucking industry especially benefits when factories do not make an effort to locate near railroad connections.

3. Adoption of the just-in-time inventory method by manufacturers benefits short-haulers because manufacturers require their suppliers to be in close proximity to their factories so that deliveries can be made quickly, and serving short routes ensures that truckers will not compete with the railroads.

4. A weak dollar helps the trucking industry since people buy American-made goods. (A weak dollar makes foreign goods prohibitively expensive.) And as a result of more manufacturing activity being conducted in the United States, more constituent parts must be transported to factories for installation in end products.

5. As far as Americans increasing their consumption of foreign-produced
    goods, transplants (foreign manufacturers in the United States) are
    preferable to rising imports. This is because manufacturing a product in
    the United States requires more transportation since all of the parts need
    to be delivered to assembly factories, whereas importing a finished prod-
    uct only requires transporting the product from the port to the retailer's
    shelves.

T I P

One telling sign that truck operators are optimistic about the *volume*
of future business is provided by the purchase of trucks. Thus, you should
track changes in the direction of net truck orders (orders minus cancelations
and deferrals). Of course, the greater the growth in net truck orders, the
more bullish the outlook becomes for the level of activity for the trucking
industry.

Rates

Changes in directions of the rates that trucking companies charge are determined
by changes in demand for trucking services as well as changes in capacity. Most of
the cyclical and secular developments that affect demand for trucking services are
discussed above. However, natural disasters are another factor that can reduce
demand for trucking services. For example, flooding on the West Coast in late
1995 reduced demand for trucking services since many crops were damaged.

Of course, the greater capacity expands, the softer pricing will become for a
constant level of demand. One factor that can increase capacity in the trucking
industry is rising deliveries of new trucks. Also, devaluation of the Mexican peso
or the Canadian dollar can add capacity since these events can result in more truckers' moving back into the U.S. market. Finally, rising levels of cabotage increase
capacity.

Truck Drivers

The issue of the availability and retention of truck drivers should be one of your
primary concerns when evaluating the merits of investing in a trucking operator.
Trucking companies have historically had difficulty recruiting, training, and retaining qualified truck drivers because truck driving is so difficult. For instance, truckers drive for extended periods of time without rest, are usually alone, sleep in their
trucks, eat in truck stops, and are away from home for days or weeks at a time.

T I P

☞ Truckers generally announce price increases for effective dates either in January or April. These announcements sometimes generate investor interest in the group. Of course, the greater the rate increases, the more bullish the outlook for the trucking operators.

Due to these hardships suffered by truck drivers, the larger trucking companies can have annual turnover rates of 300 percent, while it is not uncommon for smaller carriers to have annual turnover rates as high as 800 percent.

In order to reduce the exorbitant costs associated with recruiting, training, and certifying caused by such turnover, many truck operators wisely increase the pay of their veteran drivers. Thus, you should not automatically regard rising wages as a negative development affecting a trucking company since this measure is often effective in reducing employee turnover.

In determining the severity of the driver recruitment and retention problem, you should consider the following:

1. The fact that driver shortages are countercyclical. Thus, a stronger economy accentuates the difficulty that trucking companies have recruiting drivers because more drivers are needed. Conversely, a slowing economy helps trucking companies recruit drivers since these people have fewer job alternatives.

2. The demographics of young men. Since young men are the most likely candidates for truck driving positions, the greater the pool of young men (especially in the South and the midwest) the easier it should be to recruit drivers.

3. The vitality of competing industries. For instance, a slowdown in the construction sector is positive since more construction workers may seek employment in the trucking industry. Similarly, downsizing in the military is beneficial since more enlisted men may seek work as truck drivers.

4. The level of federal funding for driving schools. The greater the level of funding, the more potentially qualified drivers there will be, and vice versa.

5. Whether truck drivers are licensed under a state-by-state or under a national licensing system. The national licensing system is more problematic because points are added on a cumulative basis and are thus accumulated more quickly.

To illustrate how a national licensing system more quickly disqualifies truck drivers, consider the following scenario: Assume that drivers are suspended as soon as they receive three points against them. Thus, under the state licensing system, drivers would be suspended when they receive three points against them in any given state. So, if a driver had two points against him in New York, two points against him in California and two points against him in Texas, he would not be suspended under the state licensing system since he did not receive three points on his record in any particular state.

However, under the national licensing system, the same driver would have been suspended as soon as he received his third demerit (regardless of from where it was derived) since he would have accumulated three points on a national basis.

6. Laws regarding driver qualifications. For instance, the driver shortage problem will be mitigated when truck operators are allowed to hire resident aliens lacking U.S. citizenship or are allowed to hire drivers under 21 years of age.

7. The enforcement of mandatory alcohol or drug testing of drivers. Of course, the more rigorously these tests are enforced the more drivers will fail. Also, the trucking companies are especially inconvenienced when they are required to perform these tests on their applicants.

There are a few other factors that you should take into account in determining the relative power that management has relative to labor. First, you should consider the percentage of dock hours during which a carrier is allowed to use casual laborers (who are paid much less than Teamsters). The more dock work that casual laborers are allowed to perform, the better for the profitability for the company.

You should also consider the number of years that the trucking company can freeze pay of casual workers, the length of time for new workers to reach full pay parity, concessions on overtime for existing dock workers, and whether unions will submit to arbitration instead of orchestrating walkouts to settle minor grievances.

Owner-Operators

In order to alleviate driver shortages, some trucking companies rely on owner-operators (trucks unaffiliated with trucking companies and driven by their independent owners) to handle long-haul traffic. Advantages to trucking companies hiring independent owner-operators include not having to provide training, equipment, or health insurance. However, the downside to using owner-operators is that (since they are paid a percentage of the carrier's revenues) the carrier loses the benefits of being able to raise its prices since much of the revenue increase is passed on to the owner-operator. Therefore, when you believe that *rates* for trucking companies will surge, it is best to invest in those carriers that are least reliant on owner-operators.

Categories of Truck Operators

You should be aware of the main advantages and disadvantages associated with the three major segments (less-than-truckload, truckload, and dedicated contract carriage) of the trucking industry.

Less-than-truckload carriers (e.g., Arkansas Best and Yellow Corporation) carry small shipments of freight for multiple customers through a network of terminals. There are both advantages and disadvantages to the less-than-truckload carriers' hub-and-spoke system. First, the hub-and-spoke system raises high barriers to entry because less-than-truckload carriers need a whole infrastructure of terminals, dock workers, a vast sales force, and (computer) equipment to facilitate the switching of freight. On the other hand, the barriers to entry are much lower in the truckload sector since all that is needed is a truck and a truck driver.

Second, there is better retention of drivers in the less-than-truckload sector than in the truckload sector because of union bargaining and because routes are shorter.

However, one problem with the hub-and-spoke system is that a greater number of lost- or damaged-goods claims arise (than in the truckload sector) because of the additional handling that occurs at the terminals. Also, since the hub-and-spoke system results in delays at the terminals due to transferring cargo, it is not geared for the just-in-time delivery system. Additionally, the higher union concentration in the less-than-truckload sector makes these carriers more vulnerable to both strikes and the payment of rising compensation packages.

T I P

The trucking companies are major beneficiaries of improvements in communications technology. For instance, satellite tracking systems

- Permit drivers to stay in contact with headquarters, thus allowing drivers to make additional pick-ups after they have begun their runs.
- Allow truckers to keep their customers better informed as to when they can expect their deliveries.
- Allow drivers to save time by not having to stop at pay phones to make calls.
- Allow headquarters to pinpoint the exact location of their fleets which is particularly helpful when breakdowns or hijackings occur.

Truckload carriers, such as J.B. Hunt Transport and Werner Enterprises, transport freight directly from origin to destination without sorting the freight at terminals. The truckload operators have an advantage over the less-than-truck-load carriers in that their longer runs entail less loading and unloading (on a percentage basis). Also, these longer hauls make it easier for truckload carriers to arrange the back hauls. (However, management information systems are making paperwork processing easier for the less-than-truckload operators to arrange backhauls.)

Truckers are also using navigation systems that provide drivers with maps and optimum driving routes. Finally, electronic sensors are being used to monitor engine performance.

Truckers (e.g., Ryder System) that engage in dedicated contract carriage assume the internal transportation responsibilities for large companies. For example, a large retailer may hire a dedicated contract carrier to deliver merchandise from its warehouses to its stores.

Companies that rely on dedicated contract carriers benefit in a number of ways. First, dependence on truckers eliminates the problem of companies' capital commitments being tied up in their fleets and relieves such companies of recruiting, training, and certifying their drivers. Second, companies that operate their own transportation have a high level of empty miles. For example, there might be no freight for the truck to transport on its way from a store back to the warehouse. Third, companies do not have to solicit other shippers' freight to reduce these empty miles. Fourth, trucking companies offer better coverage. For instance, if a truck breaks down, the trucking company will be more likely to be able to dispatch a replacement to retrieve the freight than will a company operating its own fleet.

T I P

Dedicated contract carriers may be big beneficiaries of intrastate deregulation since deregulation lowers shipping rates. Thus, more companies may become convinced that it may be cheaper to use a dedicated contract carrier.

However, many companies will not entirely cede their transportation responsibilities to outside trucking companies. One reason many companies will choose to handle some of their own trucking is that they want to be sure that they have the capacity to meet peak or seasonal demand internally. Also, maintaining its own fleet of trucks reserves bargaining leverage for the company vis-a-vis for-hire carriers.

T I P

> Consider the percentage of rail intermodal that trucking unions allow their companies to use. Of course, the greater this percentage is the better, since the trucking company will be able to reduce its costs further.
>
> Such percentages of allowable intermodal traffic are usually negotiated between unions and management. When agreement is reached, the companies that have the lowest percentages of intermodal traffic when such agreements are reached have the most to gain. For example, assume that the unions and management agree that trucking companies should be allowed to transport as much as 40 percent of their freight via intermodal arrangements. A truck operator that transports only 5 percent of its freight intermodally has more to gain than a truck operator that transports 38 percent of its freight intermodally at the time of the agreement on intermodal traffic.

Interaction with Railroads

Trucks are more flexible than railroads since they can move goods long distances using a single vehicle. Also, using a single vehicle to make a delivery makes it easier for shippers to track their freight than is the case with railroads. Moreover, trucks do not have to bear heavy investment in fixed facilities as do the rails.

Intermodal transportation is beneficial to truckers since it alleviates driver shortages, reduces transit times, and costs about 25 percent less than highway transportation on long hauls. Nonunion carriers have more to gain (than union carriers) from intermodal since they have no unions to oppose the trucking company's contracting with railroads to have the railroad haul cargo on part of the route. Interestingly, carriers operating in the West should benefit the most from increased intermodal transportation since their routes generally cover longer distances.

However, intermodal is perceived as an inferior service since its multiparticipant nature makes it prone to delays. Consequently, intermodal shipments are often priced at a discount to all-highway moves.

Other Investment Considerations

It is best to invest in the trucking industry when

- Speed limits are rising. Higher speed limits mean that truckers can offer faster delivery while incurring fewer speeding tickets. For example, it was bullish when Congress passed a bill in late 1995 that allowed states to raise their speed limits. Some states even went further by completely abolishing their speed limits.

- The cost of trucks in terms of performance (as measured by the number of pounds of freight that can be hauled at a given number of miles per hour while still achieving a low fuel economy rating) is stable or declining. For example, a truck that hauled 72,000 pounds at 55 miles per hour in 1980 only had a fuel economy rating of 5 miles a gallon. However, by 1994, a similar truck could haul 80,000 pounds at as much as 65 miles per hour while maintaining a fuel economy rating of 7 miles per gallon. Moreover, the price of trucks did not vary significantly between 1980 and 1994.

- The percentage of business meals that are tax-deductible is rising since truckers can often write off part of the cost of their meals as a business expense. The greater the deductibility, the better.

- Fuel costs (including fuel taxes) are decreasing.

When deciding in which trucking companies to invest, you should

- Search for those trucking operators whose fleets consist of relatively new tractors and trailers. In other words, the lower the average age of a truck operator's fleet the better. One advantage of a relatively new fleet is that the operator can offer better customer service since new trucks experience fewer breakdowns. Additionally, most of the breakdowns that do occur are still under warranty. Moreover, relatively new fleets are helpful in attracting new drivers.

- Consider incidence of hijacking. More hijackings are likely to occur when truckers haul more valuable products such as computer chips.

- Search for trucking companies that have a low ratio of accidents per million miles traveled.

- Search for trucking companies that have a low percentage of deadhead miles to total miles traveled. Deadheading means returning from a delivery with an empty truck.

- Search for companies that have little exposure to roads that can be covered with snow or ice since these roads are prone to delays, more accidents, and poor fuel economy.

Regulation

Many aspects of the Interstate Commerce Commission vanished by the end of 1995. This should benefit truckers since the costs associated with filing detailed rate and route schedules will be reduced or eliminated.

However, some carriers could be hurt by less regulation. One reason is that shippers could refrain from doing business with carriers of unknown financial condition because actuarial studies have found a high correlation between a motor carrier's financial health and its accident rates. Also, insurers may demand higher premiums or even deny coverage completely due to the absence of reliable and timely financial data.

AIRLINES

The legendary Warren Buffet once said, "Don't invest in airlines. It's the worst business of any size in the world, with huge fixed costs and lots of overcapacity." I concur.

The fact that the airline industry has huge fixed costs means that airlines will maximize the use of their fleets. This overcapacity results in air travel's being commoditized. Worse still, airline seats are a perishable commodity. Once a plane has left the ground, the airline can never sell that empty seat to a customer. Since airlines do not want to miss sales and since the marginal costs of adding another passenger is negligible, price wars are epidemic in the airline industry. When the marginal cost of filling a seat is less than the average seat cost, losses are sure to follow.

Capacity

There are many reasons why the airline industry is burdened with overcapacity. Among them are the following:

- Airlines are trophy properties in that businessmen like to own airlines because they are glamorous, not because they believe they can make a reasonable return on their investment. This irrational desire to own an airline results in executives' keeping the airline running even when the prudent course of action would be to shut it down. Also, some businessmen continue to operate an airline even after they have repeatedly failed.

  For instance, Edward Beauvais lost his home when America West (which he co-founded) went bankrupt. Nevertheless, Mr. Beauvais went on to establish Western Pacific Airlines. Even pilots and flight attendants are irrationally attracted to the airline industry. For example, Kiwi Airlines was established by people who were previously dismissed by the major carriers. However, each of these pilots supplied $50,000 of start-up capital while each flight attendant contributed $5,000 just for the right to work in the airline industry.

  This intense attraction to the airline industry is problematic because there can be no shakeouts, which would help firm up prices. Similarly, layed-off mechanics, pilots, and management are reserve pools of talent that are eager to rejoin the airline industry. These people allow start-up carriers to outsource virtually everything—attendants, public relations work, and legal work. The ability to outsource reduces the barriers to entry in the airline industry. Thus, a new carrier can be launched with a single 727 rented for as little as $7,000 a month.

- Due to intense competition among airline manufacturers, planes are provided to airlines on irresistible terms. For instance, airline manufacturers sometimes grant airlines "rent holidays" in which airlines are allowed to defer their lease payments.
- Due to the massive losses that the airlines have been incurring, they have been trading wage- and work-rule concessions for stock. For instance, union employee stock option plans at UAL Corporation (the holding company for United Airlines) owns 55 percent of UAL stock. Such ownership by employees adds to industry capacity since airlines that are controlled by their workers will favor expanding their routes.
- Efforts to orchestrate mergers within the airline industry have been unblemished with success.

  Integrating employees, with different wage scales and work rules, as well as meshing together computers, routes, airplanes, and maintenance has been a nightmare. In some cases, cultures never merge, leaving companies to hold together factions as best they can like United Nations peacekeepers. With employees carrying more clout than ever in the industry, and sitting as major stockholders at several carriers, there's no guarantee new mergers would be any easier now than in the past.[3]

  When airlines expand their boards of directors to include representatives of various unions, there are simply too many people involved in negotiations regarding mergers and acquisitions to achieve agreements.

- Airplanes are being flown far beyond their projected life spans as airlines continue to find ways to extend the lives of their planes. For example, in the early 1990s, many industry observers believed that many older airplanes would be retired in view of new federal noise reduction requirements. However, many airlines simply installed "hushkits," which further preserve "zombies." Thus, there are very few retirements of airplanes.
- As the costs of landing slots, landing fees, airport fees, passenger facility fees, and fuel taxes rise, airlines try to increase the number of flights that they offer so as to better leverage their costs.
- Other countries are impressed with the effect that deregulation in the U.S. airline industry had on bringing about lower airfares, and they thus, want to stimulate competition in their markets. As a result, these governments

---

[3] Scott McCartney, "Despite Merger Hype Airline Industry Remains Fragmented," *The Wall Street Journal,* November 20, 1995, p. A1.

are reaching "open skies" agreements with the United States, which permit one nation's airlines to compete in the others' markets, thus, adding capacity to international routes.

Despite all of the structural problems that the airline industry faces in terms of excess capacity, the following factors can offer temporary relief to the problems caused by the capacity glut:

- It is favorable when aircraft orders (net of deferrals and cancelations) are declining.

- It is even better when net aircraft orders are exceeded by retirements.

- An increase in temporary groundings helps alleviate excess capacity.

- Reduced seating density can reduce capacity. However, in 1994, TWA replaced seats that it had previously removed on the theory that if it did not accommodate more passengers, such passengers would simply fly on other airlines.

- Slower turnaround times at airports would reduce capacity. However, it is instructive to note that the airlines are adamantly in favor of the speeding up of turnaround times. For instance, Southwest Airlines petitioned the FAA to allow its planes to taxi to the runway while passengers were still standing. Also, during a period of labor discord in 1995, pilots at Federal Express made a concerted effort to taxi to and from the runways as slowly as possible in order to infuriate Federal Express's management.

Price Wars

While excess capacity is one reason that price wars are pervasive throughout the airline industry, it is far from being the only reason. Another reason is that many carriers (e.g., Pan Am and TWA) benefit from filing for bankruptcy protection. Since bankrupt companies are allowed to reschedule their debt repayments and

T I P

When analyzing a major airline, you should consider the percentage of that carrier's routes that face competition from low-fare competitors. Of course, the lower the percentage, the better.

renege on their labor agreements, their cost structures are lowered. Thus, bankrupt airlines are very aggressive in lowering their ticket prices, in turn, forcing the healthy carriers to reduce their air fares.

Also, many new start-up carriers (e.g., ValuJet Airlines, Frontier Airlines, and Western Pacific Airlines) have low cost structures since they acquire small, used planes and operate with nonunionized employees. Passing part of these low costs on to customers results in the start-up carriers' taking market share away from the larger airlines. This commoditization is aggravated by most airline reservation systems' giving priority ranking to the lowest-fare flights.

Additionally, airlines have had to compete on price more intensely in recent years since they are selling more seats to discretionary travelers—that is, more seats are being sold to vacation travelers rather than business travelers. This is problematic because business travelers are more profitable than vacation travelers since the former do not need extensive advertising of low-priced tickets to prompt them to travel. Additionally, passengers are becoming more savvy about finding ways to save money on airfares.

Moreover, many industry observers fear that the diffusion of communications systems could further reduce business travel; with more fax machines, E-mail, and video conferencing, communication conducted over telephone lines may partially replace air travel. Also, these observers point out that air travel in general suffers from adverse marketing when flights are delayed due to air traffic control problems. (Incidentally, cities sometimes try to divert airport fees and the like to their cities' general coffers. Thus, these monies cannot be used to improve the air traffic control system.)

However, I do not believe that communications will present such a monumental problem for the airlines; it may in fact, actually stimulate demand for more air travel. These communication systems allow people to conduct business over wider geographic boundaries than before, but these long-distance relationships will still need to be sustained with personal meetings and interaction.

Cost Considerations

Unlike almost all other industries, airlines suffer from *reverse* economies of scale. The more cities served, the more complex the operation becomes. Merely trying to match crews with flight schedules requires a mind-numbing calculus. These problems are compounded by the airlines' seniority systems secured by unions.

Also, most airlines have high labor costs since the unions are extremely strong. In fact, virtually all employees at some major airlines belong to a union. The strength of these unions has resulted in high wages and an inflexible workforce. For example, pilots at the major carriers are paid as much as $200,000 a year for flying just 50 hours a month.

Far and away the leaders of organized labor at airlines are the pilots. Major airlines have grown so large that they can hardly afford a job slowdown by their pilots, much less an outright strike. Fixed costs are so high, and the number of pilots so large, that an airline would be forced out of business long before it could possibly train, certify, and deploy replacement pilots. For safety reasons, the government requires exhaustive and extensive pilot training.[4]

Other operating concerns include the following:

- Compensation for pilots may rise in the future if a shortage of pilots arises due to insufficient numbers of pilots being hired (trained), the mandatory retirement age of 60, and reduced numbers of pilots in the military.

- Workers' opposition to hefty compensation packages for top management makes it difficult to attract professional managers to the airline industry. Also, many airlines are ceding much management discretion to workers, giving managers little room in which to maneuver.

- Airline workers can only be pushed so far. Workers at some start-up carriers periodically try to organize unions after being told that they must buy their own uniforms, must pay for their own airport parking, and would only be paid for flight time, not for layovers. Aside from leading to more unionization, cutting wages and benefits can hurt employee morale, which can translate into inferior customer service.

The Hub-and-Spoke System

Many major airlines have replaced large parts of their point-to-point routes with a hub-and-spoke system, in which many flights from outlying areas are funneled in to a hub, at which point the passengers transfer for connecting flights to their ultimate destinations.

The hub-and-spoke system has numerous advantages over the linear system. First, the hub-and-spoke systems increase the number of cities connected without the need for direct flights between every pair of cities, thereby allowing the carrier to eliminate lightly traveled point-to-point segments. Also, the average ticket revenue per passenger increases since passengers remain on the same airline.

Nevertheless, there are numerous problems associated with the hub-and-spoke system. First, the hub-and-spoke system can wreak havoc among a multitude of flights all over the country. For example, a delayed flight from a spoke (Montreal) destined for its hub (Chicago) can delay all of the flights on which its passengers hope to connect.

Second, the hub-and-spoke system is extremely expensive to operate:

- It must be adequately staffed to facilitate the three or four times a day that as many as 50 flights are scheduled. Unlike in the restaurant industry

---

[4] Scott McCartney, "Airlines Remain at the Mercy of Their Pilots," *The Wall Street Journal* CCXXVI, no. 92 (November 9, 1995), p. 31.

where part-time employees are used to meet peak demand, airline personnel are full-time workers who cannot be sent home after a few hours of
busy activity.

- Since planes must wait until all connecting passengers have boarded
  before they depart, utilization of airplanes is reduced.

- Pilots dislike the system since they waste a lot of time on the ground.

- The system requires airlines to award excessive frequent-flier miles.

Frequent-Flier Programs

Frequent-flier programs have been one of the few silver linings in the clouds hov-
ering over the airline industry. These programs benefit the major carriers in the following ways:

- Frequent fliers generate tremendous brand loyalty. Many passengers go to
  great lengths to schedule their flights on airlines with which they are
  accumulating frequent-flier miles. Furthermore, these passengers are not
  terribly price sensitive.

- Many passengers, when redeeming their frequent-flier miles, are accompanied by someone who pays full fare.

- Many frequent-flier miles are awarded by the airlines' partners. These
  companies pay the major airlines for each mile that they award.

- Many frequent-flier miles that are awarded are not even redeemed.

- Frequent-flier miles offset the annoyance that passengers have with the
  hub-and-spoke system.

However, you should be aware of a few pitfalls associated with frequent-
flier programs. First, arbitrary revocation of the terms of frequent-flier programs
might be a thing of the past as the U.S. Supreme Court ruled that passengers can
sue airlines over frequent-flier changes. Also, the major airlines could be hurt
if the IRS declares that frequent-flier miles earned by business travelers are
taxable.

Fuel Costs

Fuel prices are a no-win situation for the airlines. When they rise, airlines'
expenses obviously increase. If the airlines try to pass higher fuel prices on to
their passengers in the form of higher air fares, demand for travel falls. If the airlines absorb higher fuel prices, their profit margins erode. When fuel prices fall,
airlines often lower their fares, triggering price wars. Finally, the airlines have
little experience in hedging fuel prices, having only done so since the end of the
Gulf War.

Analytics

The structure of the airline industry is so unattractive that you will probably not want to be a long-term investor in this industry. When asked why he invested in USAir, Warren Buffett responded by saying "my psychiatrist asks me the same thing." However, some investors like to trade airline stocks. These traders should buy shares of those airline companies that are

- Increasing their load factors (the percentage of seats filled). It is even more important that the absolute load factor (the percentage of seats *sold*) is rising.

- Demonstrating rising revenue passenger miles (one paying passenger flown one mile on one scheduled flight).

- Demonstrating rising yields (the average fare received per revenue passenger mile).

- Demonstrating an upward trend in the ratio of revenue passenger miles to available seat miles. (An airlines' available seat miles is the sum of the distance that each of its seats have flown.)

- Lowering their costs per available seat mile. (The cost-per-available-seat-mile ratio is calculated by dividing passenger operating expenses by available seat miles.)

Company-Specific Considerations

You should search for airlines that have young fleets. One reason is that maintenance costs are much lower, whereas after a plane is 25 years old its repair costs roughly double. Similarly, it is preferable for an airline to have some standardization within its fleet since standard fleets allow carriers to reduce their maintenance costs.

You should also consider how many hours, on average, a carrier's pilots fly. The closer this average is to the federal limit of 1,000 hours a year, the better use the airline is getting out of its pilots.

Additionally, you should consider the percent of a carrier's traffic that is flying at a discount. Moreover, you should consider the depth of the average discount.

Code Sharing

Code-sharing arrangements between a major carrier and a regional carrier allow each partner to advertise and sell a flight as their own when it is operated by the partner carrier. Under code-sharing arrangements, the regional airline feeds passengers to its major partner by delivering passengers to a hub for connecting services. This reduces the waiting times between connections (from one partner's flight to the other's). In return for such service, the major partner assists the regional carrier in terms of advertising and marketing. Also, the major partner usually provides the regional partner with baggage handling and flight reservations. Additionally, the passenger only has to check in once and his luggage is automatically transferred.

The majors lose less money when they cede low-density routes to the regional airlines with which they have code-sharing agreements because the major airlines can still arrange flights to remote airports for their passengers.

One problem with code sharing is that the passengers do not always know which airline they will be traveling on. This is problematic since some passengers are concerned with airline safety and service records as well as on-time performance. Passengers say that it is very difficult to get a seat allocation on a code-share flight.

Several major airlines have equity interests in the regional airlines with which they have code-sharing arrangements. Here's an investment technique you can use in this situation:

Sometimes you can buy a stock for less than the value of the shares that that company owns. This occurs when the market capitalization of the company under review is lower than the cumulative market value of the stock that the company owns in other companies. For example, assume that the company in which you are considering investing has a market capitalization of $100 million. Then assume that this company has the following equity interests in other companies:

Company	Percent Interest	Market Capitalization ($ million)	Value ($ million)
A	20%	$200	$40
B	30%	100	30
C	25%	300	75
Total			$145

In this example, the $100 million company is valued lower than the equity positions (amounting to $145 million) that it has in other companies. Moreover, the target company's operations are thrown in for free.

REGIONAL AIRLINES

The regional airlines have benefited from taking over short routes from major airlines. Major airlines often find that it is worthwhile (i.e., they lose less money if they decide) to cede their shorter routes to regional airlines since the regionals have lower cost structures. Whereas the major carriers cannot serve short-distance, low-density routes profitably, the regionals can.

There are a number of reasons why regional airlines have dramatically leaner cost structures than the majors.

1. The regionals have less-expensive and more flexible labor forces. While it is not unusual for a pilot at a major airline to earn at least $160,000 a year, it is uncommon for a pilot at a regional airline to earn as much as $60,000 a year because regional pilots are usually not as experienced and are seldom unionized. In terms of policy flexibility, some flight attendants may be allowed to begin cleaning the cabin as passengers deplane, meaning the planes are on the ground for a shorter amount of time, thereby boosting the utilization of the planes.

2. Regionals also offer fewer amenities than the majors—for example, less food and beverage service. Such cost-saving measures benefit the regionals in a number of ways: unit costs of meals are reduced; overhead is reduced since flight attendants do not have to be trained to serve meals, menus need not be planed, and contracts with food vendors do not have to be negotiated; and turnaround time can be reduced since the plane will not be delayed while waiting for the food.

3. The regionals' small planes are less expensive to acquire (or to lease) and burn less jet fuel than larger aircraft.

4. Regionals often have no sales force because code-sharing agreements with major carriers provide them with marketing and reservation systems.

TRAP

> ⊘ Regional airlines can be hurt when the workers at the major airlines have more stock in their own airlines. This is because these workers may be opposed to ceding routes since doing so would make many of those workers redundant.

Another attraction of the regionals is that they can charge relatively expensive fares for their services since their low-density routes have little, if any, competition. This is partly because code sharing stands as a barrier to entry to other regionals. Also, regionals often have a larger percentage of price-insensitive business and military travelers than the majors.

Concerns

Regulatory standards for small carriers could be ratcheted up. If small planes would have to meet more stringent safety standards, the regionals' costs would rise. Also, pilots that fly small planes can fly 20-percent more hours than those flying jets or bigger commuter planes. If pilots of small planes were only allowed to fly the same number of hours as pilots of larger planes, the regional carriers would be adversely affected.

The regional carriers often compete with Amtrack, buses, and the family car. Thus, lower train- and bus-ticket prices, as well as lower gasoline and car-rental prices would adversely impact the regional carriers.

12

Energy

INTEGRATED OIL

The fortunes of integrated oil companies such as Chevron and Texaco are inextricably linked to the price of crude oil itself. The higher crude prices rise, the more bullish the outlook is for oil stocks. The further oil prices fall, the more bearish the projections of oil stocks become. Since oil is an international commodity, you must review the global supply-and-demand picture in order to estimate the future price of oil.

Of course, you should also consider developments on the cost side of oil companies' ledgers. American integrated oil companies traditionally prided themselves on their size (in terms of revenues and employees). Also, these companies assumed a great deal of debt because they believed that prices would continue to rise indefinitely. Now, however, oil executives are becoming more focused on their companies' profitability rather than their size. As a result, they are aggressively using technology to reduce their headcount and boost their productivity. Moreover, many integrated oil companies have been reducing their debt loads to more manageable levels. Therefore, cost reduction will become a major source of the oil industry's profitability growth.

Supply

Since the 12 OPEC members have collectively accounted for roughly 40 percent of the world's oil production (and over three-quarters of the world's oil reserves) in the mid-1990s, a review of the OPEC members' oil policies is usually a sound place to begin your analysis of the world's oil supply.

While most members of OPEC would like the cartel to reduce output (and thus lift prices), these same members have a tendency to cheat on their quotas. Once one member begins to cheat, other members follow suit because they do not want to miss out on the higher prices resulting from the quota. However, this cheating by several members causes output to rise noticeably and therefore for oil prices to fall.

Nevertheless, there are circumstances in which OPEC members cannot cheat on their quotas. For instance, no member of OPEC (except for Saudi Arabia) has the resources required to meaningfully boost output. Reasons for these shortfalls include military build-ups and devastation resulting from wars. Also, the weakness of the dollar hurts oil producers because oil is sold in dollars but much of the imports into Middle Eastern countries are purchased with European or Japanese currencies.

Similarly, while Saudi Arabia has the resources to boost its output, it probably does not want to do so. As a result of being endowed with a reserve life of as much as 200 years, Saudi Arabia traditionally favored keeping oil prices relatively low so as to foster dependence on oil. However, things have changed. Saudi Arabia is in need of hard currency as much as any other OPEC member. One reason for this is that the Gulf War and the military buildup that followed were extremely expensive. Second, high oil revenues are needed to keep the more than 6,000 members of the Royal family from an internecine feud. Similarly, the Saudi government must maintain its generous transfer payments to keep its increasingly Westernized and educated population from revolting.

On the other hand, the reentry of Iraq into world oil markets would, of course, increase the supply of oil. There are a number of factors that indicate that the U.N. Security Council will eventually allow Iraq to reenter the world oil markets:

1. France favors Iraq's reentry since French companies were active in Iraqi oil exploration.

T I P

☞ The greater the percentage of output that is produced from OPEC, the better the outlook is for oil prices. While cheating often occurs, there is at least some cohesiveness among the members of OPEC.

2. Russia favors Iraqi reentry since Baghdad would once again have the means to purchase Russian weapons systems.

3. Turkey (a close U.S. ally) would benefit from Iraqi oil exports since much of Iraq's oil would flow through Turkish pipelines.

4. Other nations endorse Iraqi oil exports since this would enable Iraq to make war reparations.

5. Even the United States and Great Britain might favor Iraqi reentry if oil prices rise too far.

T I P

The closer OPEC members' quotas are to their capacity, the less risk there is of OPEC's cheating on its quotas.

You should also be aware of how the following issues and developments affect the supply of oil:

- Islamic revolutions do not result in reduced oil exports over the long run. As Henry Kissinger once said, "Even revolutionaries need hard currency."

- While the former Soviet Union (FSU) has huge oil reserves, it is difficult for the FSU to deliver its oil to export markets. First, the FSU's pipelines are a mess—the Russian government has reported that there are more than 700 major leaks each year. One reason for these leaks is that the pipelines are frequently bent as the soil contracts and expands with the drastic temperature change in some parts of the FSU. Similarly, portions of the pipe actually collapse as the supports holding them sink into marsh-lands. Second, though there may well be over 100 billion barrels of oil in Azerbaijan, Kazakhstan, and Turkmenistan, these areas are landlocked and face hostile surrounding countries that may try to claim some of these reserves as their own.

- Countries with jurisdiction over the North Sea such as Great Britain and Norway can influence production from the North Sea by changing royalty and by tax rates' being levied on the oil produced in that basin.

- Restrictive environmental regulations make it extremely expensive for large oil companies to drill for oil in the United States.

- Advances in seismic and drilling technology lower the break-even point for extracting oil. For instance, technology has recently been developed that makes it profitable to explore for oil in the Gulf of Mexico where salt layers used to distort seismic data.

- There will obviously be less supply of oil when the most prolific oil fields are producing at capacity and are running down reserves.

- There will be less supply of oil on international markets when traditional exporters are consuming more of their own supplies. This often occurs when exporters such as Indonesia are rapidly industrializing. Further, if the producing country subsidizes oil prices at the pump, further internal consumption will be encouraged.

- Major oil producers should favor higher oil prices when their production costs and budget deficits rise.

- When the incremental output from expensive new fields is not sufficient to meet incremental demand, oil producers will realize that they are better off not even spending money on bringing new production on stream. By avoiding these expenditures, oil prices will firm. On the other hand, were these producers to make large investments to produce more oil, the additional supply of oil would be a factor in eroding pricing.

- Privatizations of oil companies in developing countries will lead to more output of oil. This is because many nationalized oil companies such as Mexico's PEMEX were often used as a means to collect taxes and implement social policy. Under those circumstances, the companies did not have enough cash left to drill new oil wells or even to maintain the old ones.

- More oil will be produced when developing countries invite Western oil companies to explore for oil in their countries.

T I P

More oil tankers coming on stream may be a future indication of greater oil production.

Demand

The demand for oil is largely a function of economic activity. Thus, the greater the general economic growth is in developed countries, the better. Even seemingly small percentages of economic growth in developed countries can actually be quite significant since industrialized countries (such as the United States and Europe) have such large economies. Thus, even a 3.5-percent rate of economic growth in the United States can materially boost demand for oil.

It is important to monitor trends in gasoline usage because gasoline (which is derived from oil) accounts for 45 percent of U.S. oil consumption. Thus, environmental laws such as those concerning fuel efficiency of automobiles will reduce

T I P

☞ Free trade agreements, such as GATT, are positive for the oil industry since these agreements result in more transportation.

oil consumption. Also, the Clean Air Act, which mandates that gasoline sold in the
nation's nine smoggiest cities must be blended with ethanol, indicates that the content of oil in gasoline will be reduced. Additionally, the emergence of the electric
car could noticeably reduce oil demand.

Similarly, higher speed limits are good for gasoline sales because higher
speed limits result in fewer miles per gallon. For example, a 1984 Department of
Transportation study found that the average car got 34-percent and 17.7-percent
fewer miles per gallon at 75 mph and 65 mph, respectively, than at 55 mph.

Economic growth in developing countries is another important factor in
worldwide demand for oil. Interestingly, there should be a great deal of demand
for oil from the developing world as these emerging countries industrialize. For
instance, the transition from an agrarian economy to a manufacturing economy
will result in higher consumption of oil as will the transition from bicycles to
mopeds to automobiles.

T R A P

⊘ When manufacturing becomes more efficient, the prospects for oil
prices dim.

Price Movements

You should be aware that a number of mechanisms have been put in place for purposes of stabilizing the oil markets. First, the futures market's propensity for
spreading risk helps reduce the possibility of a sustained surge in oil prices.
Second, the United States has accumulated reserves in its Strategic Petroleum
Reserve (SPR) in Texas and Louisiana for purposes of reducing oil shocks. Thus,
the greater the number of barrels of oil (in terms of the number of days of use and
the number of days of imports) stockpiled in the SPR, the better for price stability.

The third factor that may reduce the chances of oil prices spiking is that
some Middle Eastern oil producers are making downstream investments (e.g., in
gas stations). These investments will add stability to oil prices since these producers will be less likely to cut off oil supplies when such a step would threaten their
own fuel outlets.

T I P

☞ The United States Strategic Petroleum Reserve may be lowered when the government needs money. For instance, several Senate Republicans proposed selling 39 million barrels from this reserve to help reduce the budget deficit during the federal budget stalemate in the beginning of 1996.

Investment Considerations

You should seek to invest in those integrated oil companies that have the following characteristics or are undertaking the following measures:

- A high percentage of production replacement. Failure to acquire at least as many barrels of oil in reserves as are being produced will result in the oil company's not having any oil to produce in the future.
- Low costs for finding and developing oil reserves (in terms of dollars per barrel).
- Production oil with a low sulfur content.
- Making good use of the advances in exploration. For instance, horizontal drilling allows explorers to drill vertically until they hit oil or gas, and then move horizontally to maximize production. Also, three dimensional seismic surveying can detect mineral deposits to a depth of 6,000 feet. This entails blasting the surface of the prospective area with dynamite and then sending sound waves down through the ground. These waves bounce off layers of the rocks below and are detected up by "geophones" (sensors arranged in a grid on the surface) that record an acoustical image of the ground.

REFINERIES

Refineries are used to convert crude oil into end products such as gasoline and heating oil. In determining how profitable an integrated oil company's refineries

T R A P

⊘ An oil company that has very little debt on its balance sheet while also having a very low reserves-to-production ratio can actually be in a very precarious capital situation because the company will have to spend a great deal of money locating, acquiring, and developing reserves.

are (or how profitable independent refinery operators such as Tosco Corp. or Sun Company may be), you must consider capacity within the industry as well as demand for the end products.

One problem that has plagued the refineries in the early and mid-1990s was excess capacity resulting from massive liabilities associated with closing refineries. In fact, it can cost at least $1 billion in cleanup costs to close a large old oil refinery. Thus, many refinery operators believe that they are better off running their refineries, even though they lose money, than closing them triggering big losses with no chance of recovery. However, some capacity has been reduced in the mid-1990s as a result of joint ventures such as the one between Mobil and British Petroleum.

When the price of oil futures falls, it is often worthwhile to consider investing in the refineries. Sometimes these shares fall in lockstep with the integrateds' shares when oil prices drop. However, refineries benefit from lower oil prices because oil is their primary raw material. Also, lower gasoline prices result in greater demand for gasoline by drivers, which benefits the refineries and other oil companies with downstream investments (usually gas stations).

TIP

👉 A lower dollar is helpful to the refineries and oil companies with downstream investments since people will take more domestic car trips instead of traveling abroad.

Interestingly, many oil companies are making downstream investments. For instance, oil companies are trying to make better use of their real estate by establishing convenience stores and offering fast food. In fact, Diamond Shamrock acquired National Convenience Stores and Chevron is partnering with McDonald's in the West and Southwest.

NATURAL GAS

There are many proponents of natural gas. First, environmentalists like natural gas because natural gas is the cleanest-burning fossil fuel. Natural gas is preferable to coal since coal emits sulfur (which is blamed for acid rain) and emits carbon dioxide (which causes global warming). Second, since natural gas is produced domestically, there are no adverse balance of payments considerations as is the case with imported oil.

Of course, it is most profitable for exploration companies, such as Apache Corp. and Forest Oil, to produce natural gas when prices are the highest. Like any other commodity, natural gas prices are the highest when demand exceeds supply.

Demand

The following are among the factors that affect the demand for natural gas:

- The more buoyant economic activity is, the better. For instance, natural gas benefits from rising activity at independent power plants, steel and paper mills, and petrochemical facilities.
- The colder the weather (particularly in the winter) measured in heating-degree days, the better. (Heating-degree days is a measure of the coldness of the weather, based on the extent to which the daily mean temperature falls below 65 degrees Fahrenheit. A daily mean temperature usually represents the sum of the high and low readings divided by two.)
- Electric utilities may favor gas-fired power generation since, on a kilowatt-hour basis, gas undercuts coal by roughly 25 percent. Also, gas-fired power plants cost approximately 50-percent less to build and can be brought on stream much faster than coal plants. Additionally, expiration of nuclear licences presents another opportunity for natural gas to fuel the generation of electricity. However, since many utilities and manufacturers can easily switch to oil, lower oil prices may result in less demand for natural gas.
- As the price of electricity falls due to deregulation in the utility industry, the price advantage for natural gas will narrow.
- More people are moving to the intermountain states—are heavy consumers of natural gas since it is prohibitively expensive to transport oil (an alternative to natural gas) there.
- Efficiency and conservation drive down total energy use.
- Growth in the number and usage of natural gas–powered vehicles will benefit natural gas prices.

Sources of Supply

You should be aware that for several reasons it is generally more difficult and expensive to explore for natural gas than for oil:

T I P

> The mere discussion of deregulation of the electric utility industry is problematic for the natural gas industry. This is because many utilities are placing expansion of their gas-fired facilities on hold until they determine what the consequences of a deregulatory environment will be.

T I P

👉 Rising volume of natural gas pipeline transport may be an early indicator that demand for natural gas is rising.

1. You have to drill deeper for natural gas than oil.

2. Completion costs such as the costs of capping the well to keep flow under control are more expensive for natural gas because natural gas has higher pressure than oil which means that heavier steel in the pipelines must be used.

3. Natural gas platforms tend to be further offshore than oil platforms.

4. Financing for offshore natural gas development is more difficult and expensive to obtain than for offshore oil development because gas is difficult to transport. (Pipelines are needed for gas, whereas little infrastructure is needed for offshore oil since tankers can simply pull up to the platforms.)

5. Oftentimes contracts regarding the purchase of natural gas need to be consummated before drilling begins.

T I P

👉 Incidentally, it is less expensive to drill for natural gas in Canada than in the United States because natural gas is found in more-shallow basins in Canada. Also, land is cheaper in Canada, and the Canadian government has more tax incentives for natural gas exploration.

The following are among the factors that affect the supply of natural gas:

- The higher the average rig count, the greater will be the future production of natural gas. However, you must take the efficiency gains of rig operators into account.

- The greater the number of gas well completions, the greater will be the future production of natural gas. You must also take into account improvements in recovery per well due to better technology.

- The higher gas reserves rise in the lower 48 states, the worse the price picture becomes. Additionally, aggressive additions to gas reserves/storage are problematic.

- The lower the reserve-to-production ratio falls on an industrywide basis, the better.

- In the long-term, more domestic reserves and production will come from less-conventional sources such as tight sands and coal seams.

- The more natural gas imported from Canada, the worse domestic pricing becomes. Similarly, an expanding infrastructure of pipeline capacity capable of receiving natural gas from Canada is problematic.

Natural Gas Pipelines

The profitability of pipeline operators such as Columbia Gas System and Ensearch Corp., is not a function of natural gas prices. In fact, there may even be an inverse relationship between natural gas prices and the profitability of pipeline companies because the Federal Energy Regulatory Commission (FERC), under Order 636, required the pipeline operators to unbundle their transmission services from sales services. Thus, pipeline companies sell their capacity, not the natural gas itself. Therefore, lower prices for natural gas could boost the demand for natural gas, in turn boosting the demand for natural gas pipeline operators' capacity.

Before investing in a pipeline company, though, you should consider the exposure that such company has to capacity relinquishment, which allows customers to turn back a portion of their capacity to pipelines to reduce their costs. However, the negative effects of capacity relinquishment are often slightly ameliorated by the pipelines' being allowed to charge exit fees.

OIL AND NATURAL GAS SERVICING COMPANIES

Oil and natural gas companies are aided by the oilfield servicing industry. Oilfield servicing companies perform a multitude of services for their clients. Some of

T I P

The natural gas pipeline operators, such as El Paso Natural Gas Company, that are located in the Southwest and are capable of piping gas into the northern part of Mexico may represent a promising investment opportunity. This is because it is the northern part of Mexico that is industrializing and will need sources of energy. While Mexico does have a domestic supply of oil and natural gas, these reserves are located in the southern part of that country and Mexico does not currently possess the infrastructure necessary to pipe these energy sources northward. Thus, gas must be piped in from the United States.

these services include pressure pumping (e.g., BJ Services Company), reservoir analysis (e.g., Halliburton Company), high-pressure drilling (e.g., Parker Drilling), and the provision of equipment for all phases of exploration and development (e.g., Baker Hughes).

The oilfield servicing companies benefit from rising oil and natural gas prices because the exploration companies are more active when prices are rising. Another benefit to the entire oilfied servicing industry occurs when the major integrated companies outsource more of their exploration and development work.

Offshore Contract Drilling

The offshore contract drilling business generally requires investing in long-term assets (e.g., rigs) and marketing them for short-term assignments. Thus, offshore contract drilling is a risky business. However, when analyzed properly, investing in stocks in this industry can be highly rewarding. For instance, shares of Global Marine soared over 100 percent, from 5\frac{3}{8}$ in May 1995 to over $12 by April 1996.

You should consider the following when determining which offshore contract drilling operator to invest in:

- The operator should have a versatile fleet of rigs: designed to drill both exploration and development wells, as opposed to being designed primarily to drill just exploration wells; designed to drill in a number of areas, as opposed to being designed to drill in just one area; and suitable for both oil and natural gas.

- The average age of the operator's rigs should be below the industry average. Relatively new rigs usually have less mechanical downtime than older rigs, which is an important advantage because an operator's contract may be terminated by the customer if drilling operations are suspended for a long time due to a breakdown of equipment.

- The operator should achieve high utilization rates. (The average rig utilization rate for a period is equal to the ratio of days in the period during which the rigs were under contract to the total days in the period during which the rigs were available to work. Note that this does not include the time when the rigs were down.) When rig utilization is low, operating profit margins are negatively affected due to the fact that a significant portion of operating costs (such as maintenance and depreciation) are fixed.

  Also, in determining how effectively an operator utilizes its rigs, you should consider the number of feet drilled per year and the number of wells drilled per year. Of course, the more, the better.

- The operator should be able to increase its day rates (the rates for leasing a rig for one day). However, it is best when day rates are not high enough to support the construction of new rigs.

- When day rates are moderating, the operator's rigs should be under long-term contracts.
- The operator should have a low and decreasing incidence of lost-time accidents.
- The operator's customers should pay for the operator's mobilization expenses.
- The operator should be able to obtain insurance on reasonable terms.
- The operator should not take unnecessary foreign risks.

COAL MINING

Coal mining companies such as Ashland Coal and MAPCO earn their profits by efficiently delivering coal to their customers. Since the largest end market for coal is the electric utility industry, you should understand the relationship between coal companies and the utilities.

Serving Electric Utilities

The electric utility industry is the coal industry's largest customer and consumes roughly 86 percent of coal used in the United States. The utility industry favors relying on coal since coal is cheap and highly reliable. Also, prices and supplies of coal (unlike oil and natural gas whose prices fluctuate wildly) are guaranteed under long-term contracts. These price guarantees are important because utilities earn a stipulated return on their investments that is approved by a public utilities commission. Thus, utilities need to have stable, long-term energy policies.

Another advantage of coal over oil and natural gas is that coal is very inexpensive to store. Moreover, there is no concern with coal's combustibility.

Even though coal is environmentally damaging, utilities largely prefer to rely on coal-fired electricity generation. Utilities find it more economical to install scrubbers (to reduce harmful emissions) as opposed to redesigning their power plants to run on oil or natural gas. Also, utilities are allowed to capitalize the cost of installing scrubbers. Since utilities' earnings are still largely set by a return on their capital, the higher their capital investment, the higher the utilities' potential earnings.

T I P

It is preferable that the utility industry does not buy too high of a percentage of its coal pursuant to long-term contracts. If utilities buy more of their coal at spot prices, spot prices will rise. Then these spot prices will be the basis for negotiation for future long-term contracts.

Consequences of Utility Deregulation

Due to their being able to use their monopoly status to pass their higher coal costs onto their customers, utilities have traditionally been insensitive toward the price of coal.

However, as deregulation comes about, the utilities will no longer be able to pass higher costs onto customers because there will be more competition. Thus, new supply contracts will be negotiated at lower prices. As a result, mines with low production costs should be able to capture more market share in the future.

International Developments

Greater international demand for coal and reduced supplies of coal produced in foreign countries are positive for U.S. coal mining concerns. Thus, increased economic activity and the reduction of European governments' subsidies to their coal mines benefit American mining companies. These conditions increase opportunities for U.S. companies to sell their coal abroad while reducing the threat of imports into the United States.

T I P

Deregulation of the electric utility industry could increase the demand for coal since electricity prices will fall.

The coal industry also could benefit from the electrification of developing countries. There is huge potential in doing this as there are 3,000 megawatts (MW) of installed electrical capacity per person in the United States, whereas, in China, electrical output per person wouldn't even light one 100-watt bulb for a year. At least 10 percent of the Chinese people have no electricity at all, and India and Pakistan have even less electricity than China.

However, it should not be assumed that these countries will significantly increase their imports of U.S. coal. One reason is that many of the coal mines in developing countries are owned by governments that are not concerned with profitability. Thus, these countries will continue to rely on domestic supply even though their mines are unproductive.

Also, countries such as China are huge producers of coal. In fact, China is sitting on coal reserves equivalent to more than three times Saudi Arabia's vast oil reserves. Interestingly, China favors keeping its miners busy mining coal since striking by Russian coal miners was one of the first developments that led to the unraveling of the Soviet Union. In fact, most of China's prosperity is in its coastal areas while their coal is inland. Therefore, Beijing must keep its mines open in order to try to stop the income gap between its rural and urban citizens from widening.

Coal Mining Techniques

Coal mining can be broken down into two categories: surface mining and underground mining. Surface mining involves the removal of the cover layers of soil and rock (i.e., overburden), extraction of the coal, backfilling the earth and site restoration. Surface mining is the most productive method of extracting coal—as much as 90 percent of a given coal deposit can be removed through this method.

T I P

> Even when it becomes obvious that demand for coal will soon soar, coal prices usually do not rise quickly. This is because supplies of coal can be brought to market quickly since the location and quantity of U.S. coal reserves is generally well known.

Surface mining is also a very efficient way to recover coal in terms of output per miner hour.

Another advantage of surface mining is that there are fewer regulations in force compared with underground mining. Also, coal producers only pay 55 cents for every ton of surface coal produced (versus $1.10 for every ton of underground coal produced) into the Black Lung Disability Trust Fund, which is used to provide benefits to eligible miners.

However, there are limits to the benefits of surface mining:

- Surface mining can only be used where the underlying coal seam is no more than 200 feet deep.
- A mine operator is responsible for postmining reclamation on each of its mines for at least five years after the mine is closed, meaning the earth where coal was mined must be restored to its original condition in terms of topography and vegetation.
- Rain and snowfalls can be obstacles.

On the other hand, underground mining is more labor intensive and far costlier than surface mining for the following reasons:

1. Much more infrastructure is required for underground mining.
2. Underground mines are less efficient to mine because they are significantly smaller than surface mines.

3. There is a greater union presence in the underground portion of the industry.

TIP

☞ In determining the effectiveness of a coal mining company's surface mining, you should calculate the company's overburden ratio. The overburden ratio is bank (in-ground) cubic yards of earth to coal (in tons). (Overburden is the layers of earth and rock covering a coal seam.) Of course, the lower the overburden ratio, the better.

Investment Considerations

You should seek to invest in the coal mining companies that demonstrate the following:

- A large number of recoverable tons of proven coal reserves. Moreover, a high percentage of these reserves should be recoverable using surface mining techniques (as opposed to underground mining).

- A large percent of its coal sold pursuant to long-term contracts that stipulate that the price of coal will be significantly above the spot price of coal.

- Coal with the following properties:

    1. A high Btu content. British thermal units (Btus) are a measure of a fossil fuel's energy content. Specifically, one Btu is required to elevate one pound of water one degree Fahrenheit.

    2. A low sulfur content. The second phase of the Clean Air Act (CAA) will go into effect in the year 2000 and will require utilities to stay within 1.21 pounds of sulfur dioxide emitted per million Btus combusted. Thus, those coal mines that produce low-sulfur coal will benefit from the CAA since utilities will be willing to pay more for low-sulfur coal than high sulfur coal. However, low-sulfur coal may be valued less if utilities are installing scrubbers and trading more sulfur-emission allowances. (Each pollution allowance gives the holder the right to emit one ton of sulfur dioxide.)

    3. A low ash content.

    4. High consistency in terms of grades of coal.

    5. The coal's having little surrounding rock and clay; it should be clean.

- Only a small percent of the operator's coal mined by unionized workers.

To the extent that unions exist, the company should have long-term contracts with its unions.

■ Cordial relations with its workers. For instance, there should not be a long history of strikes. Also, shift changes should occur at the mine faces so as to allow equipment to run continuously. Interestingly, it is preferable for miners to work 10 hours four days a week rather than 8 hours five days a week; this reduces the time that workers spend traveling to and from the mine face each week.

■ High productivity (the number of tons per man-days) compared with the regional average.

■ Accident rates below the industry average.

■ No overbearing legacy (retiree) costs.

■ A large percent of production coming from mines that are directly connected by conveyor to loadout facilities.

ELECTRIC UTILITIES

Publicly traded electric utilities, such as Consolidated Edison and Montana Power, are vertically integrated producers of electricity. Thus, these utilities generate, transport, package, and market electricity. Until the mid-1990s, utility stocks proved to be safe investments because the utilities enjoyed the benefits of being monopolies and, were a steady, predictable business since electricity is an essential commodity.

However, this model of stability and safety is being shattered. The following are among the challenges that the electric utilities face:

■ Slow growth. U.S. utilities are confronted with a less-than-1-percent annual growth rate in electrical utility usage in this country, which is unlikely to improve in the future. For instance, even though the number of electric appliances that consumers have in the home has been rising, there is new federal legislation that sets efficiency targets for new appliances.

■ Rising expenses. It will become more expensive for utilities to comply with environmental regulations. For example, the CAA sets restrictions on emissions of sulfur dioxide and nitrogen dioxide gases. Also, the Supreme Court ruled that states can apply tougher standards on activities (such as the generation of electricity) that result in harmful discharges into navigable waters.

■ The transformation (by regulators) of many utilities into tax collectors. For instance, *"about half of every dollar billed to Niagra Mohawk customers goes either directly or indirectly to the government or to meet government mandates. About 18 cents of every dollar on a Niagra Mohawk*

*customer's statement goes straight into federal, state and local tax cof-
fers."* [1] These policies, of course, result in the utilities becoming less
competitive relative to the independent power producers ("IPPs") and
other competitors discussed below.

Similarly, in many states, utilities and their customers are required to
bear millions of dollars of costs for social programs such Consolidated
Edison's "Say Yes To Family Math and Science." These utilities are also
required to provide low-income assistance, offer universal service, and comply with environmental regulations that often exceed federal regulations.

- The requirement by federal law that utilities buy any power IPPs want to
  sell, whether or not the utility wants or needs it. These IPPs were sanctioned under the Public Utilities Regulatory Policy Act (PURPA) of 1978
  in order to reduce dependence on imported oil and encourage the use of
  renewable energy sources such as solar energy and waste-to-management
  energy. The problem for utilities is that electricity produced by these IPPs
  is extremely expensive because the alternative sources are not efficient
  electricity generators. Also, during the energy crisis in the 1970s, several
  states based these long-term contract rates (which utilities are required to
  pay the IPPs) on high estimates of future oil and gas prices.

- Many of the utilities' industrial customers' building their own power
  plants. Utilities that lose large customers soon become burdened with
  excess capacity. Also, the mere threat of a large customer supplying its
  own power is enough to cause the utility to offer the customer lower rates.

TIP

The lower the percentage of electricity that a utility sells that is initially produced by an IPP, the better.

- The growing popularity of municipalization—when cities and localities
  create their own power companies. These municipal power companies
  buy power independently on the wholesale market while using the local
  utility's lines for delivery to customers. This "golden-rule policy" (which
  requires that transmission-line owners provide comparable service to buyers and sellers of power as it does to itself) saves the utilities' competitors
  tremendous amounts of money in the development of transmission lines.

---

[1] Toni Mack, "Don't Shoot the Power Company," *Forbes* 157, no. 8 (April 22, 1996), p. 158.

Moreover, municipal utilities can offer very low rates to the utilities' customers since their costs are lower than for-profit utilities. For instance, municipal power plants are neither burdened with collecting or paying taxes nor paying dividends.

TIP

☞ Utilities that have experience operating in other deregulated industries may be better prepared to cope with deregulation in the electric utility industry. For instance, NIPSCO Industries has experience in the deregulated natural-gas distribution industry, while Citizens Utilities is gaining experience in the deregulated telecommunications industry.

- Utilities' increasingly competing with one another. First, some background: The push for deregulation of the electric utility industry has come from businesses wanting lower electricity costs as well as from regulators desiring to spark more competition in the industry. Other proponents of deregulation point out that the excess capacity in the industry represents a waste of resources. For instance, the most common type of energy producer, the steam-powered electric plant, usually sits idle for 13 hours a day. Also, utilities must install billions of dollars' worth of generating capacity to meet a peak demand that only occurs once or twice a year.

  In 1992, FERC opened up the wholesale power market to competition. The wholesale market is made up of electric utilities and others who do not buy power for their own use, but sell it to end-use customers, such as homes, commercial buildings, and factories. However, many proponents of deregulation want deregulation to go further. These proponents are in favor of retail wheeling, requiring utilities to transmit their competitors' power directly to individuals and businesses. Third-party wheeling fees are paid when an outside producer transmits its power to the ultimate customer through the local utility's network of power lines.

  With retail wheeling, you may eventually be able to buy electricity from a generating facility located many hundreds of miles away from your home. In fact, the California Public Utilities Commission ruled in December 1995, that all California customers will be able to select their electricity supplier by 2003.

Opposition to Retail Competition

The road to freer competition will not be without its opponents. First, environmentalists oppose deregulation of the utility industry because it will bring about lower electricity prices and thus encourage energy consumption. Environmentalists also fear that deregulation would result in utilities' depleting nonrenewable resources.

Second, it will be difficult for state regulators to orchestrate deregulation. For instance, some plans that states have regarding deregulation hinge on changes in the laws of other states, federal policy, or even the policies of foreign countries. In fact, California's deregulatory plans are contingent on law changes in 13 western states, two Canadian provinces, and part of Baja California since California's electricity network is linked to these territories. Additionally, state regulators may be adverse to allowing consumers to choose their suppliers because these regulators would have to relinquish control over local rates.

Third, utility employees are averse to deregulation since their jobs could be jeopardized by mergers and acquisitions.

TRAP

⊘ You should avoid those utilities whose stranded costs represent a large percentage of their shareholders' equity.

Concerns with Deregulation

One major concern regarding deregulation is the issue of stranded power plant investments—unamortized costs of prior investments that are scheduled for recovery through regulated monopoly rates but that would not be recovered under competition. For instance, losing customers due to competition may render utility plants uneconomical to operate. Since these plants were built with regulatory sanction, the utilities believe that they are entitled to receive compensation for their stranded investments.

Second, competition impedes the industrywide cooperation needed during times of electric shortages. For example, if one region of the country faces the threat of a brownout, the local utilities would seek to wheel electricity into their regions. However, outlying utilities may decline such requests in hopes of embarrassing their competitors with a brownout.

Third, competition is not suited for the utility industry because the transmission lines are interconnected. Moreover, since electricity travels in the line of least resistance, no one utility can control the direction of electricity independently.

TIP

☞ Utilities that have low costs per kilowatt-hour are better positioned to compete in a deregulatory environment than those that have higher costs per kilowatt-hour.

Thus, in order for one utility to wheel power to another region, many other utilities would have to cooperate. For instance, if a utility in Philadelphia wanted to wheel electricity into Detroit, all of the utilities in between these cities would have to shut off their grids to incoming electricity. Failure to do this would cause electricity to be siphoned off along the way.

Reaction to Competition

In view of the increasingly competitive environment, utility companies have been trying to reduce their costs. For instance, utilities such as Northern States Power and Wisconsin Energy have been merging in order to reduce their payrolls and excess capacity and to achieve economies of scale. Also, utilities have been installing computer chips in their meters, which eliminates meter readers and makes billing instantaneous.

Some utilities are diversifying by building power plants in foreign countries. This may be a sound strategy because electricity is vital for the advancement of developing countries. Before a steel mill can be put into operation, there must be sufficient electricity to run the steel mill.

While there is huge potential for power plants in developing countries, there are also many obstacles to building these plants, including the following:

- Politics and bureaucracy. There is a great deal of anti-Americanism in developing countries. Thus, opposition to American investments is often a rallying cry for foreign politicians.

- Often as a condition for obtaining the necessary permits, U.S. utilities must engage in building the country's infrastructure (e.g., roads, ports, and housing).

TIP

☞ It is preferable for a U.S. utility to apply for the necessary permits in countries that have "single-window clearance," which means that an investor only has to deal with one office.

- International lending agencies may not be willing to finance power projects if electricity is given away or easily stolen.

- International lending agencies may not like a foreign federal government's guaranteeing its states' obligations to buy a given amount of electricity at a predetermined price.

- There are often discrepancies over the allowed rate of return because some governments are averse to foreigners' repatriating profits.

- U.S. utilities have many foreign competitors that already have extensive experience in serving emerging markets.

- Developing countries have severe capital shortages, which limits the number of power plants they can afford to commission.

- Many developing countries are inherently economically and politically unstable which makes it difficult to justify large commitments.

T R A P

⊘ Individual investors constitute a large category of shareholders of utility stocks. This is currently problematic for the industry because individual investors have traditionally been attracted to utility stocks for their safety and high dividend yields. Since the utility industry is becoming more competitive, utility stocks will be less safe, and since dividend payouts may be reduced further, fewer individual investors may commit to these stocks.

Investment Considerations

When you would like to include electric utility stocks in your portfolio, you should search for those utilities that

- Are low-cost producers and are located in close proximity to high-cost producers. When retail wheeling comes about, these utilities will be able to take market share away from their neighbors.

- Operate in regions with a growing customer count.

- Have a high percentage of power consumed by residential users in terms of total electricity consumed. This is because residential users are less price sensitive than industrial and commercial users.

- Have a low emission rate of sulfur dioxide, thus reducing the utility's spending on environmental compliance.

- Have a low average delivered cost of coal per ton and per Btu.

- Have regulators that rule on applications for rate hikes quickly.

- Have regulators that base applications for rate hikes on a projected test
  year (which is forward looking because it considers inflation and the
  higher costs associated with growth). This is better than having applications based on historical data.

TIP

☞ Higher interest rates are usually problematic for utilities since utilities carry heavy debt loads.

- Have regulators that allow the utility to earn performance incentives
  based on criteria such as customer service, fuel, and purchased-power
  cost savings and energy-efficiency programs.
- Have their electric distribution systems underground. Thus, they are less
  vulnerable than above-ground systems to severe weather.

ENVIRONMENTAL SERVICES

Many investors have misperceptions regarding the environmental services industry. The first misperception is that this is a highly secular (rather than cyclical)
industry. Based on this belief, many investors thought that the environmental companies would perform exceptionally well once the Clinton/Gore administration
took office. However, the environmental stocks did not benefit from the first few
years of the Clinton Administration. Since the economy was very weak in the early
1990s, enforcement of environmental regulations was relatively lax. In fact, envi-

TIP

☞ A change in presidential administrations usually results in a lag in
environmental enforcement.

ronmentalists joked that the White House Effect is not doing anything about the
Greenhouse Effect.

Another development that has arisen in the mid-1990s that has reduced environmental enforcement is opposition to federal environmental mandates imposed
on cities and states without federal funding. In fact, some mayors have refused to
implement federal environmental mandates. For instance, in 1994, John Bennett,
the mayor of Aspen, CO, threatened to stand in front of government bulldozers

rather than pay $12 million to clean up lead deposits from a 100-year-old silver mine, and the mayor of Philadelphia declared that the government would have to incarcerate him before he would spend $500 million for a waste-water treatment plant to protect fish in the Delaware River. Accordingly, Congress has tried to pass a "no money, no mandate" bill that would prohibit new environmental laws without federal funding.

The second misperception is that all of the segments of the environmental services industry move in a lockstep fashion. However, environmental services is, in many ways, an "either/or" industry. For example, if you have waste, you can basically do one of three things. You can burn it in an incinerator, bury it in a landfill, or recycle it. Giving business to any one of these three sectors will result in less business directed towards the other sectors.

T I P

> ☞ It is problematic when environmental laws are not allowed unless they meet cost–benefit tests.

Nonhazardous Waste Landfills

The operators of nonhazardous waste landfills such as USA Waste Services and Sanifill are an interesting investment niche. First, in a May 16, 1994, ruling on C&A Carbone v. Town of Clarkstown, the U.S. Supreme Court struck down "flow control" laws. Flow control laws gave local authorities monopoly rights to set dumping fees and to process virtually all the waste generated in their service areas. (Municipalities favored flow control laws as a method for recovering the huge sums of money that they invested in trash incinerators, recycling plants, and other costly facilities. Most of these facilities were built on the assumption that there would be insufficient disposal capacity.) Regardless, the result of less flow control is that independent landfills can attract more waste.

There are other developments occurring that will benefit the nonhazardous waste operators. For instance, these companies must now comply with Subsection D of the Resource Conservation and Recovery Act and are thus required to construct liners, leachate collection systems, and groundwater monitoring systems and to control methane release. Since compliance with these regulations costs around $500,000 per acre, smaller operators are being forced to sell their businesses to stronger operators.

In addition to acquisitions of privately held landfill operators, there are also opportunities for well-financed companies to buy municipal operations. For instance, about 25 percent of the $30 billion nonhazardous waste business is handled by municipalities. Since many of these municipalities face budget deficits, they are willing to sell their waste collection and disposal operations. The result of this consolidation is that landfill operators are able to increase their tipping (i.e., disposal) fees.

Hazardous Waste

In general, the hazardous waste landfill business is in a secular state of decline. This is because the companies that produce toxic waste as a by-product of their regular production processes are engineering new methods of production that minimize these toxic by-products. Companies are trying to avoid producing hazardous waste because the cost to dispose of it is high, the liability is ongoing, and the public relations is terrible.

However, the outlook for hazardous waste remediation companies such as International Technology Corp. and Groundwater Technologies is brighter. First, there is a good chance that the EPA will adopt a use-based standard for cleaning up Superfund sites. Such use-based tests are likely to reduce litigation, which should result in more remediation.

TIP

Water purification companies, such as Ionics and U.S. Filter Corporation, should benefit from the rising demand for ultrapure water by the semiconductor, food processing, utility, and pharmaceutical industries.

Also, the federal government is expected to dole out tens of billions of dollars in contracts to clean up military bases and nuclear weapons sites over the next two decades. Interestingly, the military sites are in need of a great deal of remediation since they were long immune to federal regulation and will have to meet the most stringent standards before being converted to civilian uses.

However, not all of this remediation will benefit environmental service companies. This is because unions, military personnel, and Department of Energy employees will all vie to complete much of the remediation work.

13

CHAPTER

Other Industries

GOLD MINING

Gold stocks are generally utilized as a proxy for gold itself. Many investors favor buying gold stocks due to their simplicity and liquidity. On the contrary, holding gold bars and gold coins represents transportation and storage risks and expenses. Thus, one of the most important considerations in determining the direction of gold stocks is to determine the future direction of gold itself. In doing so, you must analyze the supply and demand factors for gold.

In estimating the future levels of supply of gold you must consider four main factors. These factors include in-ground gold, gold held by central bankers, gold held by industry, and gold held by investors. Similarly, the major categories of demand for gold include demand by central bankers, demand by industry, and demand by investors.

You should also consider the degree of economic development of the countries that mine gold. If large a percentage of gold is mined from countries that are underdeveloped, these countries could be largely dependent on gold as a source of revenue. Thus, when the price of gold falls, the underdeveloped countries may produce more gold since they will need to maintain their trade receipts. (These considerations are applicable to all commodities.)

Since gold is an international commodity, you must analyze the output of newly mined gold on a worldwide basis. (Remember, though, that the more difficult it becomes to mine for gold, the better the pricing outlook becomes. Conversely, the less expensive it is to produce gold, the more likely it is that gold prices will fall.)

South Africa

A good starting point for this analysis is South Africa since this country accounts for more gold mining than any other. One of the main factors that could result in declining levels of output in South Africa is the very heavy expense of mining for gold there. The expense comes from their mines' being very deep, their ore grades' declining, and their gold mining companies', such as Kloof Gold Mining Company and Driefontein Consolidated, paying very high dividends, which are a drain on capital. A second reason why there may be lower levels of gold output in South Africa is that the government there may not want to substitute efficient technology for labor-intense gold mining methods for reasons of social policy. For instance, Pretoria may favor retaining its miners since each South African miner feeds between 10 and 12 people.

On the other hand, the return of South Africa into the international fold, as a result of the elimination of apartheid, may encourage Western mining companies to invest in South African mines. These miners will attempt to earn a return on their risky investments by relying on the most current technology to maximize their output of gold. However, such investments may not increase the supply of gold on a worldwide basis if such investments come at the expense of fewer mining projects in other parts of the world.

The United States

The United States has traditionally been the second-most prolific producer of gold. One of the main factors that could reduce the output of gold in the United States is heightened sensitivity to the damage that gold mining has been alleged to have on the environment. For instance, more than half of the nation's Superfund sites are due to gold mining.

As a consequence of such problems, it is very difficult to open new gold mines in the United States. Before a new mine is opened the mine owner must obtain a host of permits from a multitude of federal, state, and local agencies. Battle Mountain Gold's Crown Jewel mine in Washington, for example, had to receive 56 permits from 32 agencies before mining could begin. Moreover, these permits are very difficult and expensive to obtain. In many instances, environmental-impact studies are a precondition for being granted a permit. These studies, in turn, can consume 1,000 pages, occupy 250 people, and cost $5 million. Finally, even when miners are allowed to begin production at a new mine, it takes at least two years to develop a mine after the feasibility studies have been conducted.

An additional factor that could inhibit gold production in the United States is a proposed federal tax that would be levied on the gross gold production mined from federal lands. Proponents of this tax claim that it is not equitable that miners do not have to pay royalties on gold mined on federal land since oil companies and cattle ranchers have to pay royalties for using federal land. These taxes would raise the costs of mining and therefore would likely result in less output.

TRAP

🚫 It is important that you realize that a tax on gross production is worse than a tax levied on profits. This is because, under a regimen of taxes based on gross production, a gold mining company that loses money would still have to pay taxes based on the amount of gold coming out of its mines. However, this same mine would not be liable for taxes if taxes were based on profits since this mine would have no profits on which taxes could be imposed.

You should also consider the percentage of a company's production that derives from federal land. For instance, a company that mines all of its gold on federal land would have to pay taxes on all of its production. On the other hand, a company that did not mine any gold on federal land would not be liable for such taxes. Thus, if such tax were imposed and gold stocks plummeted, stocks of the companies that did not mine on federal land could become compelling investments.

Additionally, the investor should consider current production versus prospective production. If future production is expected to be lower than current production, the corresponding gold mining stock might become attractive because the company will be hurt less in the future than currently.

As you can now see, it is extraordinarily difficult to open new mines in the United States. In fact, Mr. K. R. Werneburg, president of Battle Mountain Gold once said, "There are only two places a U.S. mining company can go. One is abroad to mine for gold and the other is to bankruptcy court."

Thus, it is not surprising that many American gold mining companies are exploring for gold reserves in places such as Indonesia and South America. While it can take several years to obtain all of the approvals necessary to open a gold mine in the United States, such approvals can sometimes be obtained in as little as one day in South America.

It is important to note that gold mining is an extremely capital-intensive business. As discussed above, huge investments are made in obtaining the necessary permits. Additionally, even in the United States, gold mining companies

TRAP

∅ While a gold mining concern can reduce its *near-term* costs by exploring for gold in South America, the *long-term* costs associated with running that mine could well be higher than would be the case if that mine were located in the United States. This is because once the company sinks its capital in the ground, it becomes defenseless against the extortive demands of the host country. For instance, some American-owned mines have been required to build roads, schools, and hospitals under the threat of nationalization. Also, costs of operating such mines rise when they have to be protected by mercenaries. Finally, the economic benefits of foreign mines are lost when foreign governments impose gold-export restrictions.

sometimes find that is necessary to build infrastructure around their mines in order to deliver gold to its markets and to attract miners. For instance, mining companies in the United States have built roads and living quarters as well as installed electricity and water systems near their mines.

As a result of these very high fixed costs, gold mines almost always operate at 100-percent capacity. Thus, higher gold prices can lead to slightly lower production in developed countries. This is because mining companies often take advantage of higher gold prices to move into lower-grade areas, where it is less efficient to mine gold.

On the other hand, better use of state-of-the-art mining methods can lead to greater output of gold in the United States and abroad. One efficient method of gold mining is called heap leaching, which occurs when low-grade ore is crushed and placed (or heaped) on large pads, then sprinkled with a diluted cyanide acid solution that separates (leaches) the gold from the rock.

It is important to know how much sulfur is contained in the gold-bearing rock since sulfur turns into sulfuric acid when exposed to air and water. This acidic drainage, in turn, kills aquatic life. It is thus preferable, of course, to invest in a gold mining company that heap leaches gold from rocks containing very low levels of sulfur.

Another method of gold mining is called bioleaching, which occurs when bacteria is used to break down sulfide ores, in effect oxidizing them over a shorter period of time than nature would. Bioleaching is not expensive or damaging to the environment since the bacteria are naturally forming bacteria.

Elsewhere, gold mining companies have been using remote sensing devices in the form of satellite imagery as well as the application of geophysics to find gold deposits hidden in jungles or other unexplored areas.

T I P

> It is important to consider the vulnerability that a mining company has to unions. Since underground mines depend on the productivity of individual miners, they are more susceptible to union demands. On the other hand, since open pit mines use large earth-moving equipment to achieve economies of scale, they are less susceptible to union pressures.

The Former Soviet Union

The third-largest producer of gold is the former Soviet Union. Factors that could result in less production coming out of these formerly Soviet republics include a lack of spare parts, outdated technology, poor infrastructure, and the decreasing use of (inexpensive) prison labor. Also, better technology in the Western world allows western mining companies more selectivity in choosing mine sites. Thus, advances in technology make it unnecessary for these miners to tolerate arbitrary tax policies, demands for bribery, and the absence of the rule of law in the former Soviet Union. Accordingly, of the more than 8,000 mining licenses awarded in Russia between 1992 and 1994, only 2 percent included foreign companies. Additionally, the shift to capitalism can hurt output because more profit-minded governments may not produce gold where it is not profitable.

Supply and Demand at Central Banks

It is important to monitor the gold transactions of central bankers since these bankers can move the price of gold based on their buying and selling. Central banks typically hold gold as an ultimate reserve asset, as an alternative to holding currency and as a form of collateral. Central bankers also hold gold because it is a risk-free credit. For instance, a country such as Taiwan may have a trade surplus with the United States. Thus, the central bank of Taiwan would have a large part of its reserves in U.S. dollars. However, the central bank of Taiwan would risk having a foreign country's (the United States') depreciating a large part of its reserves (those held in U.S. dollars). Thus, central bankers often like to hold gold since no one country can depreciate that part of its reserves that are held in gold.

Also, developing countries often like to hold gold since they can leverage it when applying for loans from organizations such as the International Monetary Fund (IMF). For instance, the IMF often lends four times the value of gold that a borrowing country has in the form of gold reserves.

Despite these reasons for holding gold, central bankers sometimes view holding gold with disdain since gold is a non–interest-bearing asset that takes up precious vault space. At other times the pendulum swings the other way and central bankers may use the following methods to profit from their gold reserves:

- Selling call options on its gold holdings. By doing this, the central bank receives money by granting investors the right to purchase its gold.

- Engaging in leasing gold. Gold leasing begins when a mining company (indirectly) borrows gold from a central bank. Then the company sells its borrowed gold on the open market. These proceeds are then invested in mine production. The company repays its debt to the central bank by returning recently produced gold to the bank. The central bank benefits from gold leasing by charging an interest rate (which is paid in dollars) on its leased gold.

You should consider the direction of these lease rates. Higher lease rates might presage higher gold prices. When producers find that forward sales are becoming too costly, they will lease less gold and therefore will not quickly sell the gold leased to them in the open market. Additionally, when lease rates are high, some investors buy gold with the aim of lending it out at the new, higher rates.

Higher interest rates could indicate that central banks are reluctant to lend out more of their reserves. (Banks could even recall some of their gold loans.) Lease rates could move higher if gold producers are selling forward a very high percentage of their future production.

Also, it is important to realize that gold mining companies will not wish to lease gold when they believe that gold prices are going to rise. For example, it would not make sense for a mining company to borrow 100 ounces of gold when gold sells for $400 an ounce if that company's management believed that the price of gold was going to rise. The proceeds received by quickly selling this gold in the spot market would be $40,000. However, if gold prices rose to $600 an ounce, the

T I P

One factor that can lead to more gold production in other gold-producing countries is the devaluation of host countries' currencies. One reason is that the gold-producing country probably devalued its currency in order to stimulate exports (including gold). Also, as a nation's currency falls in value, international gold mining companies have an incentive to mine for gold in that country because the costs of production are lower. Finally, devaluations of currency due to reductions in that nation's interest rates are often believed to be inflationary. Fears of inflation are bullish for gold since people will want to accumulate gold, an asset that is considered a store of value.

TIP

When a country's currency reserves are growing quickly while its gold reserves are modest, that country's central bank may begin to boost its gold-buying program in order to increase the percentage of reserves held in gold.

company would end up returning gold with a $60,000 value. Thus, the gold mining company would be leaving $20,000 ($60,000 − $40,000) on the table.

Separately, gold mining companies can commit to selling their anticipated production at a specified price at a certain date in the future by entering into forward contracts. A rising level of forward selling is bullish over the long term because forward selling takes future supplies of gold off of the market. Thus, when gold that had been sold forward finally is produced, it will not add to supply on the spot market.

You should consider factors that could lead to central banks' selling their gold. The main factors revolve around needs to extricate themselves of severe financial hardship. For instance, the Iraqis sold 200 million tons of gold in 1992 as a result of the costs of the Gulf War. Similarly, Russia sold 200 million tons of gold in 1992 due to its troubled economy. (Interestingly, in the beginning of 1996, it was rumored that the United States would have to sell some of its gold reserves in order to fund government operations.) However, you should analyze the impact that such large sales have on the price of gold. When central banks are dumping huge quantities of gold onto the market and the price of gold does not fall appreciably, it is extremely bullish because this would indicate that demand is strong enough to absorb aggressive selling of gold.

Demand and Supply by Industry

You should determine whether there is an excessive or an insufficient supply of gold held by industry. Since jewelry fabrication accounts for the majority of gold used by industry, this is usually a sound place to begin your analysis—examining the inventory levels of gold held by jewelry fabricators. If these levels are high (by historical measures) and are beginning to decline, then this is a bearish situation. On the contrary, if inventories of gold held by jewelers are at low levels but are beginning to rise, it would be bullish for the future price of gold.

Another method of determining inventory levels of gold held by jewelers is to monitor the price of refined gold. Typically, gold smelted by Swiss refiners trades at a $1 premium above the spot market price. Thus, when the premium slips (e.g., to 75 cents above the spot price) it may indicate that inventories are already too high. On the other hand, when this premium rises (e.g., to $1.25 above the spot price) it may indicate that jewelry refiners are aggressively accumulating gold.

There are two other points to be made in connection with gold used for jewelry purposes. First, the higher the caratage of the jewelry purchased the better. Thus, it is preferable that more jewelry is purchased in Hong Kong where the average piece of jewelry has 24 carats (or is 100-percent pure gold) than in the United States where the average piece of jewelry has only a 14-carat rating. Second, jewelry is very price elastic. Thus, jewelers are likely to decrease their gold purchases when the price of gold is rising.

Other industrial sources of demand for gold include the dental industry, the electronics industry, heavy manufacturing such as jet engines, and the tableware industry, as gold is sometimes used as trimming on dishes and glasses. Thus, you should consider changes in demand among these industries. For example, if electronics manufacturers are becoming increasingly efficient in their production, they may use less gold in each unit that they produce. However, if the number of units that the electronics companies produce is rising, then the reduction of gold content in each unit could be compensated for.

Finally, in connection with the supply of gold provided by industry, you should consider the extent of gold scrappage. Gold scrappage comes from manufacturers of jewelry and other products in which gold is a component as well as from people's disposing of their jewelry. Of course, greater amounts of gold scrappage increase the supply of gold and therefore depress gold prices.

Demand and Supply by Investors

Traditionally, gold prices have risen during times of anticipated inflation or political turmoil because gold was thought to be the ultimate store of value. This line of reasoning was in force in the early 1990s in Asia. For instance, these nations benefited from growing disposable income. However, their citizens had a lack of confidence in their economy, few investment alternatives, and suffered from rampant inflation. Thus, in many parts of the Orient, holding gold jewelry became a form of savings. In fact, some Indian buyers are people seeking to sock away unreported income in gold ornaments, which can be explained away as inheritances or gifts. However, the ability of investors in more developed countries to use futures contracts and other financial tools to minimize their inflationary and political risks has reduced the appeal of gold as a safe haven.

Nevertheless, gold prices benefit when investors accumulate gold as a form of "portfolio insurance." Since gold has historically had a negative beta (meaning that gold prices typically rose when the rest of the stock market was falling) these investors buy gold to ensure that their entire portfolios do not fall too far. These buyers of portfolio insurance believe that their strategy is similar to buying fire insurance but hoping that it will not have to be used. Viewing gold in this manner credits gold with a value that is separate and distinct from the return that it provides.

T I P

☞ Gold prices often react positively when interest rates are lowered. One reason is that such action is often interpreted as being inflationary. Also, as interest rates fall, the opportunity cost of holding gold falls.

One way to get a sense of the prevalence of gold being used as portfolio insurance is to detect the percentage of their clients' portfolios that Swiss bankers put in gold. Of course, the higher this percentage is, the better the outlook is for gold.

Gold is usually traded in U.S. dollars. Thus, when the dollar strengthens, gold becomes increasingly expensive for foreign investors to accumulate. Therefore, when the U.S. dollar appreciates, foreign investors may want to take their profits while foreign jewelers may not be able to afford to buy gold at the higher prices (in local currencies). Thus, in the short term, a rising dollar is bearish for gold.

Finally, to gauge the demand for gold by retail investors, you should consider how quickly the prices of gold coins are rising. Similarly, you should consider the volume of coin sales. Moreover, it is particularly bullish when the markups (the difference between what dealers charge for these coins minus the prices that the dealers will pay for the same coins) on these gold coin sales rise briskly.

Trading Characteristics

The gold mining stocks are more of an asset play than an earnings play. Thus, investors sometimes buy gold stocks when the stock market has already risen a great deal. Investors also like to buy gold stocks when other stocks are trading on very aggressive earnings expectations because gold mining stocks usually do not get taken to the woodshed when they miss their earnings projections by a very minor amount.

Some analysts believe that gold stocks trade as part of a larger group of metals. Accordingly, when other precious metals (e.g., platinum, palladium, silver, and copper) have already taken off, gold may be the next to go.

Additionally, analysts have recommended monitoring the ratio of the Dow Jones Industrial Average to the price of one ounce of gold bullion. For instance, in the beginning of 1996, the Dow Jones Industrials were trading around 5500 while gold was selling for $400 an ounce. Thus, the ratio would be 13.75. According to proponents of this ratio, since this ratio has become too high, gold might be ready to surge. Such a high ratio would be considered to represent a ridiculous bias in favor of financial assets.

On the other hand, this ratio is said to be at its lowest extreme when the markets are favoring hard assets over financial assets. For instance, when gold soared to over $800 an ounce in 1980, the Dow Jones Industrial Average was trading below 1000. Thus, this ratio would have been no more than 1.25. At this point, financial assets may be undervalued and hard assets may be overvalued.

Company-Specific Considerations

When gold prices are low it may be best to invest in the lowest-cost gold producers such as Placer Dome. However, when gold prices are high it may be best to invest in the high-cost producers such as Pegasus Gold. Consider the following example:

	Company ABC		Company XYZ	
	1/96	7/96	1/96	7/96
Cost	300	300	380	380
Price	390	500	390	500
Margins	23%	40%	2.6%	24%
	(i.e.,90/390)	(i.e.,200/500)	(i.e.,10/390)	(i.e.,120/500)
Percentage change in margins		173		920

When gold prices are low ($390 an ounce on January 1996), Company ABC is more profitable (23-percent margins) than Company XYZ (2.5-percent margins) because its costs of production are lower ($300 versus $380). Thus, in January 1996, Company ABC would have been a better investment that Company XYZ. However, when the price of gold rises to $500 an ounce in July of 1996, Company XYZ is a better investment that Company ABC. Even though ABC still has wider profit margins than XYZ (40 percent versus 23 percent), Company XYZ demonstrated a greater earnings improvement than ABC. This is because XYZ's earnings rose 920 percent from January to July, during which time ABC's earnings only rose 173 percent.

Separately, the stock market will value a high-cost producer much more favorably when the price of gold rises. For instance, if a company had an average cost of production of $425 an ounce and the spot price of gold was only $400, the market would value the company's reserves at zero since it would not be worthwhile to bring this gold out of the mine. However, if the spot price of gold advanced to $500 an ounce, it would be worthwhile to mine the reserves. Thus, the reserves, which had previously been valued at zero, would now be valued as netting the company $75 an ounce ($500 minus $425).

You should also consider the valuation of a gold company's production and reserves. To do so use the following formula:

Market capitalization / (Ounces of annual production) (Price of gold)

Assume that Company ABC has 10 million shares outstanding and that these shares are trading at $20. Further assume that ABC produces 500 ounces of gold a year. Separately, assume that Company XYZ has 15 million shares outstanding and that these shares are trading at $30. Further assume that XYZ produces 1,250 ounces of gold a year. Finally, assume that gold is trading at $400 an ounce share. Thus, if the costs of production at both ABC and XYZ are the same, which is the better investment?

The answer is Company XYZ since its gold is valued lower than ABC's gold ($900 an ounce versus $1,000 an ounce). Of course, you would want to effectively buy an ounce of gold at the lowest price possible. (The calculation for ABC is $200,000,000/200,000 = $1,000. The calculation for XYZ is $450,000,000/ $500,000 = $900.)

While XYZ has the lower valuation per ounce of production, by using the following formula you should consider the valuation of the recoverable reserves that each company has:

Market capitalization / (Ounces of recoverable reserves) (Price of gold)

Assume that the market capitalizations for both companies in this example are the same as in the previous example. Further assume that gold trades for $400 an ounce and that ABC has 10,000 ounces of reserves while XYZ has 12,000 ounces of reserves. Thus, which company has the more attractive valuation?

The answer is Company ABC since each of its ounces is valued at $50 while Company XYZ's ounces are valued at $93.75. (The calculation for ABC is $200,000,000/$4,000,000. The calculation for XYZ is $450,000,000/$48,000,000.) Thus, by investing in ABC's shares you can buy gold reserves for a 46.6-percent discount to the cost of buying XYZ's reserves.

$$\frac{\$93.75 - \$50}{\$93.75}$$

Additionally, you should consider how long the gold mining company can continue producing at the same rate before its mines are depleted. In order to make this calculation, simply divide recoverable reserves by annual production. Thus, given the facts above, which company has longer-lasting reserves? The answer is Company ABC since it has 20 years of recoverable reserves (10,000/500) while Company XYZ only has 9.6 years of recoverable reserves (12,000/1,250).

Finally, when you believe that the price of gold is about to surge, you should attempt to invest in the gold mining company that has the least percentage of its future production hedged. This is because the more production that is sold on the forward market, the less of a proxy the stock is for the commodity. For instance, if gold is currently trading at $400 an ounce and you believe that gold will quickly soar to \$600 an ounce, it would not make sense to invest in a company that has already sold most of its future production at \$425 an ounce. Doing so, would result in the company missing out on an additional \$175 an ounce in profit (\$600 – \$425).

DEFENSE CONTRACTORS

The end of the Cold War presents many opportunities for defense contractors. First, the loss of hegemony by the superpowers has resulted in numerous wars, border conflicts, and dangerous peacekeeping missions. Second, lower procurement budgets have resulted in American defense contractors' becoming extremely efficient. Third, defense contractors are responding to reduced procurement budgets by aggressively diversifying.

Increasing Hostility

During the Cold War, the Soviets and the Americans had much more control over their client states since the superpowers were much more active in supporting their client states' governments, both financially and militarily. It was preferable, from the perspective of world peace, when the superpowers had their hegemony. Since a conflict between satellite states had the potential to escalate into a dispute between the superpowers and since the superpowers could exercise their nuclear options, few regional conflicts arose during the Cold War. However, the end of the Cold War (and the partial dismantlement of the superpowers' nuclear arsenals) has eroded the hegemony (and the nuclear threat) the two superpowers had previously imposed on their client states.

Reasons for the United States and the Soviets' losing their hegemony include reduced tensions between these two nations as a result of the disintegration of the Soviet Union and attempts by those former republics to move toward democracy. Another reason that Soviet and American hegemony has broken down is that neither the former USSR nor the United States can afford to subsidize their friendly allies. Moreover, increased nationalism has made the various client states less willing to abide by their superpowers' dictates.

Indeed, since the end of the Cold War hostility has increased—the United States, for example, has been involved in wars in Panama, the Persian Gulf, and Somalia. Additionally, the United States has participated in peacekeeping missions in Haiti and Bosnia as well as humanitarian endeavors in Rwanda.

Elsewhere since the conclusion of the Cold War, many small countries have attempted to settle their disputes violently as Ecuador and Peru did in mid-1995; Pakistan and India have border skirmishes from time to time; and the truce between Greece and Turkey is occasionally tested.

Also, irredentist disputes could turn violent. For instance, South Korea is contesting an island that currently belongs to Japan. Separately, several Southeast

Asian nations and China claim the Sprately Islands. It is likely that the incidence of these regional conflicts will rise since the loss of superpower hegemony reduces the chances of such disputes' escalating into global (nuclear) incidents.

Another reason that there is more hostility is that the reduced cost of weapons systems makes weapons easier to obtain and therefore more pervasive. Even undeveloped countries such as Somalia and Rwanda can afford military equipment to cause enough casualties to result in U.S. military involvement.

A further reason that there is likely to be more military activity is that politicians will again use military actions to unite their people when their country's economy is weak or when they are personally losing popularity. (The theory goes that taking military action against another country will provoke retaliation. This retaliation then provides the leaders of the country that initiated the aggression with the cover needed to argue that the retaliating country is a threat. For instance, some analysts have opined that one of the reasons that Cuba's Fidel Castro allowed the downing of two unarmed Cessnas in late February 1996 was to unify Cubans against an anticipated United States response.)

Growing nationalism is yet another source of geopolitical instability. For instance, the Chechnyans and Azerbaijanis (in the former Soviet Union) are fighting for more autonomy. Also, the Basques in Spain and the Indians in the Mexican state of Chiapas have waged war for greater self-governance. This quest (by nationalities living within the borders of a larger nationality's state) for self-rule often leads to violent insurrections and military responses.

Similarly, state-sponsored nationalist movements are another source of cross-border tensions. This is especially true when people of given nationality live in a neighboring country that the rulers of the first country would like to invade. Thus, leaders of that given nationality can take offensive measures against its neighboring countries in the name of righting alleged mistreatment of its nationals in that country. In fact, Adolf Hitler used alleged mistreatment of ethnic Germans as a rallying cry for his invasions of the Slavic countries. Today, similar scenarios are being played out in Africa and could be played out in the former Soviet republics in the future.

The United States does not only have to be concerned with regional conflicts; it has so many disputes with China that a cold war between the two could erupt. Included among the disputes that the United States has with China are China's failure to protect U.S. patents and trademarks from counterfeiting; China's human rights violations including forced abortions, systematically allowing orphans to die, and mistreatment of Tibetans; China's nuclear arms sales to nations such as Iran and Pakistan; and China's threats of military action against Taiwan. Events that could escalate tensions between the two nations are the United States' failure to renew China's most-favored-nation trade status; the United States' lobbying against China hosting international events such as the Olympic games and the United States' favoring excluding China from international bodies such as the World Trade Organization. Such escalating developments are not entirely hypothetical. In fact, at the end of February 1996 Secretary of State Warren Christopher asked the U.S. Export-Import Bank to stop financing any deals in China for 30 days as a result of Beijing's selling nuclear technology to Pakistan. The Chinese government could further escalate tensions with the United States by nationalizing U.S. investments in the mainland.

The Importance of Readiness

The result of more hostilities worldwide is that the armed forces must focus on their readiness. This readiness requires that troops have the weaponry necessary to respond to these hostilities at their disposal. Therefore, greater military tensions should equate to greater procurement. Furthermore, the troops must be capable of using the weapons at their disposal. Therefore a heightened concern over readiness means that the armed forces will have to increase the frequency and duration of their military exercises. These exercises will result in the greater utilization of weaponry. Accordingly, ammunition will need to be replaced and the weaponry itself will wear down faster, thereby warranting a more rapid replacement cycle of weaponry.

T I P

☞ The price of oil is an important factor in determining our Arab allies' ability to purchase American weapons systems. Thus, our Persian Gulf allies can buy more weaponry when the price of oil is high.

Similarly, the defense contractors that produce simulation and virtual reality devices that prepare troops for military maneuvers should benefit from rising demand. In fact,

> According to Lieutenant-Colonel Bob Birmingham, of the army's Simulation, Training and Instrumentation Command, when 18 Apaches crossed the border into Iraq to fire the first American shots of the Gulf War, only three of the 36 airmen on board had fired a real Hellfire missile before. All the others had done their target practice in simulators. But they were confident they knew what to do, and they did it perfectly.[1]

---

[1] "The Softwar Revolution," *The Economist,* June 10, 1995, Survey p. 10.

Foreign Weapons Sales

Due to increased hostilities worldwide, our allies should boost their defense budgets. For instance, there is more of a military threat and less of a budget deficit problem in the Middle East and Pacific Rim. Thus, nations in these regions have a greater need for weaponry and more resources with which to procure it.

The following are among a number of reasons why many politicians favor selling weapons abroad:

- Selling arms abroad better enables our allies to contain local conflicts without U.S. intervention.

- Selling weapons abroad lowers their production costs. This is very important since defense contractors have much smaller production runs than most other heavy manufacturers. Selling just a few more copies of an aircraft, for example, can greatly leverage the contractors' fixed costs. For instance, the Air Force projected in late 1995 that accelerating its procurement of the C-17 cargo carrier from 8 units to 15 units a year would reduce the unit price from as much as $220 million to $185 million. Thus, increasing orders of weapons by selling some units abroad greatly reduces the cost of producing each unit.

  Conversely, there have been instances where reducing the number of planes ordered was actually more expensive than producing the original numbers of planes. For example, in late 1993, it was estimated that reducing purchases of the F-22 fighter plane by $263 million would actually have increased production costs of the remaining F-22 orders by $700 million.

- Most politicians realize that if the U.S. does not sell its weapons to a foreign country, a competing country (e.g., France or Israel) will. Also, it is often compelling to deliver orders to defense contractors who are major employers.

- Foreign weapons sales are often needed to ensure the survival of parts of the defense establishment. (This is especially true during times of declining domestic procurement budgets.) Thus, it is in the interest of national security that the United States maintains an industrial base capable of efficiently and independently producing weapons systems. Similarly, it is important to encourage young people to study engineering and to keep defense industry workers adroit.

Moreover, the Gulf War should help U.S. defense contractors sell their weapons to friendly countries since the war gave the United States the opportunity to showcase the effectiveness of its weapons systems, and many of our allies are familiar with American weapons systems already since the United States fought the Gulf War in concert with a large coalition.

However, one of the biggest obstacles to U.S defense contractors' selling their weapons systems abroad is the competition with cheaper weapons from a cash-strapped Russia. (Nevertheless, potential clients are often wary of buying Russian weaponry since they are concerned about Russia's ability to service it in the future.) Another problem with the collapse of the Soviet Union is that its engineers and physicists are emigrating to other countries, thereby boosting the effectiveness of their newly adopted countries' defense establishments. Finally, South African defense contractors are likely to become more successful in selling their arms in the international marketplace as a result of the end of that nation's international isolation (resulting from the end of apartheid).

Military Spending

Investors should be careful to distinguish defense spending from procurements. The fortunes of defense contractors are more dependent on procurement than on overall defense spending. Increases in the defense budget may not benefit the defense contractors if the additional spending is directed toward nonmilitary activities such as narcotics interdiction, border patrol, humanitarian expeditions, and environmental cleanups of military bases.

Similarly, large reductions in defense spending may not hurt the defense contractors if procurement spending is not reduced; spending on other areas of the defense establishment (e.g., troop levels, compensation, and rents for foreign bases) can be reduced while the government continues to increase spending on its weapons arsenal.

T I P

There is generally consistency in increases (or decreases) in the amount of money spent on troops and increases (or decreases) in the amount of money spent on equipment. Thus, you should consider the equipment-to-men ratio. When more money is directed toward troops, future budgets can usually be expected to direct more money towards weapons procurement. On the other hand, you should use reduced spending on troop levels as a warning that spending on equipment might also be reduced.

In fact, reduced defense spending can be beneficial for defense contractors. After U.S. military bases are downsized, these smaller bases cannot do all of the work that their larger predecessors could. Thus, defense contractors (rather than the military) may become more active in modifying, upgrading, and maintaining the military's weapons systems when defense budgets fall. Similarly, the Defense

T I P

☞ You should consider the percentage of the value of a defense contractors' weapons programs that is covered by progress payments. Of course, the higher this percentage is the better. In other words, it is preferable for the government to pay 90 percent of the value of a given level of completion of a weapons program rather than 80 percent.

Department may outsource more work to defense contractors when it cannot afford to keep up with the technology that the private sector is developing.

Procurement

Unlike consumer goods manufacturers, defense contractors do not have to bear the risk of anticipating demand for their products since their weapons systems are built to order. Thus, defense contractors neither have to assume inventory risks nor inventory write-downs.

In addition, defense contractors receive progress payments from the government. These payments are based on stages of program completion and are made prior to delivery of the weapons system. Receiving money throughout the development of a program is a major advantage that defense contractors have over industrial manufacturers.

Nevertheless, defense contractors face a number of obstacles in fulfilling their contracts, particularly because they frequently bid on programs well in advance of design completion. Bidding for work before being certain of their capability to produce the weapons system presents a couple of risks. First, if the contractor cannot produce the weapons system according to specifications, on schedule and within budget, the contractor may be required to refund certain progress payments already received.

Complying with contracts is particularly problematic for defense contractors. This is not because defense contractors are more prone to violating contracts than other manufacturers. Rather defense contractors have the cards stacked against them. In almost all other industries, companies are not expected to develop perfect products on their first try. In fact, some of the best consumer goods manufacturers such as Minnesota Mining and Manufacturing gladly accept initial product failures that eventually lead to innovative product launches. However, in the defense industry, any evidence of problems in the developmental stage is pounced on by Congress and critics of the weapons programs. Since these criticisms can kill weapons programs, defense contractors have a natural tendency to deceive auditors during the development of their programs. However, upon discovery of overcharges or other discrepancies in contract compliance, the Defense

Contract Audit Agency can seek the repayment of such charges and insist on other reconciliations.

Whistleblower statutes (which protect loose-lipped employees from company retribution) increase the chance of defense contractors being held liable for repayments of contract violations since employees of defense contractors feel freer to alert auditors to flaws in the weapons systems. For instance, the FBI and the Pentagon inspector general's office searched Litton Industries' headquarters in late March 1996. The search was prompted by a sealed whistleblower suit alleging that Litton secretly padded many defense contracts. These whistleblower statutes are particularly problematic since the government can unilaterally suspend a defense contractor from receiving new contracts pending resolution of alleged violations of procurement laws.

T I P

Companies (such as Boeing and McDonnell Douglas) that generate a large portion of their business from nongovernmental entities (e.g., the airlines) are the most likely to make concessions on penalty payments.

The second problem with defense contractors' bidding on programs before the designs are completed is that the contractors do not know the inevitable problems that will arise in the manufacturing process. This often causes them to bid too low for contracts, which, in turn, leads to cost overruns.

A separate concern is that the continuation of a contract is contingent upon yearly approval of appropriations by Congress. These approvals sometimes fail to surface. (Thus, in order to increase political support for their programs, defense contractors often try to subcontract work to manufacturers that are located in the most strategic Congressional districts.) Despite the fact that, if the customer cancels a contract for its convenience, the contractor is reimbursed for its investment in the program, defense contractors often make concessions on these penalty payments.

Defense contractors have traditionally benefited from a convoluted procurement process. It used to be that industrial manufacturers could not bid for defense contracts, not because their products were inferior, but because industrial manufacturers were unfamiliar with all of the steps they needed to go through in order to sell their products to the defense department. Thus, the procurement process presented a barrier to entry, thereby limiting competition.

However, procurement reform aimed at streamlining the requisitioning process could be problematic for the defense contractors because more industrial companies could bid for defense contracts. As terms of defense contracts become less specific, more companies, particularly the most efficient industrial manufacturers, will win defense contracts at the expense of the traditional defense contractors.

Nevertheless, there is a silver lining in the cloud for defense contractors. Namely, improvements in the acquisition process could result in greater procurement.

Production

Traditionally, defense contractors were not considered to be highly efficient manufacturers, one reason being their small production runs. However, consolidation and better inventory management are improving defense contractors' manufacturing efficiency.

In response to annual procurement budgets falling from $85 billion in the 1980s to approximately $39 billion in fiscal 1996, defense contractors have been aggressively downsizing. Specifically, they have slashed their payrolls and research and development budgets. However, such aggressive cost cutting eliminates economies of scale. In order to regain their economies of scale, defense contractors have been rapidly consolidating, which allows them to further reduce their costs by eliminating the resulting redundant facilities and positions. For instance, in early 1994, Northrop Corporation merged with Grumman Corporation. Also, in early 1994, Loral Corporation acquired IBM's Federal Systems Division which

T I P

There have been few antitrust challenges by the Justice Department regarding mergers in the defense industry; the defense industry does not need competition because the government dictates what it will pay for the production of its programs. Also, most of the mergers and acquisitions in the defense industry have been reasonably priced since the defense industry is relatively mature.

had extensive operations in systems integration and other government functions. More recently, Martin Marietta and Lockheed Corporation merged to form Lockheed Martin. As a result of this consolidation, there are obviously fewer defense contractors.

Moreover, when defense spending declines, some companies divest their defense-related businesses. For example, Westinghouse Electric sought to sell the defense portion of its electronic systems business in early 1996. Also, Chrysler agreed to sell its aircraft-modification and defense-electronics businesses to Raytheon in April of 1996. Therefore, the fewer remaining defense contractors enjoy bigger pieces of the shrinking procurement pie.

Defense contractors are making great progress in shifting from the just-in-case inventory system to the just-in-time inventory method. Traditionally, defense contractors ordered large batches of components (the just-in-case method). The thinking behind maintaining large inventories of components was that the military did not want to jeopardize the nation's readiness just because a Stealth bomber was lacking one bolt. Another reason for buying large lots of supplies was that the defense contractors subcontracted parts from all over the world. Thus, in view of long delivery times, it was necessary to have spare components on hand.

However, there were drawbacks to the just-in-case inventory system: there were substantial storage costs; there was a lot of waste (because if there was a flaw in production, a large batch of inventory would be damaged); there was a greater risk of obsolescence since sporadic production resulted in the components' being irregularly improved.

Now, however, defense contractors are buying more of their inventory closer to the time that it is needed (the just-in-time inventory method). The benefits of just-in-time are the reverse of the disadvantages of the just-in-case inventory method—namely, less risk of obsolescence, less waste, and lower storage costs.

Niches of Opportunity

The United States' reluctance to accept casualties should continue to influence the kinds of weaponry that the defense department procures. Thus, the kinds of weapons systems that are least likely to result in casualties are likely to be the most popular. For instance, missiles with precision guidance systems should be in high demand since they allow accurate attacks without jeopardizing pilots or airplanes. On the other hand, there could be less demand for tanks since tanks are used in close combat (where the risks of casualties are highest).

A second theme is that surveillance equipment will be needed to monitor peace treaties. As previously discussed, hostilities should continue to flare up all over the world; however, many will be (temporarily) concluded with the signing of peace treaties. For these treaties to be taken seriously by the warring factions, they will have to be monitored with the use of surveillance equipment produced by companies such as Loral Corporation.

Interestingly, unmanned surveillance planes equipped with sophisticated cameras and radar should be a profitable niche for defense contractors. These drones are highly cost-effective. For instance, some of them can stay aloft for nearly three days. If these planes are shot down, there is no loss of life and little monetary loss since they cost just a fraction of a reconnaissance jet. Moreover, these planes can also be used for monitoring oil spills, forest fires, and national borders.

A third theme is that more antimissile missiles (such as Raytheon's Patriot) are needed to protect friendly countries against their aggressive neighbors.

Offensive missiles such as the Scud make it inexpensive and convenient for hostile countries such as Iraq and North Korea to antagonize their neighbors. Moreover, these offensive missiles are extremely difficult to detect. On the contrary, hostile countries are less likely to use offensive air forces because they are expensive to maintain, their crews are hard to train and their airbases are difficult to protect.

The final area of opportunity that will be mentioned here relates to mobility. Due to the rapidly rising number of hotspots (and their remoteness) American forces must be prepared to deploy quickly. Thus, demand for aircraft cargo carriers should rise. In fact, in mid-November 1995, the Air Force requested 80 additional McDonnell Douglas C-17 cargo carriers (32 had already been ordered). Also, growing anti-U.S. sentiment in the countries in which the United States maintains its bases will accrue to the benefit of the builders of amphibious transport vessels—such as Avondale Industries—since these ships can accommodate high troop levels at sea (i.e., away from foreign soil).

New Weapons

The defense industry is developing new classes of weaponry by converging with electronics manufacturers and telecommunications companies. For instance, the military is trying to incorporate Global Positioning Systems (directed by telecommunication satellites positioned in space) that will guide weapons to their targets. The military is also working on devising seek-and-destroy mobile launches that will be able to detect objects and determine if they are part of an enemy's weapons.

Other New Age weapons that the military is reported to have been experimenting with are being designed to render an enemy's army ineffective without engaging in combat. These weapons include the following:

- Electromagnetic waves to sabotage computers.
- Effective methods to spread computer viruses.
- Microwaves to turn off the engines of enemy tanks.
- Soundwaves to make an enemy feel seasick or to put an entire country to sleep.
- Lasers to blind an opposing army.
- Voice synthesizing to impersonate enemy commanders.
- Genetically engineered soldiers.

The military is also experimenting with nonlethal weapons such as rubber bullets as well as foams and nets that will stop and hold people in their tracks. These nonlethal weapons are being designed for peacekeeping missions against civilians as well as for domestic police forces.

Diversification

Defense contractors are aggressively manufacturing products for the consumer market. In fact, when reading through the annual reports of defense contractors, one of the primary points that will be made is that less revenues are derived from the defense industry. For instance, in its 1995 annual report, Rockwell International boasted that two-thirds of its sales came from commercial and international markets, not from defense-related activities.

One great example of a defense contractor manufacturing a product for the consumer market is GM Hughes' manufacturing its direct broadcast satellite systems. Interestingly,

> these satellite dishes [lead by GM Hughes' DirecTV] have had one of the highest adoption rates seen in consumer electronics. [Between the time of] their introduction in mid-1994 [to February 1996] 2.5 million units have been installed. In comparison, it took color TV manufacturers 10 years to sell one million TV sets; it took the VCR makers four years to sell one million units.[2]

Additional efforts by defense contractors to diversify include the development of medical imaging systems and navigation systems that are being placed in automobiles. Also, the defense industry is producing a chalky substance that can be placed along the U.S.–Mexico border that will cause trespassers to glow in the dark. Finally, the defense industry is developing "smart guns" for the police forces that will only fire if the officer to whom such gun was assigned pulls the trigger.

Other Investor Considerations

Ideally, you should search for defense contractors that have the following attributes:

- Broad program diversification. A defense contractor, the bulk of whose revenues are dependent on a few programs, could be severely wounded if these programs are scaled back or scrapped.

- A large percentage of product development funded through customer contracts. In the defense industry, it is common for the government to fund research and development through defense contractors. Government funding of research and development helps strengthen defense contractors' balance sheets and reduces their risk. However, the downside to the government's funding a defense contractor's research and development is that the government can license one contractor's patents to another

---

[2] Rita Koselka, "Blockbusted," *Forbes* 157, no. 4 (February 26, 1996) pp. 46–47.

contractor. Thus, defense contractors do not gain much value from the patents that result from government funding of research.

- Heavy involvement in developing weapons systems with dual-use technologies. These are technologies that can be used in both commercial and defense systems.

- Large backlogs. Moreover, a large percentage of these backlogged orders should be funded government orders as opposed to unfunded government orders. Also, you should make sure that these backlogs exclude unexercised options.

- Funding under cost-plus contracting rather than fixed-price contracting. Under fixed-price contracting, the defense contractor is liable for cost overruns. However, cost-plus contracting makes it much easier for the defense contractor to earn a profit on its program development.

- A long history of converting a large percentage of its options to firm orders. This high percentage indicates that the military is impressed with the performance of the contractor's work.

CONGLOMERATES

The shares of conglomerates typically perform best when the economic outlook is uncertain. Since investors do not believe that the economy will grow quickly, they will not invest in cyclicals; similarly, since investors do not believe that the economy will deteriorate, they will neither search for defensive stocks nor growth stocks. Thus, conglomerates that can expose their shareholders to a wide cross-section of the economy are a suitable investment vehicle during times of mixed economic indicators.

Another characteristic of conglomerates is that they often trade at discount valuations to the broad market averages. This is because conglomerates are underfollowed as a result of the difficulty in analyzing them. Also, these stocks are not as appealing for stockbrokers to sell because it is difficult to tell "stories" about such diversified companies.

However, these stocks can rapidly appreciate when it is revealed that management is seriously considering spinning off some of the conglomerate's units. This is because investors are confident that managers will be more accountable and motivated when they are managing independent companies rather than divisions of one massive company.

EMPLOYMENT AGENCIES

Employment agencies have become very popular investments in the mid-1990s. For example, shares of Manpower Inc. (the largest nongovernment employment services organization in the world) more than doubled from a low of $16⅞ in

TOOL

One tool that you can use for determining the outlook for employment agencies is the net hiring strength index. This index is the percentage of employers who say they will be expanding their workforce in the next quarter, net of those employers who state that they will reduce their staffs. Of course, the higher the net hiring strength index, the better. You should also consider the average amount of money that a company spends on its dismissed workers' outplacement. Typically, further into a period of downsizings, the sense of guilt of dismissing people diminishes and employers spend less on outplacement.

1994 to a high of $34⅜ in 1995. One reason for this investor attraction is the awareness of the role that these placement agencies play in relocating workers who are idle due to massive corporate downsizings. Also, when the economy is strong, employees have less loyalty toward their employers (and more career opportunities), which adds to the benefit of the employment agencies.

An interesting niche within the employment agency industry comprises firms such as CDI Corporation and Kelly Services that specialize in temporary employment. These temporary employment agencies may experience more demand in the future because there seems to be a growing disconnect between jobs and work. Thus, employers are more apt to hire people on a when-needed basis. Moreover, employers like to hire people on a temporary basis since doing so is inexpensive, is analogous to long-term interviews, and allows for easier dismissal when necessary.

TEXTILES

While the United States has lost much of its textile base over the past few decades, remaining textile makers, such as Burlington Industries and Dominion Textile are engaged in the production of fabrics, threads, and yarns. Demand for particular textiles can be estimated by determining the demand for the end products that consist of textiles under review.

There are two factors that you should be aware of when evaluating the production of textiles. First, textile companies have often found themselves competing against prison labor—an impossible position for legitimate textile mills to be in because prison wages are much lower and rent expenses are almost nonexistent. Further, there are neither employee taxes nor medical benefits for inmate workers. Additionally, prison-made goods have very low marketing expenses since many state and federal agencies are required to give the corrections department preferences at supplying goods.

TRAP

⊘ Future legislation could be detrimental to the temporary employment agencies. First, the National Labor Relations Board periodically considers new rules that would give temporary workers collective-bargaining rights. Second, the Senate Labor Relations Committee has held hearings regarding legislation that could increase temporary workers' rights and benefits. These hearings were prompted by the thinking that oftentimes temporary workers are actually permanent workers without the *benefits* of permanent workers.

Second, it is often difficult for a textile company to move some of its production offshore. This is because unions representing U.S. workers sometimes have the power to dictate the percentage of offshore-produced apparel that the manufacturer can sell in the United States.

INDEX

ABOUT THE AUTHOR

David Wanetick is the Editor-in-Chief of the *Market Maneuvers* publications. The flagship publication, *Market Maneuvers,* has been published in a newsletter format for five years and is widely quoted by the media.

Market Maneuvers is nationally read for:

- Its prescient stock recommendations. Our two best recommendations are featured each month. Each company's operations, products, strategies, financial position, financial performance, and valuation are thoroughly described.

- Its Industry Analysis section which provides a concise overview of the current status of the industries in which the recommended companies operate.

- Its Mood Of The Market column which discusses the outlook for the broad stock market.

- Its Domestic Scene column which discusses how factors such as inflation, interest rates, and employment will impact on the economy in general.

- Its International Arena article which articulates how foreign developments will affect the economy and stock market.

- Its News You Can Use section which explains how political developments will affect a narrow niche of the stock market.

- Its Tools of the Trade article which illustrates how investors should apply financial tools to the investments under their review.

Should you be interested in Mr. Wanetick's latest recommendations, you can subscribe to *Market Maneuvers* for one year (twelve issues) by remitting $145 to:

Market Maneuvers Subscriptions
305 Madison Avenue
Suite 1166
New York NY 10165
(212) 592-4141